Gender, Teaching and Research in Higher Education

Challenges for the 21st Century

Edited by

GILLIAN HOWIE
University of Liverpool

ASHLEY TAUCHERT
University of Exeter

Ashgate

Published by
Ashgate Publishing Limited
Gower House
Croft Road
Aldershot
Hampshire GU11 3HR
England

Ashgate Publishing Company
131 Main Street
Burlington, VT 05401-5600 USA

Ashgate website: http://www.ashgate.com

British Library Cataloguing in Publication Data
Gender, teaching and research in higher education :
    challenges for the 21st century
    1. Education, Higher 2. Women in education - Congresses
    3. Women - Education (Higher) 4. Feminism and education -
    Congresses
    I. Howie, Gillian II. Tauchert, Ashley
    378'.0082

Library of Congress Cataloging-in-Publication Data
Gender, teaching and research in higher education : challenges for the 21st century /
edited by Gillian Howie and Ashley Tauchert.
        p.cm.
    "Based on a conference held in the Philosophy Department of Liverpool University in
    January 2000"--Pref.
    Includes bibliographical references and index.
    ISBN 0-7546-1478-6
        1. Women--Education (Higher)--Congresses. 2. Women in education--Congresses. 3.
    Feminism and education--Congresses. I. Howie, Gillian. II. Tauchert, Ashley.

    LC1567 .G48 2001
    378'.0082--dc21
                                                                                00-065042

ISBN 0 7546 1478 6

Printed and bound by Athenaeum Press, Ltd.,
Gateshead, Tyne & Wear.

GENDER, TEACHING AND RESEARCH
IN HIGHER EDUCATION

Gender, Teaching and Research in Higher Education presents new insights and research into contemporary problems, practical solutions, and the complex roles of teaching and learning in the international academy. Drawing together new research from contributors spanning a range of international and interdisciplinary perspectives, this book discusses topics of particular importance in the UK, USA, Australasia and South Africa, including: curriculum, boundary disciplines and research assessments, the Higher Education institution, educational practice, authority and authorization, teaching and counselling. Discussion of quality audits, curriculum modifications, teaching certificates and other key topics, add to this book's value in informing current debate and providing valuable research aids for education into the 21st Century.

Contents

PART III: FEMINIST PEDAGOGIES

PART IV: ASSESSMENT AND EVALUATION

PART V: OVERSEAS PERSPECTIVES

List of Tables

Preface

Gender, Teaching and Research in Higher Education emerges from a conference held in the Philosophy Department of Liverpool University in January 2000. The conference was organised to explore the changes in the roles of women in Higher Education in the context of the new culture of efficiency.

Our thanks go out to all those who participated in the event, making it a joyful and fruitful day. The papers presented at the conference covered a wide, although intersecting, range of issues. We found those issues reflected in the contexts of America, Australia and New Zealand and decided to include a selection of papers from these countries. This in no way constitutes a full or detailed exploration of the international scene.

This was the first conference hosted by the 'Institute for Feminist Theory and Research'. More conferences are planned to take place in Liverpool and Exeter over the next few years. One day we hope to have funding for various other initiatives. In the meantime, we thank the Philosophy Department for its support of this venture and extend our warm thanks to Fran Ali, Howard Robinson, Ingrid Wasanaar, Regenia Gagnier, Angelique Richardson, Chris Willis, Jane Spencer, Sue James and Isobel Armstrong in particular for lending various support and encouragement over the last year or so. We appreciate the enthusiasm and patience of Sarah Lloyd at Ashgate Publishing, and are grateful to AUT for the discursive and campaigning context in which to develop the political theme of the feminisation of Higher Education. In addition we would also like to extend our thanks to Stacy Gillis who worked as our Editorial Assistant in the preparation of the final draft of this manuscript.

List of Contributors

Barbara Bagilhole is a Senior Lecturer in Social Policy in the Department of Social Sciences at Loughborough University. Her major research interest is in equal opportunities, covering gender, race and disability. She has published widely in this field, including a recent book (1997) *Equal Opportunities and Social Policy: Issues of Gender, 'Race' and Disability* (Addison Wesley Longman). Her most recent research projects have included looking at the experiences of women managers, academics, engineers and vicars. She is currently writing a book for Macmillan on *Challenging Women in Non-Traditional Occupations*. She has also undertaken research on men in non-traditional occupations, and pursued her research interest in gender into Europe and in a British Council funded project in India.

Alan Bleakley is a Senior Lecturer in Medical Humanities, University of Plymouth Postgraduate Medical School, and Senior Curriculum Development Manager, Cornwall College. He has been teaching in Higher Education for over 25 years, and has developed a number of innovative courses in both pedagogy and psychotherapy. He is currently pursuing a three-year research project studying how consultants teach junior doctors on ward rounds, and is writing a study on clinical judgements by doctors under conditions of uncertainty and value conflict. His current publications include (2000) *The Animalizing Imagination: Totemism, Textuality and Ecocriticism* (Macmillan), and a number of scholarly articles in educational journals re-visioning the current conventions of educational practice such as reflective practice, self assessment and lifelong learning. His previous publications include two books on the psychology of imagination and a collection of poetry.

Colleen Chesterman has been Director of ATN WEXDEV since November 1997. She has an Arts degree from University of Sydney, with Honours in English, a Masters in Sociology from Warwick University, with a thesis on women and part-time work and a Doctorate in Creative Arts from University of Technology, Sydney, with a thesis on women and biography. In universities she has taught sociology and creative writing. She has worked at senior level in the public and non-government sector, as Deputy Director of the NSW Women's Co-ordination Unit and Director of the NSW Council of Social Service and has run for ten years her own consultancy firm in planning and policy development. Her current research interest is in senior women managers and their impact on organisational cultures. She has recently completed training modules on women and mentoring for the Association of Commonwealth Universities.

Valerie A. Clifford is Associate Professor at the University of the South Pacific and Director of the Centre for the Enhancement of Learning and Teaching there. She started her career in sociology and spent six years at the University of Otago Medical School researching women's health.   She moved into academic development ten years ago at Otago, then moved to the University of Canberra and now Fiji. Her current research interests are feminist and inclusive pedagogy, academic leadership and group mentoring.

Mary S. Erickson is Associate Professor in the Department of Nursing at the State University of West Georgia, where she has taught for twenty-five years. She teaches all areas of nursing with pediatrics and women's health as her areas of interest. She has been involved with all areas of curricular development including the Department's current caring curriculum.

Jennifer FitzGerald is a Senior Lecturer in the School of English, Queen's University, Belfast. Her most recent publications have been on the contemporary African-American novelist, Toni Morrison, and on the Irish scholar, Helen Waddell, so celebrated in the 1920s and 1930s. She has been teaching on the Women's Studies undergraduate programme since 1991; she received a Queen's Teaching Award for the development of the learning journal in 1999.

Becky Francis is Senior Research Fellow at the School of Post-Compulsory Education and Training, University of Greenwich. Her research interests include gender identity and gender and achievement, and she is currently working on projects exploring these issues both in compulsory and post-compulsory education sectors. Key recent publications include: (2000), *Boys, Girls and Achievement: Addressing the Classroom Issues* (Routledge); and (1998), *Power Plays* (Trentham Books).

Allison Green teaches at Highline Community College, Des Moines, Washington (near Seattle), where she coordinates the Culture, Gender and Global Studies Department and teaches writing and women's studies. She has an M.F.A. in Creative Writing and Literature from Emerson College, Boston. Her publications include stories and poems in literary journals, and she published a novel, *Half-Moon Scar*, in 2000. Her interests include whiteness and white privilege; the intersections of race, class, gender and sexual identity in the classroom; and, issues for queer students, staff and faculty in higher education.

Erica Halvorsen is a Research Officer at the Association of University Teachers, where her interests include equal opportunities and the representation of women in higher education.

Sandra Harding is Professor and Dean, Faculty of Business at Queensland University of Technology, Brisbane, Australia. A sociologist, she has degrees from the Australian National University, University of Queensland and North Carolina State University. Her particular interests include alternative forms of industrial organization and inequality at work. She is currently engaged in a large scale national study, the Australian National Organisation Survey (AusNOS), funded by the Australian Research Council Strategic Partnerships with Industry programme. This study was completed in 2000 and will provide unique insights into work and organisation, including gender segregation at work, in Australia.

Gillian Howie is a Lecturer in the Department of Philosophy at the University of Liverpool. Her research interests include political philosophy, Kant and Hegel, and Critical Theory. She has published on various topics including feminist philosophy, gender roles, Marx and de Beauvoir. She is currently completing an analysis of the ideology of postmodernism. *The Aura of Expressionism: A Critical Study of Deleuze and Spinoza* is forthcoming from Macmillan.

Christina Hughes is a Lecturer in the Department of Continuing Education, University of Warwick. Previously she worked in the Department of Social Policy and Social Work and the Centre for Educational Development, Appraisal and Research (CEDAR), both at the University of Warwick. Her publications include (1996), *How to Research* (Open University Press, with Loraine Blaxter and Malcolm Tight), and *Mirrored Lives: Gender and Discourses of Education, Employment and Family* (Routledge, forthcoming). She is co-editor of *Gender and Education* and Assistant Editor of *Gender, Work and Organisation*. Her research interests are focused on the connections between education, employment and family in women's lives and the development of qualitative research methodologies.

Sue Jackson is a Lecturer in Women's Studies, and Co-convenor of the Women's Studies Programme at the University of Surrey, Roehampton. She is also an Associate Lecturer with the Open University, where she teaches a range of courses from pre-undergraduate to post-graduate, including accreditation for teacher training. Sue has just completed her PhD, where she combined her interests in women's studies, feminism and education to consider the position of women students in the academy. She has published widely in areas of women and learning in higher education. Recent publications include: (2000), 'Networking Women: a History of Ideas, Issues and Developments in Women's Studies in Britain', *Women's Studies International Forum*, 23 (1); and, 'To be or not to be: the place of Women's Studies in the lives of its students', *The Journal of Gender Studies*, 9 (2).

Barbara Körner is a social science scholar with a humanities and arts background. She studied in Germany and Canada, and has been actively involved in the 1980s peace/green movements in Canada and England. Her PhD thesis (Lancaster, 1997) arose out of this activism, as did her feminist consciousness. Since 1992, she has been teaching part-time in different institutions of Higher Education, and has completed research in the area of non-violence. She is now developing research interests in education, culture and identity, family relations, and social exclusion and social change.

Jen Marchbank and **Gayle Letherby** both work for Coventry University where they are often mistaken for each other. As well as researching and writing together on working and learning in Higher Education, they each have published in their separate fields of interest. Gayle's interests include feminist methodology and epistemology, reproductive identity, family and kinship. Jen's interests include policy making, feminist activism and gender, violence and resistances. Gayle is currently Co-Chair of WHEN (Women's Higher Education Network) and Jen is a former Co-Chair of the WSNA (UK) (Women's Studies Network Association).

Zoë Bennett Moore is a Senior Lecturer at Anglia Polytechnic University, where she acts as the Director of Postgraduate Studies in Pastoral Theology for the Cambridge Theological Federation. Her teaching and research interests are at the interface between feminism, education and pastoral theology. Recent articles include: (1998), 'A Midrash', *Feminist Theology*, 18; (1997/8), 'On Copy Clerks, Transformers and Spiders: Teachers and Learners in Adult Theological Education', *British Journal of Theological Education*, 9 (3); and, (1998), 'Women and the Cost of Loving: Towards Transformative Christian Practice', *Contact*, 127. She is currently working on feminist perspectives on pastoral theology.

Louise Morley is a Senior Lecturer in higher education studies and Assistant Dean of Professional Studies at the University of London Institute of Education. She was previously at the University of Sussex, the University of Reading, and the Inner London Education Authority. Her research and publication interests focus on equity, gender, power and empowerment in higher and professional education. Recent publications include: (1999), *Organising Feminisms: The Micropolitics of The Academy* (Macmillan), *School Effectiveness: Fracturing the Discourse* (co-authored with Naz Rassool, Falmer Press); (1996), *Breaking Boundaries: Women in Higher Education*, and (1995), *Feminist Academics: Creative Agents for Change*, both edited with Val Walsh and published by Taylor & Francis.

Barbara Read is Research Fellow at the School of Education, University of North London. Her research interests include gender and ethnic identity, and writing and assessment in HE. In 1999 she was awarded her PhD from the University of Bristol for her examination of the representation of Bristol's involvement in the slave trade in the city's museums and heritage sites, and the interconnections between history and local, national and ethnic identity.

Jocelyn Robson is Principal Lecturer at the School of Post-Compulsory Education and Training at the University of Greenwich. She teaches on a range of courses for staff in further and higher education and her research interests include teacher professionalism, gender and achievement, and gender and film. Publications include (1996), *The Professional FE Teacher* (Avebury); (1997), and *Girls' Own Stories: Australian and New Zealand Women's Films 1979-1996* (Scarlet Press).

Ashley Tauchert is a Lecturer in English at the University of Exeter. Her research interests include feminist theory, women's literary history, embodiment and writing, gender theory, and pedagogy. Her book, (2001) *Mary Wollstonecraft and the Accent of the Feminine*, was published by Palgrave Press. She recently received a University of Exeter 'Excellence in Teaching' award.

Karen J. Vogel has been teaching at Hamline University since 1989. She received tenure at Hamline in 1995. Hamline is a small four-year liberal arts University located in St. Paul, Minnesota. She currently teaches a variety of courses cross-listed in International Studies, Women's Studies, and Political Science, including: Gender Politics, International Organizations, Government and Politics of Eastern Europe.

Val Walsh is a freelance academic and trainer, teaching Women's Studies at the University of Central Lancashire. Her research focuses on the conditions for and obstacles to women's co/creativity, with particular reference to women artists, women in higher education, and the use of life histories to explore class and gender. Recent publications include: (1999), 'Sites/Sights to slow you down: An Interview with British Sculptor Lorna Green', *n. Paradoxa* (International Feminist Art Journal), 4; and (1999), 'Digging up tangled roots: Feminism and the Resistance to Working-Class Culture', in Paula Polkey (ed.), *Women's Lives into Print: The Theory, Practice and Writing of Feminist Auto/biography.*

Penny Welch teaches Politics and Women's Studies at the University of Wolverhampton. Her recent publications include: (1999), 'The Politics of Teaching Women's Studies', *Women's Studies Quarterly*, 27 (3 and 4); and (2000), 'Thinking About Teaching Politics', *Politics*, 20 (2).

Introduction

Gillian Howie and Ashley Tauchert

This collection of papers is a discussion of the purpose and product of Higher Education. The 1990s have seen a rapid consolidation of a new institutional and economic context in which this discussion can take place. The audit culture, initiated in the 1980s, has become over-determined with surveillance procedures. Teaching Quality Assessment (now Subject Programme Review), Research Assessment Exercise, Subject Benchmarking, Institutional Reviews, and teaching accreditation collectively determine the national criteria for Higher Education funding, personal performance indicators and professional standards. The purpose and product of education is itself affected by the predominance of these criteria of 'efficient' and 'quality performance'.

Following Lyotard, we ask 'Who transmits learning?' 'What is transmitted?' 'To whom?' 'Through what medium?' 'In what form?' and 'With what effect?' (Lyotard, 1986, p.48). Aside from a general de-funding argument, we suggest that performance criteria are *determining* the transmission of knowledge: method and content. Further, though, we suggest that the enlightened ideal of education has been transformed into the modern ideal of skills provision: laboratory skills for the scientist or committee skills for the Humanities and Arts students. This is not to eulogise the erstwhile ideal but merely to note that at least the concept of education, teaching the future citizen the enlightened ideals of autonomous critical thinking and social obligation, held a moment of political resistance or utopia. But the notion of the autonomous academic or academic practice means little when the control of the budget and its allocation occurs according to criteria which, even if rapidly internalised, are set from outside. Similarly there is no autonomy to either the learning process or decisions about the learning environment when the cost, economic and social, is borne by the individual.

We do, of course, acknowledge an increase in numbers of women within Higher Education institutions but we suggest that there is more than a coincidental connection between this and depressing levels of pay and conditions.[1] Our analysis of the feminisation of labour within Higher Education begins with an exploration of how the culture of performativity aggravates discrimination. When we start to ask questions about the criteria used to distribute goods within the system, we begin to see that 'quality control' is a euphemism for financial restriction, but we also find that a successful performance increases the ability to produce proof. This is because the receipt of a judgement of quality or merit secures the funding of research programmes, the domination of specialist fields, and the prestige of expertise. Hence, successful performance increases the ability to be right, which is why Lyotard describes the current situation as legitimation through power.

Political resistance to the culture of performativity thus takes place around two issues: epistemology and ethics. The following papers analyse how the contemporary culture perpetuates discrimination, and, feeling the weight of past generations on their shoulders, the authors look to reassess the ends of education in context of, but distinguishable from, the enlightened ideal.

The papers which follow offer a range of insights into the present condition of Higher Education and the social implications of its practices, as well as reflecting on the role of women academics and the institutionalisation of the feminist scholar. Feminist academic work on women and gender in Higher Education is immanent critique working with a remarkable level of committed self-awareness. That is not to say that we escape all prejudice or bias, or even that we will agree in any but the most clear-cut cases. However, the picture emerging from the discussions recorded in this collection represent a general consensus that the institution of Higher Education is on the cusp of impending change with hitherto unimaginable implications for the cultures and traditions it serves.

Women academics reflect here on the ways in which their work is sidelined, overlooked, cannibalised, devalued and occluded. Many struggle to continue their life-roles as primary carers, while maintaining a work-role designed to the dimensions of what is possible and desirable when someone else is responsible for this domestic work. The discussions are sensitive to, and successfully expose, the ways in which the academic institution reproduces these over-familiar sexual divisions of labour in its own procedures. In the end this collection might be said to articulate something of the many and varied voices of female academic subjects, while returning to a cluster of common themes, problems, and demands which will be familiar to all women working within the Higher Education sector today. The female academic subject – as subject (rather than object) of theory, subject (rather than object) of knowledge – is a precious hybrid creature rapidly taking on a distinctive profile against the backdrop of the exponential instrumentalisation of Higher Education. For, as Harding so aptly notes: 'while psychiatrists have endlessly studied what they regard as women's peculiar mental and behavioural characteristics [...] women have only recently begun to study the bizarre mental and behavioural characteristics of psychiatrists' (Harding, 1997, p.164). This collection is intended to mark a significant moment in the history of women's study of the 'peculiar mental and behavioural characteristics' of the institutions and their traditional inhabitants, for whom 'woman' has for so long been circulated as an object of study.

One of the most striking aspects of the work presented in this collection is its exposure of the myriad of apparently disparate and disconnected ways in which 'gender' impacts on, and can be analysed as a determining factor of, Higher Education theory and practices. 'Gender' is shown to be a determining feature in issues ranging from research grant applications (see Bagilhole), to undergraduate writing style and assessment outcomes (see Francis *et al.*, FitzGerald, and Moore), to feminist pedagogic practices in the classroom and beyond (see Welch, Körner, and Vogel), to curriculum design and the burdens of student support in the market-led culture of Higher Education (see Letherby and Marchbank, Jackson, and

Bleakley). 'Gender', in the context of a wide array of practices and procedures, has been revealed by these various arguments to be both a more complex and diffuse factor, but also a more crass and predictable one, than we had previously suspected. As Walsh argues, academia remains populated and managed by 'too many professionals who lack a conceptual framework or language for conceiving the conjunction of [...] gender, power and organisation' (p.41). Every aspect of university life is infused with 'gender' in the form of undisclosed bias. But let us be clear what we mean in this statement. 'Gender' is a contested term: between social constructivism and the discourse theories of postmodernism, 'gender' currently connotes an array of attributes largely understood in the context of identity and representation. 'Gender' might better be understood as a 'floating signifier', in the way Laclau finds 'democracy' to be 'radically ambiguous and not simply polysemous' (Laclau, 1993, p.335).[2] But, whether one understands 'gender' to be an essential attribute of sexual difference, or a constructed social imposition on the generic human subject, is in the end irrelevant to the case being presented here. The impact of 'gender' in Higher Education (and the fields of knowledge it sustains) is unarguable, and this impact is not arbitrary, but consistently monodirectional in its effects.

Women in Higher Education carry the burden of 'gender' manifested as proportionately lower pay for equivalent work, poorer working conditions, greater instability of employment, institutional sexism, overt and covert discrimination, bullying and harassment. It can no longer be argued that the onus lies with the individual women who have chosen to take on the mantle of the academic to try ever harder to achieve the standards which would demonstrate their e/quality. Academics need to recognise and address the structural and cultural barriers that exist to women's full participation as autonomous subjects of knowledge. This conclusion is not a new one for feminist activists, but the experience of having it even partially confirmed by statistical evidence, and noticed by hitherto complacent governmental bodies is, although belated, welcome.

Halvorsen's 'Gender Audit' marks the limit of the arguments in this collection in its stark demonstration of the institutional discrimination embedded in Higher Education today. Bagilhole's paper summarises what is at stake in this argument when she calls for us to 'make explicit what we've always felt to be implicit' (p.57). Very few, if any, sacred cows survive this process of explication, as Bagilhole reveals through an analysis of how traditional mechanisms intended to ensure scholarly 'quality' in practice act to amplify the lack of parity between academic men and women in status and representation. Bleakley's exploration of the 'gift' in teaching exposes the degree to which current models of teaching are instrumental, market-driven, and situated. Bleakley shows how other models of teaching are available but marginalised by the culture of efficiency. Such an alternative way of teaching, he notes, would take account of power and the context of power. The 'gift' of teaching, he says, has aesthetic and ethical dimensions standing opposed to the qualities demanded by the current instrumentalist paradigm. Morley, on the other hand, notes the increasing difficulty in finding space to experiment under conditions established by the 'process of instrumentalisation' (p.95). Indeed, she suggests that there is 'little discursive space for dissent within the regulatory frameworks of quality assurance and new managerialism' (p.104).

For others, however, feminist pedagogic practices are seen to emerge through cracks in this regulatory framework, in critical spaces in classrooms, and in female networking and models of 'care' in the curriculum. Erickson's 'Care' model finds echoes in Korner's notion of critical pedagogy through the feminist paradigm of 'consciousness-raising', and in Clifford's and Chesterman's experiences of collaborative work establishing new and creative webs of support and interaction between women academics. Erickson's account of the nursing curriculum exposes what might be considered a nodal point of overdetermined feminisation in the academy: a field of work in which the undervaluing of women's caring role meets the undervaluing of 'women's knowledges'.

Moore's paper indicates the extent to which the creative feminist academic exposes herself to 'risk' and 'danger', and underlines the argument that feminist pedagogy is 'impossible' without creativity, which is always risky, even dangerous' (p.178). Green demonstrates the impact of foregrounding the politicised 'identity' of the teacher on the kinds of things that can be taught, and makes an argument for the otherwise neglected 'community college' to be recognised as a key site for political struggles in US Higher Education. Several of the papers highlight the practical and emotive problems of isolation for feminist academic practice, partly answered by the formal and informal networks coming into evidence in recent years. Clifford, for example, highlights the severe isolation of women in academia, and the impact of isolation on challenges to institutional practices. We account for the apparent depoliticisation of academic feminist theory in our paper on the 'Cloistered' ideal shadowing the contemporary academic ideal.

A notable tension subsists throughout the work represented by this collection. Feminist activism predates feminist academia, and the work of feminist activists in academic contexts raises a new paradox. Feminist activism is rooted in an awareness of experience as the starting point for any convincing politics, yet academia demands that experience be properly theorised before it can be weighed as evidence. Some of the papers here represent versions of the 'bottom-up' argument of feminist activism, prioritising the experience of the feminist teacher and researcher, and emphasising the validity of what Jackson terms 'personal location' in the work we produce (p.24). Others emphasise the increasing inappropriateness of 'personal location' in the audit culture of contemporary academia. We have reached the crossroads.

The use of data or evidence to support descriptions of the state of Higher Education sits uneasily with the assumption that there is a peculiarly feminine epistemology. One way to resolve this would be to dissolve the knot into a relativism or pluralism: so many competing stories, so many standpoints. We believe that standpoint theory has three advantages over traditional theories of knowledge. The first is a thoroughgoing attempt to protect individual experience. The second is the assertion that some claims to know are more robust from some standpoints; and finally, the belief that epistemology ought to take subjectivity, the position of the knower, into account. From a specific standpoint within Higher Education it is obvious that some propositional claims, and methods of justification, are far from neutral. From that position, women – as feminists – are able to investigate the curious relationship between belief, justification, and institutional practice. By seeing this relationship in the context of the new disciplinary culture, we believe that we can begin to make sense of why discriminatory practices are continuing, and why it is that academics are feeling their subjectivity and autonomy erased. This feeling, that is beginning to resurface once more through a range of 'consciousness-raising' exercises, is not incidental to the economic processes to which Higher Education is submitted. The analysis of this relationship, however, requires something more robust than standpoint theory (Howie, 1998, p.109).

Harding's final chapter takes the market model of Higher Education institutions at its word, and analyses evidence of institutional discrimination from the perspective of management theory. She finds that the very 'idea that fair and objective judgements can be made and rewards allocated solely in proportion to worth, to individual merit, is, at best, naïve and, at worst, a deception' (p.285). Her pragmatic suggestions for addressing 'poor placement' in the Higher Education hierarchies expose a biased 'meritocracy' governing Higher Education procedures in the name of 'scholarship'. Her observation that the 'playing field' is already 'biased' if 'the candidate with the most publications "wins" when all that is really required is evidence of some appropriate level of productivity' has strong implications for an academic system determined by Research Assessment performance ratings (p.274).

Feminist activism is considered to have come dangerously close in recent years to transferring its political energies into purely theoretical debate, losing its will and capacity to change the world, and this point is raised in the following chapters. However, we must keep in mind that in the context of academia, theorising *is* activism, and a disregard for the formalities of theorising will ensure that feminist academic work continues to be marginalised, diminished and ignored outside the scope of its own immediate concerns. Further, though, in context of the performance culture, where truth and ethics are subjected to the demands of the market, feminist academics are opening the portals of power and privilege to scrutiny, and in the process developing new sites of resistance.

Notes

[1] In Wales, efficiency savings of over 14 per cent were made in Higher Education between 1993/4 and 1997/8. In the same period in England, the efficiency gain was 15 per cent (*Higher Education in the New Century*, submission to CSR2: 2001-4). This should be seen in context of the increase in numbers of women into Higher Education and the fall in value of salary over the last twenty years of 30 per cent.

[2]   Laclau defines a floating signifier in the following way: 'if a plurality of signifieds is joined in an unstable fashions to certain signifiers, the necessary result is the introduction of equivocality (in the Aristotelian sense). But if one can affirm that this instability does not depend entirely on the equivocality of the signifier but on the contexts in which the signifier is used, it is no longer a question of equivocality but of ambiguity and unfixity' (Laclau, 1993, pp.334–5).

References

Harding, S. (1997), 'Is There a Feminist Method?' [1986], in S. Kemp and J. Squires (eds), *Feminisms*, Oxford University Press, Oxford.

Howie, G. (1998), 'Feminist Philosophy', in O. Leeman (ed.), *The Future of Philosophy: Towards the 21st Century*, Routledge, London and New York.

Laclau, E. (1993), 'Politics and the Limits of Modernity', in T. Docherty (ed.), *Postmodernism: A Reader*, Harvester Wheatsheaf, New York and London.

Lyotard, J.-F. (1986), *The Postmodern Condition: A Report on Knowledge* tr., G. Bennington and B. Massumi, Manchester University Press, Manchester.

PART I
WOMEN IN HIGHER EDUCATION

Chapter 1

Gender Audit

Erica Halvorsen

Introduction

Academic women have long known that they are not promoted as much or paid as much, and do not, in truth, have equality with their male counterparts. From the early 1900s there has been ample evidence to support this fact, but it has not appeared to be of sufficient consequence, or importance, for steps to be taken to eradicate the discrimination that has caused it. This chapter will look at the evidence to support the argument that women academics are disadvantaged in terms of pay and promotion prospects, analyse the position of women academics now, and assess the short-term prospects of their situation improving.

In the academic year 1998/9, 130,534 academic staff were employed in Higher Education institutions (HEIs) in the United Kingdom, 45,367 (35 per cent) of them were women.[1] Half these women were on fixed-term contracts, and were therefore likely to experience the job insecurity and broader life restrictions, such as difficulty in obtaining a mortgage, that result from that kind of employment. This compares with 38 per cent of men. Of the remaining women, 3.5 per cent were employed on 'other', e.g. hourly paid, terms, which leaves a minority in permanent, either full-time or pro-rata, positions. As 60 per cent of men have permanent posts the quantifiable over-representation of women on fixed-term contracts is 6 per cent.

14 per cent of all academic staff were employed part-time, the majority of whom (53 per cent) were women; and the majority of all part-time staff were on fixed-term contracts: 57 per cent of women and 58 per cent of men. But, interestingly, even though the proportions of male and female academics who worked part time on fixed-term contracts is roughly the same, women were more successful than men in securing the few available permanent part-time posts.

The statistics

In June 1996 the Higher Education Statistics Agency (HESA) published the first set of data through which all the universities and colleges of Higher Education in the United Kingdom could be compared. Previous to that date the Universities' Statistical Record (USR) had published statistics relevant to the 'old' university sector, and the Higher Education Funding Council for England (HEFCE) had produced similar, but not always comparable, data for the now 'new' universities and colleges of Higher Education. HESA was established to collect data from the whole of the recently unified Higher Education sector and disseminate it accordingly. In the first volume it published, *Resources of Higher Education Institutions*, information about the academic staff employed in Higher Education in 1994/5 was available, so there continues to be an approximate time lag of one year between the collection of this data and its publication.[2] This is obviously disadvantageous for anyone who may wish to use that data, because it never reflects the real, accurate, current situation. Also, the readily available information in the Resources volumes is too broad for any but the most general of comparisons to be made. Supplementary data may be obtained from HESA, however, and it is this that has given the clearest picture of the representation of academics recently; at least, that is, until the publication of the Independent Review of Higher Education, the Bett Report.

In May 1999, that report identified an average pay gap between male and female full-time non-clinical academics in the 'old' universities of £4,259, and an average gap of £1,524 in post-1992 institutions in England and Wales. These figures were as at March 1998. In the Bett Report, less than a quarter (24 per cent) of the academic staff in the pre-1992 sector were reported to be women compared to 43 per cent in the post-1992 institutions; and the average pay for all full time academic staff was £31,163 in the pre-1992 sector compared to £27,061 in the post-1992 one. In November 1999, the National Association of Teachers in Higher and Further Education (NATFHE) requested salary data from HESA by institution, which was aggregated to show that, in England, academic women in both pre- and post-1992 institutions were paid £4,126 less than their male colleagues; in Wales £5,236 less; in Scotland the difference was £4,978; and in Northern Ireland £4,307. And, in April 2000, NATFHE returned to the same data set to produce an analysis of the male-female pay gap by subject area, which showed that even in 'woman-friendly' subjects, such as Health and Community Studies, which employs the largest number of women (38 per cent), there is still a £1,960 average pay gap between the genders.

These averages can be explained in a number of ways. Since they are of the pay of all academic staff, from Lecturer/Lecturer A to Professor, both the proportions of each gender on each grade and their position on the salary scale within that grade will weigh the averages in favour of one sex or the other, if the representation is disproportionate. Since 1992, when the first league tables to rank schools by their pupils' GCSE grade results were published in *The Times*, the press has had an increasing propensity to rate all the UK's educational establishments using as much of the information that is publicly available as it can. Tables are produced for schools and Further Education colleges on the basis of their A level results, and for HEIs by, among other things, the Research Assessment Exercise and Teaching Quality Assessment ratings of their departments, the grade of degree their students are awarded, and the amount of income they generate from external sources. Rankings of the different HEIs vary slightly from newspaper to newspaper due, presumably, to the weightings accorded to each of the factors in the equations each uses, but when a table is produced that presents the statistics in their baldest form, there would appear to be little room for their disputation. League tables which have been published by the *Times Higher Educational Supplement* for the last five years show the proportion of female professors, as defined by HESA's broad grade bands,[3] in individual institutions, and. They are constructed by using the HEIs' generated, and HESA supplied, data about the grade on which staff in every returning institutions are employed, and they show two things: over the five-year period, the overall proportion of female professors employed in Higher Education institutions has only increased by 2.6 percentage points, and in the academic year 1998/9 women comprised only 9.8 per cent of the professorial complement in the UK's Higher Education institutions. This figure may be, and has been, vigorously disputed by some vice chancellors of post-1992 universities, and principals of colleges of Higher Education, which have awarded certain of their staff, and not only women, the title of professor without the attendant remuneration. A ruse that holds no sway with inputters of Hesa returns who regard professors who are paid on Principal Lecturer scales as Principal Lecturers.

By applying a linear regression model to the percentages of female professors in the UK's HEIs in the five-year period from 1994/5 to 1998/9 (Table 1.1), it is estimated that, at the current rate of growth, it will be 68 years before half the academics in this position are women.

Table 1.1 Percentage of female professors in UK HEIs, 1994/5 to 1998/9

Academic Year	Female Professors (%)
1994/5	7.2
1995/6	8.0
1996/7	8.3
1997/8	9.2
1998/9	9.8

Source: HESA Individualised Staff Returns

However, relatively small proportions of either sex become professors (7.7 per cent of all academic staff in 1997/8), yet 16 per cent of all academic staff were categorised as senior non-professorial staff (i.e. Senior Lecturers and Researchers) in 1997/8, and it is from this rank that most of the next generation of professors will be drawn.[4] Some will be recruited after demonstrating their excellence outside the Higher Education sector *per se*, but the majority will be promoted from within it. Table 1.2 shows the percentage of women in senior positions over the same five-year period as that shown for professors.

Table 1.2 Percentage of non-professorial female senior staff in UK HEIs, 1994/5 to 1998/9

Academic Year	Female Senior Staff (%)
1994/5	17.0
1995/6	18.6
1996/7	20.1
1997/8	21.1
1998/9	21.9

Source: HESA Individualised Staff Returns

When compared to the percentage of women professors the figures are consistent in showing that the proportions of women professors are approximately 55 per cent *less* than the proportions of senior female non-professorial staff in each of the five years; whereas the position is reversed for men; the proportions of professors who are men increased from 11.8 per cent to 15.5 per cent *greater* than the proportions of male senior staff over the five year period.

If, for example, the same ratio were applied to the percentage of non-professorial senior women in 1998/9 as the one for men, then the percentage of professors who are female would rise to 25.3. That a quarter of professors are not female could suggest that women do not apply for professorial positions; that they apply and are not successful; or that there is a culture of institutional sexism in the UK's universities and colleges of Higher Education, and, this last, without even considering the proportions of women on the lower grades. The evidence to support any theory of institutional sexism is largely anecdotal due to the (purposefully?) obfuscatory practices adopted by the institutions. The statistics prove that there is a disproportionate number of women in the higher positions, but it is not something the heads of – at least some of – these institutions appear willing to acknowledge, as witnessed by this observation: 'some vice-chancellors of top universities offended the Department for Education and Employment's Permanent Secretary at a private dinner by pooh-poohing his concern about the lack of women in senior university jobs'.[5] It is re-enforced by the introduction of the publication of criteria by which candidates are judged and the provision of information regarding the reasons for their failure at the University of Cambridge, *only* after an unsuccessful legal challenge relating to the selection of professors in 1998.

Evidence to support the contention that women are on lower scale points within each grade is provided by the Bett Report's tables of average salaries for non-clinical academics on national pay rates, which are summarised in Table 1.3.

Table 1.3 Average salaries by grade for non-clinical academics on national pay rates

Pre-1992 Institutions

	Lecturer A	Lecturer B	Senior Lecturer	Professor
Female	£19,251	£26,531	£32,430	£41,192
Male	£19,489	£26,997	£32,971	£42,999

Post-1992 Institutions

	Lecturer	Senior Lecturer	Principal Lecturer	Professor/HoD
Female	£19,453	£26,755	£31,360	Locally
Male	£19,516	£27,315	£32,277	negotiated remuneration

Scottish Conference Sector

	Assistant Librarian	Lecturer/ Librarian	Senior Lecturer	Professor/HoD
Female	£19,630	£25,291	£30,861	£41,466
Male	£21,095	£26,169	£31,840	£41,707

Source: Independent Review of Higher Education Pay and Conditions

Table 1.3 shows that the discrepancy between male and female average pay within each grade is marginal, and does not appear to support the finding of the same report that there was an £4,259 average pay gap between men and women in the 'old' universities. However, the average discrepancy over *all* grades serves to underline effectively that women are not in the higher paid posts and that they are not promoted in the same proportions as their male colleagues. That women have been paid less and promoted less than their male counterparts has long been recognised and been the subject of more thorough analyses than a stark league table, or report into pay and conditions of *all* HE staff can provide (McNabb and Wass, 1997; Brooks, 1997), but the obsessive publication of such tables by the press, and very existence of the Bett Report, serve to focus attention and provoke debate beyond the academic community.

The RAE

Since its inception the Research Assessment Exercise (RAE) has played an increasingly dominant role in the determination of academic staff's promotion and, therefore, career prospects. The obvious reasons for this are, put simply, that the higher a department's research grading the more money it is allocated; the more money it is allocated the more prestigious its research; the more prestigious its research, the more prestigious the university becomes and the more students it attracts, thus more money is generated. The last RAE was conducted in 1996, when the HESA returns recorded 126,582 academic staff employed in the UK's HEIs. Of these, slightly over two-fifths were reported as being research active and returned in the 1996 exercise. At that time 68 per cent of the academic staff in universities were men; nearly half (46 per cent) of those men were confirmed as being research active, but less than one-third (30 per cent) of their female colleagues were entered in the exercise. For each category of staff the proportion of men who were entered in the RAE was higher than the proportion of women. The highest proportions of both sexes entered in the exercise were professors – 90 per cent of male professors and 83 per cent of female professors. The proportions of other staff entered in the exercise decreased with seniority – 60 per cent of female senior lecturers and 68 per cent of their male counterparts; 36 per cent of women who were lecturers, and 47 per cent of men in the same position were research active; 17 and 19 per cent of female and male researchers respectively were returned; and 13 per cent of women, compared to 28 per cent of men in the 'Other Staff' category are recorded as having taken part in the 1996 RAE.[6] The largest difference in proportions of each sex is on the most populous, Lecturer, grade. Two-fifths of all academic staff were on this grade at the time of the last RAE, with an approximate one-third/two-thirds split between women and men, which mirrors the gender distribution of academic staff as a whole. The considerably larger difference in the proportion of Senior Lecturers who are research active, compared to the proportion of Lecturers who are research active, and then the similar large difference in the proportions of Professors and Senior Lecturers who were entered in the 1996 RAE, are indicative of the importance published research has to grade, if not, by extension, to promotion. Purely on the basis of the data pertaining to the 1996 RAE, it would appear that if submission to the exercise is weighted more heavily in promotions' criteria than, say, teaching ability, then women have less chance of gaining promotion because they are not as research active. But does the fact that they are not as research active, in terms of RAE submissions, constitute discrimination?

Until April 2000, this theory had no substance in law. It had been tested many times within universities through their internal procedures, but each institution is autonomous and no standard had been set across the sector. In February/March 2000, an Employment Tribunal heard the case of *Dr H Mercer v London School of Economics*.[7] Dr Mercer brought claims of both direct and indirect sex discrimination against the LSE in relation to the permanent appointment of a lecturer in Business History, and the RAE respectively. Both claims were successful. Direct discrimination was proven largely because the attitude of the Convenor of the selection panel had, throughout the process, suggested that he did not want to appoint a woman. This is something particular to that case, and direct discrimination is a straightforward thing to prove when the evidence is readily available. However, indirect discrimination is notoriously difficult to establish. The Sex Discrimination Act provides:

A person discriminates against a woman in any circumstances relevant for the purposes of any provision of this Act if […]
(b) he applies to her a requirement or condition which applies or would apply equally to a man but –

which is such that the proportion of women who can comply with it is smaller than the proportion of men who can comply with it, and which he cannot show to be justifiable irrespective of the sex of the person to whom it is applied, and which is to her detriment because she cannot comply with it.[8]

In determining whether indirect discrimination has occurred or not, members of a tribunal adopt a step-by-step approach to the legislation. Here, the tribunal determined that requirement or condition imposed by the LSE was that the successful candidate had to be RAE active. In the job description this was couched in implicit terms, in the duties and responsibilities of the postholder, 'to contribute to the scholarship and intellectual life of the School by conducting research which will enhance the School's high reputation as a research-led teaching institution. Publication in books and articles in refereed journals is particularly encouraged'. It applied equally to male applicants. In order to determine whether or not the proportion of women who can comply with the condition is smaller than that of men the tribunal has to decide which group, or pool, of people they wish to use to make the comparison. In this case, they were offered two sets of statistics – the national HESA returns, and data specific to the LSE. The statistics pertaining to the LSE were subdivided into two groups, one of which informed the tribunal of the gender division of staff in the whole School, and the other dealt only with the Economic History department. The tribunal chose all academic employees of the LSE as its pool and concluded that since there were 85 female academics and 284 male academics in its employ (23 per cent and 77 per cent, respectively) at the time of Dr Mercer's application for a job at the School, 'that the proportion of women in the pool is smaller than the proportion of men in the pool and therefore less women than men can comply with the condition'.[9] In its defence the LSE attempted to justify the requirement by citing the revenue obtained by foreign students who are attracted to an institution by its high RAE rating. The tribunal did not deem it to be a sufficient defence, and determined that as Dr Mercer could not comply with the requirement at the time of her interview she had suffered a detriment and had, therefore, been indirectly discriminated against.

Unfortunately, Employment Tribunal decisions have no precedent value for other tribunals; and each tribunal is free to choose its own pool for purposes of comparison. This case is probably not, then, the watershed it was augured to be. The implications of the judgement would be enormous if the pool used here were to be enlarged to encompass academics employed in all UK HEIs because, on the reasoning adopted by the tribunal it would make the RAE itself indirectly discriminatory against women, purely because there are less women employed as academics than men. But the importance accorded to submission to the next RAE by the appointment panel at the LSE suggests that a greater proportion of more junior staff will have been submitted to the 2001 exercise, than to the 1996 one, and that a greater proportion of women will have been submitted.

The future

Research into attitudes to equal pay was carried out for the Equal Opportunities Commission in autumn 1999. The students who took part in this research were all expecting to enter employment in 2000, half were in HE and a quarter each were in FE and sixth form colleges. Both male and female students had the same aspirations in terms of level of responsibility, yet their career trajectories differed:

> Women generally expect to have lower salaries than men when they enter employment. This is essentially because they are more likely to choose industries where salaries are lower. Two out of five women were intending to go into education, health or related service industries, while men were most likely to go into research, IT or business. The great majority of both male and female students expected to have the same earnings as their male/female counterparts after both five and ten years.[10]

This last finding evidences a rather naïve faith in a system that has consistently managed to maintain lower wages for women. According to the 1998 New Earning Survey, the latest government statistics available, full-time female employees received 80 per cent of men's gross hourly earnings, and a more recent report shows an even bleaker picture. In April 1999, men in full-time employment had average gross annual earnings of £23,000 – 42 per cent higher than women.[11] In Higher Education the situation is slightly better – women earn 85 per cent of men's wages – the higher average due, possibly, to the fact that the New Earnings Survey includes traditionally higher-paying male – and lower-paying female-dominated jobs. As does the Office for National Statistics' (ONS) report which cites women's employment in the lower paid professions, such as nursing, teaching and domestic service. This cannot, though, be used to excuse the disparity in pay between men and women in the universities and colleges of Higher Education in the United Kingdom. Here, the qualifying criteria for employment are equal, the disciplines are judged, rightly, to be equal in terms of pay, and the conditions of employment are the same for both sexes.

Over the last few years the Commission on University Career Opportunity (CUCO) has worked hard to produce equality for women in Higher Education. Though opportunities for women have improved slightly since 1994, when the Commission was established, the statistics show that parity has not been achieved. Recommendation 49 of the Dearing Report argued that

> all institutions should, as part of their human resources policy, maintain equal opportunities, and, over the medium term, should identify and remove barriers which inhibit recruitment and progression for particular groups and monitor and publish their progress towards greater equality of opportunity for all groups.[12]

This accords with Recommendation 59 of the Bett Report:

> Each university and HE college should have, and publish, a clear statement of its policies on equal opportunities and of the steps it is taking to ensure equality for women and ethnic minorities.

In response, David Blunkett, Secretary of State for Education and Employment, wrote to the Chair of the Higher Education Funding Council for England to 'ask HEFCE to ensure that all institutions have equal opportunities policy statements and that they are accountable for their full and proper implementation'.[13] As a direct result, HEFCE, the Committee of Vice Chancellors and Principals (CVCP) and the Standing Conference of Principals (SCOP) set-up, and will operate, an Equal Opportunities Action Group in summer 2000, which will supersede CUCO. The group will meet for five years and has funding of £2.5 million. Its proposed role is to:

- raise awareness about, and the profile of, equal opportunities;
- develop and disseminate advice and good practice;
- commission research to underpin policy and practice development;
- monitor progress on employment performance in the sector; and
- recommend appropriate benchmarks and standards to measure progress in institutions.

This will be overseen by the Equal Opportunities Commission and the Commission for Racial Equality. If real political will exists to redress the imbalance in the salary gap between men and women in UK HEIs, and to promote equity in male/female promotion prospects, a two-pronged (at least) approach has to be taken. To eliminate the salary differential an immediate injection of cash is required, estimated as being between £200m and £400m, and ring-fenced for the purpose. A corresponding commitment from the treasury to factor this sum into every subsequent funding rise for Higher Education is also necessary. Some HEIs could afford to pay their female staff more from their own resources, but do not do so. These institutions may well be in the minority but it would be divisive, and contrary to the principles that underpin the maintenance of national pay scales and bargaining if they did. Secondly, one of the most effective ways of ensuring HEIs introduce promotions and recruitment criteria which give transparent equality of opportunity is to introduce cash penalties for non-compliance with them; or, perhaps, as the unions have argued, to reward those institutions whose commitment to their implementation shows palpable results.

Conclusion

There is no doubt that data is being, and has been, collected which gives an accurate profile of academic staff in terms of their grade of employment, age, terms of employment, cost centre assignation, mode of employment, salary etc, by institution. HESA does not collect information on academic staff who are employed on less than a 0.25 pro rata contract, nor are academic-related staff included in their returns, but the figures that they do collect show that, over the five-year period, women have been paid substantially less than men. The selection of statistics that are chosen for publication in the annual Resources of Higher Education volumes do not enable pay comparisons to be made. However, additional information can be purchased from the Agency at considerable expense, and only on its terms. It collects data on the exact salaries of the men and women employed in HEIs and chooses not to make it readily available. The publication of salary details that could lead to the identification of individuals is not to be advocated, but there is a case to be made for information which would seem to indicate discriminatory practices to be easily accessible. Of course, the information can be drawn upon by the institutions that collect it, and the Agency that collates it, and it can only be concluded that the former do not think the pay divide between male and female academic staff has been of sufficient importance to rectify the anomaly, or the latter to give it more prominence.

However, the Dearing and Bett reports have put equality on the political agenda, and this government's response to them has been encouraging:

> I am determined that the equal opportunities record in Higher Education must improve, and I am pleased to see that progress is now starting to be made. [...] want to see openness, transparency and equality of opportunity reaching the very highest levels of university governance. It is frankly not good enough that only five of the seventy two English universities and only six Higher Education colleges are headed by women, and that there are no ethnic minority heads in either category. That must change.[14]

Notes

[1]   HESA Individual Staff Record 1998/9.
[2]   *Resources of Higher Education Institutions*, 1994/5, Higher Education Statistics Agency Ltd, June 1996.
[3]   Professor includes Heads of Departments, Professors, former Universities' Appointments Panel (UAP) scale Researchers (Grade IV), Clinical Professors and those appointed Professors on a locally determined scale.
[4]   Senior Lecturers and Researchers include Principal Lecturers, Senior Lecturers, former UAP scale Researchers (Grade III), Clinical Senior Lecturers and those appointed Senior or Principal Lecturers on a locally determined scale.
[5]   Peter Scott, Comment, *Independent Education*, 24 February 2000.
[6]   Lecturers includes Lecturers, Senior Lecturers (former PCEF scale), Clinical Lecturers and those appointed Lecturers on a locally determined scale. Researchers includes all research grades except former UAP scale Researchers Grades III and IV, and those appointed on a locally determined scale.
[7]   *Dr H.J. Mercer v London School of Economics*, ET 2201988/98 (6 April 2000).
[8]   Section 1(1)(b) SDA 1975.
[9]   Para 55, ET 2201988/98.
[10]   Research Findings, *Attitudes to Equal Pay*, Equal Opportunities Commission, 2000.
[11]   *Social Inequalities 2000*, Office for National Statistics, Stationery Office, 2000.
[12]   *National Committee of Inquiry into Higher Education*, Sir Ron Dearing, Crown Copyright, 1997.
[13]   Letter from David Blunkett, Secretary of State for Education and Employment, to Sir Michael Checkland, Chairman, HEFCE, 23 November 1999.
[14]   David Blunkett, Secretary of State for Education and Employment, Speech to AUT Summer Council, 10 May 2000.

References

Brooks, A. (1997), *Academic Women*, SRHE/Open University Press, Milton Keynes.
McNabb, R. and V. Wass (1997), 'Male–Female Salary Differentials in British Universities', *Oxford Economic Papers*, 49.

HESA cannot accept responsibility for any inferences or conclusions derived from the data it has published by third parties.

Chapter 2

Transcending Boundaries: Women, Research and Teaching in the Academy

Sue Jackson

Introduction

At the heart of the structures of many academic institutions today is the question of research. Power is often in the hands of those who attract research money, and who are considered to be highly valuable assets as active researchers whose work is being included in the Research Assessment Exercise (RAE). Indeed, many established researchers are being offered posts and research money on the strength of their contributions to the RAE. Although not entirely the case, this tends to apply to men, who still hold the vast majority of senior research and senior lecturer posts. This in turn enables senior male academics to determine what counts as 'good research'. I will argue that good research methodology relies on sound epistemology, and that feminist research epistemology delivers both a critique of assumed neutrality in traditional research and suggestions for good research practice. Nevertheless, I will show that what determines 'good research practice' is guided by a male academic culture and institutional discrimination against women. It is of no surprise that feminist research carries little esteem and attracts little money within Higher Education Institutions. In this chapter, by first outlining some issues of feminist research and epistemology and then moving on to consider both the Research Assessment Exercise and the Institute for Learning and Teaching, I will evaluate the position of women in research and teaching in Higher Education. Whilst I will show that many women are keen to transcend the boundaries of more traditional academic research and teaching, the gatekeepers of the academy ensure that the work of women academics remain undervalued, with severe effects on their career opportunities and development.

Feminist research

In considering the nature of feminist research, outlining the development of feminist research, and engaging in a debate about feminist methodologies, epistemologies and theoretical perspectives, I shall show that feminist research and feminist theory inform each other and are inextricably woven together. Both research and theory give us ways to conceptualise how we think about knowledge. Within research, decisions need to be made about how a topic is investigated, what will count as evidence, how it will be collected, and how it will be analysed. This cannot be done without a theoretical positioning and engagement, so that we can rethink the findings from a different viewpoint.

Part of my engagement with theoretical research has been to consider how (feminist) research methodology relates to (feminist) epistemology and the production of knowledge. This is something which has concerned Liz Stanley in her considerations of feminist research. She has long rejected a 'theory/research' divide (see Stanley, 1990), showing how theorising requires research of some kind and, I would add, research requires theorising, a point she picks up in later analysis. More recently (Stanley, 1997), she has argued that methodology also matters because it delivers the 'facts' which are used to support a theory, i.e. the consideration of the relationship between methodology and epistemology. Methodology, she suggests, is a central component of knowledge, and so of feminist epistemology. Different knowledges about the same thing are possible, for knowledge is always grounded in point-of-view. Feminist epistemologists question the process of justification whereby something counts as a 'true' belief. Methodology matters, then, 'because it is the key to understanding and unpacking the overlap between power/knowledge' (Stanley, 1997, p.198). Moving from and between methodology and epistemology will enable a philosophical engagement with theoretical perspectives and constructions of knowledge. It is clear, then, that the debate needs to continue at an epistemological level, considering what counts as knowledge, and who has the power to define it so.

I argue, along with many others, that there is no such distinctive category within feminist research as feminist research *methods*. Sandra Harding, for instance, argues against the idea of a distinctive feminist method of research. Instead she suggests that what is more important is a feminist standpoint that engages in an intellectual and political struggle which places women's experiences at the centre of any research, rather that concentrating on using particular methods (Harding, 1987, p.27). However, this is not an uncontested view. For example, an article appeared in *Women's Studies International Forum* as recently as 1995, presented as a 'A Bibliography of Selected Readings on Feminist Research Methods' (Campbell, 1995). Indeed, many earlier attempts to consider feminist research shared a perspective that in order for research to be 'feminist', the researchers should only engage in qualitative methods, enabling women's voices to be heard and women's stories to be told in a way which had not happened in the past. In Britain, Helen Roberts' early (1981) edited collection, setting ways of *Doing Feminist Research*, certainly focused on a range of qualitative case studies. Throughout the 1980s, there was a strongly held view that quantitative methods were associated with 'male' ways of thinking, whilst qualitative methods were 'softer', better suited to a woman-centred approach. Indeed for these reasons Shulamit Reinharz, continuing her earlier work into the 1990s, also suggests that the use of interviews – especially semi-structured or very loosely structured interviews – is one of the principal research methods used by feminists (Reinharz, 1992, p.18). Indeed, interviews and other qualitative research is important work, enabling analyses and understandings to be grounded in women's lived experiences, rather than within a universalised male experience of the world.

However, others have suggested that *any* research method can be utilised in feminist research projects. For example, Liz Kelly, Linda Regan and Sheila Burton (1992) have come to the defense of quantitative methods in feminist research, showing that they can be valuable in considering a wider picture. Similarly, Toby Jayaratne and Abigail Stewart (1995) have set out some practical strategies for feminist researchers to use quantitative as well as qualitative methods. Different research methods will give insightful ways of considering issues, and a simple qualitative/quantitative dichotomy is not helpful. Feminism has added an insight into recognising the subjective nature of quantitative research, for instance, recognising that data collected here is no more objective than that collected in qualitative research. In Liz Stanley's (1990) edited collection, in which she and others have considered feminist praxis in theory and research, several contributors have given consideration to the subjective nature of quantitative research. Denise Farran (1990), for example, has written about the production of statistical information, showing that whilst statistics are seen as representations of social reality, they also construct that reality. Fiona Poland (1990) has shown how the researcher decides how to collect data, what to include, and how to present her findings; and this is as true of quantitative research as it is of qualitative. Anne Pugh (1990), in considering her feminism and her use of statistical information, says that number crunching can be useful, but the main feminist interest will come from the context and frame of reference employed. Statistics do not yield a neutral picture, but are always gathered and then interpreted via methodologies. What I have found more useful, then, is to consider a distinctive feminist methodology, or rather feminist methodologies: critical frameworks that are used in the gathering of data, and in its analysis and theorising.

What is it, though, that makes such methodologies, or critical frameworks, explicitly *feminist*? Whilst Liz Stanley (1997), building on her earlier work, warns against establishing 'truth' claims for any one version of 'appropriate' methodology, there are some features which are generally accepted as enabling good practice in carrying out feminist research. Mary Maynard and June Purvis summarise from a British perspective some of the key issues in their consideration of *Researching Women's Lives from a Feminist Perspective*. In this edited collection, they indicate that 'there is no one answer to the question "what it feminist research?"' (Maynard and Purvis, 1994, p.25). Instead, they initiate a debate around issues of methods, methodologies and epistemologies, through presenting a series of case studies which engage in their various ways with questions about what constitutes feminist research. The authors suggest that a focus on autobiographical analysis of research can be a useful tool for exploring the research process. They offer examples of research which explore personal accounts, and consider some of the parameters and boundaries within which the authors consider feminist research to be constituted. For Ann Phoenix, for instance, one of the central features of conducting feminist research is in considering the intersection of gender and 'race' in the research process, an aspect which has at times been missing from the work of other writers on feminist research, such as Shulamit Reinharz. In considering her own studies of young mothers, Ann Phoenix shows how her personal location in her work has enabled her to bring added dimensions to her work as a feminist researcher (Phoenix, 1994).

My own research methods and methodological positioning have also developed out of a commitment to feminism and to feminist research. Feminism is a central part of my identity, personally and politically, ideologically and in the lived realities of my experiences. In a very real sense it would not be possible for me to engage in anything other than feminist research – researching as a feminist – which of course in itself is not an unproblematic concept. What *is* straightforward – for me at least – is that I use my feminism to view the world through a particular and partial perspective, a perspective set in women's lives and women's experiences (see Harding, 1987). There is nothing unusual in taking a partial perspective: most of what is 'known', what counts as 'knowledge', is also particular and partial – the particular and partial perspectives of men's experiences, albeit a hidden partiality, universalised as 'truth'. I intend to make my own lens neither opaque nor hidden, and to place women's experiences at the centre of my research.

As I have shown above, then, methodology, is never neutral, and its location is always relevant to claims to 'know'. However, this is contested in the academy, which required academic work to be apparently objective and neutral. Work which acknowledges and locates itself within its subjective positioning can find itself excluded from the canon. For instance, in the discipline of psychology Sue Wilkinson, in her work on 'Why Psychology (Badly) Needs Feminism', describes how knowledge itself is seen as male (and White, and western), with an emphasis on scientific methods and a failure to recognise the subjectivity of constructions of knowledge. There is, she says, a continuing insistence in the academy between the dichotomy of objectivity/subjectivity. She describes how her own writing has been criticised as 'emotion-laden', with requests for a more 'objective' style (Wilkinson, 1991).

This has been an issue for other women researchers, too, including myself. Feminist researchers can often find themselves isolated in the academy, and gender issues are not always taken seriously. At one institution where I lectured, for instance, my work was excluded from a departmental book on Higher Education because: 'Sue's interests are in gender, which is not relevant to the topic'! Feminist research, based in women's lives and women's experiences, is often not counted in the academy as 'real' research, and work located in Women's Studies becomes problematic in the hunt for jobs or promotion. Indeed, there are no Women's Studies, Gender Studies, or Feminist Studies panels in the Research Assessment Exercise, which itself is increasingly becoming a determining factor for academic 'success'.

The Research Assessment Exercise

However, it is not just feminist researchers who can find themselves isolated in the academy. As I will go on to explore, women – whether working as researchers or as lecturers – suffer discrimination in an academy in which the odds are stacked up against them. Women, for instance, are more likely to earn less than men, are more likely to be on short-term contracts, and less likely to be in senior positions. It is, then, perhaps of little surprise that women are also less likely to have work submitted to the Research Assessment Exercise (Lodger and Eley, 1998; Wotjas, 1999). This is cause for concern for women's jobs, as academic posts today are often reliant on such submissions (see Swain, 1999). Indeed, an employment tribunal has found an institution of Higher Education guilty of sexual discrimination against a female lecturer, who was found to have suffered both direct and indirect discrimination because of the Research Assessment Exercise. Although Dr Helen Mercer had been highly praised by her institution, the London School of Economics, for both her research and her teaching, she was rejected for a job in favour of a male candidate who had less experience, but was judged by the selection panel to have higher potential for the Research Assessment Exercise. The tribunal found that the number of women on the shortlist had been cut, drawing the inference that the selection panel did not want to appoint a woman, and found that 'making RAE participation a condition of employment was discriminatory because of the lower number of women taking part in the RAE than men' (Swain, 2000, p.8).

Why, though, is it that women are less likely to have submissions in the RAE? One explanation is that women are more likely to engage in interdisciplinary research than are men. Recent surveys have shown that women are more likely than men to focus on interdisciplinary projects (Wotjas, 1999; Major, 1999). This holds true across all disciplines (with the one exception of engineering science). For example, Joyce Tait, director of the Scottish Universities Policy Research and Advice Network, states that she has 'been doing interdisciplinary research for about 25 years. I think disciplines are about staking out your territory, and I think men are a bit more territorial than women' (in Wotjas, 1998).

The Research Assessment Exercise is based within disciplines and subject areas, and women's propensity for interdisciplinary work might well be an issue here. However, it is difficult to know the extent to which this causes a lack of recognition of women's work. A study by a consultancy firm to investigate women and research, which surveyed 11,000 researchers, found their results hampered. As their questionnaire was addressed to staff in senior positions, this also meant that most of the respondents were men. However, what is clear is that traditionally male-dominated subjects like clinical medicine, engineering and the physical sciences, receive disproportionately large allocations of funding under the Exercise. Additionally, only one quarter of the RAE panel members are women, and only one seventh of the panel Chairs, with the panels Chaired by women responsible for just 10 per cent of the RAE funding.

One key issue that has concerned the Women's Committee of the Association of University Teachers is the impact of maternity leave on women academics' submissions to the RAE. In the Research Assessment Exercise which took place in 1996, there were no mechanisms for determining how, or even if, maternity leave should be taken into account in submissions to the Exercise. As a result, women's research output could be deemed inadequate, with no considerations given to the time in which the academic was absent on maternity leave, and unable to submit publications. Indeed, women academics found themselves faced with the decision to either complete a full return, regardless of their maternity leave, or to risk being left out of their institution's submission, with serious consequences for future career chances. Others, though, were not faced with such a choice: it was in many cases the institution itself which made the decision, pressurising staff to continue researching and writing throughout their maternity leave of absence. Clearly as it is only women who can take maternity leave, this represents discrimination.

In the move towards the 2001 Exercise, things were looking little better:

> Of the 60 panels, only 12 have attempted to incorporate maternity leave as a determining factor in research productivity, and these range from considering maternity leave as a factor significantly affecting individual contribution, to considering maternity leave as one of a number of unusual or exceptional circumstances (Phillips, 2000, p.13).

However, at least partly as a result of the AUT's submissions, the guidelines for the 2001 Research Assessment Exercise have since been reconsidered, and in Spring 2000 AUTwoman was able to report on its front page 'Breakthrough on RAE guidelines'. These guidelines now state:

> The situation of staff who have taken maternity leave or other career breaks, who hold part-time contracts, who are disabled, or who have been absent for long periods through illness (where this is indicated by Higher Education institutions) will be taken into account in reaching overall judgements of quality where it is indicated in submissions (AUTwoman, 2000).

This does, though, place the decision with the institution, not the individual. Women could still find that the institution has taken a decision on their submission (or non-submission) of work for the Exercise which works to their detriment. With an indication that needs to be made by the institution and not the individual, there will be many variations in practice that will effect women's submissions differently. There is no requirement on the institution to make this information available, and little is yet known about the advice and guidance institutions will offer to those responsible for completing RAE returns. In addition, more information is needed about what is meant by 'taken into account'. Will it be up to individual panels, for example, to determine what to take into account, and how? Whilst the selection of 'good research' appears to be neutral or unbiased, it is clear that this is far from the case. It is biased against women both in terms of quantity (where women can be hampered in their research and writing activities by maternity leave or care commitments) and in terms of quality (in the decisions that are made to return some individuals and not others as research active). In particular, as can be seen above, women can find themselves hindered by a focus on interdisciplinary work and qualitative research.

In a dichotomous exercise which labels academics as either research active or non-research active, women who do not have their work submitted stand little chance of success in promotions. With the odds stacked against women as researchers and academics, it is then of little surprise that women are less likely than men to apply for research grants. A survey conducted by the Wellcome Trust into why more than three times more men than women apply for research grants is addressing four questions (Lodger and Eley, 1998):

- how often do women and men apply for grants?
- does the university career affect grant-applying behaviour?
- do women and men share the same workloads?
- do attitudes towards making applications differ between the sexes?

However, there are questions that the Wellcome Trust has not asked, such as whether short-term and possibly part-time contracts make it impossible to apply for grants; or whether universities are unlikely to support applications from staff in more junior positions.

One territory that men appeared to have claimed as their own is the territory of research, leaving women disproportionately situated in the field of teaching, and in lower-paid, lower-status jobs. The Bett Report, an Independent Review of Higher Education: Pay and Conditions, published in June 1999, highlighted the discrimination apparent against women academics in all areas of teaching, researching and job promotion. Women are more likely than men to be in short-term contracts, and to be in lower-grade jobs. Even when women and men are doing work of a similar nature, what the Bett report highlighted for the first time in Britain is that men still earn considerably more than women do. In the worst cases, women academics are being paid up to £8,000 a year less than men in equivalent posts, although figures from National Association of Teachers in Further and Higher Education (NATFHE) show that at one institution the average man's salary exceeds the average woman's salary by £19,000 per year! However, even in nursing, the subject most dominated by women and where 70 per cent of lecturers are female, men earn over £1,000 p.a. more than women in equivalent posts (MacLeod, 2000). This discrepancy exists throughout research and teaching.

The Institute for Learning and Teaching

The distinction between research and teaching is of course an interesting one. For many universities, research is the defining activity, enjoying a higher status than lecturing. It is coming to be seen as the 'real' work of universities, perhaps because it is through research activities that much university funding is derived (see *Times Higher*, 1999). Indeed, the 1992 Further and Higher Education Act separated out funding for research and funding for teaching. A report from Warwick University has indicated that for lecturers there is no aspect of their work that ranks higher than research, giving high self-esteem and a sense of achievement (Evans and Abbott, 1997). It is, then, as Tom Schuller shows, 'ironic that staff defined as "researchers" are for the most part marginal in status' (Schuller, 1995, p.5). It is not surprising to find that gender is often a defining feature in locating researchers as marginal or central, with many women being engaged as hourly-paid researchers to support – often without acknowledgement – the high status research of men that leads to funding and career opportunities (see Wotjas, 1999; Guardian, 1999). The emphasis for promotion and career development is on a constant demand for research and published work.

However, it is possible that this research culture will start to change, with different criteria being adopted for promotion into positions of seniority. Following the publication of the Dearing Report, the Institute of Learning and Teaching was set up, not only developing a system of qualifications for all lecturers, but recognising and awarding excellence in teaching (see Bekhradnia, 1998; Swain, 1997). Indeed, academics who wish to be members of the Institute of Learning and Teaching will have to demonstrate a series of competencies in teaching outcomes (Utley, 1999a). However, it remains to be seen what will be recognised as 'excellent' teaching practice. Although one of the outcomes that lecturers must demonstrate does show a need to 'create opportunities for appropriate innovation in learning and teaching practice', it is debatable what such innovation means as other outcomes appear to be grounded in an academy which has become market led and vocationally based; and to focus on securing procedures already in place, with a concentration on 'assessment strategy', 'assessment criteria', 'marking schemes' and 'transferable skills'.

Nevertheless, feminist pedagogy has led the way in innovative work in learning and teaching (see Jackson, 1997), and some women academics, drawing on feminist theories of education, are creating a learning and teaching environment that moves to transcend boundaries and make border crossings into innovative pedagogic practices. These practices find ways to encourage students to draw on their personal experiences to develop both theoretical and analytical approaches to Higher Education (Jackson, 1999), and to challenge current constructions of what it means to be 'academic' (Jackson, 2000, forthcoming). Although the language of the ILT seems unlikely to encourage feminist pedagogic practice, either explicitly or implicitly, feminist pedagogy could usefully be disseminated in the academy as an exemplar of good practice.

The Institute for Learning and Teaching was set up to promote good practice throughout Higher Educational institutions, and to return the emphasis to teaching. This could have been seen as a positive move for women lecturers, who often find their work more closely associated with teaching and learning than with research. Women, often concentrated in more junior positions, are more likely to have a higher teaching workload than men. Women are more likely than men, too, to spend time on administrative and pastoral work, and still take most of the domestic responsibilities, leaving less time for research activities. It could, then, clearly benefit women if membership of the ILT meant that the teaching women are doing carried more status and value, and maybe even attract higher salaries, as institutions recognised the worth of teaching as well as of research. Nevertheless, there is concern that the ILT could create an even wider gap between teaching and research, further damaging women who are more likely to be concentrated in teaching and are already discriminated against in the RAE.

There are, then, many arguments against the Institute for Learning and Teaching. There are, for instance, concerns that universities will use membership as a way of avoiding a need to supply Continuing Professional Development for staff and yet still satisfy the recommendations of the Quality Assurance Agency. Certainly the early months of its inception have failed to see many applications. There is additionally concern that the ILT could create an even wider gap between teaching and research, and the Association of University Teachers has accused the ILT of using 'appalling stereotypes' of female academics (Baty, 2000), with its training literature described as 'absolutely inappropriate':

> The training literature at the centre of the storm includes two sample application forms advising how to get membership of the ILT. A fictional male lecturer's application is given as an example of a successful applicant, while a female lecturer's application is deemed unsuccessful. The woman is described [...] as 'a warm [...] and slightly ephemeral person' [...whilst] the man is a 'capable and innovative teacher', contributing to [...] the research assessment exercise (Baty, 2000).

Working in a 'male culture'

It is clear, then, that with teaching as well as with research male academics are taken as the norm. The 'capable teacher' who also contributes positively to the RAE, and who works competitively and individually in a market-led academy is not a model that many women would recognise of themselves. Even initiatives which might appear to be positive for women in the academy can be appropriated. Writing in 1995, Helena Kennedy asks why there are fewer women than men at the top in Higher Education. In her article, she looks at the problematic opposition between equal opportunities policies and practices and the competitive and patriarchal system on which Higher Education institutions are based. She describes the 'glass ceiling' that women hit, which is even more problematic because it is so difficult to see. 'One of the central components of the glass ceiling in academia is the mysterious and mystified ideal of an ungendered, disembodied and academic brilliance', and yet the supposed neutrality of tests of excellence, Helena Kennedy says, is 'fictional', leading to a system where 'one set of competitors – highly qualified female academics – never get off the starting blocks'. She states that 'the undervaluing of women's skills is central to their absence in the highest echelons', and the very conceptions of knowledge and excellence have to be challenged (Kennedy, 1995, p.15).

Despite the location of both the Research Assessment Exercise and the Institute of Learning and Teaching in British universities, the predominance of a male culture in both teaching and research spreads much further afield. In Denmark, for instance, often considered to be more open in terms of gender equality than in Britain, the figures for women working in Higher Education are even worse than in the UK. Only 6 per cent of professors are women, as are a shockingly low total of only 19 per cent of all university employees (de Laine, 1998). Women hold only 20 per cent of all senior lecturer and senior research posts (Gold, 1998; Hague, 2000a). For women from ethnic minority groups, the figures are even more appalling (see Hague 2000b). Where women are engaged as researchers, this is largely as short-term contract staff, with little possibilities of developing their own interests. In the sciences, women fare particularly badly. Women constitute 1 per cent of physics professors and 0.3 per cent of chemistry professors, for example. These are, of course, traditionally male areas, but it makes little difference in subjects like music, which is studied by a majority of female students, but which has only two women professors (Gold, 1998).

Jytte Hilden, Denmark's research minister, states that 'the research world favours male researchers, their themes and their angles' (see Loder, 1998). Despite well-functioning day-care institutions, enabling women to be able to work in Higher Educational institutions, the male culture of the universities discriminates heavily against women, with a real lack of women mentors and role models for both students and academics. Jytte Hilden suggests that new initiatives and a change in culture is needed if women are to succeed. Indeed, the government has set up a special programme (Female Researchers in Joint Action), although both funding and initiatives are needed at every level. Female Danish researchers are 38 per cent less likely to get some research grants than their male colleagues, and even if a grant is awarded, it is likely to be only half of that awarded to men (Loder, 1998).

At 18.4 per cent of the total, Finland has more women professors than any other country in the European Union (Seppanen, 1999), but this is still a high minority position which leaves women struggling in a male culture. Despite the fact that the proportion of women completing the examination needed to enter university is significantly higher than men, and women fill a higher number of university places than men, an education ministry report concludes that women still face gender inequality in their careers. Lusa Husu, one of the authors of the report, suggests that this inequality stems from:

> the male-orientated culture in the universities. All seems to go well for women up to the point they have their doctoral theses published. Then the opportunities for further research seems to be much more restricted than for their male counter-parts (in Seppanen, 1999).

Although all areas of academic life appear to be affected by a bias towards a male culture, scientists are particularly badly hit. European Commission conferences held in 1993 and in 1998 have confirmed this view (see Hinde, 1998). The 1998 conference heard that the under-representation of women in science is 'simply appalling'. A female Israeli delegate told the conference that for women in academic science 'at the beginning there is an iron gate, then a sticky floor; at the top a glass ceiling, and in between a hurdle race' (in Hinde, 1998).

Throughout Europe, more women are entering science, which is no longer viewed as a male preserve – at least by the increasing number of women who are taking undergraduate science degrees. However, 'waiting for women to filter naturally through to the top ranks of academia, as has often been suggested, does not appear to be producing results' (Hinde, 1998). It is not just family responsibilities that hinder women wishing to teach or research in science, important as they are. Hilary Rose has stated that academic science is a 'system where men give each other prizes' (in Hinde, 1998). She suggests that is it men who are the gatekeepers of academic science, who set and govern the rules and practices. She says:

> All the powerful positions are held, and have been historically held, by men. People can see talent in people who look like themselves. Like young people need role models, older successful people look back and see talent in people who are like they were. Whatever the desired cultural traits are, women do not have them. We have to persuade science's gatekeepers that it is possible to be 'not man' and brilliant (in Hinde, 1998).

Certainly the European Conference contained plenty of anecdotal evidence to suggest that this will be a hard lesson for men to learn: women are not taken seriously in their work, and face many negative effects due to gender discrimination.

Conclusions

It is clear then, that for many women researching and teaching in the academy, the most exciting opportunities are those which enable current boundaries to be transcended: boundaries of interdisciplinary research; of a central focus on women's lives and experiences; boundaries of constructions of 'academic; of a public/private divide; and boundaries of a dichotomous divide between research, teaching and learning. However, for many women in the academy, the gatekeepers are continuing to make these boundaries difficult – sometimes impossible – to cross. Whilst these gatekeepers continue in the main to be the white, middle-class men who dominate the academy, ensuring that the male culture of the university is dominant, women will find themselves powerless to make the challenges to bring about change. In particular, as feminist researchers and teachers, we may find ourselves particularly isolated, whilst nevertheless finding ways to engage in innovative challenges to the research and teaching of the academy.

References

'Breakthrough on RAE guidelines', *AUTwoman* (2000), 49, Spring.
Baty, P. (2000), 'Claims of "appalling" sexism rock ILT', *Times Higher Education Supplement*, 11 February.
Bekhradnia, B. (1998), 'Excellence in Teaching Must Have Prizes', *Times Higher Education Supplement*, 26 June.
Campbell, R. (1995), 'Weaving a New Tapestry of Research: a Bibliography of Selected Readings on Feminist Research Methods', *Women's Studies International Forum*, 18 (2).
de Laine, M. (1998), 'Danish Women Fight to Bring Home the Bacon', *Times Higher Education Supplement*, 6 February.

Evans, L. and I. Abbott (1997), 'Report from Warwick University's Teacher Development, Research and Dissemination Unit', *Guardian*, 13 May.

Farran, D. (1990), 'Seeking Susan: Producing Statistical Information', in L. Stanley (ed.).

Gold, K. (1998), '8.1 per cent of Professors are Women', *Times Higher Education Supplement*, 3 July.

Hague, H. (2000a), '2.3 per cent and 9.8 per cent ...', *Times Higher Education Supplement*, 7 April.

_____ (2000b), 'Stopped By the Sound Barrier', *Times Higher Education Supplement*, 14 April.

Harding, S. (1987), *Feminism and Methodology*, Open University Press, Milton Keynes.

Hinde, J. (1998), 'Flaws of motion', *Times Higher Education Supplement*, 15 May.

Jackson, S. (1997), 'Crossing Borders and Changing Pedagogies: from Giroux and Freire to Feminist Theories of Education', *Gender and Education*, 9 (4).

_____ (1999), 'Learning and Teaching in Higher Education: the Use of Personal Experience in Theoretical and Analytical Approaches', *Journal of Further and Higher Education*, 23 (3).

_____ (2000), 'Differently Academic?: Constructions of 'Academic' in Higher Education', *Higher Education, Research and Development*, forthcoming, 19 (3), December.

Jayaratne, T. and A. Stewart (1995), 'Quantitative and Qualitative Methods in Social Sciences: Feminist Issues and Practical Strategies', in J. Holland and M. Blair (eds), *Debates and Issues in Feminist Research and Pedagogy*, Multilingual Matters, Clevedon.

Kennedy, H. (1995), 'Prisoners of Gender', in *Times Higher Education Supplement*, 3 November.

Loder, N. (1998), 'Danish Women Face Research Bias', *Times Higher Education Supplement*, 15 May.

Lodger, N and S. Eley (1998), 'Probe Into What Puts Women Off Research', *Times Higher Education Supplement*, 18 September.

MacLeod, D. (2000), 'Female Trouble', *Guardian*, 4 April.

Major, L. E. (1999), 'The Bigger Picture', *Guardian*, 2 February.

Maynard, M and J. Purvis (eds) (1994), *Researching Women's Lives from a Feminist Perspective*, Taylor & Francis, London.

Phillips, D. (2000), 'Leaving Out Maternity', *AUTLook*, 214, January.

Phoenix, A. (1994), 'Practising Feminist Research: the Intersection of Gender and 'Race' in the Research Process', in M. Maynard and J. Purvis (eds).

Poland, F. (1990), 'Breaking the Rules', in L. Stanley (ed.) (1990).

Pugh, A. (1990), 'My Statistics and Feminism', in L. Stanley (ed.) *ibid.*

Reinharz, S. (1992), *Feminist Methods in Social Research*, Oxford University Press, Oxford.

Roberts, H. (1981), *Doing Feminist Research*, Routledge & Kegan Paul, London.

Schuller, T. (1995), *The Changing University*, Open University Press, Milton Keynes.

Seppanen, R. (1999), 'Male Culture Holds Back Women', *Times Higher Education Supplement*, 14 May.

Stanley, L. (1990), *Feminist Praxis: Research, Theory and Epistemology in Feminist Sociology*, Routledge, London.

_____ (1997), 'Methodology Matters!', in D. Richardson and V. Robinson, *Introducing Women's Studies* (second edition), Macmillan, Basingstoke.

Swain, H. (1997), 'New Learning and Teaching Body Set to Reward Excellence', *Times Higher Education Supplement*, 21 November.

_____ (1999), 'Jobs Insecurity Spreads', *Times Higher Education Supplement*, 10 December.

_____ (2000), 'Doctor Wins LSE Sex Bias Case', *Times Higher Education Supplement*, 14 April.

Times Higher Education Supplement (1999), '"Old Boys" Hold on to Research Funds', 1 January.

Utley, A. (1999a), 'ILT Sets its Entry Rules', *Times Higher Education Supplement*, 5 February.

_____ (1999b), 'A Club No-one Wants to Join', *Times Higher Education Supplement*, 9 April.

Wilkinson, S. (1991, 'Why Psychology (Badly) Needs Feminism', in J. Aaron and S. Walby (eds), *Out of the Margins, Women's Studies in the Nineties*, Falmer Press, London.

Wotjas, O. (1999), 'Women take Interdisciplinary Route to Research', *Times Higher Education Supplement*, 29 January.

Chapter 3

Equal Opportunities Without 'Equality': Redeeming the Irredeemable

Val Walsh

Introduction

In the 1980s in some colleges and universities in the UK, the advent of equal opportunities as a public discourse which could include and be applied to Higher Education provided an umbrella of hope and aspiration, under the canopy of which women – amongst others hitherto variously outside the academy or marginalised within it – could imagine the possibility of openly and officially working to challenge and change our conditions of service as female academics, and thereby disturb forever the habits of ingrained academic culture. The chance to take on and make history seemed in view.

However, women's experience, anecdotal evidence, research and writing since then reveal that the academy is not the safer and better place for women as academics imagined possible in those early days. Those improvements and advances which can be noted, such as a rise in numbers or seniority, appear to have been made at considerable cost.[1] What followed in many institutions might be identified as resistance or as a backlash. Another, new but familiar, credo changed the face of academia as the new managerialism began to bite.

Equal opportunities was incorporated almost immediately into Personnel, to be managed by staff with no previous interest in it, as part of a job description which centred on mechanisms of organisational control, even surveillance. The *complexity* of equal opportunities was lost, to be reduced to a general notion of 'access', and access itself was delimited to intake/income, not quality of educational experience, curriculum change and safety on campus. The *politics* of equal opportunities was sidelined as EO became a new PR mechanism, torn from its liberatory and oppositional roots, and appropriated into the rhetoric of new managerialism. This process of incorporation produced ethical chaos; a kind of organisational identity crisis, the management of which in the public domain is now called 'spin'.

This chapter is rooted in the experience of those brief years of active challenge and hopefulness inside the academy. It is informed by what has happened since. This attempt to reconsider equal opportunities in the light of its past, present and predictable 'failure' (which is not meant to deny any positive impact), starts by considering the *problematic* of equal opportunities in the year 2000, in the context of its short history and with particular reference to the (UK) academy. The chapter considers the *problem* of equal opportunities as a complex and contentious hybrid: its emotionality, its instrumentality, and its fatal flaw. I conclude that the dilemma that is equal opportunities is complex and beyond control (typically the reach of legislation) but not influence, as well as both 'simple' and daunting. Here we face the importance of 'embodiment' for equal opportunities discourse and practice. The chapter notes that while equal opportunities *as legislation* often has to face the opposition of the powerful, it also founders on the bodies of those it is supposed to help. Indeed the problematic relations involved in helping/being helped risk (re)producing dominance, subordination and stigma.

The shifting and complex problematic of equal opportunities in the academy

There exist institutions where women and other non-traditional members are still 'new' and different. Though some individual staff members may have been there for many years, they remain 'other', intruders in a place whose historical purpose has specifically worked to construct and defend the difference and differentials which render us 'woman' to the 'man of reason'; working class, disabled, 'queer' or 'ethnic' to a ruling elite whose membership may change, but whose assumptions and purposes, so deeply (and securely?) rooted in history and tradition, survive.

In institutions which have remained relatively untouched by the impact of women's movements, feminist research and scholarship, and Women's Studies, we witness not just the inertia and/or resistance of old established cultures, but also the lack of awareness that this is what they are doing; that the history of the academy is indeed a history of 'their' own dominance and control. This lack of social and intellectual reflexivity testifies to a detachment and insularity from both demographic and cultural changes in society during the last forty years, as well as more recent developments in academia, in some institutions, and in some disciplines:

> The cure for this intellectual illness requires acknowledgement of one's own perspective as a perspective, and the recognition that there are other viewpoints (Mason Mullett, 1993, p.84).

In 2000 this was not a new thought, but it remains unacknowledged or resisted by many academics and academic managers, and 'unacknowledged perspectives have enormous power to oppress' (*ibid.*, p.83). This social and intellectual insularity has consequences for any efforts to rethink our dichotomies and categories:

> Failure to recognize the interpretive dimension and the political dimension of our categories easily results in the exclusion of people from fair consideration (*ibid.*, p.81).

Implicit norms, for example concerning gender or academic identity, remain as 'natural facts', and are left undisturbed and often defended. 'Persons' are assigned to categories (of age, gender, ethnicity, class, disability, for example), but the process of categorisation is not examined. This demands *both* equal opportunities *and* intellectual work. Alastair MacIntyre's stringent observations about the historical workings of the academy with regard to what he diagnoses as the philosophical crisis of moral theory are both generally and specifically relevant to the preoccupations of this chapter:

> what I take to be the real world and its fate has remained unrecognized by the academic curriculum. For the forms of the academic curriculum (would) turn out to be among the symptoms of the disaster whose occurrence the curriculum does not acknowledge (MacIntyre, 1994, p.4).

This observation evokes the between-a-rock-and-a-hard-place location of equity work in the academy, be it activist, academic or organisational. In the UK, both the diversification of student intake and the expansion of the curriculum since the 1960s, followed by the entry of equal opportunities discourses into the organisational workings of the academy, may be taken to indicate that the longstanding state of affairs described by MacIntyre has been disturbed. However...

Equal opportunities as everyday and specialist

Academics have trained as specialists in their chosen subject discipline. Many are not familiar with feminist and postcolonial theory, or recent work on disability. Consequently, there are too many professionals who lack a conceptual framework or language for conceiving the conjunction of, for example, gender, power and organisation. This makes it difficult even to discuss the issues in a way which goes beyond rock-bottom fears and prejudices.

Most academics outside of the Humanities and Social Sciences have not had an opportunity to reflect on issues of power and communication. Some may have encountered equal opportunities training, but the field which has developed over the last thirty years – from Women's Studies to Gender Studies, Black and Ethnic Studies, Postcolonial Studies, Disability Studies, Lesbian and Gay Studies – confirms that the achievement of equal opportunities in organisations is not merely a question of mechanisms. EO is not a 'suit' to be donned as we go through the academic door. It requires us, critically, conscientiously and with humility, to reflect upon our own privileged identities, subjectivities and practices (personal and professional), and to change our ways accordingly. Professionals were once assumed to just know their subject and 'do their job'. Social awareness, interpersonal responsibility and professional accountability were not explicitly required.

The fact that equal opportunities requires as much acquired, if not experiential, knowledge and skill as any academic discipline, goes unrecognised, and this puts competent response and action beyond the reach of many academics immersed in their own (increasingly competitive and isolated) disciplines and projects. It may also be a more difficult subject to approach since academic discipline has previously assumed 'objectivity', and this precludes reflection on one's privileged identities in relation to knowledge production. The need to problematise power and dominance, the idea of subjectivity as a process relevant to knowledge production and the exercise of power, and the significance of the body in knowledge production, are all likely to be dismissed as subject-specific and not relevant.

Certainty, superiority and the 'invisible gendered subject'

The ethical demand to set aside objective certainty to implement what appears to be a personal and political project is a steep one. The consequences of such work are likely to be experienced as a diminishment of authority. Yet this is what equal opportunities asks of all of us with institutional power or privilege. For those at the 'top', more is at stake publicly, especially in the context of new managerialism, where to 'admit' to 'not knowing' or not knowing enough, about oneself, 'others', and a changing society, amounts to an admission of weakness.

The 'maturing' of the equal opportunities field has contributed to a widening gap between activists/equity 'experts', and managers charged with delivering 'equal opportunities'. Academic managers might recognise there is a problem, but the problem is identified as residing with those who think there are equity issues within the academy. For the majority of managers, an 'inability to see their own gender as a factor in inequality enables them to continue to regard equal opportunities as language from the "other"' (Whitehead, 2001b).

This lack of self-awareness and self-reflexivity renders such figures 'the invisible gendered subject' (*ibid.*). Senior academics and managers are often less experienced in and aware of gender and power than many *students* in the field of Women's Studies, for example. This relational dynamic is certainly born out by Whitehead's comparison of male and female managers in the FE sector. He found female managers were ontologically and epistemologically sophisticated, 'not just in terms of equal opportunities. but at a much more fundamental level; in terms of knowledge, understanding and self-awareness' (*ibid.*). By contrast, when asked whether gender had been a factor in terms of career progression, experience of organisational life, and ultimately broader experiences, male managers in the study appeared 'totally floored by the question', reacting with variations on 'mmm ... I don't know ... I've never thought about it ...' (*ibid.*). Whitehead comments:

> On occasions it was as if I had spoken in an incomprehensible language. The majority had no sense of what the question meant or was referring to. [...] It was like questioning the existence of the sun, sky or air we breathe (*ibid.*).

In addition to disciplinary background, generational factors may also play their part, but these intersect significantly with the more fundamental factors of gender.

The new skills and knowledge bases developed during the last twenty-five years or so, initially as a result of women's movements and feminisms, have contributed to what may be experienced as 'inappropriate' differences and differentials in understanding and operational skill, which cut across conventional demarcations of power, status and gender, and which may lead to confrontation and defensiveness. There may be a perceived need for 'cover-up': on the one hand, of ignorance and inadequacy; on the other of knowing 'too much' for your own safety, since such knowledge may be seen as a threat.

Too many in the academy have not, over these years of social change, had occasion or inclination to reflect critically and reflexively on their own identities and practices and managerialist 'spin' does not encourage 'depth', which Mason Mullett identifies as 'the part which is added when we reflect on our own experiences and see how they can be characterised by the terms available to us' (Mason Mullett, 1993, p.80). Happily, there is a rich and expanding field of research, writing and practice, which is imagining, realising and theorising these urgent issues. Unhappily, it seems at times a world apart from both the realities of lives outside the academy, and the academic and managerial practices of many inside the academy, including many of those 'in charge'.

Gender, power, organisation

Elite white men and their representatives control structures of knowledge production (Hill Collins, 1991, p.201).

Managerial and organizational sites offer an environment wherein particular gendered (masculine) scripts can be performed by men (managers) as acts of self-identity validation (Kerfoot and Whitehead, 2000, p.184).

The juxtaposition of these two statements is suggestive of the nature and complexity of the equity project in Further and Higher Education. Control and exclusion are obvious targets for equal opportunities action, and the solution once seemed simple: get in more women/black/disabled/working class academics. We now know both that that is not easily effected, and when it is, problems of control and dominance persist. Kerfoot and Whitehead spotlight the problem of abstract masculinity and its projects as performed in the workplace. What they found in their study of male managers in the new work culture of Further Education, in the wake of restructuring and the new managerialist ethos, was an increased valuation of behaviour associated with being 'manly'. Faced with the demand for increased hours, increased productivity, and displays of 'commitment' they found an emerging dominant form of masculine discourse and subjectivity, aggressively competitive, goal-driven and instrumental in its quest for achievement.

Talk of potency and control, and 'making things happen', recur in the interview material. Kerfoot and Whitehead describe this new managerialism as consonant with, and constitutive of, a form of abstract masculinity that achieves validation through control and power over others. This is a work culture which promotes 'a way of relating to the world, and to others, that renders all before it an object of conquest' (*ibid.*, p.196). Why would we expect those deemed successful in this context to assist in, or promote the delivery of, an equal opportunities environment? Rather they embody the *problem*, for example of the private/public split, organisation and power *as* masculine: power as *potestas* rather than *potentia* (see Bethke Elshtain, 1992, p.117, p.123 for discussion).[2] The failure during these years of 'equal opportunities', to address heterosexual masculinity as a problem with profound and devastating consequences *for men*, is in particular a joint failure of journalists, academics and politicians (i.e. knowledge producers, policy-makers and opinion-makers), who themselves thought they were fireproof, and did not need to change or promote change. Their gender and sexuality interfered with their abilities to do their jobs in a caring, responsible and skilful manner. Without self-reflexivity *as men* this is impossible.[3] Younger men have effectively been abandoned by other, older, more privileged and more influential men. The class, gender and poverty issues *of equality of opportunity* which have been largely left unattended, are cruelly evident. A timebomb is beginning to go off.

The incompatibility of new managerialism and equal opportunities

> Domination arises out of an inability to recognize, appreciate and nurture differences, not out of a failure to see everyone as the same. Indeed, the need to see everyone as the same in order to accord them dignity and respect is an expression of the problem, not a cure for it (Flax, 1992, p.193).

Women's lives, careers and realities defy and actively bridge neat inside/outside, public/private, mind/body binary splits. New managerialism, on the other hand, explicitly works to intensify the dichotomy between the public domain (mind) and the private domain (body) to breaking point, and hence the differences, real and required, between women and men, and between disabled and non-disabled students and staff. If equal opportunities were working properly, this would be culpable, illegal and actionable indirect discrimination and negligence of the duty of care towards employees. It would not, as at present, require *individuals* to take on their organisations, with their bodies, lives, reputations.

The gendered new managerialist model produces job descriptions and person specifications which routinely demand superhuman combinations of qualifications, skills, attributes and experience (previously the contribution of several people not one); not to mention 'total loyalty' and compliance. This actively discriminates against those who are not 'superfit'; those not served by ancillary staff who maintain and sustain their living and relationships outside the academy; and those with relational responsibilities. It works to promote competitive individualism, and as such is an explicitly elite political project which 'refuses to recognize interdependence and collective responsibility, relying instead on the survival of the fittest to bring about a healthy, efficient society' (Morris, 1991, p.83).

The 'no-limits' approach to prove commitment takes this further, producing (in addition to distress, illness and dysfunction) marginalisation, *stigma*, and potential career curtailment for those who cannot or will not 'mal/function' in this way: 'When you listen to this culture in a disabled body, you hear how often health and physical vigour are talked about as if they were moral values' (Wendell, 1993, p.234). The vigour in question is *virile* (Walsh, 1994): 'weakness' is a function/sign of a lack of virility. If virility is the primary virtue (both prerequisite and goal), where does this leave those not considered traditionally 'virile', including women and those with disabilities? How can these managerial cultures 'include' women as managers? Does inclusion have to mean collusion?

Divide and rule: assimilate and control

The question of assimilation and collusion has particular significance, even poignancy, in UK Higher Education in 2000, at a time when Black and Ethnic Studies, and Disability Studies are continuing to establish themselves. Simultaneously, and in some of those same institutions, Women's Studies has found itself rebranded as Gender Studies, or made redundant and removed from the curriculum altogether. I understand this to mean several significant things, which remind us that gender/heterosexuality (i.e. masculinity, see Holland *et al.*, 1998) is the most virulently entrenched and defended institution; and why feminists (not women) appear to be the most resisted and pathologised 'outsiders' in academia.[4]

Managers and academics can maintain a distance between themselves and these more recent developments. They continue to assume ethnicity and disability do not require a reflexive reconsideration of their own identities and positionalities, or a reformulation of knowledge production, and the relation between thought and body, thinking and living. New managerialism thinks it can handle (i.e. 'spin') these new curricular developments and incorporate them *discretely* and *without disturbing* other areas of the curriculum. Packaged, commodified, compartmentalised, these important academic developments are expected to stay away from other disciplines/subjects/academic programmes, because they are seen as self-reflexive only. They are considered additions, market segments, which while they have the appearance of equal opportunities in action, involve no perceived risk to general management, no ceding of power and privilege, no self-reflexivity on the part of managers or colleagues teaching other courses. Their presence is institutionally painless and trouble-free, for in 2000 they are identified as acceptable pedagogies, not politics.

Taking up the identity of 'change agent' is of course what feminist academics and equal opportunities activists have been doing inside the academy for some time (see Morley and Walsh, 1995; 1996). Women's studies (also a market segment) has perhaps shown itself to be too productive of real and significant change, inside the academy and out (in our lives and relationships). These changes and challenges have had repercussions for all academics and managers, not just organisationally, but because Women's Studies and feminisms explicitly write men and masculinity into their scripts.

Equal opportunities: hybrid, necessary and fatally flawed

> Thinking in terms of sexual difference is but the inaugural act in a political project that assumes women to be subjects capable of freedom and of self-signification [... It] is also a hermeneutic key that allows the modern concept of equality to be perceived as a principle which is false in its logical foundation and homologizing in its concrete effects (Cavarero, 1992, p.45).

> 'Equality', like other central political categories, is a contested term; but whereas 'equality' in some of its possible meanings can encompass 'difference', no sense of

'equality' compatible with a genuinely democratic citizenship can accommodate subordination (Pateman, 1992, p.28).

The problem of equal opportunities lies not just in the practical difficulties of implementation: overcoming opposition, the challenge of organisational, cultural and curriculum change, the reallocation of resources, the exhaustion of maintaining its processes, but in its *deep* address to the 'whole' person, not just in our professional capacities, but in relation to our selves and others.

The complexity and hybridity of equal opportunities also lies in its identity as both organisational and academic, both politics and ethics; rooted in values of democracy, social justice, and an ethic of care, which while the subjects of study inside the academy, are identified with the social and political worlds outside. Equal opportunities is a rank outsider seeking to take up residence in institutional domains previously considered neutral. It reworks the public/private divide identified with *will* on the one hand, and *desire* on the other. The *emotionality* of its purpose and processes is combined with an *instrumentality*, and this mix of heart and mind makes its identity suspect, its status low, particularly in institutions historically devoted to the hierarchical maintenance of Reason. Its instrumentality presents a particular problem to academics who think of themselves as 'professional' and 'expert', and who have been accustomed to professional autonomy.

In addition, the marketisation of new managerialist equal opportunities, and the categories it constructs and deploys (such as gender and disability) are problems in themselves. Gender, for example, always means looking at women in relation to normative standards developed in relation to men. The fatal flaw of equal opportunities is that, as with new managerialism, it reproduces and reinforces differences as singular, fixed and hierarchical; its categories work to infantilise and stigmatise; and it is viewed by its opponents as overly instrumental in the cause of 'vested interests', and as mechanistic and shallow by activists (Bethke Ekshtain, 1992).

Because of the way 'equality' ranks and denies differences, Jane Flax suggests we replace it with *justice*, as a more useful (though not simple) antidote to relations of domination. This might get round the problem of assimilation, of having to eliminate our 'difference' before entering the public world (Flax, 1992, p.194). As Bethke Elshtain put it: '*Does the new woman have to become the old man?*' (Bethke Elshtain, 1992, p.123). The idea of justice is an ethical and political one, and as such antithetical to the new managerialist academy, where the emphasis is on skills rather than ideas (Whithead, 2001a, p.11). However, equal opportunities has shown itself to be 'about gaining power, not changing it' (Cockburn, 1991, p.217): access without alteration (see Rhode, 1992). It started out as aspirational and strategic, and about care not just justice, but as Braidotti warns, 'feminist thinking cannot be purely strategic' (Braidotti, 1992, p.189), not least because it is also an ethics. But good things can come out of bad, and the rhetoric and practices of new managerialist equal opportunities have helped make visible the problem of 'equality' as a discourse. Equal opportunities has proved itself more *complex* a project than was originally thought; it has shown itself to be *incomprehensible* in environments where there is an insufficient experiential and knowledge base, together with a demonising of the 'political'. It has, perhaps unavoidably, shown itself *irredeemable* in reproducing the stigma of 'difference'.

It is evident that equal opportunities is not just about explicit denigration or simple omission. If it were, improvement resulting from legislation would be more evident than it is. The field of micropolitics, focusing as it does on how power is relayed through everyday practices, contributes to our understanding of the obstacles to women's professional efficacy and advancement: it 'exposes processes of stalling, sabotage, manipulation, power bargaining, bullying, harassment and spite' (Morley, 1999, p.5). But 'these power-laden microprocesses are notoriously difficult to challenge through policies for equality' (*ibid.*, p.97). Relational thinking, however, enables us to raise questions about 'who is exercising control (and) who defines what is to count as a legitimate interest or need' (Mason Mullet, 1992, p.85).

The philospohical, political and ethical questions raised by equal opportunities are incapable of being illuminated or much advanced by legislation. However, once we understand what equal opportunities cannot do, we can reframe it and give it new direction and purpose. Debra Rhode argues for a shift from difference to disadvantage, which 'produces a different set of questions and removes men's physiology as the standard against which all claims appear only additional' (Rhode, 1992, p.153). More contextual analysis is possible and the political problem becomes 'not equality for women but quality of life for all individuals' (*ibid.*, p.154). In employment settings, the issue becomes, 'not whether gender [age, ethnicity, disability, sexuality, class] is relevant to the job as currently structured, but how the workplace can be restructured to make [gender, age, ethnicity, disability, sexuality, class] less relevant' (*ibid.*, p.155).

Many differences which feature within equal opportunities discourses and action cannot be masked or hidden, so 'safety' is a luxury many cannot achieve. Legislation may be able to provide redress after the event, but may do little to protect us beforehand, to secure safety and dignity on a daily basis. In pathologically hostile environments, to be identified *as* black, *as* disabled, *as* gay, *as* old(er), *a*s woman, *as* working class, constitutes a body project in which the presentation of self demands continuous (and skilful) attention and management. Our individual power to 'control' and manage our own embodiment and its readings is curtailed by a political economy.

Embodiment: positionality and/or stigma

Western culture has set very high priority on the production of the sexed body, situating the variable sexuality on top of the list [...] Sexuality as power, that is, as institution, is also a semiotic code that organizes our perception of morphological differences between the sexes (Braidotti, 1992, p.185).

As I moved back into the world, I also began to experience the world as structured for people who have no weaknesses (Wendell, 1993, p.223; see Potts and Price, 1995).[5]

As society has become more dominated by visual media and rhetoric over the last forty years, we have witnessed the increased marketisation of sex and sexuality. Heterosexism struts its stuff all the time and everywhere, with few challenges. As Vron Ware observed, 'We are all prisoners of gender' now (Ware, 1992, p.254). It is a decade since Cynthia Cockburn first wrote about the consequences for women of 'the sexualisation of social relations in organizations' and 'the heterosexism of such workplace culture' (Cockburn, 1991, p.138). Since then, in the period of equal opportunities (such as it is), the picture has become publicly clearer, through research, press coverage, documentary and dramatisation.[6]

The accelerated entry of women into the workplace and the professions since the 1960s has produced an environment which carries over the sexual arrangements and distinctions in society. For heterosexual men in particular, this renders the public domain more like the private domain: both the home front (identified with emotion, mothers, 'wives') and the leisure/pleasure front (identified with sex, 'lads' and lovers). No education or training has been provided for coping with these complexities, which, as the weekly toll of reported cases of sexual harassment, bullying, intimidation, discrimination and rape shows, gives aberrant heterosexist opportunism a free hand.

Equal opportunities legislation offers nothing to ameliorate these pathological relations. Coping with oppression in the workplace is an additional and potentially draining *workload.* In poverty, isolation, fear and subordination, women's ontological desire remains secret, suppressed, inchoate, barely a dream. The material, social and cultural changes of the years of feminism, working-class politics, black politics, lesbian and gay rights, and now disability politics, have contributed to a partial realisation for some women of what is possible when these constraints begin to be lifted. Women are among those who have built a bridge between the inside and the outside of the academy. During these years, women everywhere have exhibited stamina and creativity in buckets. But what of our continuing vulnerability?

Any new model must *embody and support diversity and sustainability*, and be heartfelt: fuelled by cultural action rather than driven by political ideology. In other words, it must be owned at every step, rather than imposed; a product of diversity more than policy. With the disability lobby at last entering these debates, this is beginning to happen. The power relations of manager and managed are subject to change once people and their various and multiple constituencies refuse representation, and speak *both* as and for themselves, *and* as party to a 'rainbow' coalition. This is not the instrumental and strategic construction of consensus. Risk, chance, uncertainty continue to attend this highly political, creative, social and cultural process, this time as functions of our hopeful, adventurous and courageous spirits, rather than as the unknown, the different, the dreaded 'other'.

Notes

[1]   Women at the height of their careers are resigning, suddenly moving sideways, or leaving at short notice: in frustration, exhaustion, anger; from ill-health; or to avoid ill-health, to get out alive. And not just in isolation, but in clusters: eight here, five there …

As we know when calculating the carcinogenic impact of nuclear power stations, it is the clusters which are significant. But how do we testify/document the distress and despair, the assimilations and departures of women in academia, without pathologising them? (See Steedman, 2000; Walsh, 1997.) After writing this note, news of research commissioned by NATFHE from the Higher Education Statistics Agency, to mark thirty years of equal pay legislation, arrived, showing that only nine Higher Education institutions in the UK employ women over fifty-five as Senior Lecturers, as compared to a hundred who employ men of the same age; and 67 per cent of these pay them less than men of the same age. This item sits alongside several other articles in a section on Equalities, including what is described as 'a pioneering agreement on equal opportunities in employment' (see in same issue Breen, 2000; Prabhudas, 2000).

2 *'Potestas*, one Latin term for power, especially political power, control, supremacy or dominion. *Potentia*, another Latin term for power understood as might or ability, efficacy, potency, especially "unofficial and sinister"'. Fascinatingly, these contrasting usages demarcate historically roughly the boundaries of male and female forms of power' (Bethke Elshtain, 1992, p.117).

3 At the BSA study group on auto/biography summer conference this year, men were in evidence doing such self-reflexive work: Mikko Innanen, David Jackson, Saul Keyworth, Marti Silvennoinen, Andrew C. Sparkes and Brett Smith, and Arto Tiihonen.

4 See Brown Packer, 1995; Butler and Landells, 1995; Dossor, 1995; Edmands, 2000; Epstein, 1995; Flann, 1994; Kerman, 1995; Morley, 1999; Varley, 1999; Walsh, 1995, 1998.

5 Key 'weaknesses' might include being identified as with dependants, disabled, 'ethnic', female, gay, ill, (single) mother, old(er), poor, 'ugly', working-class.

6 See Boseley, 2000; Buxton, 1999; Gillan and Ward, 2000; Reeves, 2000; Riley-Jones, 2000; Taylor, 2000; Toynbee, 2000; Weale, 2000; Wilkinson, 1999; Wylie, 2000.

References

'Ageism and Sexism Scandal' (2000), *Lecturer*, 24 July.

'Partners for Equal Opportunities' (2000), *ibid.*

Bethke, E. (1992), 'The Power and Powerlessness of Women', in G. Bock and S. James (eds).

Bock, G. and S. James (eds) (1992), *Beyond Equality and Difference: Citizenship, Feminist Politics and Female Subjectivity*, Routledge, London and New York.

Boseley, S. (2000), 'Women Told to Remove "Safe" Implants', *Guardian*, 7 June.

Braidotti, R. (1992), 'On the Female Feminist Subject, or: From "She-Self" to "She-Other"', in G. Bock and S. James (eds).

Breen, S. (2000), 'Engaging Hearts and Minds against Discrimination' (interview with Bert Massie, the first chairperson of the Disability Rights Commission), *Lecturer*, 16 July.

Brown, P. (1995), 'Irrigating the Sacred Grove: Stages of Gender Equity Development', in L. Morley and V. Walsh (eds).

Butler, A. and M. Landells (1995), 'Taking Offence: Research as Resistance to Sexual Harassment in Academia', in L. Morley and V. Walsh (eds).

Buxton, J. (1999), 'Better balance between job and personal life is the new work ethic: new employers', *Guardian*, 6 January.

Cavarero, A. (1992), 'Equality and Sexual Difference: Amnesia in Political Thought', in G. Bock and S. James (eds).

Cockburn, C. (1991), *In the Way of Women: Men's Resistance to Sex Equality in Organizations*, Macmillan, Basingstoke.

Dossor, D. (1995), 'Grievance', in L. Morley and V. Walsh (eds).

Edmands, M. (2000), 'Pride After Prejudice' (interview with Yvonne Thompson), *Guardian*, 5 February.

Epstein, D. (1995), 'In Our (New) Right Minds: the Hidden Curriculum and the Academy', in L. Morley and V. Walsh (eds).

Fineman, S. (ed.), (1994), *Emotion in Organizations*, London, Sage.

Flann, H. (1994), 'Fear, Loyalty and Greedy Organizations', in S. Fineman (ed.).

Flax, J. (1992), 'Beyond equality: gender, justice and difference', in G. Bock and S. James (eds).

Gillan, A. and L. Ward (2000), 'Prostitutes imported into slavery', *Guardian*, 30 May.

Hill Collins, P. (1991), *Black Feminist Thought: Knowledge, Consciousness and the Politics of Empowerment*, Routledge, New York and London.

Holland, J., C. Ramazanoglu, S. Sharpe and R. Thomson (1998), *The Male in the Head: Young People, Heterosexuality and Power*, The Tufnell Press, London.

Innanen, M. (2000), 'Concepts of fathers among Finnish young people', paper presented at BSA study group on auto/biography summer conference, University of Leicester, 1-3 July.

Jackson, D. (1998), *Screaming Men* (poems about men and masculinities), David Jackson, West Ridgeford.

_____ (2000), 'Ageing Men Aren't Dinosaurs', unpublished paper.

Journal of Further and Higher Education (2000), special issue, '(En)Gendering Management: Work, Organization and Further Education', 24 (2), June.

Kerfoot, D. and S. Whitehead (2000), 'Keeping All the Balls in the Air: Further Education and the Masculine/Managerial Subject', in *Journal of Further and Higher Education*, 24 (2), June.

Kerman, L. (1995), 'The Good Witch: Advice to Women in Management', in L. Morley and V. Walsh (eds).

Keyworth, S. (2000), 'Physical Education, the Gender Game and Heterosexism', paper presented at BSA study group summer conference, *op cit*.

MacIntyre, A. (1994), *After Virtue: A Study in Moral Theory*, London, Duckworth.

Mason Mullett, S. (1993), 'Inclusive Philosophy: Feminist Strategies for the Recovery of Persons', in D. Shogan (ed.).

Morley, L. (1994), 'Glass Ceiling or Iron Cage: Women in UK Academia', *Journal of Gender, Work and Organization*, 1 (4).

_____ (1999), *Organising Feminisms: The Micropolitics of the Academy*, Macmillan Press, Basingstoke.

Morley, L. and V. Walsh (eds) (1995), *Feminist Academics: Creative Agents for Change*, Taylor & Francis, London.

_____ (1996), *Breaking Boundaries: Women in Higher Education*, Taylor & Francis, London.

Morris, J. (1991), *Pride against Prejudice*, The Women's Press, London.

Pateman, C. (1992), 'Equality, Difference, Subordination: the Politics of Motherhood and Women's Citizenship', in G. Bock and S. James (eds).

Potts, T. and J. Price (1995), '"Out of the Blood and Spirit of our Lives": the Place of the Body in Academic Feminism', in L. Morley and V. Walsh (eds).

Prabhudas, Y. (2000), 'How Family-Friendly is Your Employer?', *Lecturer*, July.

Reeves, R. (Director of Futures at the Industrial Society) (2000), 'The Way We Work: A Word to the Wise', *Guardian*, 7 June.

Rhode, D. L. (1992), 'The Politics of Paradigms: Gender Difference and Gender Disadvantage', in G. Bock and S. James (eds).

Riley-Jones, A. (2000), 'Mothers Without Men', *Guardian Weekend*, 10 June.

Shogan, D. (ed.) (1993a), *A Reader in Feminist Ethics*, Canadian Scholars' Press, Toronto.

_____ (1993b), 'Feminist Ethics for Strangers', *ibid.*

_____ (1993c), 'Conceptualizing Agency: Implications for Feminist Ethics', *ibid.*

Silvennoinen, M. (2000), 'The Subjectivity of a Sports Researcher at Stake', paper presented at BSA study group summer conference, *op cit.*

Sparkes, A.C. and B. Smith (2000), 'Narratives of Self: Scholarship, Literature or Something Else Altogether', paper presented at BSA study group summer conference, *op cit.*

Taylor, D. (2000), 'Nice and Sleazy Does It', *Guardian*, 11 May.

Tiihonen, A. (2000), 'Autobiographic Storymaking as a Way to Understand Body Experiences, Masculinities and Sports Culture', paper presented at BSA study group summer conference, *op cit.*

Toynbee, P. (2000), 'The Two Sides of Life', *Guardian*, 12 May.

Varley, J. (1999), 'Reflections from the Science Front', paper presented at WHEN (Women in Higher Education Network) conference, University of Salford, 29 November.

Walsh, V. (1994), 'Virility Culture: Academia and Managerialism in Higher Education', in M. Evans, J. Gosling and A. Sellar (eds), *Agenda for Gender* (discussion papers on gender and the organisation of Higher Education), University of Kent at Canterbury (Women's Studies Committee).

_____ (1995), 'Transgression and the Academy: Feminists and Institutionalization', in L. Morley and V. Walsh (eds).

_____ (1997), 'Interpreting Class: Auto/biographical Imaginations and Social Change', in P. Mahony and C. Zmroczek (eds), *Class Matters: 'Working-class' Women's Perspectives on Social Class*, Taylor & Francis, London.

_____ (1998), 'Women up Against Art Education: History or Practice?', in *Drawing Fire* (The Journal of the National Association for Fine Art Education), 2 (3).

_____ (2000), 'From Tangle to Web: Life Histories as Feminist Process', in P. Anderson and J. Williams (eds), *Identity and Difference in Higher Education: Feminist Perspectives* (forthcoming).

Ware, V. (1992), *Beyond the Pale; White Women, Racism and History*, Verso, London and New York.

Weale, S. (2000), 'The End of the Tribunal', *Guardian*, 2 February.

Wendell, S. (1993), 'Toward a Feminist Theory of Disability', in D. Shogan (ed.).

Whitehead, S. (2001a), 'Woman as Manager – A Seductive Ontology', in *Gender, Work and Organization*, 8 (1) (forthcoming).

_____ (2001b), 'The Invisible Gendered Subject: Men in Education Management', in *Journal of Gender Studies* (forthcoming).

Wilkinson, H. (1999), 'Better Balance Between Job and Personal Life is Key Demand of the New Work Ethic: New Workers', *Guardian*, 6 January.

Wylie, I. (2000), 'In Search of the Perfect Boss: Women Are the Fairer Sex After All. Right?', *Guardian*, 5 February.

Chapter 4

Against the Odds: Women Academics' Research Opportunities

Barbara Bagilhole

Introduction

This chapter reflects on some potential barriers to women's likely success in the academic, research community. It utilises previous research in this area by the author and others in the field, and some observations from recent interviews with a small sample of seven senior and experienced women academics; Professors or above.

Research is essential for career success in universities, and it dominates teaching in terms of status and rewards. This situation is likely to continue and increase. There are signs from the government that the symbiotic relationship between research and teaching is no longer regarded as inviolable. There may be more teaching-only staff, and even whole departments, and institutions in the future. It will become more important to gain research income for success in academic careers. Those who can obtain Research Council and research contract income are supported and encouraged by universities, whereas those who teach are viewed as second-class academics. However, women do not apply for research grants in the same proportion as men (Loder and Eley, 1998).

In the light of this, the chapter identifies various issues and themes that may have a detrimental effect on women's ability, or inclination, to compete with men for these important research rewards. Firstly, I consider how women's lack of seniority and their different roles from their male colleagues, contribute to their lack of success. Women academics continue to be predominantly found at the bottom of the hierarchy, and their roles both outside and inside the academy have been found to affect their careers. These first two factors are seen as accentuated by Higher Education's lack of progress in equal opportunities. Secondly, I consider the role of gatekeepers in keeping women in their place. The issues of networking, peer-reviewing and refereeing, and composition and decisions of research funding committees are thus investigated for gender implications. I suggest ways in which we might consider women's systematic inclusion in all gate-keeping activities in academia, and contend that unless exclusion becomes inclusion this negative circle for women is likely to continue to be reinforced.

Where are the women academics?

The under-representation of women, particularly at the higher levels of the academic occupational ladder has been a well-documented, persistent phenomenon for many years. In 1990, the Hansard Society Commission Report highlighted the fact that the increase in women students had not been accompanied by any significant increase in the percentage of women in academic posts. It described British universities as 'bastions of male power and privilege' (p.68). The progress report six years later (Hansard Society Commission, 1996) was not optimistic of women's progress: 'Generational change does not appear to have done the trick and the evidence suggests that waiting for it to do so may well take a long time'.

Statistical evidence shows that women have an unequal chance when attempting to enter the academic profession and when they arrive, they are promoted more slowly than men and are more likely to leave. A Government commission (IRHEPC, 1999) set up as an 'Independent Review of Higher Education Pay and Conditions' of university staff made particular mention of the fact that women academics remain under-represented and under-paid in British universities. Also, the Association of University Teachers (AUT) (1999) showed that inequalities exist between women and men in starting salaries, salary at renewal of fixed-term contracts, operation of promotion procedures, probationary requirements, access to pension benefits, allocation of discretionary pay, and part-time and hourly pay rates.

For women academics, there is a sharp decline in their representation from Lecturer grades through to Professors. Whilst only 31 per cent of all academic staff are women, this minority position is reduced to 21 per cent for Senior Lecturers and Researchers, and even further to only 9 per cent of Professors (Table 4.1).

Table 4.1 Full-time academic staff in all UK HEIs, 1997/8

	% Women	% Men
Professors	9	91
Senior Lecturers and Researchers	21	79
Lecturers	35	65
Researchers	37	63
Other grades	39	61
Total	31	69

Source: Table 16, Resources of Higher Education Institutions, 1997/8 (HESA, 1999)

This data on academic staff (defined as full-time employees whose primary function is teaching and/or research) collected by the Higher Education Statistics Agency (HESA) enables some broad insights into the location of academic women, and their distribution across teaching and research activities in UK institutions. Whilst women represent 31 per cent of academic staff in universities and colleges, they are more likely to be 'research only' or 'teaching only' staff than 'research and teaching' staff. For research-only staff their chances for successful, long-term participation in the academic community are limited by their terms of employment (Ramsden, 1996).

What do women academics do?

Outside the academy

The career-breaks, and responsibilities for family care work, which women are more likely than men to undertake (*Social Focus on Women*, 1998), militate against their career development, in the HE context, which defines relevant experience and merit in ways that favour male career-trajectories. Bagilhole (1993) found that only 56 per cent of her sample of women academics were married or had a partner, and only 30 per cent had children. Many had chosen not to have a conventional family life, in favour of their career. The following quote from a woman academic sums this up:

> There is a difficulty in combining the conventional role of a woman, family, children, with the expectations of a successful academic. Successful women academics have to demonstrate that they are more committed to the task in hand, and better. If you are accepted as a successful teaching then you become an honorary man.

This is an important decision when competing in an 'institutionalised context governed according to the male life cycle' (Acker and Warren Piper, 1984, p.242). Women can succeed in Higher Education, but they do so at a price (Thomas, 1990). For Dudovitz (1983) the separation between academic work and women's lives is a sham. In the eyes of critics the two are inseparable. This highlights the problems for women of combining an academic career with family life. The implications for women academics are that they may be viewed as a liability to departments in terms of research contribution and thus perpetuate and strengthen the discrimination against women Researchers working within UK HE. The following quote from a senior woman academic is a reflection on these phenomena:

> We're half the population so if half the prestigious jobs aren't going to women there's got to be a reason. At its most benign, it might be something like, in order to get them you have to have been playing the power structures rather longer than many women can, because of their fractured careers.

Inside the academy

Further, examining what kinds of activities academic women are engaged in is also revealing. The gendered division of domestic labour is often mirrored in the academic workplace, where women academics carry disproportionately higher teaching, pastoral, and administrative loads, circumscribing their participation in research. Men retreat into research, and this is seen as legitimate, whereas women take on the role of nurturing students (Bagilhole, 1993; Goode and Bagilhole, 1996; Deane *et al.*, 1996; Tothill, A., 1998). The following quote from a woman in Bagilhole's (1993) study illustrates this:

> Women do all the teaching and caring for students whilst the men do the research. One of my male colleagues sticks a note on his door telling students when they can see him – a couple of hours a week. In other words his door is never open to students. Because women care more they get overloaded with day to day administration and students. So they can't do research and publishing, which is necessary for promotion. There's a need for what women do well to be equally valued within academia.

Spending more time with the students presents women with the problem of shortage of time for research activities, and damages their career because these duties were not recognised or rewarded by the university. The academic system rewards research and publications, activities exhibited more by men than women.

Women are also typically concentrated on departmental and faculty committees, which are not decision-making bodies (Bagilhole, 1993; Brooks, 1997). This low-level servicing work has negative consequences for their career advancement. It does not feature in official measures of productivity, simultaneously limits the time available for the research and publishing necessary for promotion, and equips them only poorly for service on more 'high-level' Boards such as those within the Research Councils. One of the senior women commented:

> Women tend to be the ones who take caring roles in departments because they're so damn good at juggling priorities. They get loads of administrative tasks to do. So the burden on women is disproportionately skewed towards their role as managers, often at a fairly low level in departments. They're often the programme tutors, the ones who give more time to students.

This kind of 'cultural annexation' (Spurling, 1996) is sometimes referred to as constituting a 'glass wall' rather than a 'glass ceiling'.

Lack of progress on equal opportunities in Higher Education

Despite the growth of interest in, and concern for, equal opportunities issues in Higher Education, there seems to have been a general lack of success in affecting the position of women academics, as can be seen from the figures above. Most institutions continue to make patchy progress on an agenda of enhancing women's access to current systems and structures.[1] There appears to be a disparity between paper policies and effective implementation (Burton and Weiner, 1993; Heward and Taylor, 1993). Whilst the first survey by the Commission on University Career Opportunity of equal opportunities policies in universities showed some progress, a lack of proactive moves were detected. For example, whilst more than 90 per cent of universities had written equal opportunities policies, only 42 per cent provided training for staff responsible for recruitment. Similarly, the follow up study found that whilst 58 per cent of institutions were monitoring promotions by gender, 80 per cent reported that no action was taken on the information derived (Bagilhole and Robinson, 1997). Even more recently, the findings of an AUT survey (1999) highlighted the widespread practice of circumventing normal appointment procedures in order to bring in 'star' academics to boost Research Assessment Exercise ratings, and hasty promotions of such appointees, in complete disregard of formal procedures, in order to retain them.

Gatekeepers

Within Higher Education institutions Academia values reputation above all, and reputation is heavily dependent upon integration into formal and informal networks in the research community. Women are less likely to have access to these networks (O'Leary and Mitchell, 1990; Bagilhole, 1993). 'Generally, the university is a "man's world" and the old boy network is influential' (Sutherland, 1985, p.25). Success in the academic market place requires a high level of educational attainment, but moving through the system of rewards and status requires knowing colleagues who can provide guidance, support and advocacy to the newcomer. The following quote from Bagilhole's (1993) study demonstrates women's experience:

> Particularly in research, you see it going on. Men giving advice to other men in private. Sporting activities brings them into contact with staff from other departments, which gives them opportunities that I don't have. Then they make more of the right decisions about research and so on. I've no access to the grapevine. They intertwine well and it helps their work.

Women have particular difficulty in securing access to this 'colleague system' that allocates resources, research support, and opportunities to publish (O'Leary and Mitchell, 1990). Network connections are crucial ingredients in professional career success, and looked for in promotion decisions (Halsey, 1992). They bring mutual career benefits, information exchange, contacts for research resources, career planning, professional support and encouragement, and connections to influential people.

Women academics being in a minority have fewer role models and informal networks than men. They lack sponsors or mentors; supportive relationships where older and experienced academics contribute to younger colleagues career development. 'The structure of the academic hierarchy puts women in the situation of being judged only by those of the opposite sex on a great many occasions' (Sutherland, 1985, p.15). There seems to be an undervaluing and stereotyping of women as part of the male institution. This is more problematic than overtly discriminatory behaviour. Often inadvertent, sometimes well-intentioned it often seems so 'normal' as to be virtually invisible, yet creates an environment that wastes women's resources, takes time and energy to ignore or deal with, undermines self-esteem, and damages professional morale. It leaves women professionally and socially isolated, and makes it difficult to keep informed about professional matters and promote views. Through it 'women are marginalised and to some extent, alienated' (Thomas, 1990, p.181). A comment from a woman academic in Bagilhole's (1993) study sums this up:

> Whether it's deliberate or not, most people making decisions see women as good at some things and not appropriate for other things. It's so subtle, they think that they're being objective but they're not. Women are filtered out. We need to make explicit what we've always felt to be implicit.

In research funding bodies The Research Councils in the UK have a considerable effect and influence on an academic's career success. They offer the most prestigious and career enhancing research grants for academics. A previous track record in the ability to attract this sort of external research funding is often now openly requested in academic job advertisements. However, women are less likely than men to apply for and receive external funding for research (Hawkins and Schultz (1990); Loder and Eley, 1998). Bagilhole (1993) found that nearly a half of the women in her study were less successful than their male colleagues in obtaining external funding. The following comment relates a perceived reason for this from a woman academic in her study:

> The men don't want to use you for collaborative research because you're not part of the network and they feel they can't profit from you. It's subtle, what you get asked to do and what you don't get asked to do.

It is useful to examine the research application process for any factors that might impact differently on women and men. Again, at the interface between academics and their success in research applications, are gatekeepers involved in peer-review and the peer refereeing process. This system often lacks transparency and therefore is open to question in terms of subjectivity or bias that might intrude. In this particular context, it might be interrogated for any potential bias against women academics.

In Sweden, Weneras and Wold (1997), given open access to the national peer-review process for research funding by their government, revealed that nepotism and sexism were rife. They found that for a female scientist to be equally rated, she needed to be 2.5 times more productive than the average male applicant. In addition, although policy did not allow reviewers personally affiliated with an applicant to process that particular application, 'neutral' committee members compensated by raising their scores when judging applicants affiliated with one of their peers.

Importantly for research careers, there continues to be a great commitment to peer-review in the UK on the part of Research Councils, and prestigious journals. However, the conduct of peer-review in the UK has been the subject of continuing and extensive debate. The Boden Report (1990) assessed the peer-review system and concluded that 'there were no practical alternatives to peer-review for the assessment of basic research', and the Director General of the Research Councils once more confirmed their commitment to it in 1994. The Royal Society (1995) examined peer-review and highlighted the issue of track record. The tendency towards conservatism, through which established academics are discouraged from moving into new fields where they have no previous track record, was noted as a major drawback of the system. What was not acknowledged was the differential impact the requirement for a track record can have on women academics, who are disproportionately on short-term contracts, and who, even if they are in permanent positions, more often take career breaks than men. The report also drew attention to the need for transparency in terms of peer-reviewing and decision-making panels, and of feedback being given to applicants by these panels. The report concluded that: 'It is not self-evident that peer-reviewers can be wholly neutral' (p.7).

The question of female 'visibility' and lack of senior academic positions can be crucial for the peer-reviewing process. These are important structural constraints in the research community for women. As McAuley (1987) pointed out: 'This community expressed in research validating committees and funding bodies is predominantly male in its composition [...] there is a tendency to give awards to people who are "known" – and these tend to be men' (p.166). As a male Professor in the Goode and Bagilhole (1996) study explained:

> You make a contact, you build up a relationship, the organisation trusts you because you've produced for them. Therefore getting their support for further programmes is a lot easier. You can almost get to a situation where you're saying well, if the idea's come from that guy, it's all right – don't ask too many questions, give him the resource [...] when you get the forms in to referee for grant applications – and I do hundreds of them – the first question is like, Who is this guy? And you have to answer that – and if you look and say, well I don't know this guy from a bar of soap – whereas if you look and say, oh yeah, it's him again, he's really good at this and that and the other and he's got loads of equipment, and you put yeah, yeah, good facilities. It's almost Catch 22.

In the area of research funding bodies, attitudes and approaches towards equal opportunities and peer-reviewing vary (Fenton, 1998). Leat (1998) also revealed differences within a single type of funding body, in terms of the application procedures used, kinds of information required, and assessment methods practised. As an example of good practice, the Wellcome Trust's Policy and Research in Science and Medicine Unit (PRISM) undertook a gender evaluation of the trusts funding, which revealed little difference in success rates between men and women who applied. However, it also found that four times as many men apply and are awarded project grants as women, five times as many men applied for programme grants than women, and twice as many men applied for Senior Research Fellowship in Basic Biomedical Science as women. As a consequence the Trust now tries to ensure that there is female representation on the membership of all its Panels and Interest Groups with responsibility for decision-making on applications. It has also started recording information related to the gender and race of grant applicants in line with recommendations from the Equal Opportunities Commission.

The Boards and Committees, which make decisions on the success of research applications in Research Councils, are high level academic peer-review bodies capable of attracting the confidence and support of the wider academic community. This requirement for academic status is interpreted in terms of the demand for members with appropriate seniority (Professorial or equivalent), and previous research track record, which, given women's position in the academic hierarchy, has immediate implications for their inclusion. Also, the Research Councils do not use open advertisements for Board membership, but rather the procedures for selection of members mirrors the above peer-review process. Visible and known senior academics are asked to sit on Boards and Committees making decisions, and given the above issues, this would appear to be more likely to be men than women. There is another issue involving Board membership, which also differently impacts on women and men academics. The institutional breakdown of Board membership into pre-1992 and post-1992 universities is important. Members from old universities tend to predominate, where the number of women academics is considerably fewer.

Women academics are disproportionately distributed in new universities and thus disproportionately affected by the pattern of research grant allocation by Research Councils. A study of research allocation has shown that old, elite universities are increasing their share of the research funding. The UK's twenty large universities with medical schools (the Russell group) secure 75 per cent of all research awards and contracts, 70 per cent of research students, and 75 per cent of research-only staff. These research staff and students have trebled since 1980. This increasing dominance of the old universities has come at a time when the total number of institutions competing for research grants has doubled. The pre-1992 universities take only 4.5 per cent of all research funds, 3 per cent of research council awards, and 9 per cent of research students (Major, 2000). The following comment from a senior woman academic illustrates the disillusionment that reflects this pattern of resource allocation:

> You're a woman in a multi-disciplinary field from a small institution − you think 'what's the point?' [...] The scholarship here is as good as anything I've met anywhere else, but one has this prejudice to meet about old/new universities [...] So there's that kind of climate of: 'It's a waste of time, it's all stitched up by the old boys − and some old girls − it's not worth the opportunity cost of spending all that time and emotional energy'. And I think that's very sad because [...] you know the old phrase, 'If you always do what you've always done, you'll always get what you've always got'. And if we need anything in British scholarship, it's a bit more innovation at the moment.

Conclusions

The factors outlined above, continuing disadvantaged career opportunities and lack of seniority, impact upon women's research activity. However, the level of this disadvantage is made more difficult to expose because the accurate measurement of women's research has not being addressed. For example, neither the gender composition of Research Assessment Exercise (RAE) panels, nor information on the gender balance of those entered for RAEs, has been systematically collected. However, the Higher Education Funding Council (HEFCE) has plans to do so for the 2001 RAE. In fact there is a systematic failure throughout HE to collect and monitor gender statistics. Data on academic staff held in various locations are incomplete and categories used by the different bodies collecting information are insufficiently compatible with each other to allow accurate comparisons to be made. For example, the format in which the Higher Education Statistics Agency currently publishes data is problematic for calculating the disciplinary distribution of academic women. Staff data are recorded by gender and by cost centre, but cost centres do not correspond to disciplines or subjects.

Cockburn (1995) insightfully articulated the issue of women's lack of representation on political decision making bodies: 'Women's relative absence deepens women's silence, and so the cycle goes'. This is also the case in academia. Peer-review is an important issue, and female representation in these gate-keeping positions is important. Some progress in this direction has already been made by the Committee of Vice-Chancellors and Principals of the Universities of the UK (CVCP) initiative to create a Women in Higher Education Register.[2] Using a centralised resource such as this comprehensive database of eligible academics could increase the numbers of women involved in this process and enhance effective and fair identification of suitable peer-reviewers. However, importantly, this needs proactive measures on behalf of universities and Research Councils.

In broad terms, the peer-review system importantly contributes to academics' success in research careers and may work against women because of their relative lack of seniority, visibility, and track record, because they are more likely to be on short-term contracts, have fractured careers, and different roles in academia. In terms of overcoming such potential barriers, it is essential that women are included in all the 'gate-keeping' procedures throughout the research application process.

Notes

[1]　However, it should be acknowledged that post-1992 universities have made more progress than pre-1992 universities, in the proportion of women in senior positions.

[2]　The stated objectives of the register are to: make accessible the skills and expertise of women in HE for the benefit of the economy and culture of the country; address the current inaccessibility, under utilisation and under representation of women in the corridors of power; provide a foundation to address and research significant issues for women: training and development programmes; initiatives to improve utilisation, equality of opportunity and outcome; retention and returner schemes; and participation, progression and promotion; facilitate a resource centre and networking base for women in HE; raise the profile of women in HE; demonstrate commitment to the progress and contribution of women in HE; and give the impetus to senior women to discover the power and uses of IT.

References

Acker, S. and D. Warren Piper (eds) (1984), *Is Higher Education Fair to Women?*, SRHE/Open University Press, Milton Keynes.

AUT (1999), *AUT Update* 55, 28 January.

Bagilhole, B. (1993), 'Survivors in a Male Preserve: a Study of British WomenAcademics' Experiences and Perceptions of Discrimination in a UK University', *Higher Education*, 26.

Bagilhole, B. and E. Robinson (1997), *A Report on Policies and Practices on Equal Opportunities in Employment in Universities and Colleges of Higher Education*, Commission on University Career Opportunity, Committee of Vice-Chancellors and Principals of the Universities of the United Kingdom (CVCP), London.

Boden Report (1990), Advisory Board for the Research Councils' Working Group on Peer Review.

Brooks, A. (1997), *Academic Women*, Society for Research into Higher Education/Open University Press, Milton Keynes.

Burton, L. and G. Weiner (1993), 'From Rhetoric to Reality: Strategies for Developing a Social Justice Approach to Educational Decision-Making', in I. Siraj-Blatchford (ed.), *'Race', Gender and the Education of Teachers*, Open University Press, Buckingham.

Cockburn, C. (1995), 'Women and the European Social Dialogue: Strategies for Gender Democracy', V/5465/95-EN, Equal Opportunities Unit, European Commission.

Deane, E., L. Johnson, G. Jones and N. Lengkeek (1996), *Women, Research and Research Productivity in the post-1987 Universities: Opportunities and Constraints*, University of Western Sydney, Nepean, HE Division, Evaluations and Investigations Division, December.

Dudovitz, R.L. (1983), 'Editorial' in R.L. Dudovitz (ed.) (1983), *Women in Academe* Pergamon Press, Oxford.

Fenton, N. (1998), *Mediating Social Science*, Sage, London.

Goode, J. and B. Bagilhole (1996), *Whose University? The Impact of Gender*, Research Report of the Gender Studies Research Forum, Loughborough University.

Halsey, A.H. (1992), *Decline of Donnish Dominion: The British Professions in the Twentieth Century*, Oxford, Clarendon Press.

Hansard Society Commission Report (1990) *Women at the Top*, Hansard Society for Parliamentary Government: London.

Hawkins, A.C. and D. Schultz (1990), 'Women: the Academic Proletariat in West Germany and the Netherlands', in S.S. Lie and V.E. O'Leary (eds), *Storming the Tower: Women in the Academic World*, Kogan Page, London.

Heward, C. and P. Taylor (1993), 'Effective and Ineffective Equal Opportunities Polices in Higher Education', *Critical Social Policy*, 37.

IRHEPC (1999), *Independent Review of Higher Education Pay and Conditions*, Chaired by Sir Michael Bett, HMSO, London.

Leat, D. (1998), *Faith, Hope and Information: Assessing a Grant Application*, York, York Publishing Services Ltd.

Loder, N. and S. Eley (1998), 'Probe Into What Puts Women Off Research', *Times Higher Education Supplement*, 18 September.

Major, L.E. (2000), 'Cream and Crumbs on the Plate', *Guardian Education*, 9 May.

McAuley, J. (1987), 'Women Academics: A Case Study in Inequality', in A. Spencer and D. Podmore (eds), *In a Man's World. Essays on Women in Male-Dominated Professions*, Tavistock Publications, London.

O'Leary, V.E. and J.M. Mitchell (1990), 'Women Connecting with Women: Networks and Mentors in the United States' in S.S. Lie and V.E. O'Leary (eds), *Storming the Tower: Women in the Academic World*, Kogan Page: London.

Ramsden, B. (1996) 'Academic Staff: Information and Data', in R. Cuthbert (ed.), *Working in Higher Education*, Society for Research into Higher Education/Open University Press, Milton Keynes.

Royal Society (1995), *Peer-review: An Assessment of Recent Developments. Social Focus on Women* (1998), Office of National Statistics/Equal Opportunities Commission.

Spurling, A. (1996), 'Women and Change in Higher Education', in Eggins, H. (ed.), *Women as Leaders and Mangers in Higher Education*, SRHE/Open University Press, Milton Keynes.

Sutherland, M. (1985), *Women Who Teach In Universities*, Trentham Books, Stoke-on-Trent.

Thomas, K. (1990), *Gender and Subject in Higher Education*, Open University Press, Milton Keynes.

Tothill, A. (1998), *Women in Research*, Report on the Centre for Social Science Development of the Human Sciences Research Council. Audit of Women Researchers in the Humanities and Social Sciences at South African Universities and Technikons.

Weneras, C. and A. Wold. (1997), 'Nepotism and Sexism in Peer-review', *Nature*, 387.

PART II
MODELS OF HIGHER EDUCATION

Chapter 5

Institutional Discrimination and the 'Cloistered' Academic Ideal

Gillian Howie and Ashley Tauchert

Introduction

The modern university dates back to Europe's high Middle Ages, from the twelfth-century models of Paris, Bologna, Salerno and Oxford, during the period referred to as the 'Latin Renaissance'. Events preceding, and then following, the establishment of Oxford and Cambridge demonstrate the integral ties between clerical authority and scholarship. From 1280 onwards, private money, often linked to the Church, was used to fund various university colleges. Lay, rather than clerical, money funded many of the post-Reformation Oxbridge colleges, but their continuing alliance was reflected in the theological bias and cloistered geography. The official association was not properly broken until the Oxford and Cambridge Act, which included the abolition of religious tests. This ecclesiastical coupling was prevalent too in the foundation of the Scottish Universities at St Andrews, Glasgow, and Aberdeen. Although there had often been tension between political authority and the quasi-autonomous universities, the system of university education actually first expanded mainly due to the demand for facilities for dissenters – those unwilling to take the religious test. The new universities included University College and Kings College, London, as well as Durham. Later expansions were driven by the need for trained specialists in science and engineering to manage and augment the modernisation of industry in the middle nineteenth century and, finally, through Robbins the contemporary system of Higher Education emerged between 1955 and 1975 (Scott, 1984; Moodie and Eustace, 1974; Ross, 1976).

This paper explores the assertion that the modern university is the result of a process of accretion, as much as of evolution or reform (Scott, 1984, p.5). We agree with Scott that there has been a significant shift in the general conception of knowledge within Higher Education and we also propose an underlying continuity. The Renaissance of the sixteenth century, the scientific revolution of the seventeenth century, and the Enlightenment of the eighteenth, appear to have had little immediate or obvious impact on the processes of Higher Education today. However, the liberal and modern universities share certain characteristics. Amongst other things, the Enlightenment inherited from the Renaissance a division of subject matter into rhetoric and mathematics. In its turn, the Enlightenment, clarifying the epistemological foundations of scientific endeavour, presented us the axis: individual as knower and individual as natural object, which can be investigated and known. This axis forked out in the expansion of the university system, sometimes one having precedence and sometimes the other. The idea of a 'knowing subject' was reified in the arts and humanities as the cultural or civilising force; while the 'natural object' was established within various scientific projects. Other natural sciences relied upon the epistemological method which explained that some things could be known beyond a shadow of doubt, whilst others could only be believed.

The modern university is the university of liberal modernity, and its academic work is governed by various Enlightenment, humanistic, beliefs. The project of Enlightenment then bequeathed us the concept of a subject who could (and should) use his or her own understanding, be neutral to context, and who would be able to come to know and categorise the empirical world. The ideal of an academic, unhampered by his or her embodied state, is the organising motif that has remained through the process of accretion. We have adopted the concept of 'cloister' to suggest an historical patrilineage between the humanism of the Renaissance, the Enlightenment and Modernity; between the medieval, the liberal, and the modern university; the religious past and the secular present.[1]

Schuller describes the collegiate organisation as a form of democracy but points out that 'the notion of academe as a community is Athenian with myriad low-status employees who would not recognise themselves as participating in a collegial democracy' (Schuller, 1995, p.7). We would like to add to this that the university was, and remains, Athenain in one further sense. It was not until 1878 that women were permitted to take degrees, and then not as full members in Oxford until 1920 and Cambridge until 1948. Women studying for their London degree found themselves in women-only lectures and had to leave by a side entrance; women studying in Cambridge lived so far away from the centre that lecturers had to arrive by train. Even until the 1970s it was assumed that women graduates would either become teachers or work part-time, thus managing the conflicting demands of career and parenting.[2]

There are various explanations available for the figures presented in the current Gender Audit of Higher Education, which demonstrates the notable degree to which women staff remain clustered in lower-paid and lower-status posts. We contend that there is more than a coincidental relation between the history of the cloistered university and the institutional discrimination currently evident. The thoroughly liberal, Enlightenment, principle of fairness would suggest that benefits should be distributed according to merit regardless of contingencies associated with embodied states, such as gender and ethnicity. The Gender Audit suggests one of two things: either women academics are not of sufficient merit to ascend through the 'hierarchy', or the criteria for distribution are suspect. We contend that criteria and mechanisms for distribution might appear to be rational and neutral, but manage to incorporate select values and thereby constitute the conditions for the repetition of the same. As Ashby once said, 'an institution is the embodiment of an ideal' (1966, p.6). Appearances of a neutral ideal in almost all cases conceal bias in practice. The group benefiting from the status quo, from the bias, tends to be of a type: male and white. And it is this group that hangs most fervently onto the belief that neutrality is possible and more often than not achieved.

Therefore, for the sake of a more robust critical enquiry, we intend to begin an exploration of how the institution embeds principles which favour a select group; how beliefs and values circulate with hegemonic vigour; and how academics are inculcated into – and inculcate – the belief that neutrality is a matter of clear and detached judgement. Male and female academics all learn the language of neutrality, but a woman lives the dissonance between what any 'neutral' observer would claim to be the case and what she 'knows'. We maintain that a successful female academic must repudiate this knowledge, must appear to have detachment yet be competitive, must agree that the public and private are distinct spheres of endeavour and disavow her own knowledge that one supports and is the life-blood of the other. In short, to be admitted into the cloister, the female academic must pretend not to know what she does know, and know what she does not. She must feign an impossible disembodiment, which means in fact faking the masculine position. We call this self-repudiating female subject Athenic, and conclude that women have recently been included within the Athenian community as Athenic subjects, only to constitute the 'body' of low-status employees, who are rarely – if ever – recognised as fully participating members of the college government.[3]

Institutional embodiment

Each university is intrinsically a political body with its own system of government and self-regulation, bound by rules and regulations, the most prominent being its statute or charter. Within these general limits the university will normally have a set of statutes which contain general legislation about detailed decision-making practices, academic curricula, nature and kind of degrees, and perhaps some disciplinary procedures. One consequence of these rules is to establish a complex and hierarchical system of rewards and sanctions. Although the offices are ranked, we also find that that there is often an informal chain of command or a 'collegiate', Masonic, spirit.[4] It is clear that power is possessed, some individuals are authorised to act and are so authorised by the procedures and rules which distribute or protect entitlement.

The dominant ethic of the liberal university, the precursor to the modern, was to take responsibility for initiating, and entrusting, a cohort of the next generation into the intellectual and cultural tradition. Although the modern university has tended to be more pre-occupied by the exigencies of civil society and industry, it used to see itself as providing for an intellectual elite who could, if they so chose, stand aside from pedestrian occupations. The legal concept 'university' refers to a 'body incorporated for the purposes of learning and possessing endowments and privileges'. The university has indeed embodied, and still does embody, various normative principles and privileges guaranteeing the perpetuation of strata and privilege. These principles organise the body of the institution itself and can be witnessed in the determination of space (for example in the architecture, the physical accessibility to buildings, the structuring of the lecture theatre), and of time (for example with efficiency studies, teaching rotas, distribution of administrative tasks). These same principles cascade through disciplines, constraining and informing the subject matter, whilst ordaining the methods of assessment which we apply, both to ourselves and to our students. By identifying these principles with the concept of 'cloister', we can demonstrate why it is that equal opportunity policies have not, and can not, succeed.

Critiques of disembodied neutrality gained a profile on the academic scene from the 1970s (Goodlad, 1976, p.61). Academic work was undertaken to assess and explain the discordance between the liberalised policies of inclusion, the agenda of equal opportunities, and political realities. One of the conclusions drawn was that modernised structures managed to include women into 'the order' in such a way that formal liberal demands could be met without any substantive changes occurring. The structures determine the roles of men and women by distributing privileges, sanctioning specific practices, and circulating politically charged representations. If we develop this insight, that apparent neutrality often conceals bias, and analyse how power is distributed across, and distributes within, the practice of Higher Education, then we might begin to get some sense of the effects of the university as an organisational mechanism. In short, we suggest that it is possible to examine each Higher Education Institution as a body that is endowed with, and endows, power and privilege. Furthermore – as the Gender Audit demonstrates – these institutions reproduce the cloistered model and thereby privilege some kinds of bodies over others.

Gatens argues that we can apprehend degrees to which the 'body politic' has 'developed in a manner which has assumed that its occupants have a male body' (Gatens, 1992, p.125). She emphasises the sexual specificity assumed by institutions: 'It is the male body, and its historically and culturally determined powers and capacities, that is taken as the norm or standard of the liberal individual', women achieve this standard on condition that they 'elide their own corporeal specificity'. As female academics we are conscious of the manifestations of institutional embodiment as an accumulation of apparently disconnected instances of sexist assumptions or sexual discrimination. These range from the mundane to the criminal: a quiet departmental expectation to be available to teach twilight hours; accrual of pastoral care duties; problems with committee selection and roles; toilets with no provision of sanitary bins or baby changing facilities; sexist jokes in the lecture theatre and staff room; local struggles to maintain parity in pay and promotion. These represent diverse, and sometimes trivial, consequences of latent structures and practices concealed beneath the skin of the androgynous university body.

Institutional embodiment locates normatively embodied subjects in the systems and architecture of social institutions. With a sweeping overview, the procedures and rules which establish rank, the description of systems of distribution of sanction and privilege, appear gender-neutral. An example might be the Research Assessment Exercise. The RAE procedures were designed to be gender-blind, and appear to be so until we explore their underlying assumptions; assumptions which, in the end, have resulted in the systematic exclusion of a number of people (particularly women) from participating in the exercise and, consequently, left them in a worse position in terms of their own university hierarchy and career.[5] We have found that the procedures and the culture of Higher Education are two sides of the same coin; both bearing the stamp of institutional embodiment.

Consistent with this finding is our apprehension of numerous key points of agency within the university system; places where decisions are taken as to the distribution of some good. At the promotions gateway, for instance, stands a keeper (an individual or committee) making decisions about, amongst other things, the quality and quantity of a candidate's work, the soundness of disposition, the strength of spirit, the apparent collegiality, indeed, decisions about 'clubability', and offering explanations for performance indicators. Explicit monitoring of the procedures governing promotions in and between institutions would fail to reveal an essential connection between input and output. Indeed, many decisions are taken 'off-site' and merely confirmed according to the monitoring situation. One reason for this is that decisions and inferences are based on beliefs, and because social location is relevant to belief formation, and because gender is a – perhaps the – notable feature of social location, gender will always have a significant influence on decision-making, however gender-neutral the manifest procedures we devise aim to be.

But these beliefs, assumptions, or motives that guide our inferences, and govern the gate-keeping in institutions, are rarely conscious or explicit. Lorde describes the mythical norm underpinning Western cultural forms and processes as identifiably 'white, thin, male, young, heterosexual, Christian and financially secure' (Lorde 1990, p.282). Weiss adds that 'people' who do not meet the specifications of this 'mythical norm' 'are designated as the abject other, doomed to exist in those uninhabitable, unliveable regions that Butler reminds us are, in point of fact, densely overpopulated' (Weiss, 1999, p.99). In Higher Education these can be seen to span out as the notable regions of casualised labour; short-term, fixed-term or part-time contracts. The discriminatory practices and cultures currently in evidence, then, can be understood as symptomatic of the institution maintaining its coherence; given that coherence is in most cases structured and organised around a partial identification of human variables. We can read traces of this partial coherence in the kinds of assumptions institutions make about individuals. For example, when devising teaching strategies it has often been assumed that all academics are available to teach evening hours. Those who are not so available to the institution are considered, at best, special cases. It is not so much that Vice-Chancellors are still arguing that men and women come into their understanding to a different measure, but that the space carved within the social practice for 'progressive rational deliberation' or scientific 'advancement' assumes a normative self at least temporarily free from passions and/or relational *restrictions*. These assumptions, once embedded in practices marginalise and exclude those who are visibly 'encumbered' in any way.[6] Public deliberation and activity thus remains dependent upon, but in denial of, any connection to the 'private' sphere of quotidian or life-sustaining activities. Although few academics are actually clerics now, some would like to think they still are, and all can be treated as though they were, because it can be assumed that someone else (usually female) is still doing the ecclesiastical washing.

The body of disciplines

The notion that we study the 'best', or examine works that the 'greatest' minds have produced, or analyse the 'most significant' events, rests on a plethora of shaky received ideas. These ideas relate to the nature of the discipline in question, its situational concomitants, the nature of human abilities in general, of human excellence in particular, and the role that social order plays in all this (Nochlin, 1994, p.98). The bias evident in the construction of module content is well documented. The conditions of truth, the rules of the discipline, are immanent within each discipline and can only be disputed within the bounds of a debate that is already, for example, philosophical or scientific. Susan Hekman refers to the 'disciplinary matrix' whereby 'the concepts of the discipline define the appropriate objects of study in the social world' and '[e]ach discipline defines what objects are worthy of study' so that 'aspects of social reality that are not conceptualized in the disciplinary matrix cannot become the object of investigation'. She concludes that '[w]hat counts as "logical" analysis is, thus, constituted by the disciplinary paradigms of the investigator's social-scientific community' (Hekman, 1999, p.72). There is no real proof that the rules of the game are either sound or robust other than the fact that consensus is extended to them by experts. And who counts as an expert? Someone authorised within the game, and usually by seeded players.

It is, though, currently fashionable within certain disciplines to subject content matter, the notion of canon and proof, to critical scrutiny and to accept that the canon is a construction from a particular viewpoint: a choice. It is rare, however, that this insight actually leads to a revision of the curriculum, except as a historical aside, as a separate module, or in interdisciplinary research work. There is often a dissonance caused by the intellectual arguments concerning subject position and the fact that no real account is taken of unacknowledged value systems; the presence of an intruding subject in the selection of historical narrative. Even modules introducing the idea that there are alternative perspectives tend to do this as part of the historical narrative.

If we maintain that the critique of value neutrality has any purchase, then we need not only to revise module content but also to appraise propositions which claim to be true and to apply, and to encourage others to apply, a re-appraised epistemological method. Many academics, especially in the humanities and social sciences, now accept that social location ought to be taken into account but still balk at endorsing two implications: that reason, and research methodology, are less than supra-historical; and that it would be consistent to revise our modes and categories of assessment. An empiricist academic, a fully believing Humean scholar, would now be caught on the horns of a dilemma. The philosophical conclusion, that reason is a slave to the passions, would have to be held in abeyance whilst she or he marked exam scripts or reviewed a peer's journal article. Similarly, feminist scholars find they are advising their students to write about *parler-femme* using the three principles of logic and fully formed sentences. If the 'view from nowhere' is no longer a sustainable philosophical position, and one can abandon this without embracing relativism, then there are consequences for, among other things, methods of assessment. The idea that methods of assessment can discern objective quality or merit depends on the possibility of impartial acts of judgement and otherwise 'neutral' concepts. This is not to take a position on the realism of 'quality', either sceptical or relativist, it is to raise the matter of judgement. Manifest neutrality in almost all cases, we contend, disguises bias.

The scene of 'passing'

Academic practice establishes, and then requires a performance of, a scene of assessment, in which the supplicating subject presents itself to the academic body with a plea for entry. We have already noted one of the ways in which judgements concerning quality organise a body of material. Now, we would like to suggest that these same judgements block or grant access to the body politic itself. To enter the academy and pass through its subsequent portals we encounter a number of identifiable 'gates'. A 'gate' might be said to announce itself though the language of 'passing'. Graduation, for example, itself is often marked by a Vice-Chancellor stating 'I admit you'. Entry or exclusion is decided by a system of passing and grading subjects. A 'higher' grade offers higher level access to the academic body: where the language of 'height' denotes recognisable social hierarchies within and between institutions. A 'fail' (ungradable performance) excludes a subject from entry altogether (unless it is considered 'condonable'). We contend that the idealised characteristics witnessed in the physical organisation of the institution are replayed in the formalised scene of assessment.

Short-cutting various arguments, let us note that certain characteristics have been marked as 'masculine' and others as 'feminine'. These historical markings have little to do with actual characteristics of qualities possessed, and more to do with ideal images of male and female subjects. The qualities historically aligned with masculine subjectivity tend to be those which are the essential building blocks for any epistemology which either assumes or concludes with the possibility of detached neutral judgement. If we apply the Gatens model to our context of the cloistered university, it would seem reasonable to assume that the subject interpellated, or performed, by academic practices would be a token of the ideal type of masculinity; even though the academic subject ensconced in his or her life of the mind is presented as neutral to sex or gender. We would expect criteria to reward skills and characteristics historically associated with male-embodied subjects, and conversely to ward off, devalue and denigrate skills and characteristics historically associated with female-embodied subjectivity.

The scene of assessment determines passes, fails, and grades academic subjects according to received values of academic practice. These criteria, or descriptors, we maintain, represent deep assumptions about the normative subject assumed by academia by recording what kinds of skills or qualities are expected in an ideal performance at the moment of assessment. Passing, as understood by Queer and Postcolonial theory, connotes the phenomenon of *passing as* the normative subject.[7] Our parallel example is that we demand of a student that she should learn to *pass as* someone who can think or know in neutral terms, when neutrality has already been colonised by the male subject. Indeed, we even teach 'tricks of the trade': how to write indirect speech, how to assert third person authority, and so on. Students pass if, and only if, they can *pass as* (at least an approximation of) an ideal thinker. A female academic must, by definition, already have learnt to 'play by the rules', yet often feels compromised; for the institution demands of the subject at least an approximation of the masculine values it embodies. This approximation is easier for a male-embodied subject to enact as the whole system reiterates and supports his performance.

It is not merely a question of whether one passes or fails but also a matter of the quality of the pass. If we compare local assessment criteria for 1st and 3rd class marks we do not find opposite qualities, but rather a continuum between coherence and incoherence, between command of a great space of cultural knowledge and lack of command altogether. Similarly, we find a continuum from authority over one's material (marked by critical distance) to absence of authority (marked by the chaos of proximity), a continuum between focus and immersion, or transcendence and immanence. Underlying all this in the moment of assessment is the belief that familiarity with dominant modes of grammar, spelling and punctuation, not only deserves reward but coincides in itself with clear thought. Clear thought is compared to the mess of feelings, emotional blurred vision of the third-class student or academic: the pure Cartesian mind above the pure body of immanent failure.

We grade peers and students alike on the 'quality' of written work. In all disciplines – except, perhaps, Women's Studies – specific things have been required and become associated with 'quality'. The work, for example, ought to be presented in an argumentative, often combative, style where the reader's interest is captured and the opponent 'defeated' (Mouton, 1989). We expect the work to follow through a linear argument, to develop a coherent thread of reasoning, to provide 'scholarly' rather than anecdotal or personal evidence, and to conclude with balanced judgement.[8] An appeal to intuition is tolerated when it is considered co-extensive with 'rational insight' rather than some woolly appeal to emotional affects: clear light as opposed to the dark continent. Let us be explicit. It is not our contention that men and women think differently. We are merely highlighting the fact that judgements of 'quality' often presume not just an epistemology but also an ontology. The assumptions that the 'empirical' world coincides with logical form, that we can isolate parts from wholes and speak from a detached vantage point are inherited from Enlightenment philosophy. These ideas may not be obsolete, but they ought to be made visible, then perhaps contested. Derrida warns us against the 'autism of closure' (1982, p.135). By this he means that if we attempt to exist without changing terrain, if we merely repeat what is implicit in the founding concepts and the original problematic, then we risk confirming and consolidating that which we are allegedly deconstructing. The contention here is that feminist theory is judged according to 'standard' modes of assessment, and that because feminist approaches run counter to 'acceptable' standards of rigour they are thus ruled out. To be included at all, feminism within the academy has had to become depoliticised.[9]

We have seen that the possibility of assessment is premised on the possibility of neutral judgement. This possibility is grounded in the concept of an unencumbered transcendental subject and an original split between the empirical and the intelligible, a split redolent of the historical cloistering of academia. The distinction between the empirical and the intelligible, between what is knowable and what can only be believed, excludes from consideration, except in the softest areas, the practical aims, ends or orientation of the enquiry itself. The anti-realist tendency within Enlightenment thought, to describe ethics as a matter of taste, has fed seamlessly into the modernisation and appropriation of the university body itself.[10]

The disciplined body

Our principle claim in this section is that despite what one might expect, even the proponents of equal opportunities will find themselves floundering in the political context post-2000. The reason for this is that the process of increasing productivity tends to aggravate the situation of discrimination by facilitating the conditions within which strata and privilege can reproduce. We suggest that this reproduction occurs through the body of the university, which can be seen to be functioning as a well-disciplined machine.

A tactic of training entered the confines of academia during the eighteenth and nineteenth centuries, tied to the emergence of what Foucault has described as a 'disciplined' society. This does not mean that, through the 'massification' of education, the ends of Higher Education changed from the production of an intellectual elite to vocational training, because the ends had always included at least an element of practical application. Rather, the educational system itself became a disciplinary machine, reproducing itself through self-surveillance. We have already touched on the two characteristics that made the university disposed to this: its form of management, and the nature of testing.

First, norms were already present in the setting and testing of oral and written examinations as well as religious testing. From the beginning, non-conformity was, quite literally, an exclusionary act. Testing is a form of hierarchical observation, which introduces the individual into a field of documentation, through procedures which correlate individual data within various systems. This body of knowledge makes it possible to clarify categories, determine averages, and to fix norms. Secondly, a university administration was historically a diverse and shifting group, constituted both by professionals and by academics and, as an administrative wing of the body, held a fairly low status. Ashby once suggested that 'the British system almost eliminates the administration as a power point' (Ashby, 1970, p.11). However, once this bureaucracy was professionalised, there could be, and was, an imperceptible shift into a more hardy form of self-regulation, facilitated by the fact that academics were quite acclimatised to imposing managerial demands on themselves under the auspices of 'self-government'.

Organisational effectiveness and stability, guaranteed by the bureaucracy, was necessary to the expansion of the institution and then required by the expanded system. Uniformity of treatment, standardisation and routinisation were elementary principles in a system that was now called upon to deliver 'efficiently' according to calculable rules. This impacts on the standard of teaching and research possible as well as the content. 'The fact remains', writes Lyotard, 'that since perfomativity increases the ability to produce proof, it also increases the ability to be right: the technical criterion, introduced on a massive scale into scientific knowledge, cannot fail to influence the truth criterion [...] De facto legitimation' (1986, p.46). Such instrumental patterns of behaviour and thinking not only run counter to the critical spirit of academia, but also manage to reinforce latent 'prejudice'.

Let us take the RAE as a case in point. With this exercise, we can see a number of the elements we have already discussed. First, it is a perfect example of the principle of performativity. The exercise, triggered by governmental efficiency targets, is supposed to be concerned with the quality of research in Higher Education Institutions. But we can detect a slippage from the meaning of quality as something outside measurement, to there being specific criteria which something of quality needs to fulfil, and finally to quality being something which can be thoroughly quantified in itself. At the point of quantification we find education becomes identified with the instrumental provision of goods – rather than 'the good'. This itself fits neatly into the utilitarian tendency within liberal Enlightenment.

Aside from a general de-funding argument, if Lyotard is right, then increased productivity does not lead to a decentralisation of academic authority, but rather reproduces the existent authorities. There are a number of reasons for this. By setting up standards and authorities, work can be judged as close to, or far from, the ideal. This allows the space for partial or political judgement to be disguised as an analysis of 'academic rigour'. Such judgement then determines who has access to further funds and to status within the universities. In turn, it is those with status who constitute the peer group that counts, and from which will be drawn the next generation of peer-reviewers; whether in the Teaching Quality auditing procedures, or as RAE panels, or as peer-reviewers for journals and publishing houses. The process of academic legitimation, therefore, rests upon, and is itself justified by, an original epistemological belief in unbiased, reflective, judgement, but in fact serves largely to produce deep strata of discrimination through the collegial system of peer review and the consequent distribution of goods.

The stated purpose of the RAE is to produce ratings of quality research and these ratings are subsequently used in the determination of grants for research at the institutions. The RAE requires from the institution a high degree of information. All staff, whether research active or not, are accounted for. Each is, or constitutes, a block unit of assessment. Departments have to produce detailed plans about future programmes, expansions, future teaching and this, in turn, requires the members of staff to reveal their own plans. In addition, each department is expected to include information relating to indices of research excellence. The highly intrusive nature of the exercise is quite apparent and the continual measurements, as well as our own thwarted attempts to produce standards and targets, is a mutilating experience. All academics are subject to these criteria and regulate their work accordingly. The academic, at once subject and object, produces the work by which his or her authority will be judged. Because these criteria are mostly hidden from view, except the exhortation to produce a quantity of research, the academic experiences acute anguish and stress. This stress is most acute when work is submitted for quality appraisal that calls into question the criteria and mechanisms; hence especially true of feminist work.

Despite the diversity of power centres within the university, the body politic has always been an oligarchy; those involved in the government of the institution were few in number. These few now pursue ends at odds with 'the good', define 'good' in terms of performativity, and subordinate the institution of higher learning to existing powers. There is an interesting tension here. All policy initiatives need to be validated by various committees, even down to the departmental level. However, the impression is that the process is one of implementation rather than authorisation. What was once a fraternal Athenian contract has become a self-regulating, self-monitoring disciplinary practice. It has been claimed that the university is predicated on the view that those who teach and research ought to be free from constraint, or even detailed supervision, and that university governance used to be more concerned with context than with substance (Moodie and Eustace, 1974, p.22). This perhaps explains the enlightened ports of critical, if not practical, resistance within the system today.

The Athenic woman

The Hansard Society's Commission on 'Women at the Top' examined the under-representation of women in various senior posts and concluded that the barriers to women's equality in Britain are general and pervasive (David and Woodward, 1998, p.15). They include outmoded attitudes about the role of women, direct and indirect discrimination, and inflexible working practices. Within European Union policy terminology, 'flexible employment' is advocated as a means of resolving not only unemployment but also underemployment and enhancing equal opportunities. Perrons notes that: 'flexible working was said to provide opportunities for people to combine paid work and family life, and simultaneously enable employers to make efficiency gains by matching labour supply to immediate employment needs'. There is an obvious contradiction at the centre of the concept. Flexibility is often identified with the notion of autonomy, self-direction and self-guidance, ideas which, as we have seen, are close to the enlightened academic heart. But, when the ends of educational practice have been appropriated into a general system of efficient, market-driven provision, then flexibility actually means casualisation and erosion of anything approximating autonomous working patterns. As the Gender Audit demonstrates, when the security of the job diminishes, the number of women increases, and this exacerbates any problems that may exist within the system. It is unsurprising that the inclusion of women into the body politic has coincided with loss of overall status, falling remuneration, and a steeply diminishing quality of working conditions. The causal connection runs from the latter to the former but is supported by the fact the once women are settled within a profession, even as low status employees, the profession itself faces a harder task to be taken seriously by the other governing bodies.

Tactics of exclusion have often been linked to attempts to maintain an ideal pure community. This tactic was successful in the cloistered university until the civil rights movement, when a general liberalisation of opportunity forced the fraternity to open the gates protecting the Athenian democracy. But inclusion into the body politic has meant little, as the university itself is already a masculine entity, which manages to perpetuate and reproduce itself in a myriad of ways. These ways remain largely hidden and disguised by various claims to neutrality. We have suggested that the surveillance and discipline, to which we tend to subject ourselves and others, also manage to reproduce the same discriminatory practices whilst causing academic docility and anguish. The situation of the modern female-embodied academic was raised, with characteristic prescience, by Woolf when she reflected on her exclusion from the material and cultural bastions of academic power in the 1920s: 'I thought how unpleasant it is to be locked out; and I thought how it is worse perhaps to be locked in' (Woolf, 1982, p.24). The 'choice' between exclusion and assimilation remains a harsh one for women who find themselves on the 'inside' today. We argue that most women academics experience an antinomy between their embodiment and various institutional practices; a dissonance. However we suggest that this almost inevitable failure to meet the normative ideal of academic practice is a *positive* failure, since it gives an insight into our own position, and the latent processes which are the conditions for the educational experience.

Because the discursive mechanism of Higher Education is a system, we suggest that any further liberalisation process will only occur through collective agitation. This liberalisation process, the demands for transparency and quality control, has a positive and negative role. It is disciplinary by nature but also suggests points of exchange most exposed to view and accountability. The recent sex discrimination case (Mercer v LSE) demonstrated this dual function by exposing the limit of institutional sexism, embedded in structures designed ostensibly to maintain and improve 'quality' in academic practice, as well as the site at which such structures can be exposed as discriminatory.[11] Future RAEs will need to be conscious of, and perhaps take advice on, the discriminatory potential of any 'neutral' criteria, as well as the ways in which such criteria are interpreted by institutions and gatekeepers. Other identifiable gates that could be analysed include research council grants, application procedures, and the system of anonymous peer-reviewing. Here, we would like to ask to what degree anti-feminist 'gate-keeping' – in the name of 'quality' – represents the permissible face of the latent misogyny of the academy?

Notes

[1] Although we are concentrating on the individual Higher Education institution, we recognise that no analysis would be complete without the idea of a Higher Education system being expanded to include research bodies, funding councils, secretaries of state etc. and any gender audit contending with the interrelations of all these features.

2   A questionnaire conducted in 1984 at Liverpool University discovered a prevailing attitude that women were not interested in long-term careers, and were earning pin money.

3   In the sense of female-embodied subjectivity stranded in a patrilineal mode of transmission: Athena, born from the head of the father/god after he had incorporated/cannibilised the pregnant mother; Athena as the one who excuses the symbolic matricide which underpins social and symbolic patrilineage and its manifestations as patriarchy. For Irigaray, Athena symbolises women 'whose one begetter is the head of the Father-King [...] Completely in his pay, in the pay of the men in power, they bury beneath their sanctuary women in struggle so that they will no longer disturb the new order of the home, the order of the polis, now the only order' (Irigaray, 1995, p.37).

4   *Times Higher Education Supplement* (13 March 1998) reported that at least eleven UK universities have 'affiliated Freemasons' lodges. A spokesperson for the United Grand Lodge of England likened the university lodges to 'office five-a-side football teams'.

5   See the description of the Mercer v LSE case finding in Erica Helvorsen's 'Gender Audit' in this collection.

6   The 1984 Liverpool questionnaire also uncovered various interview questions which ranged from asking female candidates how the candidate might manage to do full-time work with a family to what time off the candidate might need to look after sick children. One was asked whether she intended to have children, and another one was asked whether her husband was aware of her application.

7   Gail Weiss discusses Nella Larson's novel, *Passing*, in terms of 'the complex emotional investments that produce a racialised body schema and in turn shape the formation of a (white) body image ideal' (Weiss, 1999, 29-30). See also Zack, 1997; *Diacritics* 24 (2-3) (Summer 1994), special issue 'Critical Crossings', J. Butler and B. Martin (eds).

8   This remains true in 'soft' disciplines, like English, where the incontrovertible judgement might take the form of a claim to the absence of incontrovertible judgement in the case of a given text.

9   Lovendsuki and Randall describe academic feminism as a deradicalisation of feminist theory and link this to the more general rise of 'municipal feminism', the filtering through of women and feminist theory into public institutions, including, but not exclusively, Higher Education. We contend that the university scene of assessment contributed to, but did not cause, this deradicalisation.

10   MacIntyre argues that due to the critical impulse of the Enlightenment, the foundations of moral judgement were scrutinised and, without either a theological or Aristotelian frame of reference, this led to relativism or to the utilitarianism of the market.

11   Employment tribunal held on 28-29 February and 1 March 2000, in chambers 2 March 2000. The applicant was H.J. Mercer, the respondent LSE. The tribunal chair was Ms A.M. Lewzey. The decisions of the tribunal, on direct and indirect discrimination were unanimous in favour of Mercer.

References

Ashby, E. (1970), *Masters and Scholars*, Oxford University Press, Oxford.

Ashby, E. and M. Anderson (1966), *Universities: British, Indian, African. A Study of the Ecology of Higher Education*, Weiden and Nicolson, quoted in Moodie and Eustace (1974), *Power and Authority in British Universities*, Allen & Unwin, London, p.23.

David, M. and D. Woodward (1998), *Negotiating the Glass Ceiling: Careers of Senior Women in the Academic World*, Falmer Press, London and Washington.

Derrida, J. (1982), *Margins of Philosophy*, tr. A. Bas, Harvester, Brighton.

Diacritics, 24 (2-3) (Summer 1994).

Foucault, M. (1977), *Discipline and Punish*, tr. A. Sheridan, Penguin, Middlesex.

Goodlad, S. (1976), *Conflict and Consensus in Higher Education*, Hodder & Stoughton, London.

Hekman, S. (1999), *The Future of Difference: Truth and Method in Feminist Theory*, Polity Press, Cambridge.

Irigaray, L. (1995), *The Irigaray Reader*, Whitford, M. (ed.), Blackwell, Oxford.

Lorde, A. (1990), 'Age, Race, Class, and Sex: Women Redefining Difference', in Ferguson *et al.* (eds), *Out There: Maginalization and Contemporary Cultures*, MIT Press, Cambridge.

Lovenduski, J. and V. Randall (1993), *Contemporary Feminist Politics: Women and Power in Britain*, Oxford University Press, Oxford.

Lyotard, J. (1986), *The Postmodern Condition: A Report on Knowledge*, tr. G. Bennington and B. Massumi, Manchester University Press, Manchester.

Macintyre, A. (1985), *After Virtue*, Duckworth, Guildford.

Moodie, G. and R. Eustace (1974), *Power and Authority in British Universities*, Allen and Unwin, London.

Moulton, J. (1989), 'A Paradigm of Philosophy: The Adversary Method', in A. Garry and M. Pearsall (eds), *Women, Knowledge and Reality: Explorations in Feminist Philosophy*, Routledge, London and New York.

Nochlin, L. (1994), 'Why Have There Been No Great Women Artists', in Herrman, A. and A. Stewart (eds), *Theorising Feminism: Parallel Trends in the Humanities and Social Sciences*: Westview Press, Oxford and San Francisco.

Perrons, D. (1998), 'Flexible Working, the Time of Our Lives?', in *AUT Woman*, 45, Autumn.

Schuller, T. (1995), 'The Changing University? A Sketch Map with Coda', in T. Schuller (ed.), *The Changing University?*, SRHE/Open University Press, Buckingham.

Scott P. (1984), *The Crisis of the University*, Croom Helm, London and Sydney.

Weiss, G. (1999), *Body Images: Embodiment as Intercorporeality*, Routledge, London and New York.

Woolf, V. (1982), *A Room of One's Own*, Granada Publishing, London and New York.

Zack, N. (ed.) (1997), *Race/Sex: Their Sameness, Difference and Interplay*, Routledge, New York.

Chapter 6

Teaching as Hospitality:
The Gendered 'Gift' and Teaching Style

Alan Bleakley

Tolerance of ambiguity: teaching as artistry

During the late 1930s, in an act of prejudice against 'black' music, the Nazi Party effectively banned playing and listening to jazz, or syncopated and improvised music. This was an attempt to discursively produce identities of an upright nature, marching to the same regular beat characteristic of military bands. Authoritarian music was used to iron out intolerably complex, syncopated, polyphonic personalities, to produce regular, anal-obsessive types – killjoys – who marched without questioning orders, and ordered others to march, thus denying improvisation. Theodore Adorno's (1950) classic post-war study on the 'Authoritarian Personality' pointed to a central and enduring trait of the authoritarian type: *intolerance of ambiguity*. To play, or appreciate, improvised, complex, syncopated music such as jazz, one must be tolerant of ambiguity. Donald Schon's (1987) model of the 'reflective practitioner', the inspiring and confident teacher, has tolerance of ambiguity as its central value. To teach as if one were an inspired musician improvising a solo requires such tolerance of ambiguity. It also requires letting go of the music as it emerges, now offered as a freely-given gift to the audience, however appreciative or unappreciative.

The mindset of intolerance of ambiguity, and subsequent inability to improvise or syncopate a style, surely has little or nothing of value to offer teaching, for it would offer students the opposite to an aesthetic experience – a literal anaesthetising or numbing. Yet such a killjoy attitude permeates the dominant discourse of education that is the 'governmentality' (Gane and Johnson, 1993; Foucault, 1997) inhabiting managerialism. This discourse, defined by technical-rational efficiency, utility and economic accountability, has been colonised by the values of the market economy.

This chapter explores the possibility of a shift of emphasis from teaching grounded in a market economy to teaching grounded in a gift economy, where teaching as *techne* is replaced by an *ethos* of practice, with deep concerns about the aesthetics or style of practice. Such a shift must however be embedded in a wider change for it to be successful – from a 'masculine' order of brash, militaristic marching music that normalises into a common identity, to a 'feminine' order of subtle improvisation, that explores difference: rapid key changes, interesting harmonies and syncopated rhythms. The argument for the necessity of such a shift centres on the value of gift-giving, where the gift is given freely, and where teaching is configured as a gift. A starting point to the debate on the gift can be found in Nietzsche's *Thus Spake Zarathustra*. In the section on the 'Gift Giving Virtue', Zarathustra says that students repay their teachers badly if they remain as students, for the student must outstrip the teacher, losing the master to find herself. Nietzsche describes gift-giving as both a 'necessity' and an 'art'.

Schon (1987) refers to teaching through reflective practice as 'artistry'. It is not a technical occupation. The 'necessity' of gift-giving through teaching, described by Nietzsche, sees teaching as a vocation, or better, a compulsion. Bertolt Brecht's (1950) poem 'Giving' says, 'What I possess I cannot treasure/ Without a mind to pass it on'. There is no choice in giving the gift, which is not owned by the giver and neither will it be treated by the recipient as capital if the economy is shifted from a market culture to a gift culture. In what Georges Bataille (1988) calls a 'restricted economy', where Protestant and Capitalist values coincide, gifts are never *given* freely, but commodities are *exchanged*, with interest. In a 'general economy' of expenditure, the gift is not an investment but a necessary blowing-off of excess, which may in fact turn into a spending of what one does not have.

We must however be cautious about beginning with Nietzsche as we argue for a feminist basis to teaching as gift-giving, where Nietzsche describes gift-giving as a 'virtue'. Virtue has the same root as 'virile', which is a synonym for 'masculine'. One smells a rat with Zarathustra's formulations, that somewhere along the line, the teacher *does* invest in the students. However this happens, it will surely be another case of what Hélène Cixous and Catherine Clément (1986) call 'the Empire of the Selfsame', the assimilation or absorption of the Other into the desires of the self, in identity, rather than recognition of, and response to, difference. The gift given freely is a primary ethical gesture of difference.

The dominant discourse of managerialism, that Stephen Ball (1990, p.157) calls an 'imperialistic discourse', constructs teachers as technical-rational performers, informed by economic and political values, marginalising other values such as the aesthetic and social. Learning is framed in terms of 'credits', as commodities bought by students – who are constituted as 'customers' – and cashed in on graduation in the employment market. The teacher is further constructed as manager (of learning environments) and salesperson in a retail business. The metaphors are those of the business world, where the signifiers are 'market' terms. A secondary discourse constructs the teacher within a pastoral care identity. Here, teacher supports student as mentor and quasi-therapist in the facilitative role, rather than the authoritative role of subject specialist. The value system underpinning and informing this role is that of the social and interpersonal. Paradoxically, the managerial and facilitative discourses share a similar language – 'bonds', 'securities', 'trusts', 'interest' – but inflect it quite differently. This usage is compounded in comforting terms such as 'Investors in People'. Such words have quite different meanings for the social worker or counsellor in contrast to the stockbroker or financial advisor. Indeed, the economic community has come to colonise the therapeutic, where your personal investment analyst or financial advisor manages your portfolio with great interpersonal skill, giving monetary matters a human face (Bleakley, 1992).

Teaching can however resist both the authoritative discourse of managerialism and the facilitative discourse of humanistic counselling, to offer a praxis underpinned by the aesthetic and the theoretical value domains, as the 'artistry' of critically reflective practice (Bleakley, 1999). Such practice is grounded in tolerance of ambiguity, uncertainty, dissensus, uniqueness and value conflict – contexts that can be seen as opportunities rather than threats. Here, teaching acquires a taxis towards the aesthetic and ethical (*ethos*), away from the economic, the political and skills of personal relating (*techne*). Teachers are then constructed as those who practice artistry rather than a set of technical skills, and 'quality' is not 'assured' through instrumental and bureaucratic means, or crude managerialism, but through the relative depths of passion of intellectual inquiry. Schon grounds effective teaching not in the application of propositional knowledge, as a technical mastery, but in an articulation of practical or procedural knowing that draws upon tacit knowledge – where we know more than we can tell (Polanyi, 1983).

The 'new managerialism', with its emphasis upon technical performance and obsession with the instrumentalising of that performance, is blatantly phallogocentric. More so, as its central instrument of quality assurance is the judgmental masculine gaze that is also intolerant of difference – judging according to generalised rather than localised standards, stripping away the *eros* of practice as indulgent, and replacing it with the *logos* of rational efficiency. Within such a climate of polyphemic surveillance, as Foucault (1977) suggests, the eye is trained to turn inward as a self-surveillance and self-stricture. Then we become paranoid practitioners, afraid to experiment or imagine in case we fail or are found out, hooked on the less demanding and more readily satisfied 'lite' culture of competences ('good enough') and 'plain English' (reduction to the simplistic). Here, we are afraid of the unctuous, the fecund, the rich, oily complexities and uncertainties of practice in what Schon (1987) calls the 'swamp' of uncertainty, as opposed to the 'high ground' of technical-rational mastery.

The fecund is also the generous and excessive. What is striking about the 'new managerialism' is its Puritan, mean-spirited attitude, or its inability for generosity. This is reflected in an inability to care. Carol Gilligan (1982) in particular has pointed to the differences between a masculine ethic of 'rights' and a feminine ethic of 'care'. The former is based on abstract principles of reciprocity in an economy of commodity exchange. The latter is based on interpersonal needs and responsibilities in an economy of gift exchange. This leads us to clearly differentiate between a 'commodity' and a 'gift'. Where learning is framed as a commodity to be sold by institutions through their salespersons – the teachers – then we move into the culture of learning credits and student loans. Study becomes an investment, the teacher managing the learner's beginning portfolio. Where learning is framed as a gift to be given freely, there is no expectation of return on an investment. Rather, the libido of the occasion rests entirely with the ethical gesture of giving itself, in the spirit of academic interest. Indeed, what traditionally animates such a gift-giving is that the gift itself is inhabited by a 'free' spirit, like Ariel, in *The Tempest*, fearing imprisonment or boarding-up (Vaneigem, 1994). From the point of view of the restless spirit of knowledge, there can be no intellectual 'property', no recognition of ownership or patent. The spirit must circulate without hindrance, as Marcel Mauss (1990) suggests in his classic essay on 'The Gift' in archaic societies, first published in 1924 (see also Schrift, 1995, 1997; Godelier, 1999).

The root of the word 'gift', as Mauss shows, is a deconstructionist's delight. For 'gift' means both 'giving' and 'taking', and is both a 'present' and a 'poison'. It is then a *pharmakon*, or 'healing poison', inherently paradoxical. Gift giving is then fraught with difficulty. It is, for Jacques Derrida (1992) an 'impossibility', for in accepting the gift, the recipient cancels its nature as a gift. The conditions of possibility for the gift (no obligation, no exchange or return) are also the conditions of its impossibility. For Emmanuel Levinas (1969), the gift must, paradoxically, be received with *ingratitude*, so that the giver does not absorb the gift-giving activity back into herself, as self-congratulation, thus cancelling the nature of the gift as an ethical gesture of recognition of the radical difference of the Other in relation to the self.

Mauss and the duplicity of the gift

Marcel Mauss (1990) suggests that the apparently simple act of giving a gift is in fact riddled with duplicity. Describing ceremonial gift exchanges in cultures in Melanesia and the north-west Pacific coast of America (where an orgy of gift-giving, the 'potlatch' occurs), Mauss notes that a gift apparently generously offered is in fact acquired by 'formal pretence and social deception' (*ibid.*, p.1). Michael Taussig (1999, p.62), in a commentary on gift-giving, friendship and sacrifice, observes that the gift is 'in theory voluntary, disinterested, and spontaneous, but is in fact obligatory and interested'. Gift giving leads to a social contract, which we might now describe as shot through with corruption. There is then a contradiction inherent to the gift, that of obligation, shadowing its etymology as both 'poison' and 'present'. Taussig (*ibid.*) describes 'the impossible but necessary coexistence of generosity and calculation' as the anatomy of both the gift and of friendship as a gift.

Following Mauss' analysis, Bataille (1988) anatomises the frenzied and anxiety-provoking cycle of giving and returning that characterises the potlatch. The extreme example is the high Aztec culture, locked into excessive blood sacrifice as gift to the sun, which will rise the following day thanks purely to this daily feast of sacrificial blood. The gift is now transformed into massive obligation, parodying even the excesses of the potlatch. Bataille points to the difference between a Puritan restricted economy (production economy) in which a gift is kept, or invested, thus forming the basis for capitalism, and a general economy (consumption economy) in which excess must be blown off, or consumed. The general economy of gift exchange culminating in the potlatch calls for gifts not only to be reciprocated, but also substantially increased. This obligation leads to a terrible anxiety. In both restricted and general economies, the spirit of the gift – an inherent animation that keeps the gift circulating – is annulled. The gift, with its animating spirit, is either stopped in its tracks, where it is treated as capital; or it is distorted into an anxiety-provoking pathological growth, an inflation now running out of control, where it carries an obligation of doubling.

In each case, the economy in question creates a subjectivity or identity: for the restricted economy, that of the capitalist investor; for the general economy, that of the consumer and the now obligated recipient. In neither case is there a freely-given gift. Translating these economies into the teaching and learning situation, the restricted economy characterises our current dominant model of education as a commodity exchange, where students invest in knowledge for supposed future employment. In the general economy, students are forever obligated to the gifts of teachers, unable to return the gift and double it.

Levinas and the gift in heteronomy: no apple for the teacher!

John Locke's view of property rights and ownership, developed in the late seventeenth century, would describe a gift as something one keeps and does not circulate, thus initiating capitalism. In an economy of commodity exchange, objective relations are established. In contrast, within a gift economy, subjective relationships are established. Indeed, the point of the gift is to cement relationships. However, to shift from an ethics of rights based on abstract principles to an ethics of responsibility and care based on quality of relationship, may land us in another difficulty – that of grounding teaching in the pieties of liberal humanism. Here, teaching is seen as facilitative of personal growth, based upon a supposed (and prior) symmetrical relationship between teacher and learner. Levinas (1969) warns against such humanistic practices, for they do not respect *difference*. Rather, they offer a totalising relationship that is potentially inhumane.

If we were to apply the ideas of Levinas to pedagogy with integrity, teaching and learning, for so long soaked in a tepid humanism, would be revolutionised. Further, if we read Levinas through the ideas of French feminists, we would consider many dominant pedagogical practices as not only unethical, but also as explicitly gendered, the masculine privileged over the feminine. Levinas is one of a body of thinkers who take as their starting point Hegel's Master–Slave dialectic, in which there is no slave without master, and no master without slave. Each is known by difference from the other, not by some intrinsic identity. The subject is constituted by, and subject to, the discourse of the Other. Humanism, by contrast, is narcissistic: the self is considered to be transparent and open to introspective mapping, identical to itself, unitary and originary. The Other is then only understood as he or she is absorbed into the self, becoming property of the self, or 'selfsame' (*propre*). This offers a totalising of the Other, both an assimilation and assassination. Levinas, amongst others, suggests that identity is rather a condition contingent upon everything that happens to the person. The subject, constructed in terms of the discourse of the Other, is subject to that discourse, not master of it.

The self that does not totalise the Other but goes out to it, is also not autonomous but *heteronomous*, concerned with alterity, or difference, and not identity. It is a self filled with aversion to, or repugnance for, self-absorption. The movement to the Other, which is a facing-up to, a confrontation (literally *con-*

frons, which means 'with the forehead') is an emptying out, as an ethical gesture. To refuse this gesture is to refuse the Other as different, and this, as Luce Irigaray (1993) points out, is especially sensitive where the encounter revolves around gender difference.

By resisting the absorption of alterity into identity – or what Jill Robbins (1999) calls 'the play of the same' within a 'habitual economy', and Levinas, the 'imperialism of the same' – we engage in an act of generosity. Jacques Derrida (1999) reads this generosity as a 'welcoming'. Such generosity resists all taxis of the imperialism of the same (absorption, assimilation and empathic identification), whose extremes can be seen in the radical extermination of difference through racism, misogyny and totalitarianism. Further, where the emptying-out move of generosity coincides with the invitation to an Other to walk into the space created in difference, we engage in an act of hospitality. For Levinas, such an ethical action also recognises the radical asymmetry that necessarily exists between self and the Other – not an asymmetry of hierarchy or dominance, but one of horizontal difference.

Radical alterity challenges the dominant humanistic discourse of education. The latter encourages autonomy in both learners and teachers and then is potentially narcissistic and totalising of the Other. 'Autonomy' is a notion gendered male, for it reflects the self-serving Odyssean journey in which all events are subsumed under the motifs of homecoming and self-revelation – Joseph Campbell's (1988) 'monomyth' of the hero's journey, written in the wake of soldiers returning home from the Second World War. We need only remind ourselves of the position in which Odysseus' extended homecoming – otherwise, a long night at the pub – places Penelope, who sits at home, knitting, patiently awaiting his arrival. 'Accidents' do not take Odysseus out of himself, but are further incorporations of, or resistances to, the Other, who is relentlessly outwitted and slain.

Humanistic notions of collectivity as a plurality of the 'I', and as empathy and dialogue in an effort towards consensus, are further examples of a totalising of the Other, an inability to tolerate incommensurability, radical asymmetry, difference or alterity, and dissensus. It is only when we dissolve such humanistic notions of community and intersubjectivity as plural of the selfsame, and its associated Kantian morality of 'right conduct', that we can engage with the ethical question of how to face another without totalisation. This is a matter for Levinas not of *theory* of the gift economy, but *acts* of generosity and hospitality, gift-giving and reception of the Other, that move through the apparent barriers of the impossibility of the gift and the inability for authentic hospitality. Both are possible impossibilities. From this position of erasure and negative capability, in which the essentially patronising humanistic discourse is interrogated and challenged, we may engage with the relationship between a teacher and learner as one of generosity and hospitality. We will however be frustrated and constrained if we attempt to enact this impossible possibility within a phallocentric commodity exchange economy, dominated by the mythical stance of the hero and the Odyssean myth of homecoming.

Levinas (1969, p.70) warns us not to totalise the Other through socialisation into an agenda of 'demagogy, psychagogy, pedagogy'. There are two discourses that can maintain the radical asymmetry or non-totalizing relation between self and other: generosity and language. Both offer a departure *without* return, against the grain of 'the Ulysses theme' (Stanford, 1992). Further, generosity and language can be conflated simply as the gift of language. Such generosity towards the Other offers a framework for teaching that is non-possessive, but can it be seen as a gift given freely? As mentioned earlier, in Levinas' scheme, this would require, paradoxically, ingratitude on the part of the student, because gratitude merely cycles the gift back to the giver. Intolerance of ingratitude would also deny the value of the gift, for some reciprocity would then have been expected. We must not take Levinas' prescription too literally – as an excuse to rationalise poor teaching, or to turn teaching into a 'thankless' task. We have all had 'ungrateful' students who have apparently thrown our efforts back in our faces. Rather, we could see Levinas' 'ingratitude', applied to an educational setting, as the common response of bewilderment of students upon first reception of new and complex ideas, demanding texts, difficult skills and value conflicts. Typically, first contact with such ideas and practices ends in frustration, puzzlement and even hostility. The teacher need not apologise for this, nor feel hurt by the student's response, seeking consensus or symmetrical understanding. For if the content is good and well represented that in itself will do the work. There is no apple for the teacher in this formulation.

An application of Levinas' model to educational practices would challenge models that configure the teacher student relationship as symmetrical, and focus upon the experience of the learner in a valorising of autonomy. Through the latter, the learner is constituted as an independent, reflective agent, and the teacher as a facilitator aiming to build a relationship of symmetry. The contrasting Levinasian model, however, should not be read as a retreat into authoritarianism or conservatism. Rather it offers a radical rethinking of the orthodox and naturalised humanistic position that, upon critical inspection, reveals a totalising at work, where the discourse of the Other is absorbed into the discourse of the self, as 'selfsame'. Levinas describes the 'nonself-identical' as an act of recognition of difference without marginalisation.

In applying Levinas' scheme to teaching, the habitual or restricted economy of pedagogy as a business enterprise and commodity exchange, or a normalising discourse of managerialism, is disrupted. Issues of reciprocity, debt, circulation, symmetry, implying a closed system of ideological, intersubjective exchange, are interrupted, and teaching is offered as a gift without return or an act of hospitality. Levinas (1969, p.258) says, 'the relationship with another puts me into question, empties me of myself, and does not let off emptying me – uncovering for me ever new resources'. The ethical gesture that recognises the Other and does not totalise the Other, is described as 'a word of honour' (*ibid.*, p.202). The faces of students met in gaze or glance do not invite us to probe their psyches. Neither do we totalise with knowledge or attempt to totalise knowledge itself. Rather, we might face up to the Other's face in treating it, as Michael Taussig (1999, p.224) suggests, as a 'fetish'. The fetish, with its emanating power, draws you to it, or educates your attention to its presence, so that you *must* gaze upon it. At this point of mutuality, that Taussig calls a 'crossing', there is always the possibility of defacement, when something precious is despoiled. Levinas says that we must not 'look' upon the Other's face, but access it, as if glancing off.

In *Totality and Infinity* Levinas describes the importance of the 'more than I contain', which is the presence of the radical Other. In Socratic teaching, we draw out what the student knows. This is maieutic teaching, where we assume content common to both teacher and student. But the responsibility of the teacher is surely to bring the student face to face with what she does *not* know. Derrida (1999, p.17) describes Levinas' view of teaching as a 'welcoming', 'where ethics interrupts the philosophical tradition of giving birth and foils the ruse of the master who feigns to efface himself behind the figure of the midwife'. Maieutics 'teaches me nothing' for it only reveals to me what I am already in a position to know, in the position of 'selfsame'. In Levinas' (1969, p.51) model, the learner can also take the role of a welcomer of teaching 'to *receive* from the Other beyond the capacity of the I, which means exactly: to have the idea of infinity'. Levinas makes a critical distinction between an 'idea' and the 'thought' that appropriates the idea for the thinker. In teaching, the idea is allowed to flow over, where act precedes comprehension, and the student welcomes this idea as an 'expression' of the teacher.

While this looks like a face-to-face relationship, in fact there is no emphasis upon intersubjective relationship, but rather an encounter with an unknown third in commonality of glance, where both learner and teacher have an asymmetrical relationship to knowledge that cannot be totalised. The teacher welcomes the Other as student in an act of hospitality, in a 'non-allergic reaction', as the student welcomes neither the personality nor the technique of the teacher, but the fact that the idea was released before its appropriation as thought or intellectual property. The coincidence of the freely-given gift and its acceptance without obligation defines a condition of hospitality. The gift of teaching becomes an act of saying rather than giving, of saying the impossible in the face of the self-evident indeterminacy of both knowledge and relationship. Levinas (*ibid.*) thus says that 'teaching does not come down to maieutics; it comes from the exterior and brings me more than I contain.'

Levinas' 'radical asymmetry' model of relationships applied to teaching is seductive, for it seems to offer a neat way of avoiding totalising the Other, as learner. Also, it offers a strong challenge to the pieties characterising humanistic accounts that can be reduced to a variety of narcissisms. However, his model does not address gift-giving, friendship, relationship or hospitality as *gendered*. Returning to Zarathustra's (or Nietzsche's) dilemma, it is easy to frame the ability to empty out in an ethical gesture as a virtue, a kind of virility, maintaining the giver in a place of masculine authority and mastery. Could there be a way through this male economy while still remaining within the economy of the gift? Lewis Hyde (1999) suggests that there is an *eros* of the gift, indeed an *eros* of property itself, and that this is the function the majority of art-making serves in our culture, where it stands outside the notorious elitism of the art market. For most artists do not enter this elite and become 'best sellers', gaining from an inflated and highly distorted corner of the commodity exchange economy. Transferring this to academic life, we could remind ourselves again of Schon's description of teaching as artistry. Here, teaching is described as an aesthetic and ethical practice (Bleakley, 1999). This view resists reduction of teaching to a technical operation governed by use value, and learning to a commodity governed by market forces and exchange value. We could challenge the Lockean notion of 'intellectual property' from this perspective, seeing intellectual property as part of a libidinal economy which restores the erotic to intellectual life. However, there is a more telling response to masculine gift economies, which Hyde fails to refer to in his work on 'the Gift' and the erotic life of property. This is the work of French feminists such as Hélène Cixous, Catherine Clément and Luce Irigaray. Their work on the gift could only have been written out of a woman's experience, where it refers to a woman's body not only as potential, primary gift-giver in birthing, lactation and menstruation, but also as the source of a unique form of *writing*.

The freely-given gift and feminist pedagogy

To give and not return, or wish for return, is the ethical gesture that Levinas proposes, but proposes with no reference to a dominant patriarchy. The feminist critique would reject the Odyssean heroic/homecoming myth that underpins 'occidental' patriarchy and constructs woman as the patient wife waiting for the husband to return from work, or the pub. The freely-given gift is only possible within a feminine economy that is characterised by a rejection of the selfsame in an opening to the Other and difference (beginning in the difference of gender). A masculine economy confronts generosity and hospitality with a distinct lack of ease and scepticism, where gift-giving implies debt, and hospitality may lead to usurpation by the Other. These, for Cixous, are tell-tale signs of a masculine fear – that of castration, of not holding on to what one has got, and of wanting to draw the other into the selfsame in order not to risk loss, or expenditure. Phallocentric desire is a desire for appropriation concealing fear of loss.

Feminist critique often makes a distinction between a masculine and feminine economy. A masculine economy is based on appropriation, following the law of property acquisition. Locke had defined private property as any natural object that is 'cultured' or 'worked' by a human being. This is precisely how women have been positioned within the male economy: as property to be exchanged, bought and sold, for example through marriage ceremonies; or as prohibited from private ownership where the man is the property keeper. Levi-Strauss (in)famously declared woman-as-exchange-commodity as a universal principle. We can see this operating powerfully in male-dominated medical practices such as gynaecological examination and treatment, where women's bodies are treated as property of medical opinion, inscribed through the male diagnostic gaze (Foucault, 1976; Lacquer, 1992).

A feminine economy grounds the gift in the body, with its possibility of maternal gifts, where the right to life is more important than the right to property. Gift giving does not seek profit or return, but relationship. Cixous and Clément

(1986, p.87) suggest that the ethical gesture of the gift resists the 'Empire of the Selfsame' or the culture of an ownself. Thus, 'if there is a self proper to woman, paradoxically it is her capacity to de-propriate herself without self-interest'. The woman 'doesn't create a monarch of her body or her desire', as masculine sexuality does where it gravitates around the penis, or the Symbolic order does where it gravitates around the Phallus or the Name-of-the-Father, as Master Signifier. It is as if the man 'were more directly threatened in his being by the nonselfsame than the woman'. While Cixous recognises that there may be no such thing as a free gift in practice, she asks if the woman is more capable than the man of escaping the laws of return and capitalisation. The answer is 'yes', where the male psyche is driven by 'phallocentric narcissism', desiring the 'plus-value of virility, authority' and so forth. The woman in contrast gives and gives of herself without the desire of recovery to a centre, or the recovery of expenses. Rather, she is able to engage in 'pouring out' to the other. The woman's 'rising' is not erection. But diffusion. Not the shaft. The vessel' (*ibid.*, p.88). For Cixous and Clément, *writing* is particularly of the woman. This is 'not a provocation' but follows from the fact that 'the woman admits there is an other' (*ibid.*, p.85). Only in such recognition can a gift be freely-given. Writing is not essentialised, but must be *referred* to the feminine, or as a trait that comes back to women more often than men. 'Feminine writing' for Cixous is tempered as 'writing said to be feminine'. Writing comes out of body, and women are 'more' body than men. Writing is also a constant cutting off and release, and the umbilical imagery here is more of the body of women than of men. Such release again challenges the monomyth of the hero's journey that ends in self-congratulatory homecoming.

Teaching can be seen as feminine 'writing', where it resists return to the selfsame, and comes out of the body, as a style. In a teaching-learning relationship based on 'noncoincidence, asymmetry', the teacher and student would be in a relationship in which 'each would keep the *other* alive and different' (*ibid.*, p.79). Given also that patriarchal language permeates education, as Irigaray points out there is no neutral or equal within such a framework of privilege. One of the gifts of feminist pedagogy is of course the creation of a feminine language of desire for learning as passion informing technique, that Joanna Frueh (1996) punningly calls an 'erotic faculty'.

Conclusion

This chapter focuses upon the teaching, rather than the research, policy framing, or public liaison, role of the Higher Education practitioner. Teaching is configured as: (1) a gift given freely and (2) an act of hospitality, within (3) a feminist framework of (4) a gift economy as opposed to a commodity exchange economy. The gift is given freely through recognition of difference and resistance to totalising the Other through identity (the 'property' of the self and the 'Empire of the Selfsame'). These four factors run counter to the normative, patriarchal practices of teaching as (1) a technical practice, (2) demanding reciprocity, within (3) a phallogocentric framework of (4) a market-driven commodity exchange economy valorising intellectual property. Since education policy has been colonised by political interests driven by economic concerns and informed by a managerial discourse, practitioners are subject to accountability in terms of 'quality assurance' mechanisms, which constitutes them as repressive bureaucrats rather than expressive artists.

Against this background, what does 'the Gift' model of teaching offer for policy? First, the gift economy offers an *eros* of teaching and learning, rather than a *logos*. Pedagogy is seen as subject to aesthetic and ethical considerations that are marginalised in technical-rational, efficiency approaches, underpinned by economic and utilitarian considerations. The aesthetics and ethics of a teaching style, involving elements such as grace, presence, artistry, connoisseurship, tacit understanding, elegance and imagination are rarely discussed in the literature on teaching practices. Even the growing body of work on 'reflective practice' beyond Schon has tended to reinforce both the humanising and technicising of the term, failing to fully anatomise 'practical artistry', or even debate its implications (Bleakley, 1999).

Second, the gift economy questions the humanistic model that focuses upon the autonomy of the learner, or the learner's experience, at the expense of a comprehensive account of the teaching process. Where the teacher is constructed as a supporter of learning, a facilitator, this does not account for a range of possibilities in the teaching role. Such a symmetrical relationship again invites totalising of the Other by the self, encouraging identity at the expense of difference. 'The Gift' model emphasises the value of heteronomy, or radical alterity, rather than autonomy. Further, there is a danger in simply switching emphasis from a rights-based property culture of objective relations to a responsibility-based culture of subjective relations if the latter continues to treat subjectivity itself as property.

Third, there is a strong argument that 'the Gift' model can only be realised within a feminine, libidinal economy. The current exchange-led market economy moulds education and constructs teachers as managers of learning and salespersons of knowledge and skills, where students enrol as 'customers'. This Lockean 'property rights' approach by implication locks up the woman, as both practitioner and student, in a cultural legacy where women exist as property of men, and this is most strongly represented in the phallogocentric language of education generally and learning contracts specifically. As long as this language and its derived practices are privileged, a language of feminist pedagogy, incorporating models such as teaching as gift, cannot gain a foothold, for it has to represent itself through masculinised language and then is merely totalised by that language. As Irigaray properly insists, a feminine language must be established in difference, and this language may be one of the *desire* for teaching and learning.

Such language will necessarily be transgressive. It will counter the legal and business terminology characterising both policy documents and texts in Higher Education. Returning to the jazz metaphor employed earlier, policy marches to the standardising tunes of military bands, everybody marching to the regular beat. Such beats do not even follow that of our closest pulse, the body's heartbeat, which is syncopated. Quality assurance systems straighten us out; they do not encourage innovation or improvisation. They cannot tolerate the blues of failure through experimentation, and the highs of improvisation through innovation. They reject the complexity of multiple rhythms and unlikely chord sequencing, and the sinuous and fluid melody line, which, collectively, echo a genealogy of the 'feminine'.

Why do we despair with teaching? Why do we want to leave it, much as we love it? There are easy targets for blame: the RAE producing a publications and conferencing factory; the bureaucratisation of teaching through quality assurance; the 'dumbing down' of student expectations; the desiccation of the lecture experience, and so forth. However, there may be another reason – that we always have and always will want to walk away from teaching even as we do it, because that is the very nature of teaching as a gift. It requires us to follow its intrinsic trajectory of unhooking, of leaving home, of the will to not return. Such a taxis challenges the patriarchal Odyssean homecoming, through an ethical gesture of emptying out to the Other, however the gift is received, even in ingratitude. This is a response to a calling, where the gift *must* be given, as an ethical imperative. In other words, passionate teaching can be nothing other than a vocation or style of life.

References

Adorno, T., E. Frankel-Brunswick, D.J. Levinson and R. Sanford (1950), *The Authoritarian Personality*, Harper, New York.

Ball, S. (ed.) (1990), *Foucault and Education: Disciplines and Knowledge*, Routledge, London.

Bataille, G. (1988), *The Accursed Share, Volume 1.*, Zone Books, New York.

Bleakley, A. (1992), 'Greens and Greenbacks', *Spring: A Journal of Archetype and Culture*, 52.

_____ (1999), 'From Reflective Practice to Holistic Reflexivity', *Studies in Higher Education*, 24 (3).

Campbell, J. (1988), *The Hero with a Thousand Faces*, Paladin, London.

Cixous, H. and C. Clément (1986), *The Newly Born Woman*, University of Minnesota Press, London.

Derrida, J. (1992), *Given Time: 1. Counterfeit Money*, The University of Chicago Press, London.

_____ (1999), *Adieu To Emmanuel Levinas*, Stanford University Press, Stanford.

Foucault, M. (1976), *The Birth of the Clinic*, Tavistock Publications, London.

_____ (1977), *Discipline and Punish: The Birth of the Prison*, Penguin Press, London.

_____ (1997), *Ethics: Subjectivity and Truth*, Allen Lane, Penguin Press, Harmondsworth.

Frueh, J. (1996), *Erotic Faculties*, Routledge, London.

Gane, M. and T. Johnson (eds) (1993), *Foucault's New Domains*, Routledge, London.

Gilligan, C. (1982), *In a Different Voice*, Harvard University Press, Cambridge, Mass.

Godelier, M. (1999), *The Enigma of the Gift*, Polity Press, Cambridge.

Hyde, L. (1999), *The Gift: Imagination and the Erotic Life of Property*, Vintage, London.

Irigaray, L. (1993), *je, tu, nous: Toward a Culture of Difference*, Routledge, London.

Lacquer, T. (1992), *Making Sex: Body and Gender From the Greeks to Freud*, Harvard University Press, London.

Levinas, E. (1969), *Totality and Infinity*, Duquesne University Press, Pittsburgh.

Mauss, M. (1990), *The Gift: The Form and Reason for Exchange in Archaic Societies*, Routledge, London.

Polanyi, M. (1983), *The Tacit Dimension*, Peter Smith, Gloucester, Mass.

Robbins, J. (1999), *Altered Reading: Levinas and Literature*, University of Chicago Press, London.

Schon, D. (1987), *Educating the Reflective Practitioner: Toward a New Design for Teaching and Learning in the Professions*, Jossey-Bass Ltd, Oxford.

Schrift, A.D. (1995), *Nietzsche's French Legacy: A Genealogy of Poststructuralism*, Routledge, London.

_____ (ed.) (1997), *The Logic of the Gift: Toward an Ethic of Generosity*, Routledge, London.

Stanford, W.B. (1992), *The Ulysses Theme: A Study in the Adaptability of a Traditional Hero*, Spring Publications, Dallas.

Taussig, M. (1999), *Defacement: Public Secrecy and the Labor of the Negative*, Stanford University Press, Stanford.

Vaneigem, R. (1994), *The Movement of the Free Spirit*, Zone Books, New York.

Chapter 7

Lifelong Yearning: Feminist Pedagogy in the Learning Society

Louise Morley

Introduction

Feminist pedagogy for empowerment has always occupied a precarious position in Higher Education. However, its central principles now seem to be disappearing completely from a system more concerned with quantifiable outputs than complex pedagogical processes. Without wishing to appear 'golden ageist', by setting up a binary between 'then' and 'now', I wish to argue that recently, there has been a discursive shift away from concerns about pedagogy and the social context of learning, power relations, and the problematisation of authority. The emphasis on teaching and learning now in Higher Education is firmly located within cognitive structures and the acquisition of technical skills and measurable competencies. Policy documents stress the need for transferable skills and employability (Dearing, 1997). In this chapter, I shall be arguing that human capital theory, stressing the causal links between education and national prosperity and international competitiveness, is a major driver in educational policy today. The current focus on utilitarianism and applied knowledges is often packaged in democratised concepts such as the 'Learning Society' and 'Lifelong Learning'. These policy discourses suggest a process of instrumentalisation, with teachers and learners constructed as relay points in a new mode of capitalist regulation.

Quality, rather than equality, dominates the change agenda in Higher Education. Within the ethos of performance indicators and measurement, nebulous concepts concerned with the affective domain have no place. There has been a taxonomic objectification of learning processes throughout the education system – a static tabularisation and reductivism of complex pedagogical issues. The subject of Higher Education has been recast and reduced to the status of a potential worker, rather than a multi-dimensional citizen. Whereas education has always been a form of cultural capital enabling social distinction, Higher Education has recently been more overtly commodified and reduced to its exchange value on the labour market. It is now a product one buys, rather than a process one enters. Hence the justification for introducing fees for undergraduates. Students are no longer constructed as recipients of a welfare service, but consumers of an expensive product, with ensuing rights, responsibilities and entitlements. It is my belief that this recasting has profoundly influenced both social relations and pedagogical processes in Higher Education.

Within the rhetoric of the learning society the Higher Educational product is constructed as ideologically neutral and benign. The more one has, the better; and the more people who gain access to it, the more society will benefit. A question I wish to explore in this chapter is whether the political projects of feminist and critical pedagogies have a place in the rhetoric of today's learning society, and whether forms of intervention aimed at personal and collective empowerment are naive humanistic anachronisms in today's mass Higher Education system.

Educating the masses: quality, standards and normalisation

After the 1992 Further and Higher Education Act, the number of universities in Britain increased from 46 to 112. There was a rise in the number of students from 900,000 to 1,800,000 (from 15 to 33 per cent). The budget for Higher Education was £11 billion (Watson and Bowden, 1999). In the changing culture of the public services, questions were raised about value for money and public accountability relating to outcomes of public investment. Massification implies a type of chaos in need of regulation, exacerbated by the fact that there is considerable product variety in Higher Education. There is currently a moral panic over standards (the more means worse/dumbing down debate), and inflation of certification in Higher Education.

There have been changing relations between Higher Education and the state, with a juxtaposition of political and intellectual authority. Quality has become a regime of truth in the academy, reinforced by performance tables and financial consequences. Maintaining standards has involved identifying reference points and comparability indicators such as subject benchmarks. Academic disciplines, award bearing institutions and professional and statutory bodies all had to be 'quality assured'.

It is important to stress that there are now at least two accounting systems for academics. Just as academics were acclimatising to research assessment, the government introduced quality audits for teaching. These two systems are often experienced as oppositional with excellence in teaching sometimes seen as a distraction from research and publication (Morley, 1995). The Institute of Learning and Teaching (ILT) opened in June 1999. As part of the quality industry, this aims to provide professional development for university teachers. Membership is not yet mandatory (not a licence to practice), but is sometimes built into lecturers' probationary period. The ILT is developing a national accreditation scheme; a portfolio of Continuous Professional Development programmes, and a register of members. The system of auditing teaching has moved from quality control to quality assurance with the emphasis now on how quality is embedded in systems, structures and mechanisms. It is not just a question of the external gaze, but more an issue of how the academy looks at itself. Attention is paid to outcomes such as student completion rates and classification of degrees and also to organisational arrangements for getting students to that point.

To some, quality assurance represents a form of consumer empowerment, introducing accountability into dominant organisations of knowledge production, and information to potential consumers (Luke, 1997). Quality audits are perceived as transformational devices which allow questions to be posed about whether equity provisions are measures of excellence, for example arrangements for students with special needs. The scrutiny of organisations is seen as a refreshing challenge to elitism and to disciplinary authority (Luke, 1997). For others, quality technologies represent an example of surveillance and regulation, with a primary aim to render employees more docile, compliant and governmentable (Ball, 1997). The standardisation implied in quality assurance could also suggest a technology of normalisation and a type of institutional isomorphism. The technology of quality assurance is perceived as a reductive input/output model. It is seen as a process of impression management and performativity, with performance indicators socially and politically constructed. The technology is thought to mask the ideology and value base of what is considered excellent at this particular political and historical moment (Ball, 1997). Like all systems of power, quality assurance can be read and experienced as both oppressive and creative.

The overhaul of Higher Education is part of the modernisation project, originated by the Conservative Government and continued by New Labour. (Watson and Bowden, 1999). New managerialism has been inserted into academia, with the accompanying values, drive systems and rationalities (Clarke and Newman, 1997; Morley, 1997; Power, 1997). The UK Higher Education system is now the most externally monitored system in the world (Watson and Bowden, 1999). The measurement of outcomes and the establishment of an audit culture has had an impact on pedagogical relations. Increasing client responsiveness is alleged, with new partnerships between universities and employers and industry.

There is an intertextuality between Higher Education reform and post or neo Fordist employment regimes. For example, the Dearing Review (1997) discusses the shift from a manufacturing-based economy to a service sector, with the requirement for new skills. New qualifications have been introduced such as professional doctorates, and new modes of delivery established such as distance learning, email courses and internationalised franchises. There is an increasing emphasis on multi and reskilling, flexibility, new technologies, a knowledge-based economy and portfolio careers. User-friendly provision has been introduced into Higher Education, such as credit accumulation transfer, accreditation of prior learning, modularisation and multiple entrance points. However, these can also be perceived as evidence of pedagogical fragmentation, with negative consequences for group formation and continuity and peer interaction.

Changing student demographics

Almost a third of young people in Britain now go into Higher Education from school. The Age Participation Index for 18-19 year olds has risen to approximately 32 per cent. The percentage of female undergraduates in the UK has doubled since the publication of the Robbins Report in 1963 (Brooks, 1997). However, only 35 per cent of postgraduate research students in the UK are women. Women students and academics still remain concentrated in certain subject areas such as education and the humanities. Women still represent only 14 per cent of the students reading engineering and technology (QSC, 1996). Women are often accused of investing in the 'wrong' disciplines, i.e. within the current rhetoric of choice, they are constructed as poor choosers. Questions are not usually raised about the pedagogies associated with certain disciplines.

There is often a remediation ethos surrounding women and education, rather than questions about why certain disciplines are more privileged than others. The gendering of the Higher Education product itself is rarely questioned in mainstream inquiries. Gender is often seen as a background variable, rather than as a construct embedded in learning processes. For example, learning is often conceptualised as a result of an interaction between former experiences and the educational context (Kolb, 1984; Entwistle, 1981). The fact that former experiences are often gendered is frequently overlooked (Severiens and Ten Dam, 1998).

When gender is considered, there are often dangers of homogenisation, that is, women are treated as an undifferentiated group; and essentialism, that is, women are thought to have inherently different ways of knowing, thinking, learning, feeling (see Belenky *et al.*, 1986; Gilligan, 1982). When gender is intersected with other structures of inequality such as social class, 'race', disabilities, sexualities, age, more disturbing statistics emerge. For example, Modood (1993) points out how student demographics in elite universities remain relatively unchanged and that ethnic minority students remain concentrated in certain post-1992 universities, predominantly those located in London and the Midlands.

Working-class students are still very under-represented in the academy. Students with working class parents constituted a mere 6 per cent of the intake in 1990/91 and this slowly rose to 12 per cent by 1998 (Watson and Bowden, 1999). Even with the necessary entry qualifications, people from backgrounds in the lower three of the five social classes are only 70 per cent as likely to enter universities and colleges as people from the top two social groups (Reay, 1998). There are references in the Dearing Review (1997) to the under representation from lower socio-economic groups 'leading to socially divisive consequences'. There is the veiled suggestion that Higher Education in particular, and lifelong learning in general, have corrective and redemptive powers. Concerns about social inclusion can be found in references to 'our society'. 'our economy', 'quality of life', 'communities', 'to maintain a cohesive society'. However, there could be an equity paradox (Morley, 1997) in so far as the transition from an elite to a mass system has produced considerable concerns about the quality of the Higher Education product. Just as members of under-represented groups access the academy, they are told that the product is potentially flawed and their achievements of limited value.

Mature students represent one of the biggest new markets for Higher Education. From 1979 to 1996 the number of entrants over twenty-one years of age rose from 24 to 32 per cent. However, the term 'non-traditional' learner is still used. Influential policy documents such as the Dearing Review (1997) name the section that deals with student diversity 'Widening Participation in Higher Education by Ethnic Minorities, Women and Alternative Students' (Coffield and

Vignobles, 1997). There are normative constructions of the student embedded in this terminology, with women and ethnic minority students, positioned as 'other'. Many universities still think of the ideal student as a 'bachelor boy', unencumbered by domestic responsibilities (Edwards, 1993). In the Dearing Review (1997), women are usually only referenced in relation to widening participation, as consumers of a neutral educational product. Equity and social justice issues are frequently reduced to concerns about access. Pedagogy is not perceived as a gendered consideration. The consumer base/demographics may be changing, but the question remains as to whether this has influenced epistemologies, research processes and agendas and organisational cultures (Morley, 1999).

The Learning Society: opportunities for all or social coercion?

The Learning Society is a seductive discourse. Its authority is underlined by the use of the definite article 'the'. It is pertinent to ask what is changing in Higher Education in terms of student experiences, demographics and life chances. The rhetoric of the Learning Society has gained greater currency than concerns with equity and diversity ever did in Higher Education in Britain. For its product champions, it represents opportunity and democratisation. For example, Christopher Ball (1991) argues that the idea of a learning society rejects privilege – the idea that it is right for birth to determine destiny. He sees it as transcending the principle of meritocracy, which selects for advancement only those judged worthy and rejects as failures those who are not.

For others, such as Macrae, Maguire and Stephen Ball (1997), it is perceived as an ambitious, manipulative and somewhat evangelical and redemptive project. The Learning Society is a disembodied discourse in which learners and teachers are degendered, declassed and deracialised. It is premised on the Enlightenment assumption of a universal subject. I would argue that there are at least three ways in which the Learning Society masks issues of inequality:

- it ignores barriers to participation, such as social structures, the gendered division of labour;
- it ignores the complexities of social positioning, habitus, gender and classed expectations;
- it ignores psychic narratives/internalised oppression re. worth, self-efficacy, confidence.

The Learning Society is driven by a market ideology. The ideology of the Learning Society is influenced by human capital theory, which suggests that national prosperity depends on individual and collective cultural capital. Justification is produced in the form of statistics which offend national pride. For example, by 1991 Britain was 18th in terms of living standards amongst the 24 countries of the OECD, and 8th among the then 12 of the European Union. The recent Moser Report on literacy and numeracy (1999) indicates that 20 per cent of Britain's adult population has difficulties with literacy, and that Britain is second only to Poland in having the lowest literacy rates in Europe.

Both globalisation and human capital theory emphasise wealth creation, rather than wealth distribution. The latter is often summarised in terms of social justice, but this remains undertheorised in the rhetoric of the Learning Society. Milliband (1994, p.17) reminds us that by 1993 10 per cent of the population owned 50 per cent of the nation's wealth and 25 per cent owned around 71 per cent; 75 per cent of the population had to get by with 29 per cent of the remaining wealth. In a society dogged by class stratification and inherited wealth, it is questionable whether the top 25 per cent gained their wealth via education!

The key to national prosperity is linked to the needs of industry and commerce, rather than to social, interpersonal, affective and aesthetic processes. Bottery (1990) has described this as a move towards a 'GNP morality of education'. Within the Learning Society only certain types of knowledge and learning are valued and validated. The domestic sphere and women's unpaid work are ignored. The Learning Society is a rational discourse suggesting a quantitative relationship between input and output. This aspect can objectify learners, positioning them as pieces of clay to manipulate for purposes of national prosperity. In the construction, complex relays of power are more difficult to capture.

The Learning Society is grafted onto existing, historic oppressions and inequalities. It is a new basis on which social divisions are re-established and re-legitimated (Macrae, Maguire and Ball, 1997). For example, technology and the notion of an information society are central to the discourse. There are new forms of social inequality that are built on differentiated access to the means of communication, learning and knowledge. As Newman and Johnson (1999) argue, cultural capital is necessary in order to be able to download relevant information from the World Wide Web. The Learning Society also works to privilege those individuals who possess the necessary cultural and material capital to be able to access the 'better' routes and credentials (Macrae, Maguire and Ball, 1997). Certain social groups are more able to decode the relative values of different educational pathways. Writing of cultural capital, Bourdieu (1984, p.142) argued:

> One of the most valuable sorts of information constituting inherited cultural capital is practical or theoretical knowledge of the fluctuations in the market in academic qualifications, the sense of investment which enables one to get the best return on inherited capital in the scholastic market or on scholastic capital in the labour market, for example, by knowing the right moment to pull out of devalued disciplines and careers and to switch into those with a future, rather than clinging to the scholastic values which secured the highest profits in an earlier state of the market.

There is a powerful discourse of multiskilling and flexibility, suggesting that employees/students are forever in deficit and must keep struggling to update, change and reskill. This can be a potent mode of regulation and surveillance, making individuals easier to govern and control. The continuous improvement rhetoric is reminiscent of the Japanese concept of *kaizen* (Morley and Rassool, 1999). It could also be argued that there are religious connotations of original sin and redemption.

The Learning Society is also linked to the notion of a risk society (Beck, 1992). That is, in the age of uncertainty and flux, social actors need to indemnify themselves against the risk of unemployment, redundancy and loss of social status. Checklists and taxonomies of competencies, subject bench marking, qualification values, performance indicators could be perceived as offering some certainties and exactitudes in a risk society (Morley and Rassool, 1999). It is worth considering whether the notion of risk is gendered and racialised, i.e. are some members of society more at risk than others?

The Learning Society overlooks the equity paradox, graduate unemployment and the risks of inflation of certification (Morley, 1997). The access movement disregards the way in which qualifications lose value when they are no longer indicators of distinction. Schumpeter (1976) expressed the fear that the expansion of Higher Education proceeds faster than the development of the labour market's capacities to absorb the graduates so produced, leading to un/underemployment and potential political instability. In other words, massification of Higher Education, while purporting to heal social divisions, could be creating another social underclass.

Pedagogic practice as cultural politics

So where do the new regimes of quality, standards and the Learning Society leave the liberatory concerns of radical educators? Like many feminist academics (Ellsworth, 1989; Gore, 1993), I am aware that feminist pedagogy could appear as yet another metanarrative or regime of truth. I am conscious too, that in the context of quality assurance, commodification and outcomes-oriented education, many of us now take fewer pedagogical risks. Indeed, many of the students I interviewed for a study on academic feminism (Morley, 1999) rejected process-oriented feminist pedagogy in favour of more tangible products such as teacher-led lectures. Group work and experiential learning were perceived as too anecdotal, imprecise and wasteful of precious time. For several younger students, the notion of lived experience as the author of knowledge was felt to privilege the mundane and deprive them of opportunities to engage more fully with theory. The consciousness-raising aims of the 1970s and 1980s were often experienced as intrusive and as a transgression of pedagogical authority. These views are open to a range of readings. Are they examples of reflexivity promoted by critical educators, or evidence of the extent to which dominant discourses of new managerialism speak us? Freire (1996, p.84) observed how a pedagogy that focuses on production and consumption 'without any preoccupation about what we are producing, who it benefits, and who it hurts' is certainly not a critical pedagogy. The reconstruction of students as consumers or customers can lead to an individualism and time urgency verging on greed (Skeggs, 1995).

The accusation of 'golden ageism' can be an effective mechanism for silencing resistance to new regimes of truth, So, once again, at the risk of appearing to promote golden ageism, I would first like to revisit (critically) some of feminist pedagogies' aims and intentions. Some key features include:

- Challenge to authoritarianism of traditional modes of pedagogy.
- Challenge to the active/passive or expert/empty vessel 'banking' model of education.
- Emphasis on dialogue, rather than transmission.
- Consciousness-raising and reflexivity.
- Centralisation of power relations, i.e. pedagogy constructed as social as well as cognitive exercise.
- Connections made between pedagogical disempowerment and socio-political powerlessness.
- Liberatory/emancipatory/transformatory aims and intentions.
- Personal/experiential knowledges valued as highly as abstract/propositional knowledges.
- Emphasis on critical engagement, rather than regurgitation of received knowledges. Students encouraged to produce own ideas and values rather than reproduce those of dominant group.
- Interconnections stressed between ideology, power and culture.
- The classroom perceived as a microcosm of wider power relations and inequalities.
- Belief that educational practices and knowledge are socially constructed, i.e. always produced within particular social and historical conditions.
- Pedagogy does not just take place in classrooms e.g. media.
- Knowledge is seen as situated, partial and exclusionary.
- Praxis – action informed by critical engagement with theory.
- Democratisation and emphasis on voice, participation and negotiation.
- Students constructed as subjects, participants or shapers, rather than objects to be worked on.
- Boundary/border crossing – across disciplines, forms of identity and difference.
- Recognition of internalised oppression, the social construction of ability, confidence, self-esteem.
- Links between personal and social change.

Feminist, Postcolonialist and Marxist educators have attempted to rethink fundamental relationships between language and experience, pedagogy and human agency, and ethics and social responsibility as part of a larger educational project (Leach and Boler, 1998). Education has been theorised as the social and institutional expression of cultural value and cultural reproduction, that is, reproduction of the universal subject (Martin, 1998). The concept of agency, promoted by Freire (1994), and also by Debord (see McLaren and Leonardo, 1998, p.240) suggests a consciously articulable form of praxis grounded in critical self-reflexivity. This begins as micropolitical discourse which is linked, via pedagogical interventions, to macropolitical structures. Agency is not bifurcated from structure but rather derives from reflexive evaluation of how structured discourses produce experience (Nadesan and Elenes, 1998). Within the context of consciousness-raising, students are encouraged to examine assumptions in dominant discourses critically; to recognise the contingent nature of all social articulations and to evaluate how their identities are constituted through hegemonic articulations. Feminist and critical pedagogies wish us to recognise, engage and critique any existing undemocratic social practices and institutional structures that produce and sustain inequalities and oppressive social identities (Leistyna *et al.*, 1996).

Power relations have played a central role in evaluations of intelligence and academic worth. Giroux (1996, p.100) argues that the culture of the university has been one of 'exclusion, one that has ignored the multiple narratives, histories, and voices of culturally and politically subordinated groups'. As a counter to this, disclosure, life history and narratives of the self are believed to contribute to bridging the gap between personal and propositional knowledges. The voice discourse has been a prominent feature of pedagogies for empowerment (Morley, 1998). Within the context of quality assurance, the student voice is located in course evaluations, rather than in life history or experiential learning. Students' experiences are now more firmly located within the framework of customer care and consumer entitlements such as course handbooks, student charters and opinion surveys. Self-actualisation and consciousness-raising are not part of teaching quality audits!

Feminist educators have posed questions about the meaning of canonicity (who decides which texts are considered great, essential and classic), and whose values, interpretations and goals constitute the foundation of Higher Education. Enlightenment traditions based on the notion that knowledge-production is only realisable via objective inquiry, universal reason and absolute truth have been vigorously contested (see Maynard and Purvis, 1993). There has been severe criticism of positivism's attempts to deny the authority and identity of the knowledge producers (Fine, 1994). Tierney (1996, p.145) asks:

> How is knowledge conceived? Whose interests have been advanced by these forms of knowledge? How has what we have defined as knowledge changed over time? How does the organization's culture promote or silence some individuals? How are some topics marginalised and others promoted?

These aims all seem rather ambitious in relation to today's mass system where the focus is on preparing students for the work force. Indeed, the Conservative reform agenda of education was based on a set of beliefs which suggested that attempts to reveal the underlying power relations that structure educational policies, processes and practices had corrupted the academic environment. The new model abstracts education from the challenges of developing a critically conscious, socially responsible and politically active citizenry (Leistyna *et al.*, 1996). Macedo (1996) argues that the instrumentalism present in today's mass system of Higher Education anaesthetises students' critical abilities. By privileging the pragmatic requirements of capital, there is a domestication of the social order for its own preservation and reproduction. The preoccupation with socially decontextualised teaching and learning releases pedagogy of its social responsibility.

Hybridity and transgression

Feminist educators have to navigate a range of contradictions in the academy (Morley, 1999). Attempts to cross boundaries have resulted in substantial amounts of emotional labour that might no longer be feasible within the current intensified employment conditions of the academy (Morley, 1998). The combination of greater central control as the system has expanded with a lower unit of resource has left academics time-urgent and boundaried in relation to opportunity costs. The student: staff ratios moved from 9.3:1 in the old universities and 8.4:1 in the former polytechnics to an overall figure of 16.5:1 (Watson and Bowden, 1999). Feminist pedagogy is resource intensive and can challenge learners in ways which are no longer compatible with commodified, industrialised relationships in the academy (Malina and Maslin-Prothero, 1998). For example, supporting students through identity displacement and reformation, the unlearning of hegemonic certainties and the complex dynamics of group diversity demands an altruism and generosity that goes unrewarded in the current system of outcomes-based Higher Education.

There has been a major ideological shift, away from the liberal and sometimes radical model of personal development and self-actualisation that existed in some parts of the academy, towards a functionalist approach to Higher Education. Universities now exist to provide education, training and cultural induction which are conducive to the development of the prevailing socio-economic system (Watson and Taylor, 1998). There has been a distinct technological steer in Higher Education planning, with concerns about the relative rates of return for public funds (DES, 1985).

New managerialism, quality and the drive towards measurement and outcomes represents a new form of organisational masculinity for feminist educators to negotiate. The use of crude quantitative outcomes overrides consideration of areas such as the affective domain, values and self-efficacy. The forces of globalisation mean that attention is increasingly focused on macro considerations to the exclusion of microprocesses of power. With the 'McDonaldization of Higher Education' (Hartley, 1995), delivery mechanisms for teaching and learning no longer need to be tied to a particular educational institution or site (Newman and Johnson, 1999). According to Bernstein (1990), the Web represents a form of invisible pedagogy. In the electronic age of virtual experiences, the clean lines of cyberspace could displace the messiness of embodied pedagogy. Identities are no longer embodied and can be transformed and concealed.

Academic survival depends on an ability to both criticise and perform dominant discourses of regulation and control. Apple (1999, p.8) points out how 'forms of solidarity are being fractured ideologically and materially'. A compliance culture has developed. There is little discursive space for dissent within the regulatory frameworks of quality assurance and new managerialism. In a keynote address at an international conference on Women's Studies, Rosi Braidotti (1999) argued that today's social imaginary is the monster, the mutant, the hybrid. I believe that this image can also be applied to women in Higher Education. The transgression of boundaries has been a feature of academic feminism. While Higher Education has not yet been subjected to a national curriculum, performance, impression management and impersonation have played a major role in academic survival (Gallop, 1995). This process is gendered, with feminist educators caught between a commitment to an international movement for social change while simultaneously being forced to perform practices that act to strengthen masculine modes of regulation in the academy. This can lead to a sense of alienation, or corrosion of character (Sennett, 1998) that is profoundly disempowering. From this hybridised and somewhat beleaguered location, perhaps it is no longer feasible (if it ever was) to claim to empower others.

References

Apple, M. (1999), 'Freire, Neo-Liberalism and Education', *Discourse*, 20 (1).

Ball, C. (1991), *The Learning Society: Interim Report*, RSA Journal.

Ball, S.J. (1997), 'Good School/Bad School: Paradox and Fabrication', *British Journal of Sociology of Education*, 18 (3).

Beck, U. (1992), *Risk Society*, Sage, London.

Belenky, M. *et al.* (1986), *Women's Ways of Knowing: The Development of Self, Voice and Mind*, Basic Books, New York.

Bernstein, B. (1990), *Class, Codes and Control, vol. 4*, Routledge, London.

Bottery, M. (1990), *The Morality of the School: The Theory and Practice of Values in Education*, Cassell, London.

Bourdieu, P. (1984), *Distinction*, Routledge and Paul, London.

Braidotti, R. (1999), Keynote address, Gender and Generations Conference, University of Tromso, Norway, June, 1999.

Brooks, A. (1997), *Academic Women*, Open University Press, Buckingham.

Clarke, J. and J. Newman (1997), *The Managerial State*, Sage, London.

Coffield, F. and A. Vignobles (1997), *Widening Participation in Higher Education by Ethnic Minorities, Women and Alternative Students*, 5, The National Committee of Inquiry into Higher Education.

Dearing, R. (1997), *Higher Education in the Learning Society* (the Dearing Report), National Committee of Inquiry into Higher Education, London.

DES (Department of Education and Science) (1985), *The Development of Higher Education into the 1990s*, HMSO, London.

DfEE (1999), *Improving Literacy and Numeracy: A Fresh Start*, the report of the working group chaired by Sir Claus Moser, Department for Education and Employment, London.

Edwards, R. (1993), *Mature Women Students*, Falmer Press, London.

Ellsworth, E. (1989), 'Why Doesn't This Feel Empowering? Working Through Repressive Myths of Critical Pedagogy', *Harvard Educational Review*, 59 (3).

Entwistle, N. (1981), *Styles of Learning and Teaching: An Integrated Outline of Educational Psychology*, John Wiley, Chichester.

Fine, M. (1994), 'Dis-stance and Other Stances: Negotiations of Power Inside Feminist Research', in A. Gitlin (ed.), *Power and Method: Political Activism and Educational Research*, Routledge, London.

Freire, P. (1996), *Letters to Cristina*, Routledge, New York.

Gallop, J. (ed.) (1995), *Pedagogy: The Question of Impersonation*, Indiana University Press, Bloomington Indiana.

Gilligan, C. (1982), *In a Different Voice: Psychological Theory and Women*, Harvard University Press, Cambridge MA.

Giroux, H. (1996), 'Doing Cultural Studies: Youth and the Challenge of Pedagogy', in Leistyna, P. *et al.* (eds).

Gore, J. (1993), *The Struggle for Pedagogies*, Routledge, New York and London.

Hartley, D. (1995), 'The McDonaldization of Higher Education', *Oxford Review of Education*, 21.

Kolb, D. (1984), *Experiential Learning*, Prentice-Hall, Engelwood Cliffs, NJ.

Leach, M. and M. Boler (1998), 'Gilles Deleuze: Practising Education through Flight and Gossip', in M. Peters (ed.), *Naming the Multiple: Poststructuralism and Education*, Bergin and Garvey, London.

Leistyna, P. *et al.* (1996) (eds), *Breaking Free: The Transformative Power of Critical Pedagogy*, Harvard Educational Review, Cambridge, MA.

Luke, C. (1997), 'Quality Assurance and Women in Higher Education', *Higher Education*, 33.

Macedo, D. (1996), 'Literacy for Stupidification: The Pedagogy of Big Lies', in P. Leistyna *et al.* (eds).

Macrae, S., M. Maguire and S. Ball (1997), 'Whose "Learning" Society? A Tentative Deconstruction', *Journal of Education Policy*, 12 (6).

Malina, D. and S. Maslin-Prothero (eds) (1998), *Surviving the Academy: Feminist Perspectives*, Falmer Press, London.

Martin, B. (1998), 'Luce Irigaray: One Subject is Not Enough – Irigaray and Levinas Face-to-Face with Education', in M. Peters (ed.) (1998).

Maynard, M. and J. Purvis (eds) (1993), *Researching Women's Lives from a Feminist Perspective*, Taylor and Francis, London.

McLaren, P. and Z. Leonardo (1998), 'Jean Baudrillard: From Marxism to Terrorist Pedagogy', in M. Peters (ed.) (1998).

Miliband, D. (ed.) (1994), *Social Justice: Strategies for National Renewal. Report of the Commission for Social Justice*, Vintage, London.

Modood, T. (1993), 'The Number of Ethnic Minority Students in British Higher Education: Some Grounds for Optimism', *Oxford Review of Education*, 19 (2).

Morley, L. (1995), 'Measuring the Muse: Creativity, Writing and Career Development', in L. Morley and V. Walsh (eds), *Feminist Academics: Creative Agents for Change*, Taylor & Francis, London.

_____ (1997), 'Change and Equity in Higher Education', *British Journal of Sociology of Education*, 18 (2).

_____ (1998), 'All You Need is Love: Feminist Pedagogy for Empowerment and Emotional Labour in the Academy', *International Journal of Inclusive Education*, 2 (1).

_____ (1999), *Organising Feminisms: The Micropolitics of the Academy*, Macmillan, London.

Morley, L. and N. Rassool (1999), *School Effectiveness: Fracturing the Discourse*, Falmer Press, London.

Nadesan, M. and A. Elenes (1998), 'Chantal Mouffe: Pedagogy for Democratic Citizenship', in M. Peters (ed.) (1998).

Newman, R. and F. Johnson (1999), 'Sites for Power and Knowledge? Towards a Critique of the Virtual University', *British Journal of Sociology of Education*, 20 (1).

Peters, M. (ed.), *Naming the Multiple: Poststructuralism and Education*, Bergin and Garvey, London.

Power, M. (1997), *The Audit Society*, Oxford University Press, Oxford.

QSC (Quality Support Centre). (1996), *UK Higher Education in the 1990s, Diversity: Too Much or too Little?*, Open University Press, Milton Keynes.

Reay, D. (1998), '"Always Knowing" and "Never Being Sure": Familial and Institutional Habituses and Higher Education Choice', *Journal of Education Policy*, 13 (4).

Schumpeter, J. (1976), *Capitalism, Socialism and Democracy*, Allen & Unwin, London.

Sennett, R. (1998), *The Corrosion of Character: The Personal Consequences of Work in the New Capitalism*, Norton, New York.

Severiens, S. and G. Ten Dam (1998), 'Gender and Learning: Comparing Two Theories', *Higher Education*, 35.

Skeggs, B. (1995), 'Women's Studies in Britain in the 1990s: Entitlement Cultures and Institutional Constraints', *Women's Studies International Forum*, 18 (4).

Tierney, W. (1996), 'Academic Freedom and the Parameters of Knowledge', in P. Leistyna, *et al.* (eds) (1996).

Watson, D. and R. Bowden (1999), 'Why Did They Do It? The Conservatives and Mass Higher Education, 1979–97', *Journal of Education Policy*, 14 (3).

Watson, D. and R. Taylor (1998), *Lifelong Learning and the University*, Falmer Press, London.

Chapter 8

Pedagogies of, and for, Resistance

Christina Hughes

Introduction

It is indeed our common experience as women that we are often the butt of male joking. Indeed, this is a significant aspect of men's claim to power through their assumed right to abuse in what has traditionally been passed off as an insignificant social encounter. Even in the closest of intimate and caring relations, such as the family, women are expected to absorb such violation, in the name of joking. Yet, as is the case with other socially violated groups, women know that the encouragement to 'laugh off' the lived effect of our violation is an invitation to laugh against ourselves. It is to participate in the staging of our own humiliation (Williams, 1991, p.167). When women identify such practices as premeditated acts of abuse and when we resist this violation by challenging its perpetrators to take responsibility for their acts we are often accused of being 'man hating' (Lewis, 1993, p.33). *Lighten up!*

No, someone has not read this paper before you, leaving their notes on the page for those that come after to witness, to be amused by, to respond to or just to be irritated. The comment 'lighten up' that is written against Lewis' text represents one of those common occurrences in academic life as readers scribe themselves onto the page. I found this comment written in a library copy and I have replicated it here because it encapsulates the issue at the heart of this paper. This is student resistance to knowing feminism.

When set against a piece of text that is discussing women's refusal to be the butt of male jokes, the comment 'lighten up' appears rather ironic. To my feminist eyes it suggests a certain lack of critical reflexivity on the part of this particular scribe. Yet the absence of critical reflexivity around gender issues is a common occurrence in my own, and seemingly others, classrooms. For example, Thompson and McGivern (1995) indicate the reluctance of students taking management courses to become involved in discussing gender issues. They note that this is particularly so in relation to men's engagement with the topic. However, it would be a mistake to assume that it is only men who are resistant to feminist knowledge.

Nor is such resistance only to be found during 'non-feminist' courses. Women taking programmes devoted to the study of women's lives similarly voice their suspicions that the educator has 'got it wrong'. In teaching Women's Studies, Deay and Stitzel (1998) found that they came to dread a number of student responses. These include the focus on the exceptional where, for example, students would challenge a feminist perspective on gendered labour markets by pointing out that their mother was a doctor or they knew a woman chief executive. It would also include assertions that we are now in a post-feminist world where sexism was a thing of the past. As Lewis (*op. cit.*) also points out, to suggest otherwise is to risk being judged of committing that heinous crime of being anti-men.

My own personal experiences of these forms of resistance to feminist ways of knowing have been perplexing and disturbing for a number of reasons. The first reason is that I am passionate about feminist scholarship. Feminism now offers a highly sophisticated array of philosophical and political perspectives that represent real challenges to dominant knowledge systems (Code, 1995). Resistance to knowing feminism represents, for me, the loss of knowledge that opening this treasure chest of potential offers. The second reason is that student resistance represents a failure on my part to be an effective teacher. It suggests that my endeavours to find classroom practices that open up new spaces for knowing that will enthuse and create pleasure are not proving to be successful. The third reason relates to the politics of feminism that are embedded in the 'critical' of feminist pedagogic approaches to teaching and learning. Critical feminist pedagogies seek to create new ways of being in the world that will contribute to the achievement of social justice. Resistance highlights the continuing success of systems that are maintaining social *in*justice. This is not a post-feminism age. The political struggle is as urgent now as it ever was.

Nevertheless, the concept of resistance is a difficult one for the critical educator. Resistance can too easily be read as false consciousness that is somehow a flaw in the student requiring the teacher to correct.[1] How then does one disrupt known oppressions that have colonised the subject whilst recognising one's own pedagogic practices are also attempts to colonise? How does one respect the learner's right to refuse certain knowledges especially when one believes in their usefulness and their empowering potential? And how does one go beyond the idea that the teacher's role is to provide remedies for resistance in order to create the 'feminist' subject, particularly when this is one of a number of subjectivities, never fixed but always in process?

In addressing these questions, I begin with an outline of the key concerns that are addressed by feminist teachers working with post-structuralist theory. This is because post-structuralism provides a framework for understanding issues of resistance that proved to be so problematic for the social learning theories of early second-wave thinking.[2] I then present three vignettes taken from post-structuralist pedagogic practice. Each vignette contains a different conceptualisation of resistance and in consequence offers different pedagogic responses. In conclusion I explore the paradoxical nature of resistance when it is viewed in terms of the liberatory philosophies that underpin feminism.

Post-structuralist feminist pedagogies

Tisdell (1998) highlights four concerns that are central to feminist post-structural pedagogies: subject position as sexed, raced and classed; the construction of knowledge; which voices we hear and listen to; and authority. Although these have always been feminist pedagogic concerns, post-structuralism has presented a number of challenging insights. Following the continental 'linguistic turn', post-structuralism has focused on relationships between discourse, power and subjectivity and has highlighted how language constructs our experience of reality and shapes the processes of knowledge acquisition. The role of language is not unproblematic because language conveys a range of meanings, never fixed or static. Thus, post-structuralism tends to 'stress the shifting, fragmented complexity of meaning (and relatedly of power), rather than a notion of its centralised order' (Beasley, 1999, p.91).

This has at least four implications. First, there is always ambiguity in the meanings we share in the everyday. Post-structuralism challenges the idea that there exists 'a single, literal reading of a textual object, the one intended by the author' (Barone, 1995, p.65). Although some readings are certainly more privileged than others, interpretation cannot be controlled. We each bring our own knowledges, experiences, values and meanings to the text. This calls into question the transfer of intended meanings between teacher and learner (and vice versa) so that authorial (teacher) authority is never guaranteed. It means that we have to acknowledge the ways in which we each produce our own meanings and our own knowledges.

Second, the fragmented and multiple model of power challenges assumptions that power is both a possession and can only be exercised by those with authority above us. Building on the work of Foucault, some post-structuralism takes up a model of power in terms of a matrix or capilliary. This is important because it allows us to recognise that we all have power. In addition, because power is constituted through discourses, people can be positioned as powerful and non-powerful. This means that we can acknowledge the inter-relations of discourses of 'race', class and gender and come to understandings of how, for example, women exercise power over other women or over men. In addition, this model of power assumes a degree of human agency because it challenges the idea that we are simply passive bodies waiting to be colonised by ideologies into a state of false consciousness. Rather where there is power there is also resistance.

Third, post-structuralism emphasises the shifting, changing nature of identity construction. The self is positioned by, and importantly positions itself within, the socially and culturally constructed patterns of language we label discourse. Thus 'practices create subjectivities so that no real human subject exists prior to the social practices within which she is subjected' (Walkerdine, 1989, p.206). The focus on the self as process is an important aspect of some forms of feminist post-structuralism because it highlights the potential for change.[3] It is linked to Foucauldian analyses of power because here power is not simply repressive but is also productive. Rather than assuming, as in some forms of feminism, that patriarchal power represses the person I *really* am, post-structuralism illustrates how the operations of power and discourse produce identities.

Fourth, feminist post-structuralism highlights how the binaried nature of language shapes our gender identities and possibilities. Language is organised in terms of hierarchical binaries of which male-female is the classic example. 'The structure of language and the dominant storylines combine, with powerful effect, to operate on our conscious and unconscious minds and to shape our desire' (Davies,

1997, p.9). In consequence, some post-structuralists argue for the development of critical literacy which will deconstruct binaries in order to illustrate how they construct regimes of truth and so demonstrate, as Davies puts it, how they create 'what we might call speaking as usual' (*ibid.*).

These aspects give rise to five principle areas of study (Tisdell, 1998). First, following the claim that discourses of gender, 'race', class or sexuality are interrelated, we need to study how our positionality produces specific subjectivities and ways of knowing the world. Second, because truth claims are bracketed out, we need to ask how do liberatory discourses contain within themselves the potential to be oppressive? Third, because we are interested in shifting identities, we raise questions such as: How do identities of learners change as the knowledge they acquire in the classroom challenges previously known 'truths'? Fourth, following principles of deconstruction, we emphasise specific binaries such as man-woman, reason-emotion, and show how each term draws on the other for its meaning. The aim is not to replace the dominant term with another but to find a new third position outside of binaried thought because this is seen to hold the potential to create new, as yet unknown, subjectivities. Fifth, there is a recognition of the limited capacity for teachers to facilitate social action. This arises from both a response to, and a critique of, modernist narratives of progression where assumptions are that science will lead us toward a better future.

Let me illustrate these ideas through the inter-relationship of positionality, knowledge construction, voice and authority, with reference to Tisdell. Broadly, positionality is concerned with how issues of gender, class, ethnicity and sexuality affect the kinds of knowledge we believe are legitimate, the voices that are heard and silenced in the classroom, and how our authority is configured. In discussing positionality in relation to knowledge, Tisdell provides an example from teaching a class on adult development. An African-American woman in her class proposed to write an assignment on African-American women's hair and its relationship to adult development. As a White woman, Tisdell notes how she initially found it difficult to see the relevance of the subject matter to the topic. She notes how she viewed hair as *not relevant* knowledge until the student persuaded her that it was and the work was eventually produced.

This example highlights many of the issues of post-structural concern. For example, it brings to our attention the need to challenge assumptions about who are the teachers and who are the learners in respect to who has authoritative knowledge. The African-American women in Tisdell's class were the real teachers about this issue both in terms of a challenge to dominant knowledges in this field and in terms of the implications of her positionality as a White woman teaching this course. The example also illustrates how we need to deconstruct our binaried assumptions. Whilst the African-American woman may have felt safe enough to voice her interests, a post-structural reading would challenge the binary of safe-unsafe. Rather, as Tisdell notes, it would ask 'Who was it safe for?' and 'What are the conditions for that safety?' Thus, the student was not as 'safe' as those students who had picked a more standard topic.

The examples that follow explore these issues further. Overall they focus on the connections that are made between people's resistance to knowing and the subject positions they do or do not take up. In saying that, each example contains a different approach to how resistance is conceptualised. In consequence, they offer alternative pedagogic responses. The first example highlights how student interest in the practical implications of knowledge produces a need for practice based responses to resistance (Titus, 2000). Titus focuses her analysis of student resistance she encountered during a pre-service teacher training course on the question: How is this stuff going to make us better teachers? She illustrates how the view that we are all actively engaged in the production of our own knowledges can be put to good use.

The second example puts a psychoanalytic understanding at the heart of the analysis (Pitt, 1997). This reflects Ellsworth's comment that we are 'subjects split between the conscious and the unconscious' (1989, p.316). Pitt highlights how psychological defences are threatened by new insights. She uses the concept of the unthought to do this and explores the inscribing role of discourses in relation to sexuality. Her example is drawn from the responses of two women taking a Women's Studies course.

The third example is drawn from research into masculinity in school classrooms (Davies, 1997). Whilst the context may be different from that of Higher Education, there are many salient lessons. In addition, our attention is drawn away from the resistant learner to the seemingly non-resistant teacher. Davies draws our attention to the need to constantly engage in critically reflexive practice when we are presented with the 'good' teacher or when we believe ourselves to be 'good' feminist teachers. She illustrates how modelling and encouraging non-stereotypical gender behaviours are insufficient when we seek to challenge hegemonic discourses. Davies' message is that the teacher should provide learners with the tools that will enable them to deconstruct discourses for themselves.

Example one: a pedagogy for technocracy

By categorising and analysing student evaluation forms, Titus (2000) is able to explore student demands that Higher Education should produce useful knowledge. She is looking to identify the postures that are taken up by women and men trainee teachers and to develop appropriate pedagogic responses. Titus rejects the idea that resistance is a barrier to learning. Rather, she argues that it can be productively engaged in the feminist classroom and so she emphasises aspects of student, and teacher, agency. Resistance is not conceptualised in terms of false consciousness but in terms of an active struggle to deal with the contradictory and indeterminate nature of social life and to create meanings of one's own. The feminist teacher's role is, similarly, to actively engage with resistance by using the beliefs and real life experiences of students as the basis for pedagogic intervention. The aim is that this intervention will be productive of identifications that feminism offers useful, and practical, knowledge.

Titus offers four student postures in relation to knowing in the feminist classroom. These are: denial, discounting, distance and dismay. She also offers four associated pedagogic practices that are constructed around these postures.

Accordingly, Titus seeks to engage with students' needs for relevant, practice-based knowledge by offering relevant, practice-based techniques. Within dominant concerns that Higher Education teaching should be built around tested systems of technocracy, she therefore offers associated feminist technologies of knowing.

For example, Titus illustrates how a denial that gendered oppression is a reality arises from students' experiences that they neither feel oppressed nor do they feel that they are oppressors. These denials can be understood in terms of women and men's refusals to take up identity positions of victims or victors. She suggests that this denial offers some degree of emotional protection and the pedagogic task is to avoid prescriptive statements as these are more likely to reproduce rather than challenge predominant individualist explanations for inequality. For example, when Titus asks students for their views on the reasons for school failure they respond that this is due to a lack of hard work or because of inadequate parenting. Titus suggests that one way of moving students beyond such individualist rationales is to present them with evidence of positive historical change before one moves to areas where discrimination exists. This facilitates the beginnings of a more reflective engagement with the veracity of individualist explanations.

Discounting takes a hierarchical view of worthwhile knowledge. Accordingly, discounting is the tactic taken up by students when they believe that knowledge of gender issues is less important than other knowledge. Students evaluating the course stated that less time should be taken up with feminist concerns, analyses and related discussions and material. Here feminism is viewed as either mere opinion or a point of view, or it is relegated to the status of a special interest. The assumptions that feminism is biased and subjective are challenged through a series of field exercises. These included the collection of data on classroom interactions and the analysis of advertising images. Titus argues that once students have collected their own evidence of the dominance of male interaction in the classroom or the ways in which advertising produces gendered subjectivities, they are in a better position to deconstruct the ways in which gender is internalised and reinforced in these subtle ways.

Titus describes distancing as the position taken when students recognise there is a gender problem but that they believe it is nothing to do with them. They ascribe the causes of sexism as either an inevitable consequence of biology, something that happened in the past or is derogatory to men. The result is that such students believe that the teacher is trying to blame someone, or something, for the existence of gendered oppression when there is no-one to blame. The teacher, in such situations, quickly becomes viewed as man-hating, as stereotyping or as exaggerating the existence of sexism. Titus suggests that in such situations the teacher should choose a topic that is close to students' interests. She gives the example of student research that highlights the disparity of wage levels in all aspects of teaching and illustrates how their anger as such evident injustices can be used to direct their interests to further investigate the impact of institutional structures and the complexities of their own lives.

The final category that Titus draws attention to is that of 'dismay'. This is the paralysis that can follow a recognition that gender oppression exists but it appears there is little the individual can do to change things. Titus suggests that such students are not resistant to feminism but they do feel confused, unsettled, depressed and overwhelmed. In response, Titus suggests it is important to give students examples of concrete activities to bring about change. Feminist approaches to the teaching of science, mathematics and technology or policies to combat sexual harrassment are the examples that Titus offers.

Example two: a pedagogy of the unthought

Pitt problematises the dynamic of resistance by looking at two different responses to the topic of lesbianism in an introductory Women's Studies course. Student A argued that lesbianism was a personal choice and had no place in a course on women's oppression. In contrast, Student B argued that not enough attention was being paid to issues of sexuality and lesbianism. Pitt notes that initially one could read these responses rather stereotypically where student B clearly represents the learner whilst Student A is resistant to knowledge about lesbianism.

If we take up the stereotypical reading we might assume that Student A could not engage with the topic of lesbianism because she is not a lesbian herself. Student B, in the process of coming out, clearly could. Our role as educator would be to encourage Student A to be more 'open-minded' and to recognise that her (unconscious) resistance is related to a refusal to acknowledge the dominance inherent in her position as a heterosexual woman. Our response to Student B would be one of alacrity through encouraging more self-directed work to enable her to know more about her emergent identity.

In fact Pitt argues that both women are resistant learners. Her conceptualisation of resistance is based on two aspects of the unconscious. The first is 'the refusal to accept the relevance of certain knowledge to oneself. Covered over by such a refusal is a powerful and largely unconscious desire to ignore one's implication in the knowledge one already holds' (Pitt, 1997, p.129). The second is that the moment of resistance rests on what Pitt conceptualises as the 'unthought'. The 'unthought' is that identity is not innate but is the result of investing in a range of identificatory positions. As a result, the 'unthought' is dangerous because it is a threat to one's sense of self that continually requires being reproduced and reassured.

Pitt reverses the notion that identity precedes identification by suggesting that identification is the first necessary step to realising one's senses of self. In other words, rather than assuming that to identify with lesbianism one has to already be lesbian, Pitt argues that one first has to identify with lesbianism to become lesbian. A similar comment could be made with regard to heterosexuality. Thus, it is through the processes of identification with the discourses of heterosexuality that one takes up, and is taken up by, this identity.

The problem for the educator is posed in an entirely new way. No longer can we assume that Student B is learning or can see the 'truth'. Nor can we argue that Student A is resistant and will not acknowledge the 'truth'. Instead, as Pitt argues 'For Student A, the unthought is that heterosexuality conditions femininity and not the other way round; for student B, the unthought might be the possibility that being lesbian is an effect of identifications rather than a matter of identity' (1997, p.135).

Moreover, Pitt adds a further dimension to her analysis. This is that students' responses are likely to be reinforced through the pedagogic demands of Women's Studies. Despite considerable critiques of dualism within feminist theorising, Women's Studies courses are not immune to identificatory polarisations. Built into such courses is a dynamic that requires students to identify with polarised subject positions. For example, 'Am I feminist or non-feminist?' or 'Am I gay or straight?' In addition, and like other subjects of study, Women's Studies offer the promise of finding certain 'truths'. One of these is that the learner will find their 'true' identity.

By drawing attention to the pedagogic rationales in courses of study, Pitt's analysis highlights how the 'unthought' is not simply a manifestation of the individual psyche but is reinforced by curricular demands. The categories of straight/gay, White/Black, woman/man are often presented as ready-made. These oppositional binaries set up the very oppositional responses that were evidenced in Student A and Student B. For Student A the ready-made identity was heterosexuality. For Student B the ready-made identity was as lesbian.

Pitt argues that feminist educators need to accept their complicity in these processes particularly when student resistance is read as a failure to achieve the 'correct' consciousness. In this feminist educators need to problematise the notions of truth that feminism, and other liberatory discourses, purport to offer. They need also to work to overcome these binaries through engagement with the differences inhabiting Women's Studies classrooms.

Example three: a pedagogy for critical literacy

Davies' focus on critical literacy highlights the importance of equipping learners not simply with knowledge but with the tools through which they can become their own knowledge-producers. Davies gives us the case of a teacher named Mr Good. In fact, Mr Good is not resistant to the idea of disrupting traditional gender identities. Indeed, as Davies' pseudonym indicates, Mr Good appears to engage in the essential strategies of deconstruction that might lead to the acquisition of new identities. Nevertheless, Mr Good's pedagogic approach remains flawed.

Mr Good wishes to challenge stereotypes of macho masculinity by making it possible for boys to take themselves up as literate, oral beings. To achieve this, Mr Good does what Tisdell indicates is essential for post-structural pedagogues. He draws attention to his own position with respect to the topic he is teaching. His pedagogic approach is, therefore, not one of the objective, detached bystander to knowledge. It is one that draws on his personal interests, feelings and ethics. In addition, his classroom practices challenge, in a supportive way, dominant ideas of masculinity. For example, during a discussion of the war in Iraq and the plight of the Kurds, Mr Good does not privilege the rational over the affective. Instead he asks students to express their emotions. He then explores the negative feelings associated with war in relation to their own lives and provides a safe space to do this. Yet he also challenges macho responses so that when a boy suggests that killing can be a solution to a problem, Mr Good responds that this would not be the case in their situation. He then takes another boys' suggestion that working together is a better response.

One reading of Mr Good is that he is opening up spaces for these children in which masculinity can be constructed in a range of ways beyond machismo. Through his responses Mr Good suggests there are many ways in which masculinity can be 'done'. Much of this incorporates the notion of the 'new man' within traditional forms of masculinity. Boys in Mr Good's class were able to read poetry without feeling self-conscious. They were able to play football and to know about wars and planes. They were able to engage with philosophical and moral issues and speak out their feelings. Overall, we might congratulate Mr Good for extending the possibilities through which, in this case, boys can become men.

Nevertheless, Davies argues that Mr Good does not go far enough. This is because Mr Good does not offer the students in his class the tools through which they could engage with and critique the discourses that are made available to them. Mr Good's pedagogy is, in many ways, analogous to the differences between multi-cultural and anti-racist approaches. Multi-cultural approaches open up the range of permissible cultural identifications. Anti-racist ones seek to illuminate for White people their complicity in dominant racisms. Mr Good is opening up for these children a range of alternative cultural identifications. However, he does not offer the children in his class 'the kind of reflexive knowledge that would allow them to see what is happening and to critique the various discourses that are made available to them' (Davies, 1997, p.25).

This reflexive knowledge includes that of the practices of deconstruction upon which critical literacy rests. Deconstruction contains two strategies. These are overturning and metaphorisation (Garrick and Rhodes, 1998). Overturning seeks to change the embedded hierarchies in language so that the dominant and marginal terms are recognised as such. One of feminisms' aims, for example, has been to expose the dominance/marginality of man/woman discourses. However, it is insufficient to seek a reversal of the binaries in terms of dominance/marginality. This retains hierarchical ways of knowing and being. Through metaphorisation one seeks to hold in play the relation of the two binaried terms so that you can illustrate how they are dependent on each other for their meaning and how one continuously threatens the hegemonic power of the other. For example, because the meanings of femininity are drawn from masculinity, as what it means to be feminine changes so does what is means to be masculine. Yet to retain their hegemony, dominant terms incorporate aspects of counter-discourses. Feminist critiques of macho masculinity, for example, become incorporated into ideas of masculinity through discourses of the 'new man' that say that 'men have feelings too'.

Arising from these features, there are three pedagogic tasks that could be undertaken. First, there is a need to generate a level of critical literacy that enables learners to recognise multiple discourses. Second, there is a need to facilitate a critical awareness of the ways in which the self is contradictorily positioned as colonised and coloniser and as oppressed and oppressive within these discourses.

Third, there is a need to embrace, as one's own, the multiplicity of positions with which one wishes to identify.

Essentially, Mr Good does not hold in play the variety of meanings ascribed to masculinity. He does not explore the ways in which these meanings rely on each other. Nor does he explore the potential to create new meanings. In this, then, Mr Good does not give the children in his classroom the tools through which to become fully critically literate and thereby able to understand how their positioning could change through resisting dominant meanings or changing them.

Conclusion

I have been concerned in this paper to illustrate a variety of ways in which feminists place their responses to resistance in the classroom within post-structuralist pedagogic approaches. Thus, the example from Pitt illustrates that we need to take account of the implications of specific curricular demands in producing identifications within the learning process. Her example highlights how courses of study build on ready-made identifications that require deconstruction. Titus further illustrates the significance of the curriculum by attending to how trainee teachers seek 'useful knowledge'. The approach taken up by Titus highlights the significance of working with the positions and voices of learners in developing feminist pedagogic techniques. She illustrates how student concerns to be a 'good' teacher means they are excited about their learning but they expect that their training will provide them with practical and effective 'methods' in the classroom. Davies' analysis reinforces this point by illustrating how the 'good' feminist teacher needs to do more model feminist behaviour or offer teacher-directed new ways of knowing. In the development of curricular technologies, there is also a need to provide students with the tools of deconstruction in order that they can become their own knowledge producers.

In addition, each example highlights several key issues when responding to student resistance. Perhaps the most significant of these is that of the dangers in viewing resistance as the result of false consciousness. As each example illustrates, pedagogic practices may indeed provoke or reinforce the very responses that they intended to disrupt. They may produce denial or dismay, they may produce a dis/identification with lesbianism or heterosexuality or even the 'new man'. In addition, they highlight the tensions that resistance exposes in liberatory discourses. Feminism, for example, is based on a truth narrative that men oppress women. Post-structuralism suggests that this is not always the case. Feminism contains within it the unitary category 'woman' as its founding subject. Post-structuralism suggests there is no founding subject but that identities are constituted within discourses. Feminism promises a better world by following the 'feminist' way, or, of course, ways. Post-structuralism questions the possibility of this. We may simply produce different, not necessarily better, worlds.

Resistant learners also call into question the liberator's truth claims of having superior knowledge. Yet the perplexity many of us experience at such resistance draws attention to a key disjunction in any emancipatory project. This is the way that liberation and subjugation go hand in hand. Our concern at learners' resistance to the knowledge we offer rests in our belief in the legitimacy of our projects. We believe we do have 'better' knowledge at least some, if not most, of the time. In liberating the resistant learner the danger is that we may seek to subjugate their preferred or prior ways of knowing. As educators, we are appropriators of the subject even though we might prefer to think of ourselves as relatively benign ones.

If nothing else, resistant learners expose the educator's attempts to colonise. They call into question the efficacy of the knowledge we offer in terms of learners' lives and experiences. It is not the radical educator's job to indoctrinate. Our task is to open up possibilities. This involves taking responsibility for the material effects of these very pedagogic practices. Not to do so would mean that we have not understood that resistance is a discourse of struggle lying at the heart of any critical pedagogy (Lewis, 1993). Feminism may be a challenge to dominant systems of thought but it also represents a threat to the investments that many woman have made in their identities and in the life practices arising from this. To not respect these investments is to fail in our responsibilities as critical educators. It is to forget that a liberatory pedagogy should never become a dogma.

Notes

[1]   Titus makes this point exceptionally clearly.
[2]   A fuller discussion of this point can be found in Francis, 1998.
[3]   See Belsey, 1997; Davies, 1994 for fuller discussion of this point.

References

Barone, T. (1995), 'Persuasive Writings, Vigilant Readings and Reconstructed Characters: The Paradox of Trust in Educational Story Sharing', in J. Hatch and R. Wisniewski (eds), *Lie, History and Narrative*, Falmer Press, London.

Beasley, C. (1999), *What is Feminism?* Sage, London.

Belsey, C. (1997), 'Constructing the Subject: Deconstructing the Text', in R. Warhol and D. Herndl (eds), *Feminisms: An Anthology of Literary Theory and Criticism*, Macmillan, Basingstoke (Revised Edition).

Code, L. (1995), 'How do we Know? Questions of Method in Feminist Practice', in S. Burt and L. Code (eds), *Changing Methods: Feminists Transforming Practice*, Broadview Press, Peterborough, Ontario.

Davies, B. (1994), *Poststructuralist Theory and Classroom Practice*, Deakin University Press, Geelong.

_____ (1997), 'Constructing and Deconstructing Masculinities through Critical Literacy', *Gender and Education*, 9 (1).

Deay, A. and J. Stitzel (1998), 'Reshaping the Introductory Women's Studies Course: Dealing Up Front with Anger, Resistance and Reality', in G. Cohee, E. Daumer, T. Kemp, P. Krebs, S. Lafky and S. Runzo (eds), *The Feminist Teacher Anthology*, Teachers College Press, New York.

Ellsworth, E. (1989), 'Why Doesn't This Feel Empowering?', *Harvard Educational Review*, 59 (3).

Francis, B. (1998), *Power Plays: Primary School Children's Constructions of Gender, Power and Adult Work*, Trentham Books, Stoke on Trent.

Garrick, J. and C. Rhodes (1998), 'Deconstructive Organisational Learning: The Possibilities for a Postmodern Epistemology of Practice', *Studies in the Education of Adults*, 39 (2).

Lewis, M. (1993), *Without a Word: Teaching Beyond Women's Silence*, Routledge, New York.

Pitt, J. (1997), 'Reading Resistance Analytically: On Making the Self in Women's Studies', in L. Roman and L. Eyre (eds), *Dangerous Territories: Struggles for Difference and Equality in Education*, Routledge, New York.

Thompson, J. and J. McGivern (1995), 'Sexism in the Seminar: Strategies for Gender Sensitivity in Management Education', *Gender and Education*, 7 (3).

Tisdell, E. (1998), 'Poststructural Feminist Pedagogies: The Possibilities and Limitations of Feminist Emancipatory Adult Learning Theory and Practice', *Adult Education Quarterly*, 48 (3).

Titus, J. (2000), 'Engaging Student Resistance to Feminism: "How is This Stuff Going to Make Us Better Teachers?"', *Gender and Education*, 12 (1).

Walkerdine, V. (1989), *Counting Girls Out*, Virago, London.

PART III
FEMINIST PEDAGOGIES

Chapter 9

Feminist Pedagogy and Power in the Academy

Penny Welch

Introduction

> Feminism recognizes education both as a site for struggle and as a tool for change-making (Briskin and Coulter, 1992, p.249).

This chapter explores the relevance of feminist pedagogy for university and college teachers who want to teach in ways that promote solidarity, equality and respect for diversity. I will argue that individual and collective reflection on the relationship between our values and our methods opens the way to adaptations and innovations that benefit students, restores our sense of professional confidence and strengthens our ability to challenge some aspects of the conditions of Higher Education in the UK today. The everyday experience of many academics is characterised by unacceptable workloads, an increase in external scrutiny, and declining salary levels and job security. Enjoyment of teaching is undermined by large class sizes and the demands of academic administration; pleasure in research reduced by the competitive ethos of the Research Assessment Exercise. A survey by Gail Kinman and Fiona Jones for the Association of University Teachers (AUT) found that 25 per cent of those questioned had suffered a stress-related illness in the past year and that 75 per cent of the total sample felt that their institutions and their working conditions had undergone too many changes in recent years (Kinman and Jones, 2000). This is not the best climate in which to suggest initiatives which require additional work and energy, but the approach that I am suggesting makes issues of power central and is aimed at individual and collective self determination for teachers, as well as for students.

Contradictions of the 1990s

My concern with feminist pedagogy comes from my experience of teaching Politics and Women's Studies in Higher Education and from the dilemmas and contradictions involved in challenging certain features of the academy from the inside. I started reflecting systematically on the possibilities of constructing a feminist pedagogy in the early 1990s when student numbers expanded significantly and student groups became more diverse in terms of class, colour, age and educational background. Women's Studies became particularly popular with students and was regarded favourably by institutional management for its contribution to equal opportunities and wider access. A little earlier, the Enterprise in Higher Education initiative, despite its origins in the Government's desire to make graduates more entrepreneurial, had given renewed legitimacy to student-centred teaching and active learning. All these developments, however, had a negative side. The growth in student numbers was not matched by an appropriate increase in resources. As teaching staff workloads became heavier, management appropriated the discourse of 'learning facilitation' to assert that academics could cope with larger class sizes, if only they changed their methods. There was a danger that progressive developments in pedagogy, and in participation rates, would be associated in the minds of many colleagues with overwork and attacks on their professional autonomy. I feared that students in the developing mass Higher Education system, especially those from previously underrepresented groups, would have a less satisfying learning experience than their predecessors.

Bigger classes in Women's Studies meant that it was much harder for me to use informal teaching methods aimed at linking personal experience, academic study and feminist activism. My own opportunity to maintain the activism that had informed my teaching for many years was also curtailed because of my increasing workload. I decided that, for a period, I would concentrate on what I could contribute as a professional educator to the promotion of equality and social justice. I was also motivated, as were many other public sector professionals at this time, by fears of job insecurity and the desire to stop any further restrictions on my professional autonomy. I needed to construct and implement a pedagogy that was congruent with my values and enabled me to offer classes in which all students could get intellectual, academic and personal benefit. In particular, I wanted to involve all students in classroom interaction and to ensure that all their perspectives and concerns were addressed in ways that challenged any sense of not being entitled to be in Higher Education.

The construction of a feminist pedagogy

I turned first to writings on feminist pedagogy and evaluated their relevance to my own situation.[1] bell hooks, the Black American feminist writer and teacher, was the most inspiring source I found. Her classroom practice and educational theory are firmly located within her understanding of relations of domination and oppression in the wider society. She warns, '[f]eminist pedagogy can only be liberatory if it is truly revolutionary because the mechanisms of appropriation within white supremacist, capitalist patriarchy are able to co-opt with tremendous ease that which merely appears radical or subversive' (hooks, 1989, pp.50–51). She also led me to Paulo Freire, the Brazilian educator, who worked with the rural and urban working class in a number of 'Third World' countries from the 1960s onwards. From bell hooks, I took the idea that all forms of domination could and should be challenged in the feminist classroom (hooks, 1989). In the work of Paulo Freire, I found the concept of liberatory education as a joint endeavour between teacher and students (Freire, 1972). I then turned to Carl Rogers, the white American psychologist, for insights on interpersonal relations in the classroom and his writing convinced me that teachers have to show students that they are valued and trusted (Rogers, 1951). I came to the conclusion that a feminist pedagogy could be constructed on the basis of three principles:

- to strive for egalitarian relationships in the classroom;
- to try to make all students feel valued as individuals;
- to use the experience of students as a learning resource (Welch, 1994, p.156).

Despite the fact that my pedagogy is built on non-feminist as well as feminist sources, I wish to identify it as feminist pedagogy to signal that it is part of the only body of educational writing in English that systematically deals with inequalities of gender, colour and sexual orientation in the Higher Education classroom and with the conflicts that arise out of difference. While the challenge to traditional pedagogies that it represents originated within the Women's Studies project, the extensive literature, now available, shows the applicability of feminist pedagogy across the curriculum. It may be, however, that those outside Women's Studies who want to teach in a way that promotes equality and respect for difference might prefer an alternative formulation. The three principles can be translated into three prohibitions to teachers in their relations with students – do not dominate, do not humiliate, do not indoctrinate. Either version can provide us with a benchmark by which to evaluate the usefulness of the literature on innovation in learning and teaching in the UK. Not enough of that work, even now, foregrounds the diversity of students' social and personal characteristics or the affective dimension of classroom interaction.

The potential of feminist pedagogy

Egalitarian relationships in the classroom

Except when students use unfair criticism or discriminatory behaviour to undermine a teacher whose position in the institution is insecure, academics have more power than students within the academy and often outside it. No classroom, in a formal educational institution, can be an entirely egalitarian place because the teacher has power conferred on her/him by the institution in order that s/he can organise the students' learning, grade their work and play a role in the accreditation of their achievement. Teachers who wish to can, however, give up the power to control or dominate students without relinquishing overall responsibility for what happens in the classroom. Sharing power and responsibility with students can be achieved in a number of different ways. Tutors can refuse to pose as experts who possess all the knowledge that students need and instead define the classroom as a place where a joint endeavour for understanding takes place. They can engage in negotiation with students, either individually or collectively, over some aspects of the course (Schniedewind, 1983). They can seek to solve problems that arise in class through open discussion.

Classroom participation is central to a more egalitarian approach and can be encouraged by the use of small group work, whole class discussion, inviting both affective and cognitive responses to the topic (Ruggiero, 1990) and the integration of academic and personal knowledge (Omolade, 1993). Independent thinking is also supported by these approaches and can be further developed through opportunities for placements with outside agencies and assessment tasks such as projects, presentations and learning diaries. Fairness, openness and transparency in the assessment process through the use of clear, published criteria, some elements of self or peer assessment and rapid feedback are vital.

By establishing as norms the principles of equal access to classroom resources and the treatment of everyone with respect, teachers can also promote interaction in the classroom that does not reproduce the social inequalities between students – of status, living standards or opportunities – that exist outside it. Ensuring that students are treated equally in the classroom irrespective of their opinions, intellectual ability or social skills is harder to achieve, but the tutor can set a good example by receiving each individual or group contribution positively. Students themselves recognise that some contributions are more insightful or useful than others but, in my experience, most prefer a request for a little more explanation or the low-key correction of a factual error to being told that they are 'wrong' or have missed the point. Fear of negative reactions from tutors or other students is likely to be a significant factor in inhibiting student involvement in class activities.

If relationships in the classroom are as egalitarian as possible, the feelings of fear and distrust that are often a barrier to learning are reduced, freeing students to engage actively with the subject matter. The conditions for students to experience the pleasures and complexities of being egalitarian and to strengthen their ability to challenge inequality in the wider society can also be created.

Valuing students as individuals

While classroom relations based on mutual respect and cooperation go some way towards providing the individual recognition and acknowledgement that students require, tutors need to show they value students as individuals outside the classroom too. Remembering names, saying hello on campus, keeping regular times for consultation, really listening when students raise academic or personal concerns ought to be basic to professional practice but busy staff may sometimes forget their importance (Bignell, 1996).

The messages that the teacher conveys when giving feedback on assessed work are perhaps the most significant. Returning assignments promptly with constructive comments and making it clear that it is the work, not the student, which is being judged, shows respect for students and their efforts. Even when class sizes are too large for teachers and students to get to know each other well, showing students that they are valued as individuals can remove their feelings of being anonymous and unrecognised within the university or college, counteract any fears of not being entitled to be in Higher Education and increase their self-esteem in ways that facilitate their learning

Using the experience of students as a learning resource

This basic tenet of feminist approaches to teaching is open to a multiplicity of interpretations. Teaching teams should regularly discuss what they mean by it, what their theoretical understandings of the relationship between experience and knowledge are and how they going to apply those understandings in the classroom. Each of the following quotations emphasises a different facet of what the use of experience might mean:

> In terms of feminist pedagogy, the authority of the feminist teacher as intellectual and theorist finds expression in the goal of making students themselves theorists of their own lives by interrogating and analyzing their own experience (Weiler, 1991, p.462).

> When I am teaching history and politics, my students can bring their experience, insights and questions to classroom discussions. I assist them by adding the factual, analytical and contextual information that illuminates and expands their insights. The method works well to empower students, drawing them out, helping them to make sense of what they already know and have experienced (Omolade, 1993, p.34).

> Race matters because teachers and students are 'racial and racialized' beings. The inclusion of our historical and social locations as they relate to power, oppression and privilege has the potential to be a compelling component in the construction of curriculum (Curtis, 1998, p.138).

Constructing feminist theory on the basis of white, Western women's experience was a major theoretical and political weakness within the Women's Liberation Movement in Britain and the USA, which was often reflected in the content and approach of Women's Studies. Challenges by Black feminists in the early 1980s (Davis, 1981; Hull *et al.*, 1982; Amos and Parmar, 1984), led to new efforts to build a feminist politics that recognised inequalities and differences between women. The more recent development of postmodernist intellectual perspectives, that cast doubt on the validity of making any generalisations based on social categories such as 'women', reinforce an emphasis on the diversity of women's lives and experience. On the other hand, post modernism can also be interpreted as undermining the shared subjectivity that provides a basis for political action. Razia Aziz (1992, p.304) argues that 'if a feminism of difference is to compete with reactionary forces for the spaces caused by political schisms, it needs to incorporate both the deconstruction of subjectivity and the political necessity of asserting identity'.

The question of the classroom conflict which can arise out of discussions informed by personal experience of issues such as racism and heterosexism, needs to be considered by teachers and discussed with students.[2] Using personal experience is not an easy option, but a well thought-out strategy can illuminate the relevance of the subject matter to everyday concerns and so increase students' motivation to study and deepen their understanding of the subject matter. Through linking their own experience with the topics under discussion and engaging with a wider range of perspectives on the issues than those that might be provided by the academic literature alone, students can also develop insights that have a positive impact on their personal, professional or political lives.

Benefits for teachers

It is not my intention to minimise the difficulties faced by anyone who wants to teach in a way that is congruent with a set of principles that are not widely accepted in the institution and which may challenge the role Higher Education plays in Western capitalist society. It is also important to recognise that the amount of scope teachers have to resolve the problems they encounter will vary according to their own social characteristics and status in the institution. For me, however, the balance has been overwhelmingly positive.

The impact of the pedagogy I have outlined is obviously greater when issues of inequality and difference are part of the subject matter of the module. Even in classes where this is not the case, however, learning and teaching methods based on the principles of feminist pedagogy do seem to generate greater engagement with the topic by students, more active learning within the classroom and a stronger willingness to show independent thinking in assignments. Not all students enjoy participatory learning in class, but they do appreciate the handouts, the detailed resource lists and the clear guidance on assessment requirements that are also part of the approach I am advocating. Implementing feminist pedagogy requires plenty of detailed planning by the tutor but I find this increases my sense of professional competence in a way that the preparation of conventional lectures and seminars does not.

Responses from colleagues

When I facilitated a workshop on feminist pedagogy in 1993, participants stressed the constraints of institutional regulations, hierarchical management structures, student numbers and the relative powerlessness of many academic staff. At a workshop on egalitarian relationships in the classroom in 1996, members of the group were more confident about sharing power with students and promoting an atmosphere of mutual respect in the classroom but hesitant on how to intervene when discussions of inequality and difference produced personal conflict between students. At the workshop in Liverpool in January 2000, I asked participants to identify some of the obstacles to organising teaching, learning and assessment in ways that promote equality and respect for diversity and to suggest how these difficulties might be overcome. They identified institutional pressures, the political and cultural climate and the weight of demands on academics are the central problems. Networking within and between institutions, research into issues of equality and diversity in learning and teaching, individual and collective reflection and collective professional action were put forward as solutions.

The pressures and climate within Higher Education today are not the same as those ten years ago when I sought a solution through feminist pedagogy. In the next section, I will give an overview of the changes of the last twenty years and a summary of the present situation. I will then suggest some areas where there is scope for feminist action to improve aspects of learning and teaching in ways that restore some of the autonomy and influence Higher Education teachers have lost.

Changes in the UK Higher Education system

The changes in Higher Education in the UK over the last twenty years are substantial. In 1998/9, there were 1,845,757 students following Higher Education programmes (HESA, 2000) compared to 778,000 in 1979/80 (DES, 1986). Full time undergraduate numbers have doubled, with even larger increases in part timers and postgraduates. The Dearing Report (*Higher Education in a Learning Society*, July 1997) pointed out that unit costs per student had decreased by more than 40 per cent in the preceding twenty years, partly due to under-investment in infrastructure. The transition to a mass system of Higher Education has also been funded by underpaying staff and obliging students to meet more of the costs of their Higher Education. In 1990, entitlement to benefits was withdrawn from most full time students, grants were frozen and top up loans introduced. In 1995, the mature student allowance was taken away and in 1998, maintenance grants were abolished and tuition fees imposed on full time undergraduates. While tuition fees are means-tested and income-contingent loans are available for living costs, the financial burden on most students is considerable. Many students undertake part time, low paid work and worry about both the impact of this on their studies and the debts they will have to repay after graduation.

The expansion of Higher Education has been accompanied by significant extension of central government control over it. The 1988 Education Reform Act removed polytechnics and colleges of Higher Education from local authority control but increased central government control over them and the universities through the new funding arrangements managed by the Funding Councils. The 1992 Further and Higher Education Act abolished the binary divide and set up a single funding council that also had the function of assessing and rewarding research and teaching quality. Restrictions on the amount of funding and the way it could be spent meant that institutions tried to keep down costs and secure income from other sources. Through all these measures, the Conservative government encouraged universities and colleges to adopt the behaviour and values of the market, notably competition and responsiveness to consumer demand.

One purpose of increased government intervention was to subordinate the functions of the Higher Education system to the economic needs of the country. The White Paper of 1987, *Meeting the Challenge*, which paved the way for the 1988 Education Reform Act, stated, 'above all, there is an urgent need, in the interests of the nation as a whole, and therefore of universities, polytechnics and colleges themselves, for Higher Education to take increasing account of the economic requirements of the country [...] The Government and its central funding agencies will do all they can to encourage and reward approaches by Higher Education institutions which bring them closer to the world of business.' That statement seems quite tentative, however, when compared to this extract from the recent Greenwich speech by David Blunkett, Secretary of State for Education in the current Labour government. 'Universities need to adapt rapidly to the top-down influences of globalisation and the new technologies, as well as the bottom-up imperatives of serving the local labour market, innovating with local companies, and providing professional development courses that stimulate economic and intellectual growth' (DfEE Press Release, 15 February 2000). David Blunkett expressed a similar instrumental view of the role of Higher Education in the lives of individuals when he justified tuition fees and loans with reference to the increased earning power of graduates (DfEE Press Release, 23 July 1997).

Current climate and conditions

Some undergraduates seem to share the view that the value of advanced study lies entirely in the utility of the qualifications it leads to in the labour market. This disturbs many academics, undermines good student-staff relations and may even make innovation in teaching and learning methods appear to be an inappropriate concession to consumerism. Increased competition between institutions and between academics in the same institution for funding and status can also have a detrimental effect on relationships between colleagues, reducing their ability to preserve collegiality in the face of increased managerialism within institutions. While some academics accept readily the need to be accountable to the public for the programmes they offer and the standards of the qualifications they confer, many others find the detailed regulations and demands of the Quality Assurance Agency unnecessary and unwelcome. There is a similar mixture of opinion on the Institute for Learning and Teaching with some colleagues emphasising its potential to raise the profile and/or improve the quality of Higher Education teaching and others fearing its ability to impose narrow definitions of 'good practice' and to undermine professional autonomy.

From a perspective that values equality and diversity, there are some positive aspects, however. Not only have participation rates in general increased, but those of white and Black women and Asian men have improved significantly over the last decade. Moreover, the current Government is making widening participation and equal opportunities key priorities for the funding council and institutions. In his speech to the AUT Council in Eastbourne, May 2000, David Blunkett announced plans, including 'opportunity bursaries', to increase the proportion of young working class people entering Higher Education (*Times Higher*, 12 May 2000). The Higher Education Funding Council for England (HEFCE) set up a high profile "Action on Access' team in January 2000 to oversee the widening participation strategy (HEFCE Press Release, 12 January 2000). Together with the Committee of Vice-Chancellors and Principals (CVCP) and the Standing Conference of Principals (SCOP), it also established an Equal Opportunities Action Group in April 2000 to promote equality for all staff (HEFCE Press Release, 17 April 2000).

All these developments and initiatives provide political and educational spaces in which all staff in Higher Education can get involved in building new internal networks. They also offer new scope for making links between the institution and the communities around it in the interests of promoting a social justice agenda. Teachers and learning support staff can also benefit from the funding available in each institution for the implementation of a learning and teaching strategy and from the work of the new Subject Centres supported by the Funding Councils (HEFCE Press Release, 21 December 1999). Subject-based research into learning and teaching is eligible for the Research Assessment Exercise and the Economic and Social Research Council is sponsoring a large scale research programme into learning and teaching at all levels.

Notwithstanding these possibilities, underlying problems remain with the Government's stance on equality of opportunity. Any connection between the level and nature of student funding and the under-representation of entrants from the manual working class is publicly denied (David Blunkett's Eastbourne speech to the AUT, *Times Higher*, 12 May 2000). The dramatic fall in full time applications from mature students since 1995, and particularly since 1997, is taken as a sign that much of the demand has been previously met (*Times Higher*, 5 May 2000). The way that student indebtedness seems to be shifting choice of degree subjects away from some of the social sciences that foreground issues of social justice and towards subjects that appear to be more vocational is not highlighted as a problem. The current hierarchy of esteem within the sector is challenged only by exhortations to the most socially exclusive institutions to attract and admit more high achieving students from inner city comprehensives. The charging of differential tuition fees according to the relative prestige of the institution remains a distinct possibility.

The future of feminist pedagogy

While the precise nature of the opportunities to advocate and implement feminist approaches to teaching, learning and the curriculum will vary according to subject area and institution, there are at least three areas in which official concerns and feminist aims are likely to coincide:

- The application of feminist pedagogy to enhancing tutor-student interaction in the classroom, building on ideas of shared power and responsibility, mutual respect and cooperation, the exploration of differences in experience and perspectives. If feminist pedagogy can be shown to enhance student learning, satisfaction and retention, it may become more firmly embedded in the academy.
- The revision of the curriculum so that it does not perpetuate existing hierarchies of power and esteem. What is studied in Higher Education should extend beyond the UK, USA and Europe, should address global inequalities and include non-Western intellectual traditions. If the focus of particular modules has to be predominantly on the UK, then issues of difference and inequality within society can be incorporated into many, if not all, subjects. Even if Higher Education institutions are not convinced by the social justice arguments

for a much wider curriculum or are resistant to the development of new interdisciplinary areas, they may be more favourably disposed to the view that the curriculum should reflect what is currently referred to as 'globalisation'.

• The development of research and innovation projects on feminist approaches to communication and information technologies. The case study literature is well developed in the USA (Hesse-Biber and Kesler Gilbert, 1994; McCulley and Patterson, 1996; Parry, 1996) and shows how networked classrooms, e-mail discussion groups, computer-assisted learning packages and the internet can facilitate cooperative, interactive and vocationally-relevant learning for diverse groups of students.

Success in any of these projects will, of course, create new dilemmas and contradictions for those who want to change Higher Education from the inside, but the overall direction will be progressive. Remember also that the proactive and creative role of academics in the pursuit of new knowledge is a protection against the worst aspects of control and surveillance:

> Precisely because fundamental research involves going beyond the frontiers of established understandings, good academics cannot be told what to do; they defy control; and the kind of creativity required cannot be commanded by an academic master, still less delivered to a management order (Dearlove, 1997, p.57).

Notes

[1]   See Edney and Langton, 1974; Smith, 1982; Culley and Portugues, 1985; hooks, 1989; Ruggiero, 1990; Danaan, 1990.
[2]   See Cannon, 1990; Morley, 1993; Essed, 1994.

References

Amos, V. and P. Parmar (1984), 'Challenging Imperial Feminism' *Feminist Review*, 17, July.

Aziz, R. (1992), 'Feminism and the Challenge of Racism: Deviance or Difference?', in H. Crowley and S. Himmelweit (eds), *Knowing Women: Feminism and Knowledge*, Polity Press, Oxford.

Bignell, K.C. (1996), 'Building Feminist Praxis out of Feminist Pedagogy: the Importance of Students' Perspectives', *Women's Studies International Forum*, 19.

Briskin, Linda and R. Coulter (1992), 'Feminist Pedagogy: Challenging the Normative', *Canadian Journal of Education*, 17.

Cannon, L.W. (1990), 'Fostering Positive Race, Class, and Gender Dynamics in the Classroom', *Women's Studies Quarterly*, 1 and 2.

Culley, M. and C. Portugues (1985) (eds), *Gendered Subjects: The Dynamics of Feminist Teaching*, Routledge & Kegan Paul, Boston.

Curtis, A.C. (1998), 'Creating Culturally Responsive Curriculum: Making Race Matter', *The Clearing House: a Journal of Educational Research, Controversy and Practices*, 17.

Danaan, L. de (1990), 'Center to Margin: Dynamics in a Global Classroom', *Women's Studies Quarterly*, 1 and 2.

Davis, A. (1981), *Women, Race, and Class*, The Women's Press, London.

Dearlove, J. (1997), 'The Academic Labour Process: from Collegiality and Professionalism to Managerialism and Proletarianisation?', *Higher Education Review*, 30.

Department for Education and Employment Press Release, 23 July 1997.

_____, 15 February 2000.

Department of Education and Science (1985), *The Development of Higher Education into the 1990s*, HMSO, London.

_____ (1986), *Projections of Demand for Higher Education in Great Britain 1986–2000*, HMSO, London.

_____ (1987), *Meeting the Challenge*, HMSO, London.

Edney, M. and T. Langton (1974), 'Feminist Subversion', *Spare Rib*, 20.

Essed, P. (1994), 'Making and Breaking Ethnic Boundaries: Women's Studies, Diversity and Racism', *Women's Studies Quarterly*, 3 and 4.

Freire, P. (1972), *Pedagogy of the Oppressed*, Penguin, London.

Hesse-Biber, S. and M. Kesler Gilbert (1994), 'Closing the Technological Gender Gap: Feminist Pedagogy in the Computer-Assisted Classroom', *Teaching Sociology*, 22.

Higher Education Funding Council for England Press Release, 21 December 1999.

_____, 12 January 2000.

_____, 17 April 2000.

Higher Education Statistics Agency Press Release, 2 May 2000.

hooks, b. (1989), *Talking Back: Thinking Feminist, Thinking Black*, Sheba , London.

Hull, G.T., P.B. Scott and B. Smith (eds) (1982), *All the Women are White, All the Blacks are Men, But Some of Us are Brave*, Feminist Press, Old Westbury, N.Y.

Kinman, G. and F. Jones (2000), 'Working in Higher Education: the Relationship Between Perceptions of Change, Working Conditions and Psychological Health', cited in Hartley-Brewer, J., 'Academics Stressed out by Rising Tide of Bureaucracy', *Education Unlimited*, 14 April 2000, <http//:www.educationunlimited.co.uk>.

McCulley, L. and P. Patterson, (1996), 'Feminist Empowerment through the Internet', *Feminist Collections*,
<http://www.library.wisc.edu/libraries/Womens.Studies/fcmain.htm>

Morley, L. (1993), 'Women's Studies as Empowerment of "Non-Traditional" Learners in Community and Youth Work: A Case Study', in Kennedy, M. *et al.* (eds), *Making Connections: Women's Studies, Women's Movements, Women's Lives*, Taylor & Francis, London.

National Committee of Inquiry into Higher Education (1997), *Higher Education in a Learning Society (Summary)*, <http://www.leeds.ac.uk/educol/ncihe/sumrep.htm>.

Parry, S. (1996), 'Feminist Pedagogy and Techniques for the Changing Classroom', *Women's Studies Quarterly*, 3 and 4.

Rogers, C. (1951), 'Student-Centred Teaching', in Rogers, C. (1951), *Client Centred Therapy*, Constable, London.

Ruggiero, C. (1990), 'Teaching Women's Studies: the Repersonalization of our Politics', *Women's Studies International Forum*, 13.

Schniedewind, N. (1983), 'Feminist Values: Guidelines for a Teaching Methodology in Women's Studies' in C. Bunch and S. Pollack (eds), *Learning Our Way: Essays in Feminist Education*, The Crossing Press, New York.

Smith, B. (1982), 'Racism and Women's Studies', in Hull *et al.* (eds).

Times Higher Education Supplement, 5 May 2000.

_____, 12 May 2000.

Weiler, K. (1991), 'Freire and a Feminist Pedagogy of Difference', *Harvard Educational Review*, 61.

Welch, P. (1994), 'Is a Feminist Pedagogy Possible?' in S. Davies *et al.* (eds), *Changing the Subject: Women in Higher Education*, Taylor & Francis, London.

Useful websites

Association of University Teachers, <http://www.aut.org.uk>
Committee of Vice-Chancellors and Principals, <http://www.cvcp.ac.uk>
Department for Education and Employment, <http://www.dfee.gov.uk>
Economic and Social Research Council, <http://www.esrc.ac.uk>
Education Unlimited, <http://www.educationunlimited.co.uk>
Higher Education Funding Council, <http://www.hefce.ac.uk>
Institute for Learning and Teaching, <http://www.ilt.ac.uk>
National Association of Teachers in Further and Higher Education,
    <http://www.natfhe.org.uk>
Quality Assurance Agency, <http://www.qaa.ac.uk>
Research Assessment Exercise, <http://www.rae.ac.uk>

Chapter 10

Feminist Pedagogy and Personal Engagement in Higher Education

Barbara Körner

What is this 'civilisation' in which we find ourselves? What are these ceremonies and why should we take part in them? What are these professions and why should we make money out of them? Where in short is it leading us, the procession of the sons of educated men? (Virginia Woolf, *Three Guineas*).

A teacher in a Passau school refused in 1943 to start lessons with the usual prayers for Hitler, but instead prayed with the young people for 'our soldiers and our enemies, including Black people who must give their lives in this war so that there will be peace [...] This incidence led to great concern among people hearing about it. A small minority regarded it as a near heroic act of taking a position. For many others it was outrageous, 'disloyal' or simply stupid. To take a risk such as this or even greater was at that time unthinkable for most people in Passau (Anna Elisabeth Rosmus, *Out of Passau*, my translation).

Take care that your hearts won't be empty when your hearts' emptiness is what is counted on! Do the useless things, sing the songs not expected from your mouths! Be awkward, be the sand, not the oil in the wheel of the world! (Günter Eich, *Träume*, my translation).

Introduction

In this contribution, I offer reflections on my teaching practice in Higher Education, collected and refined over the last seven years while teaching a range of undergraduate and postgraduate courses, in different settings and disciplines, at three institutions in the South West of England. Some of this teaching has been in Women's Studies, and some in Sociology and Politics; all has been part-time, hourly paid, i.e. on the margins of academic business. I am interested in identifying ways of teaching/learning which are induced, in my case, by a consciously feminist pedagogy, and which represent something radically 'different' in the academy.

The pedagogy I am describing is characterised by personal engagement which demands of students and myself to 'be real' as people while in the education situation, and to engage with our learning and each other, in recognition of diverse identities and power relations. The current trend, though, is to move further away from participatory and engaged forms of learning in HE, in accordance with a market-led model of fee-paying students as consumers, measurable learning outcomes, and quality assurance accountancy. This has led, for example, Louise Morley (in this volume) to suggest that feminist pedagogy is not possible in HE at the moment. My position is that it is vital at this point to put an effort into countering current trends, and to make creative use of our feminist-inspired and other radical teaching/learning experiences. As a critical intellectual and a university lecturer, I therefore wish to contribute to a dialogue about the social change potential of teaching approaches in HE. These are critical times, and I believe there is a need for 'unexpected songs', for subversive action, alternative culture, resistance; for real education and learning which can throw into question and by-pass the negative, numbing effects of the instrumentalist, business-as-usual dynamics which are increasingly intruding in academic life. A critical concern with HE pedagogy therefore is a question of cultural politics (cf. Giroux, 1992).

While fundamental ethical issues are at stake in this reflexive discussion of teaching/learning in HE, my focus here is on the details of practice. Much of the literature on critical and feminist pedagogy tends to be highly theoretical (Ellsworth, 1989; Lather, 1992; Stone, 1994), and I argue that closer attention also needs to be paid to the process of teaching, or more precisely, how pedagogical principles translate in the details of how we teach. What actually happens in the classroom is very complex, and will be viewed differently by participants, yet I believe it is important to make more attempts to share teaching experiences and open up reflection and discussion.[1] With my reflections I would like to invite debate to centre around the *detail* of practice experience in teaching/learning, and to take a positive focus on what is *possible* as opposed to what is problematic in terms of feminist/critical contributions in Higher Education.

The account of teaching practice here is based firstly on my ongoing reflexive review of what happens with particular modules, and specific classroom processes, session after session and year after year. Innumerable talks have occurred following teaching sessions, mostly with my partner, also a teacher in HE, and I have recorded many reflections, as a result of which I have changed and developed teaching practice. Secondly, I have collected written documents such as module descriptions and course evaluations. Thirdly, students have given me feedback on my teaching both written and verbal, spontaneous and solicited. I have also conducted a small survey of ex-students with whom I am still in contact, and have received ten responses for the twenty questionnaires I sent out. Twelve students/ex-students have read and commented on drafts of this paper. Classroom dynamics and assessment emerged as the two key areas of interest in this reflexive research, and personal experience/engagement and attention to process and power relations as the main issues.

In the following discussion, I first introduce some of the fundamental conflicts that have arisen from a conjunction of feminism and the academy since the 1970s. In the second section, I explore the different epistemology underlying a personally engaged, feminist teaching approach in Higher Education, by examining consciousness-raising as an evolving concept of communication which is able to incorporate attention to difference and power relations. I then present a reflexive account of my teaching experience, identifying specific practices under the headings of lecturer engagement, student engagement, and engagement with each other, or group process. In section four I present student responses to my teaching approach and critically evaluate some of the obstacles to personal engagement in Higher Education as I have experienced and negotiated them. I conclude by arguing for the possibility and importance of a personally engaged pedagogy in Higher Education at the present time.

The academy and feminist pedagogy: 'keeping it real'

Universities have been described by feminist and other radical critics as major centres of White, middle-class patriarchal privilege and power, 'harbouring' the values of our great Western 'civilisation' (Campbell, 1992), as male-dominated hierarchies where existing power relations get reproduced through competitiveness and through the myths of objectivity and meritocracy (Rich, 1975; Ramazanoglu, 1987; cf. Bourdieu and Passeron, 1990). Yet, in the context of the 'second wave' of feminist organising from the late 1960s onwards feminist curricula and Women's Studies were established in many universities in the Western world. Women, Black and working-class people in Europe and the US had fought for centuries for the privilege of a university education, and the importance of claiming an education has been well documented as an integral part of liberation movements (Davis, 1982). Not surprisingly however, feminist activity within academia has been described as an 'uneasy alliance' (Lowe and Lowe Benston, 1991), and its presence raises uncomfortable questions about the quality of education offered, and pedagogical and epistemological models used in Higher Education.

My own experience may shed some light on the conflicts at stake. I have certainly experienced my education as a privilege. Studying philosophy and German at Freiburg and Berlin, I have had the experience of an overall exciting, self-directed approach which gave me the space to do my own learning, and on this basis form intellectual community with others. Privilege comes with responsibility: as part of this I have insisted on taking the academic values displayed on old university buildings – pursuit of truth and libertas – at face value, and interpreted them as an obligation to engage with the world, and attempt to do meaningful and transformative work. Researching for my PhD in England, during and after ten years of involvement in 1980s peace, 'green' and anti-nuclear movements, and while developing my feminist politics, I have increasingly felt that I needed to claim this space of personally engaged scholarship actively for myself within the academy. When it came to teaching, I wanted to facilitate the same opportunity of real, engaged learning for my students as well. It became clear very soon that this meant asserting *difference*, and that I had a struggle on my hands to protect the integrity and academic credibility of an approach which contravenes the perceived 'neutrality' of expert academic knowledge production.

Talking about feminist pedagogy certainly precludes the appearance of academic neutrality, impartiality or 'value-freedom' which, for example, has been advocated by Martin Hammersley (1992) and contested by Caroline Ramazanoglu (1992), among others. Women's Studies, which as a discipline and a movement carries an ethos of women-centredness, therefore has been exposed to the full weight of academic hostility to liberatory purposes within university education. Recent campaigns against the threatened closure of Women's Studies programmes or Centres in the UK can be considered as efforts to protect a space fought for since the beginnings of the women's liberation movements in the 1970s, a space where women's experiences are taken as an indicator of social reality and a starting point for theory (Bowles and Klein, 1983; Stanley and Wise, 1993). Within this context, the most paradigmatic struggles for the possibility of a feminist-inspired pedagogy in HE, I suggest, do not take place very visibly, but are subtly embedded in the daily practices that are part of teaching. These struggles involve an awareness of and constant assertion against deeply entrenched institutional conventions and hegemonic practices which hinder personal, political or critical engagement. It is on this level, when it comes to actual teaching and assessment that doubts have been expressed about the viability of feminist politics in the academy. In her 'teacher's tale' for example, Mary Evans (1983) describes how easy it is to slip into traditional academic practices in our concrete day-to-day work in HE. It seems very hard to do something fundamentally different – the pull is to replicate the same old structures. This has led for example Angela Karach (1992) to write about the in-built 'dislocation' and devaluing of mature women's experience as people when they are students, including in Women's Studies. In an open letter to *Trouble & Strife*, Nanette Herbert expresses similar disenchantment:

> As a working class lesbian, I feel that Women's Studies has alienated me from my own experience. I have been taught that my own personal experience is not as important as the 'theorists' [...] I feel therefore, that instead of adopting a patriarchal academic method, Women's Studies should either challenge it or get out. We need to get back to consciousness-raising and grass-roots feminism or at least try to make a stronger link between the reality of women's lives and academic theory. At the moment, they are poles apart (Herbert, 1992, p.4).

Keeping feminist theorising vitally relevant for students' lives, I believe, is a worthwhile challenge. The recognition that there is a fundamental ethical struggle embedded in the detail of our teaching practices can serve as positive validation for our work, especially when its boundaries are constantly being reassessed under the banner of quality assurance and efficiency. It allows for fundamental questions to be asked, such as what is 'efficient' when it comes to education? Do we aim for reflexive individuals who are able to analyse the power relations and processes they are part of, or students who are simply able to reproduce what lecturers and those in positions of power over them expect, as in the 'banking education' described by Paulo Freire (1972)? Ends and means seem intricately connected here, and the agenda of a feminist-inspired pedagogy would indeed seem to contradict the apparently wished for 'outcomes' of a managerially-driven university system. Yet a public debate about the ethics of a university education and responsible citizenship remains missing or perhaps gets increasingly lost within a culture of counting quality ratings, student numbers and pass rates. Once this debate gets under way, we may find that there is considerable agreement that in these postmodern times of globalising changes, self-thinking individuals are needed more than ever: people (lecturers, students, researchers, administrators) who are able to be creative about solutions and resistance and support, who have the courage of their convictions in taking positions and making statements, who engage with their lives and times.

Consciousness-raising, communication and personally-engaged teaching/learning

Most of the teaching which has inspired the pedagogy I am describing has been in feminist theory, and the majority of my students have been women. I have been concerned to validate experiential knowledge in its specificity and diversity in the classroom, and feminist theories of women-centred politics and consciousness-raising have had an important influence on the principles behind my teaching. Men in my classes have been expected to move beyond usual gender dynamics in bringing and examining their own experiences. While this process has been a certain challenge for women and men in mixed groups, in most cases the inherent conflicts have been used constructively by the men involved to further their academic and personal learning. Sharing our experiences in groups has been instrumental in developing my particular personally engaged teaching approach.

There are epistemological principles involved in a consciously political, personally and critically engaged teaching approach in Higher Education which, as noted above, are in fundamental conflict with a 'neutral', expert-knowledge-provider paradigm of university education. The feminist concept of consciousness-raising, I suggest, is an essential theoretical source of such engaged pedagogy. Consciousness-raising was developed as a foundation of feminist knowledge-making in the US and Western Europe during the 1970s and 1980s, when women forming autonomous groups produced critical analysis of gender relations and systematic, patriarchal oppression through an exchange of personal experience.[2] The fundamental recognition that the personal is political had a liberating effect, overcoming the isolation of women who believed their experiences of violation, depression, unhappiness were exceptional or self-induced, and unspeakable. This process implied a paradigmatic re-connection of theory and experience. As Michèle Barrett has said:

> In a sense the early women's liberation practice of 'consciousness-raising' was based on the recognition of the fact that each woman's experience needed to be made collective in order to be understood; that is, it needed to be theorized (Barrett, 1987, p.32).

The process of getting together with other women to talk openly and validate each other's experiences frees us from the notion that the 'truth' about our reality can be given only from above, by those with power over us, the experts. By telling our own stories of our reality, in our own words, we achieve a sense of autonomy, a fundamental degree of freedom from male-centred forms of intellectual authority. This reflexive process of knowledge-making resembles what Belenky *et al* (1986) have identified as the stage of 'constructed knowledge', where the subjective and objective, the rational and emotional, intuitive knowledge and knowledge of the world as perceived by others are integrated.

Consciousness-raising groups of the 1970s have been challenged particularly by Black feminists as potentially exclusive and 'imperial' (Amos and Parmar, 1984; hooks, 1984). There was a tendency that yet another hegemonic group, namely White, middle-class, heterosexual women universalized from their specific experiences. It is important to realize, as Morwenna Griffiths (1995, pp.55ff) suggests, that accounts of experience need to stay open for revision and change. I would argue that, while not many 'consciousness raising groups' exist any longer, at least not publicly, the principle has evolved to include reflexive awareness of the social locations from which personal experiences are being spoken and interpreted. It is applied in various situations where women talk to each other about, for example, working conditions and family life etc. and gain critical understanding about social reality from such an exchange of experiences. Chan Lean Heng (1996) in 'Talking Pain' for example describes the constructive use of a consciousness-raising approach in educational work with factory workers in Malaysia. In my experience, such consciousness-raising frequently does take place in the classroom.

What is most significant here, I suggest, is the process of communication, the quality of the talking and listening which enables complex and inclusive ways of perceiving each other's different experiences and truths. Communication is certainly not in itself a tool of liberatory social change. On the contrary, most communication is part of daily interactions which reproduce inequality, eg. through discriminatory jokes, stereotyping, business talk. Yet Jürgen Habermas' optimistic view (1971; 1984) ascribes 'communicative action' with the 'lifeworld' power to counter the systematic distortions of 'instrumental reason' in modern bureaucracies, through the condition of mutual understanding of partners in a dialogic speech situation. Audre Lorde (1984, pp.114ff), similarly, appeals to the potential of mutuality in a situation where, specifically, women acknowledge the power relations and inherent distortions attached to their different experiences, and manage to communicate with openness and respect. She emphasises that such mutuality – as respect for different equals – implies a preparedness to engage in conflict, to confront deep-seated fears of 'difference', and the anger and pain associated with this struggle (Lorde, 1984, pp.110ff, 124ff). Morwenna Griffiths emphasises that learning from other women's experiences requires an active effort at listening:

> This means making the effort to understand the context in which they speak. It takes time and trouble. It needs to be undertaken in the knowledge that understanding will be imperfect. It also needs to be taken in the knowledge that the listener may find herself changed by the encounter (Griffiths, 1995, p.44).

If communication across difference involves openness to the possibility of change, fear of difference might be explained as fear of change. Related to this can be the anxiety associated with a changed perspective on our lives which has been provoked in the consciousness-raising exchange with other women (Bartky, 1990).

Personal engagement with others in a communication situation involves the openness to uncertainty, and the taking of the risk to show feelings, in knowledge of the fact that such vulnerability will customarily be seen as a weakness, as unprofessional, or unwise exposure. In my experience, the discomfort created through such challenging exchanges can become the most powerful impulse for learning and change. Communication processes then hold the potential for creating respectful relationships and meaningful knowledge. In the classroom, such open and engaged communication challenges both the universalism of the one ('neutral') truth passed on by the expert-teacher, and the relativism of a postmodern chorus of different voices where privilege and oppression are no longer recognised or challenged.

Experiences of teaching in Higher Education: principles and practices

From the beginning of my part-time lecturing career in England I have experimented with methods that could facilitate a way of learning which goes beyond the purely academic while incorporating it. The first year of my third year Sociology module ('European Feminist Thought') in particular provided the ground for developing my teaching approach, and in subsequent years and different contexts I have persisted in the effort to provide opportunities in the classroom to connect theory and experience. I have attempted to create situations where exchanges could take place that would allow people to listen to each other's different experiences and perspectives on social life, and where the hierarchical and disembodied aspects of a university education would intrude as little as possible on this interactive learning process. From intuitive beginnings, these efforts evolved quickly into a consciously feminist and anti-oppressive pedagogy which I have now come to term 'personally engaged'. The 'difference' of my approach, while clearly distinct, is often subtle, and embedded in the detail of what I do. Personally engaged teaching/learning entails for me three aspects: lecturer engagement, student engagement and engagement with each other/group process. These aspects are of course interconnected, and I will now illustrate them by listing some of the details of practice I tend to employ in my teaching.

Lecturer engagement

Teaching for me begins with my own critical and personal engagement with the world and with the material I am teaching, i.e. my own continuous learning, for life more than the career. While this is a fundamental attitude, I consciously use techniques to make it explicit, such as:

- bringing my work/interests into the classroom, and a bit of myself, sometimes feelings; offering personal experience and reflections;
- clearly stating to students that I have a position on things, and am not presenting 'the truth'; that students must feel free to question what I say; that sometimes I act as participant in discussions while overall facilitating the

learning process – not 'non-hierarchically', but in awareness of teacher power; acknowledging that I am learning from the students;

- staying real as a person while in the role of lecturer, and being serious about the work we are doing at all times, not going through the motions; making myself vulnerable at times, as a way to create trust, and as an opening for others to connect with themselves, and each other.

Student engagement

My teaching practice involves facilitating the students' personal and critical engagement with the material of the module, in a process through which students can own their learning. This includes making a demand on students that their learning goes beyond academic achievement and is able to touch them in terms of their lives. I use the following guidelines for my practice:

- If possible, I construct a programme together with the students during the introductory sessions, which is usually a series of workshops. This means the curriculum can be owned by students to some degree, and students are given space to use their creativity and develop thinking. I make suggestions on how to organise workshops creatively, and I do at least one myself, to fill gaps, to model, and to involve myself, in place of more formal lectures.
- I explicitly validate the use of personal experience. For example in module descriptions, engagement and reflexivity are listed as skills to be developed, both in discussions and coursework.
- I strategically build in group exercises with a focus on life experience.
- Students are sometimes being challenged on their views or behaviour in class.
- Modules are assessed by coursework if at all possible.
- Students are encouraged to do something non-conventional, for example creative or autobiographical in coursework (as well as in workshops), to work collaboratively, and use media other than written text (if they have the means to do so).
- I provide no lists of essay titles, but instead give careful guidance for coursework. I agree with individual students their particular, self-chosen focus and title, share enthusiasm about the work, provide references and sometimes lend resources. I offer feedback on drafts and essay tutorials, if possible in a group. Students are encouraged to read and comment on each other's work.
- One out of eight of my marking criteria, which I make available in writing, relates to the degree of engagement in student work: personal engagement/positioning/reflexivity.
- In discussing the use of personal experience in coursework, I usually draw attention to the risk of being labelled 'anecdotal', 'polemical' or 'self-indulgent', and that therefore students need to take extra care with referencing relevant literature, to show they have done their academic 'homework'. I have also repeatedly shared my conviction with students that engaged work will be better, more convincing work, and often, the process of assessment has been rewarding for me and students.

- I try to give thorough and careful feedback on coursework, and if possible, discuss results with students.

The list above relates to modules I lead myself. In cases where I lead seminars for someone else's module, or (part) exam assessment is involved, I have to alter my practice accordingly, for example build in exam revision sessions. However, I have found there is still space to encourage students to engage fully with the work of the module.

Engagement with each other/group process

Personally engaged teaching means engaging with the students as people. This includes respecting what students bring as individuals, and what each of us can learn from each other, as well as paying attention to group process, i.e. differences and power dynamics in the classroom. My strategies include:

- preparing myself to meet people, to enjoy our exchanges, and make a connection on a human level;
- building into courses spaces for a continuous reflection on process, notably 'check-in' at the beginning of sessions, and evaluation at the end;
- engaging in discussions and personal exchange, to coax out of each other, create together and clarify critical analysis about the world we live in as women, and men, of particular class, skin colour, ethnicity, sexuality, age, and other differences of experience;
- applying critical consciousness about social relations also to power relations that exist between us in the group, including as lecturer and students, and as women (and men) of different backgrounds;
- acknowledging that such an engaged process of learning means communication skills, including skills of constructive criticism and reflexivity, need to be developed; as part of this discussing and agreeing on process (sometimes I have suggested the principle 'speak for yourself and listen to others with respect'); keeping a check on the different speaking space people take;
- making my reflections on process available from time to time, including about my mistakes; thereby also inviting students to reflect more actively on 'what's going on', for example expressing discomfort, anger, and difficult feelings, as well as offering positive feedback;
- willingness to engage in conflict if necessary: for example confront discriminative behaviour or comments, disruptive or dominating behaviour, giggling;
- recognising and dealing with us/them divisions (repeated polarisation and aggravation in discussions) – for example of feminists versus reluctant feminists, mature versus young students;
- responding in a dynamic, non-defensive way to student criticism; being 'with the students' in case of conflict;

- not aiming to be liked by and socialising with students, but having professional relations as mutual (not equal) learners/colleagues, and showing acceptance and positive regard; acting as facilitator of both academic and personal learning.

To summarise, my approach has been to be open about my own engagement and the process of modules right from the start, and this, together with written module descriptions, including marking criteria, acts as a kind of contract for the work we do together, which I explicitly review from time to time. In my modules, my own value-base as a feminist was always obvious, and I made clear that students could not just 'study' feminism but were required to engage with it. There have been moments in modules where I have 'spoken my mind', and it has usually changed dynamics positively, and led to students taking their learning more seriously. Through my approach, I demand the full presence of students in the process of teaching/learning and do this through 'modelling'. I am there as feminist, academic, learner and teacher, human being, and attempt not to 'hide' behind a role or a 'safe' process which means that the power relationships are explored rather than minimised. This may present a difficult situation for some students, and tends to be challenging for all involved.

Student responses and critical evaluation

Students have responded quite distinctly to my teaching approach, recognising that this was 'different' from the mainstream approach, both in the focus on active participation and the centrality of personal experience, in seminar programme, discussions and assessment. Responses have been quite strong and clear, with some students being enthusiastic, inspired, thriving with this approach, and wanting all teaching to be 'like this', and others wanting more lecturing, and/or seeing the focus on process as a bit time wasting. For example, these are statements from a formal course evaluation:

> More formal input from lecturer needed. Having lectures would be good as no lectures make people stressed and worried. Need more structure.

> A totally brilliant approach. Thoroughly enjoyable and very enlightening. We are encouraged to engage with the subject on a personal level.

This polarised response points not only to different student motivations and expectations of HE, but more significantly, I believe, to the fact that my approach 'stood out' from the usual academic experience, and that this has created tensions for students. I want to start further discussion by listing some of the many positive, validating comments I have received from students and ex-students. Many have appreciated the difference of the learning experience offered:

> [...] like one candle being lit by another [...] sometimes you learn more from who a person is than from what they tell you.

[…] experience of the course has been a lifeline.

We are expected to engage with the subject matter, not to blindly write pages of notes, which of course is the best way to learn. In short, we are being treated like responsible adults and not like school children.

[…] empowering as well as validating my life experiences […] allowed me to reflect on such personal experiences within a feminist framework and consider this in the light of other women's realities.

[…] there was very little input from you and we had to use our brains and have discussions.

[…] facilitated a raising of awareness without placing yourself 'above' the students. This empowered us to own our work and focus on issues important to us.

[…] made people *think* more deeply […] you were made a more real person.

Glad I have had the experience […] it was at times extremely challenging to me as a student.

Yet even students who recognised its benefits have tended to be torn between this approach and mainstream academic conventions and demands. One ex-student offers an explanation:

Looking back now I feel it may have been difficult for some students to fully explore some of the personal issues; for very different reasons. First, the mature students are a generation of passive learners; part of their socialisation has been about the transmission of knowledge from 'experts'. Anything that deviates from this is uncomfortable in its uncertainty. Secondly, the younger students felt they did not have enough life experience to participate in the same ways.

This reflective comment points to some of the obstacles facing an engaged teaching/learning approach in HE. I have found that I had to deal with three main difficulties. Firstly, there is the expectation of academic expertise. Making yourself vulnerable and refusing to just 'deliver' information, admitting mistakes and that you are also learning from the students throws into question academic credibility. It may create insecurity in students. For me, there is extra work involved in re-assuring myself and students that the work we do is 'academic enough', and in making up for the personal engagement by taking extra care in teaching academic skills and providing students with references etc. Students have sometimes commented that the creative workshop exchanges seemed too 'enjoyable' to be 'work'. On the other hand, I find myself guarding against the re-current slide into an assumed role of provider of knowledge, which I experience as profoundly stifling. Recently, I have experienced that lecturer-engagement is definitely endangered in the context of a conservative institutional culture, in which modules are being routinely assessed by exam.

Secondly, there may be reluctance about sharing experiences. This reluctance may be grounded in a diversity of valid responses to the teaching situation and may point to important issues of power and group dynamics. Students are to different degrees willing or able to engage, and this needs to be accepted. It tends to be mature students who are more 'comfortable' with my approach and benefit more immediately, but this is not always the case. I have found that larger, diverse groups (of ten to twenty students) are easier to work with than the very small Women's Studies groups in which a lot of expectation has rested on a few individuals, and this pressure is exacerbated when individual students do not for some reason engage as much as others. There is a fine line here between challenging students to engage and creating situations where students may feel pushed to 'disclose' and make themselves too vulnerable. In my sessions, active participation is voluntary as a rule, although I model engagement and address students as full, engaged human beings. In specific exercises in which students are asked to make connections between an emerging critical/feminist consciousness and key life events, control over what to say after individual work rests with students. The work is mainly for themselves, and the other function of the exercise is to create a space for real listening, and development of trust in the group. What is important here is that the purpose of any sharing of personal experiences is clear, that students have control over what they share, and that the process is as safe as possible, ensuring respect and confidentiality.

This is as true for assessment. Through my approach to assessment, students have felt both validated and liberated to do their own work, but also challenged and worried. The invitation to make personal positioning and personal engagement explicit conflicts with how students have been trained to write essays, and in the third-year Sociology module which I led for five years we have had many discussions on mainstream prohibitions to use the first person singular – 'I' – in essays. We have dealt with some conflict and anger around my marking power, and about students being asked to produce work for my modules in different ways and to different criteria. Yet often, inspired and inspiring work has come out of the courses I have taught, and high marks have usually been endorsed by external examiners who have sometimes commented especially favourably on the more adventurous, and collaborative pieces of work. An ex-student reflects on the assessment process: 'I have taken from this module a real confidence in creating a rigorous "standpoint" at the outset of any piece of work such that the use of the first person is both contextualised and validated'.

Thirdly, there are potential difficulties concerning conflict. In many cases, especially in the modules running over two semesters, I have been aware of an emotional process evolving over the lifetime of the seminar group, with different stages such as enthusiasm, conflict and resolution. In modules and individual teaching sessions, there has been conflict to various degrees, over such issues as gender, sexuality, class, racism, age, teacher power and having men in the group. Where they have been expressed, conflicts have usually been used constructively, and I have argued elsewhere that confronting conflict and discomfort carries an important potential for social change, moving people on in their lives and critical consciousness (Körner, 1997, 2000). Conflict over feminist convictions has been most tricky in my experience, and perhaps increasingly so, as 'feminism' is becoming more of a 'dirty word'. Obviously, in a feminist-led module on feminism, this conflict will feature in one way or another, and one student said how understandable this was:

> If you put yourself in the place of the students, some of whom may lack confidence in their roles as learners, and how exacerbated this might be by also feeling they are not 'good enough' feminists.

In one particular module where a strong polarisation occurred between perceived feminist and anti-feminist elements in the group, I did not manage to get the balance right between my personal point of view and lecturer authority. This meant that the destructive aspects of conflict were not overcome in this case. This incident made it even more evident to me that the success of my approach depends on reflexivity, i.e. on a self-critical review of the power dynamics I am involved in as lecturer. As one ex-student commented:

> Does the tension between the feminist and the 'academic' lecturer aspects belie the intrinsic nature of the power relationship characterising student/lecturer-positions? Even if both are feminist!

The group process has certainly benefited when there was more time for trust to develop, and to move beyond both the initial 'courting' stage, and the conflict stage. Sometimes, speaking my mind has led to upset or even tears. But I have always managed to address conflict (between me and students and within the student group) when it arose, rather than ignoring it. What was most important was to have a chance to pick up on dynamics, and offer reflections at crucial moments, and also, not to hesitate to communicate with individual students outside class when something seemed to be wrong. An ex-student commented on this:

> Do you remember writing three of us a note to say sorry about having a go at us because we'd lost the plot for our seminar? This was a really significant act for me – that you'd bothered to send each of us a note and not just the 'leader' of the seminar group. That was about you as a person, not a feminist, nor a lecturer. I think this is the essence of what you call 'staying real'.

Personal engagement as a possibility in Higher Education

While all these years I have been aware of and worked with the tensions discussed above, the overarching impression of these reflections on my teaching experience is that a personally engaged, feminist-inspired pedagogy is possible in HE. Throughout times of self-doubt, ups and downs of being happy with courses and not so happy, making mistakes and agonising about power dynamics etc., I have never let go of a deep conviction that there is an important significance in an engaged approach in HE which is beneficial to academic life and students' experience at university, and I have certainly received a strong sense of validation from students for this approach. As one ex-student commented: 'this kind of engaged learning was what I had hoped for when coming to university'.

Yet in discussing this approach with other HE lecturers in a public forum, I have found that people tended to focus on problems rather than possibilities; on the limitations of such engaged work within the institution of HE, and on the students wanting to be consumers of educational services. I explain this reluctance with what I call a culture of fear which is taking hold in our times of economic decline, re-structuring and increased administrative loads etc. I argue that students have a right to lecturers who engage personally with their work, and that more rather than less energy should be put into making such engagement more possible and acceptable. In the present British context of increasing commodification of life and relationships, cultural vacuity, demoralisation and brutalisation, I believe it is especially important, as teachers, to work to support inspiration, be inventive, creative, 'cultural workers' (Giroux, 1992), to help keep spirits alive, to resist and counter prevailing trends. I suggest that my experience has something to offer that 'works', in a subversive kind of way, within academia – a teaching/learning situation which allows and demands of people to be 'real' with each other, based on mutual respect, and owning of the learning process, in acknowledgement of lecturer power and responsibility.

What makes it possible to maintain such an approach, in my experience, is mainly a continuous attention to power relations, or in other words a process-oriented reflexivity. As Rossiter *et. al.* (1998) have discussed in regard to feminist approaches to mental health care, this involves questions of ethical practice: how to deal with concrete issues of power in teaching practice while regarding the larger social context with its structures of domination in which HE pedagogy (including theorising it) is institutionally embedded. Engaged lecturing involves seeking the balance between taking a position, and not taking over; between an exchange of experience and academic skill learning; between being open and human in the teaching situation and not reneging on the responsibility of lecturer authority. I have used the paired concept of 'teaching/learning' to indicate mutuality in the education process. While engaged teaching/learning is not non-hierarchical, I believe it enables teachers and students to be involved in a process of learning together where something can 'happen' between people, in recognition of differences and power relations, and where change can take place. In this sense such an approach offers a 'difference' beyond the academic business of getting students through their degrees. To be maintained within the daily work in the academy, this approach needs constant review and renewal and never gets 'easy' or comfortable – as violinist Nigel Kennedy said in a radio interview: 'if you get complacent, that's the enemy of good music'. I will end with the words of an ex-student who noted that: 'We need more research on these alternative teaching styles to move us on from the "malestream" we currently endure'.

This piece of work would not have been written without the support, interest, participation and inspiration of students and ex-students, as well as colleagues who have encouraged me and provided spaces to reflect on teaching practice. I want to thank students and ex-student-friends for their input and for reading and commenting on drafts, in particular Gina Airey, Helen Charlton, Sylvie Gomez, Sharon Martin and Anne Verhamme. I am grateful to

Sam Wakeham for her courage in speaking out and stepping out of line in support of my teaching approach, as well as heart-warming validation and encouragement, and wish to thank my ex-partner, Avril Butler for all the hours of listening, our dialogues about practice ethics, and her constructive feedback on the final drafts.

Notes

[1]   Cf. hooks, 1989, 1994; Lubelska, 1991; Currie, 1992; Weiler, 1995; Morley, 1999.

[2]   MacKinnon, 1982; Spender, 1985; Kelly, 1989; Bono and Kemp, 1991.

References

Amos, V. and P. Parmar (1984), 'Challenging Imperial Feminism', *Feminist Review*, 17.

Barrett, M. (1987), 'The Concept of Difference', *Feminist Review*, 26.

Bartky, S.L. (1990), *Femininity and Domination: Studies in the Phenomenology of Oppression*, Routledge, New York.

Belenky, M.F., B. McVicker Clinchy, N. Rule Goldberger and J. Mattuck Tarule (1986), *Women's Ways of Knowing: The Development of Self, Voice, and Mind*. Basic Books, New York.

Bono, P. and S. Kemp (eds) (1991), *Italian Feminist Thought: A Reader*, Blackwell, Oxford.

Bourdieu, P. and J.C. Passeron (1990), *Reproduction in Education, Society and Culture* (second edition), tr. R. Nice, Sage, London.

Bowles, G. and R. Duelli Klein (eds) (1983), *Theories of Womens' Studies*, Routledge, London.

Campbell, K. (ed.) (1992), *Critical Feminism: Argument in the Discipline*, Open University Press, Buckingham.

Currie, D. (1992), 'Subject-ivity in the Classroom: Feminism Meets Academe', *Canadian Journal of Education*, 17 (3).

Davis, A. (1982), *Women, Race and Class*, Women's Press, London.

Ellsworth, E. (1989), 'Why Doesn't This Feel Empowering? Working Through the Repressive Myths of Critical Pedagogy', *Harvard Educational Review*, 53 (3).

Evans, M. (1983), 'The Teacher's Tale: On Teaching Women's Studies', *Women's Studies International Forum*, 6 (3).

Freire, P. (1972), *Pedagogy of the Oppressed*, tr. M. Bergman Ramos, Penguin, Harmondsworth.

Giroux, H. (1992), 'Resisting Difference: Cultural Studies and the Discourse of Critical Pedagogy', in L. Grossberg, C. Nelson and P. Treichler (eds), *Cultural Studies*, Routledge, New York and London.

Griffiths, M. (1995), *Feminisms and the Self: The Web of Identity*, Routledge, London.

Habermas, J. (1971), 'Der Universalitätsanspruch der Hermeneutik', in J. Habermas, D. Henrich, Niklas Luhmann and J. Taubes (eds), *Hermeneutik und Ideologiekritik. Theorie-Diskussion*, Suhrkamp, Frankfurt am Main.

_____ (1984), *The Theory of Communicative Action. vol.1: Reason and the Rationalization of Society*, tr. T. McCarthy, Heinemann, London.

Hammersley, M. (1992), 'On Feminist Methodology', *Sociology*, 26 (2).

Heng, C.L. (1996), 'Talking Pain: Educational Work with Factory Workers in Malaysia', in S. Walters and L. Mnicom (eds), *Gender in Popular Education. Methods for Empowerment*, Zed Books, London.

Herbert, N. (1992), 'Letter to the Editor', *Trouble and Strife*, 25.

hooks, b. (1984), *Feminist Theory: From Margin to Center*, Southend, Boston MA.

_____ (1989), *Talking Back: Thinking Feminist – Thinking Black*, Southend, Boston MA.

_____ (1994), *Teaching to Transgress: Education as the Practice of Freedom*, Routledge, New York.

Karach, A. (1992), 'The Politics of Dislocation: Some Mature Undergraduate Women's Experience of Higher Education', *Women's Studies International Forum*, 15 (2).

Kelly, L. (1989), 'Our Issues, Our Analysis: Two Decades of Work on Sexual Violence', in C. Jones and P. Mahony (eds), *Learning Our Lines: Sexuality and Social Control in Education*, Women's Press, London.

Körner, B. (1997), *Critical Passion: A Feminist Theory of Non-Violence and Social Change*, University of Lancaster, unpublished PhD thesis.

_____ (2000), 'Social Exclusion in Movements for Social Change: Towards a Politics of Difference', paper presented at Sociology and Social Policy/Social Work Departmental Seminar Series, University of Plymouth, 21 March 2000.

Lather, P. (1992), 'Critical Frames in Educational Research: Feminist and Post-structural Perspectives', *Theory into Practice*, 31 (2).

Lorde, A. (1984), *Sister Outsider. Essays and Speeches*, Crossing Press, Freedom CA.

Lowe, M. and M. Lowe Benston (1991), 'The Uneasy Alliance of Feminism and Academia', in S. Gunew (ed.), *A Reader in Feminist Knowledge*, Routledge, London.

Lubelska, C. (1991), 'Teaching Methods in Women's Studies: Challenging the Mainstream', in J. Aaron and S. Walby (eds), *Out of the Margins: Women's Studies in the Nineties*, Falmer Press, London.

MacKinnon, C. (1982), 'Feminism, Marxism, Method, and the State: An Agenda for Theory', in N. Keohane, M. Rozaldo and B. Gelpi (eds), *Feminist Theory: A Critique of Ideology*, Harvester, Brighton.

Morley, L. (1999), *Organising Feminisms: The Micropolitics of the Academy*, Macmillan, London.

Ramazanoglu, C. (1987), 'Sex and Violence in Academic Life, or You Can Keep a Good Woman Down', in J. Hanmer and M. Maynard (eds), *Women, Violence and Social Control*, Macmillan, Houndmills.

_____ (1992), 'On Feminist Methodology: Male Reason Versus Female Empowerment', *Sociology*, 26 (2).

Rich, A. (1975), 'Toward a Woman-Centred University', in F. Howe (ed.), *Women and the Power to Change*, McGraw Hill, New York.

Rossiter, A. with C. de Boer, J. Narayan, N. Razack, V. Scollay and C. Willette (1998), 'Toward an Alternative Account of Feminist Practice Ethics in Mental Health', *Affilia*, 13 (1).

Spender, D. (1985), *Man Made Language*, Routledge, London.

Stanley, L. and S. Wise (1993), *Breaking Out Again: Feminist Ontology and Epistemology*, Routledge, London.

Stone, L. (ed.) (1994), *The Education Feminism Reader*, Routledge, New York.

Weiler, K. (1995), 'Freire and a Feminist Pedagogy of Difference', in J. Holland and M. Blair (eds), *Debates and Issues in Feminist Research and Pedagogy: A Reader*, Open University Press, Clevedon.

Chapter 11

Offensive and Defensive: Student Support and Higher Education Evaluation

Jen Marchbank and Gayle Letherby

Introduction

In this chapter we examine the interconnections amongst and between current methods of evaluation in Higher Education, modes of student support and our roles and identifications as feminist pedagogues. We are concerned in particular with issues of student evaluation of tutors and teachers and student support provided by and/or expected of tutors and teachers by students and by the institution. We are interested in the political implications these issues can have for those working in Higher Education. Overall our focus is on the contradictions and tensions within the system and between our political practices and the system that we, and others like us, face. The philosophy which produces 'mission statements' and 'strategic plans' also likes to encourage notions of self-development and personal responsibility amongst students yet, at the same time, the systems which support this form of rhetoric actually encourage individualism and 'charter' type mentalities.

Feminism in the academy has historically been concerned with the critique of knowledge and knowledge production, with the critical examination of the academy itself and professional practice.[1] We add to the latter part of this debate here with particular reference to what we perceive as the danger of feminist pedagogical styles being unconsciously appropriated by management in order to maintain student numbers and satisfy league table criteria. Associated with this we also consider how an over-concentration on 'service' can lead to a deprofessionalisation of the academic job. Our own experience as two female academics who identify as feminist and whose 'jobs' in the institution include teaching, administration and pastoral work with students (as well as research) are clearly relevant. To this end we draw on our own experience and those of colleagues at our own and other similar institutions. Although we focus on the auto/biographical we aim to locate our experience within structures and contexts and demonstrate that our experience can only be understood with reference to the social (Mills, 1959; Ribbens, 1993; Stanley, 1993).

Contemporary Higher Education

Many writers have commented on the impact of recent changes and innovations in HE such as semesterisation, modularisation, open and distance learning and on the institutionalisation of quality control through, for example, Teaching Quality Assessment (TQA) visitations and Research Assessment Exercise (RAE) deadlines (e.g. Thorn and Cuthbert, 1996; Evans, 1999). The relationship between all of this and dominant political ideologies has also been considered in detail. For example:

> We see increasing dependence upon mass lectures, reduced contact hours and deteriorating staff-student ratios characterised as 'streamlined servicing' by 'good' departments and faculties (Dever, 1999, p.219).

As such, these developments have been driven by economic rather than academic criteria:

> Many changes in Higher Education in the last decade or so have been related less to knowledge production and pedagogy than to ideological and market concerns. [the] 'entrepreneurial' trend, has affected both working and learning conditions and, in a knock-on effect, the nature of student/tutor relationships (Letherby and Shiels, forthcoming).

Clearly, New Right ideology has had an impact on Higher Education both in terms of 'the entrepreneurial spirit of the market' (Epstein, 1995, p.59) and also in terms of the focus on the individual rather than the collective (reflected not least we think in the drop in popularity of sociology and the rise of psychology). Feminist and other critical pedagogies have sought to develop liberatory teaching and learning practices alongside student empowerment (see for example Davies, Lubelska and Quinn, 1994; Morley and Walsh, 1995; Morley and Walsh, 1996). However, as Morley (1995) has argued, empowerment has been adopted by the new right and, in this context, has lost its liberatory meaning. It has become associated with the development of individualism and the skills required for self assertion and advancement rather than any analysis of the roots of powerlessness and the structures of systemic oppression (Lather, 1991 cited in Morley, 1993). Add to this the rise in student numbers (64.4 per cent from 1983 to 1994 whilst staff numbers rose only 11.4 per cent over the same period) and serious tension in the system is inevitable (Court, 1996).

The result is that lecturers (and support staff) in universities are now expected to provide a service and this service, like other aspects of working in Higher Education, is gendered. This is relevant both to the provision of pastoral care, which as Cotterill and Waterhouse (1998) note, has become feminised and low-status and to teaching, where women teachers and feminism, and any subject perceived as 'soft' and/or 'political rhetoric', are devalued (Evans, 1997; Letherby and Shiels, forthcoming). As Skeggs (1995) has observed, students embark upon Higher Education confident in their right to assess and critique provision due to the economic and personal investments they have made for a successful education.[2] A major aspect of contemporary Higher Education is quality assurance induced and management monitored check systems such as TQA and RAE. Not only do universities face external moderation and review through such agencies but the existence of these practices has encouraged the development of a particular management focus within institutions to ensure improved performance on the criteria valued by the producers of league tables which appear in the media. Although league tables claim to be looking at the system it is actually individuals who are in the firing line. This is a result of the fact that internal evaluation systems have become skewed towards avoiding student attrition (ie student drop-out) and proof of quality assurance. These internal systems, student participation in consultative meetings at module, course/programme and school/faculty level and a variety of evaluation forms may be admirable but when used for both internal and external monitoring have potentially sinister implications for staff. This is further complicated by the growth of the 'charter' mentality which the check systems compound and encourage. Contemporary academics have given students various opportunities to criticise and check them whilst encouraging a culture in which students expect academics to 'solve' all their academic and personal problems.

With all of this in mind, and as feminists working in the academy, we are aware of further personal and political tensions: we do want our students to feel empowered through and within their educational experiences with us and we do feel that we have a responsibility to the women and men that we teach. Like Welch (1994) and Walsh (1996), we too think that feminist pedagogical practices go beyond the exchange of knowledge and should also influence our relationships with students. Yet, we are uncertain of the value of some of the current quality assurance systems both for ourselves and for students.

Support, evaluation and feminist pedagogy

Personal support as a political issue

A recent survey of British students (conducted in an agricultural college) reviewed the stress factors affecting students, listing issues such as the transition from home to college/university, examinations and finance in addition to the social concerns affecting all young adults as causes of student problems (Monk and Robson, 1999). One conclusion of this survey was that students who attended straight from school were less well able to adapt to the needs of Higher or Further Education than those with previous college or work experience, resulting in the college having to teach life skills:

> The areas where training was most needed were, unsurprisingly, financial management, communication, language, discipline, reliability, motivation, social skills, personal hygiene and the 'less headline worthy health issues' such as hepatitis (Monk and Robson, 1999, p.335).

However, Monk and Robson do question if this is the responsibility of institutions of education given that many of the problems facing students originate outside college walls. Nonetheless, recognising that there is a correlation between personal development and academic achievement they conclude that 'it is in the enlightened self-interest of academic institutions to provide a good pastoral care if they wish to achieve their goals of academic excellence' (Monk and Robson, 1999, pp.336-7).

Whether student support has developed through such 'enlightened self-interest' or genuine altruism institutions do now offer a range of services. Student support involves many aspects of the university: from the Chaplains and Student Union Welfare Officers to Student Services Counsellors. However, with reference to our own experience and those of colleagues elsewhere, we notice an increased reliance of students upon academic staff, or rather certain academic staff, and indeed we believe that our pedagogical approach encourages this. As feminist teachers we are keen to ensure that our students enjoy their learning and develop more than simply academic knowledge. Hence, within our classrooms a range of teaching modes are employed and we further develop additional transferable skills for example; communication, group work, analytical thought, use of information technology. Although we are very aware that such pedagogical approaches are not the prerogative of feminists alone, we believe that the fact of our being both women and feminists increases students' perceptions of our roles.[3] Our teaching practice as feminists includes such elements as the encouragement of the view that knowledge is inclusive not exclusive and we strive for non-hierarchical classrooms, in which students are empowered by active participation. As Lubelska (1991) amongst others has outlined, the approaches and content employed in the feminist classroom aim to achieve not just intellectual development, but also a more private and personal transformation in each student. However, sometimes the message that this seems to create and to be received by students is that we are supportive not just of their independent and collaborative learning development but also of them as individuals in a way that other staff are not. In fact, we have both experienced cases of students refusing to work collaboratively whilst simultaneously making demands upon us as staff to develop them individually (see Letherby and Marchbank, 1999a).

Our opinions regarding the nature of the contemporary student body are informed by experiences of student recruitment and admissions as well as undergraduate teaching. The drive for increased recruitment along with government targets for recruiting under-represented groups and the focus upon attrition rates clearly causes tension between the desire of Admissions and Course Tutors/Programme Leaders to admit marginal students and a lack of resources to provide academic, let alone pastoral care. As two Course Tutors we have witnessed an increasing number of students with either academic or pastoral difficulties requiring our assistance. We are not alone in this (see, for example, Cotterill and Waterhouse 1998). This is not an argument for social exclusion; the numbers of students has increased without adequate consideration for resource implications. Universities have developed a range of support services but increasing numbers of students wish to receive support not from the professional counsellors but from their Course Tutor (or equivalent) – someone they seem to perceive as 'belonging' to them. It certainly seems to us that students are increasingly expecting an individual service – reflected not only by requests/demands to re-mark assignments that do not achieve the desired grade, but by requests of us to help in making decisions about significant life events.

Indeed, our position as feminist teachers or perhaps just as women encourages a caring image and we are frequently sought out not just by students on our own courses but others as well. We often see students who prefer to talk to us than to the male member of staff to whom they have been allocated for pastoral support. We know that some of our male colleagues are also seen as approachable by students but on the whole it appears to us that the majority of people approached in this way are women. Although we are keen to ensure that our students resolve their problems it is neither appropriate or suitable for untrained, unsupported individuals to be the main providers of pastoral care for students. This, we believe, is one aspect of the proletarianisation of the (female?) academic job. Even if we wished to be able to provide such care, it is not possible given the other structural demands such as teaching, graduate supervision, administration and research.

As individual staff members we also feel tensions, not least of which being the tensions created by the other tasks required of us in terms of teaching, administration and research. In many cases, the pastoral role of academic staff is neither given recognition in terms of time, nor is it recognised in terms of promotion and performance review.[4] For the ambitious, or even for those who simply want to be good at their job, pastoral support, at the levels demanded, can be viewed as a hindrance to achieving those aims.

Student support and staff evaluation

Various support systems have been introduced into Higher Education institutions providing for both student support and feedback. These include tutor office hours, Course Consultative Committees and tutor groups. However, students frequently avoid these formal systems, time slots available in office hours often remain without appointments or students simply fail to turn up to fulfil their appointments, preferring to catch us after lecturers or simply by knocking on our doors when it is convenient to them. 'I Know You're Busy But ...' often demonstrates the multiple demands on contemporary students (Cotterill and Waterhouse, 1998, p.14); whereas 'You're Never In ...' denies the multiple demands on contemporary academics (Barnes-Powell and Letherby, 1998).

Consultative Committees exist so that students from each course can meet with teaching staff and discuss common concerns, the aim being to offer an opportunity for working through any difficulties faced by student groups collectively. Increasingly, however, these are seen by students as an opportunity to make complaints. Recently a colleague in another university told us about a note that their second year student representatives posted on the notice board prior to a consultative meeting. This note literally asked for student 'complaints' that the representatives could take to the meeting. In this we are reminded of an acrimonious trade dispute.

Many universities pride themselves on their systems of student consultation. However, the election of student representatives is often a staff duty and in our own institution and elsewhere it becomes increasingly difficult to find volunteers to be reps, or for those elected to actually attend. Why we wonder? Several explanations are likely including the amount of coursework students have and the fact that they have to juggle this with other work and domestic responsibilities, and the nature of the process, i.e. school/faculty-wide meetings are often boring for students. Nonetheless, it is also a reflection of student apathy, and an indication of a reluctance towards the collective discussion and resolution of issues. Gone is the student activism and collectivism of the 1970s and 1980s (see for example Crowley, 1999). Perhaps this is not surprising for, as we have argued elsewhere:

> as the 'common cultural senses' of most of our students 'would have been constructed almost entirely within or against the dominant discourses of the New Right' (Epstein, 1995, p.59), what more can we expect from Thatcher's 'children' (Letherby and Marchbank, 1999a, p.179).

Student review and evaluation is a valid, vital and valued aspect of each teaching year. However, we see certain problems with existing systems. In many institutions each module, staff member and course/programme is assessed by the simple system of issuing students with a multitude of computer generated and read questionnaires. Like Clouder (1998) we have reservations as to the epistemological value of this feedback. If there is little epistemological merit in such evaluation why use it? Cynically, it could be argued that evaluation of this nature is used to satisfy a demand for 'value for money' and costs little except the anxiety and labour of staff members whilst keeping those same staff in constant check. As students are requested to rate us via ticking a series of boxes it can foster an atmosphere in which students think not that they are part of a system of review and development but of grading us – virtually sending out the message that what we do throughout the year is not teach but be involved in a year-long interview procedure. In addition, such a review procedure encourages students to be negatively critical and leaves staff having to justify their knowledge and teaching approach. Interestingly, in a recent article in the 'Agony Aunt' section of the *Times Higher Education Supplement* (7 January 2000) the question of how to encourage students to return such feedback forms when lecturers themselves are unsure of their relevance was raised. The three replies all focused on the importance of ensuring that students are given feedback on their feedback. There was also some advice on how to encourage students to be critical and some criticism of tick box questionnaires. From our perspective these replies ignore important political issues and although Brian Mitchell's, an Associate Dean at the University of Wolverhampton, reply starts with the sentence: 'Make sure that none of your staff sees student feedback as something that threatens or undermines their position' there is no advice as to how this is to be achieved. Indeed his second sentence implies that management believe that tutors and teachers are determined to remain unchallengable: 'Some members of staff are reluctant about giving students the right to a forum or any form of authority' (*THES*, 7 January 2000). There are other concerns regarding such assessment procedures, not least that they can be abused by an organised group of students who could cause problems for a staff member based not on ability but on politics or prejudice.

Politics, practice, and the feminist pedagogue

It is our experience that although institutions have been able to develop several support systems it appears that some students do not consider other, more skilled, pastoral services preferring to bring all their issues to their tutor. We are no doubt remiss in this area in the presentation of ourselves as approachable but we do feel at times that this approachability is abused both by students and our employers. We find that we cannot stop ourselves from feeling resentful when it seems that more students each day 'need to speak to us' whilst at the same time are given increasing opportunities to criticise amongst other things the support that we give. We have both been described – both verbally and on assessment questionnaires – as being 'never available' (which often means that we are busy attending to the requirements of other students) even though we feel that the amount of time we spend talking with or working for students (i.e. writing to Local Education Authorities and potential employers, talking to parents, negotiating extensions and special examination arrangements etc.) increases every term. The current systems then encourage students to be both offensive and dependent and leaves us no choice but to be defensive and to work over and above our professional capabilities just to get our jobs done without too much hassle (from both sides).

Recent educational history is relevant here. In 1992 the binary divide in British Higher Education was, in theory, abandoned with the abolition of the title 'polytechnic' and the granting of university status to these institutions. In practice, post-1992 universities are routinely referred to as 'new' as opposed to the 'old' universities. We are interested in differences between these two tiers and suspect (but acknowledge that our sources are anecdotal) that there is still more of a culture of 'independent learning' amongst students in the 'old' institutions.

Of course, there have always been students in trouble. One of us has several years experience in student welfare which informs this discussion. In the early and mid-1980s Jen was a student union officer in charge of developing student welfare services. In addition to employing a trained counsellor and welfare adviser, Jen was involved in developing what was to become a network of support systems. The idea was to create an integrated range of services so that no matter where a student sought support they would receive the service their particular problem required. The university and the student union between them devised networking and links that meant that the relevant professional within the union, health service, counsellors and the university could be accessed by all students. This was a system reliant on information exchange and a knowledge amongst all staff and volunteers of what services were available where.

As part of this Jen became very aware that pastoral care performed by academic staff was as unrewarded in the 1980s 'old' universities as in the 1990s 'new' universities. However, what appears to be different is the level of demand placed not on all the professional services but upon academic staff. It appears to us that what has changed is that institutions have increasingly developed support systems but that a concomitant change is an ideological change in the student body.

As undergraduates neither of us ever went to a member of academic staff with a personal problem. It was not that we did not have them, nor did the staff appear unapproachable, it just did not feel appropriate to talk about our personal concerns in this forum to people who could do nothing to help. By contrast we have each been approached by students with whom we have no academic nor course management contact because their friend, another member of staff or the security guard in our building has told them that we are 'nice'! We have also experienced students knocking on our door when we are displaying a 'do not disturb sign' to ask if that includes them, and had students barge into our offices without knocking, and been verbally threatened and abused within our offices for our 'failure' to be in when they wish to see us. It appears to us that we are in a situation whereby students have received messages that we are not only sympathetic to their problems but 'on tap' and that it is their right to demand that we solve their problems for them.

Increasing access has introduced new students to university, students not necessarily equipped with the social skills to survive. When this is coupled with academic difficulties, such as non-traditional educational profile and the other pressures upon them (e.g. in relation to work, family etc.) we could be viewed as setting students up to fail or raising unrealistic expectations. Students who come to us from situations of small groups with a large number of contact hours, either from school, college or access, can find university daunting not just academically but socially. Combine this with the increasing service culture attitude of 'I'm paying your wages' and we can end up in a situation of students expecting us not just to teach them but to ensure that they succeed. However, we would argue that many students have always juggled such a combination of issues and responsibilities and we wonder if what we are currently witnessing is an increase in individualism manifesting itself in a reluctance to deal with issues collectively, to provide peer support and an expectation that we as Course Tutors will provide a 'one stop service'. Indeed, this is supported by the systems established which condone and even encourage this kind of culture.

This sounds incredibly negative about students. Part of the problem is that the structures (of the institution) exclude support for the staff member except in the most minimal sense. However, both of us have experienced students offering us support particularly as part of a community of Women's Studies (both as lecturers and Jen as Course Tutor and Gayle as a Personal Tutor), an expression of their view that we are 'all in it together'. Specifically some talk to us about how they feel that others are rude and/or demanding and disrespectful and comment that they think that we perform beyond the 'call of duty'. Interestingly though these comments still take place within the monetary discourse as even the most supportive students express their right to a service. Student support of us was also evident when we conducted our 'Why do Women's Studies?' research – certain students made comments on their anonymous questionnaires which were political in their support of us.[5] These comments were critical not of us but of the restrictions upon Women's Studies and us imposed by the institution and the limits of resources. This is the positive angle of the encouragement we give to our students to be reflexive regarding their educational experience, sometimes reflection does not result in purely negative comments but in the development of an understanding that we too are human.

Dilemmas and 'solutions'

We have real concerns for the future generations of tutors and students in Higher Education and feel that unless these are recognised 'things can only get worse'. As many other writers in this area have argued stronger support networking is one of the ways to survive in Higher Education and clearly this is true for students as well as tutors (Gray, 1994; Marchbank, Corrin and Brodie, 1993). In addition, although this chapter demonstrates that power is not unidimensional (we do not accept the simplistic equation that staff are always those with power and students always those without) we do acknowledge that in an institutional context the balance of power remains with staff and not students and therefore, it is our role to seek solutions.[6]

Dever (1999), addressing the difficulties of feminist pedagogy within the current Higher Education climate, argues that it is possible to counter what she observes as a move back away from liberatory methods of teaching towards the 'banking' system denounced by Freire (1970).[7] She sees this retrograde drift as creating not only 'conservative notions of "knowledge transfer"', but also leading to student passivity, isolation and competition, perhaps another manner in which mass Higher Education negates collective approaches to student concerns and self responsibility (Dever, 1999, p.221). Dever goes on to argue that it is possible to overcome this trend:

> This means working to recover, retain or reinforce that sense of the political and politicised context of learning that was once so central an element on our programmes, but which have been displaced or diluted in recent years [...] One defining aspect of Women's Studies [...] could well be our renewed commitment to alternative understandings of the contract between teachers and students [...] to fostering a learning environment that enables them to locate themselves in history and to question the adequacy of that location both politically and pedagogically (Dever, 1999, p.221).

Although we respect the politics and intentions behind this statement we are skeptical that this can be achieved in the existing system as the dominant political legacies which we observe working through the individual and the system, coupled with feminist attempts to put politics into practice can leave us with students who believe that individual support from staff is theirs by right and not something that they can give and receive as part of a collective student group. In fact, Dever is not the first feminist to remind us that it is hard to be a feminist pedagogue, but what is needed is to just keep trying to 'relinquish our ties to traditional ways of teaching that reinforce domination' (hooks, 1989, p.52).

It is clear that in the decade between bell hooks' and Dever's encouragement to keep up the 'good fight', little has actually changed. Maintaining 'the cherished stereotype of the feminist classroom as a scene of perpetual collaborative bliss' does not permit us any room for change nor solutions (Schilb, 1985, p.256 cited by Coate Bignell, 1996, p.323). However, just as feminist theory and pedagogy have challenged the claims of others to be holding the 'truth', it is now time for us to question the nature of the role of feminist pedagogy in the increasingly bureaucratised and marketing driven world of Higher Education for, as Evans has pointed out, we cannot 'simply assume that we are unaffected by the changes currently taking place' (Evans, 1999, p.11).

As feminists we want our solutions to focus on the collective too, and, indeed, the support we get from each other, from like-minded colleagues (within and outside of our institution), and from some students is invaluable. Increasingly though this feels less like a solution and more like a sticking plaster. We do not want to shut ourselves off from the student population or to be so formal in our teaching and pastoral work that students are frightened to ask our assistance, yet neither do we want to join the increasing number of academics on long-term sick leave or-ill health retirement who are literally sick of the job.

Notes

[1] See for example: Woolf, 1977; Culley and Portugs, 1985; Rich, 1986, Lubelska, 1991; Coate-Bignell 1996; Bagilhole and Goode 1998.

[2] Although our focus is on gender, we appreciate the relevance of other differences e.g. sexuality, age, disability, ethnicity (see for example, Maguire, 1993; Marchbank, Corrin and Brodie, 1993; Bhopal, 1994; French, 1998).

[3] For example, the use of Freirian approaches in adult and community education.

[4] See: Cotterill and Waterhouse, 1998; Harris, Thiele and Currie, 1998; Bell and Gordon, 1999.

[5] A research project to investigate why students elect to study Women's Studies, their experiences as Women's Studies students and an exploration of the attitudes towards Women's Studies across one university and in comparison with other universitites.

[6] See: Barnes-Powell and Letherby, 1998; Letherby and Marchbank, 1999b.

[7] Freire (1970, p.46) stated in the 'banking model of teaching': 'Knowledge is a gift bestowed by those who consider themselves knowledgeable upon those whom they consider to know nothing'.

References

Bagilhole, B. (1994), 'Being Different is a Very Difficult Row To Hoe: Survival Strategies of Women Academics', in S. Davies *et al.* (eds) (1994).

Bagilhole, E. and J. Goode (1998), 'The "Gender Dimension" of both the "Narrow" and "Broad" Curriculum in UK Higher Education: Do Women Lose out in Both?', *Gender and Education*, 10 (4).

Barnes-Powell, T. and G. Letherby (1998), '"All in a Day's Work": Gendered Care Work in Higher Education', in D. Malina and S. Maslin Prothero (eds), *Surviving the Academy: Feminist Perspectives*, Falmer Press, London.

Bell, S. and J. Gordon (1999), 'Scholarship – the New Dimension to Equity Issues for Academics', *Women's Studies International Forum*, 22 (6).

Bhopal, K (1994), 'The Influence of Feminism on Black Women in the Higher Education Curriculum', in S. Davies *et al.* (eds) (1994).

Clouder, L. (1998), 'Getting the "Right Answers": Student Evaluation as a Reflection of Intellectual Development?', *Teaching in Higher Education*, 3 (2).

Coate-Bignell, K. (1996), 'Building Feminist Praxis out of Feminist Pedagogy: the Importance of Students' Perspectives', *Women's Studies International Forum*, 19 (3).

Cotterill, P. and R.L. Waterhouse (1998), 'Women in Higher Education: the Gap Between Corporate Rhetoric and the Reality of Experience', in D. Malina and S. Maslin Prothero (eds), *Surviving the Academy: Feminist Perspectives*, Falmer Press, London.

Court, S. (1996), 'Coping With Overload: The Use of Time by Academic and Related Staff in Universities in the UK and the USA', paper presented SRHE Annual Conference: Working in Higher Education, December.

Crowley, H. (1999), 'Women's Studies: Between a Rock and a Hard Place or Just Another Cell in the Beehive?', *Feminist Review*, 59.

Culley, M. and C. Portuges (eds) (1985), *Gendered Subjects*, Routledge and Kegan Paul, London.

Davies, S., C. Lubelska and J. Quinn (eds) (1994), *Changing the Subject: Women in Higher Education*, Taylor & Francis, London.

Dever, M. (1999), 'Notes on Feminist Pedagogy in the Brave New (Corporate) World', *European Journal of Women's Studies*, 6 (2).

Epstein, D. (1995), 'In our (New) Right Minds: the Hidden Curriculum in the Academy', in L. Morley and V. Walsh (eds) (1995).

Evans, M. (1997), *Introducing Contemporary Feminist Thought*, Polity Press, Cambridge.

_____ (1999), 'Feminist Pedagogy in the Uni-Business', *Women's Studies Network Newsletter*, 32.

Freire, P. (1970), *The Pedagogy of the Oppressed*, Penguin, London.

French, S. (1998), 'Surviving the Institution: Working as a Visually Disabled Lecturer in Higher Education', in D. Malina and S. Maslin Prothero (eds), *Surviving the Academy: Feminist Perspectives*, Falmer Press, London.

Gray, B. (1994), 'Women in Higher Education: What are we Doing to Ourselves', in S. Davies *et al.* (eds).

Harris, P., B. Thiele and J. Currie (1998), 'Success, Gender and Academic Voices. Consuming Passion or Selling the Soul', *Gender and Education*, 10 (2).

Letherby, G. and J. Marchbank (1999a), '"I Don't Want to be Empowered, Just Give Me a Reading Pack": Student Responses and Resistance to Different Forms of Teaching and Assessment', in M. Pearl and P. Singh (eds), *Equal Opportunities in the Curriculum*, Oxford Brookes University, Oxford.

_____ (1999b), 'Empowering and Enabling or Patronising and Pressurising?: Opening Dialogues with Marginalised Voices', paper delivered at Gender and Education International Conference, Warwick, April.

Letherby, G. and J. Shiels (forthcoming), 'Isn't He Good, but Can We Take Her Seriously?: Gender Expectations in Higher Education', in P. Anderson and J. Williams (eds), *Identity and Difference in Higher Education: Feminist Perspectives*, Ashgate Publishing, Aldershot.

Lubelska, C. (1991), 'Teaching Methods in Women's Studies: Challenging the Mainstream', in J. Aaron and S. Walby (eds), *Out of the Margins: Women's Studies in the Nineties*, Falmer Press, London.

Maguire, M. (1996), 'In the Prime of their Lives?: Older Women in Higher Education' in L. Morley and V. Walsh, *Breaking Boundaries: Women in Higher Eeducation*, Taylor & Francis, London.

Marchbank, J., C. Corrin and S. Brodie (1993), 'Inside and "Out" or Outside Academia: Lesbians Working in Scotland', in M. Kennedy, C. Lubelska and V. Walsh (eds), *Making Connections: Women's Studies, Women's Movements, Women's Lives*, Taylor & Francis, London.

Mills, C.W. (1959), *The Sociological Imagination*, Penguin, Harmondsworth.

Monk, A.S. and I.B. Robson (1999), 'The Increase of Psycho-social and Stress-Related Problems in UK Agricultural Colleges: The Wardens' Experience', *Journal of Further and Higher Education*, 23 (3).

Morley, L. (1993), 'Women's Studies as Empowerment of "Non-Traditional" Learners in Community and Youth Work Training', in M. Kennedy *et al.* (eds), *Making Connections: Women's Studies, Women's Movements, Women's Lives*, Taylor & Francis, London.

_____ (1995), 'Empowerment and the New Right', *Youth and Policy*, 51, Winter.

Morley, L. and V. Walsh (1995), *Feminist Academics: Creative Agents for Change*, Taylor & Francis, London.

_____ (1996), *Breaking Boundaries: Women in Higher Education*, Taylor & Francis, London.

Ribbens J. (1993), 'Facts or Fiction?: Aspects of the Use of Autobiographical Writing in Undergraduate Sociology', *Sociology*, 27 (1).

Rich, A. (1986), 'Towards a Women-Centred University', in A. Rich, *On Lies, Secrets, Silence: Selected Prose 1966-78* [1973], Virago, London.

Skeggs, B. (1995), 'Women's Studies in Britain in the 1990s: Entitlement Cultures and Institutional Constraints', *Women's Studies International Forum*, 18 (4).

Stanley, L. (1993), 'On auto/Biography in Sociology', *Sociology*, 27 (1).

Thorne, M. and R. Cuthbert (1996), 'Autonomy, Bureaucracy and Competition: the ABC of Control in Higher Education', in R. Cuthbert (ed.), *Working in Higher Education*, SRHE and Open University, Buckingham.

Times Higher Education Supplement (2000), 'Agony Aunt', January 7.

Walsh, V. (1996), 'Terms of Engagement: Pedagogy as a Healing Politic', in L. Morley and V. Walsh (eds) (1996).

Welch, P. (1994), 'Is a Feminist Pedagogy Possible?', in S. Davies *et al.* (eds) (1994).

Woolf, V. ([1938] 1977), *Three Guineas*, Penguin, Harmondsworth.

PART IV
ASSESSMENT AND EVALUATION

Chapter 12

Creative Risk-Taking: Feminist Pedagogy and Assessment Criteria

Zoë Bennett Moore

Introduction

This chapter seeks to examine the issues raised for feminist pedagogy by the need to deliver measurable and comparable assessment criteria for programmes in Higher Education. It does not propose new theory but is an exercise in reflection on the practice of implementing feminist pedagogical strategies which derive from established theoretical and practical principles.

I have recently taken up a newly-created post with Anglia Polytechnic University, as Director of Postgraduate Studies in Pastoral Theology. This post is offered in partnership with the Cambridge Theological Federation, a consortium of several institutions training people for ordained and lay ministry in various branches of the Christian church. My main teaching work is related to a taught MA in Pastoral Theology, a course with annual enrolment figures of around fifty. The student body comprises men and women from the ages of about twenty-five to seventy, lay and ordained, some of whom are in initial training for various forms of Christian ministry, others using the course as in service training. I am involved therefore in teaching mature students on a course with a strong vocational element.

Both the maturity of the students on the course (some experience of Christian ministry is a prerequisite for admission) and the way in which the subject matter is related to their vocation is important for the nature of the course teaching and assessment. Vocation here is meant not just in the sense of a job which must be done competently, but also in the deeper sense of a perceived calling which implicates the students' whole lives, beliefs and identity as persons. For those who take the optional 'Feminist Perspectives on Pastoral Theology' module both the maturity of experience and the sense of vocation give a particular edge and importance to the introduction of feminist topics and feminist processes of education. It is important to bear in mind that many branches of the Christian church have some significantly patriarchal beliefs and practices which will be part of the day to day experience of most participants on the course. For example, Bristol University's Department of Theology published research in March 2000 concerning women priests in the Church of England indicating that 'women priests are frequently the victims of bullying and intimidation from male clergy', that 'women were being denied senior posts within the Church' (women may not in principle be bishops in the Church of England at present; it appears they are also denied other positions in practice) and that 'female clergy found it harder to get jobs and were more likely to be working in unpaid positions'.[1] Exploring the theoretical and practical dimensions of such issues is important, and brings significant existential situations and emotions to the forefront of the learning experience.

'Feminist Perspectives on Pastoral Theology' has been part of the MA since its inception nearly five years ago. To put it in context, there has been both an undergraduate and a taught MA programme in Women's Studies at Anglia Polytechnic University (the validating university) for many years, but the Cambridge Theological Federation (the actual teaching context) has had less significant formal teaching of feminist or gender issues, and, with two of its other main awards validated by the University of Cambridge, is locked into a fairly traditional mode of education.

In this chapter I will specifically discuss issues raised by the assessment of the module 'Feminist Perspectives'. The module is delivered in twelve two-hour class sessions, with eight to fourteen students in the class group. Typical groups comprise both men and women, some of whom are completely new to feminist ideas and methods. It is, in my experience, perfectly possible to work with both men and women using the teaching styles and assessment methods of feminist pedagogy, although particular issues are raised for the men concerning how and in what ways their own experience is engaged. A truly feminist approach is best achieved if the men are willing to feel their complicity in patriarchy first and their own oppression second, entering into 'the moment of being accused' and thus grasping at a deep level 'the heart of feminist theology' (Bennett Moore, 1998, p.30).

We seek through classwork and reading to uncover both the problematic relationship between women and the Christian religion and the potential for good which comes from a feminist critique. Radford Ruether has expressed clearly the critical principle of feminist theology as 'the promotion of the full humanity of women' (1983, p.18). This, taken with the commitment of feminist theology to the priority of women's experience (Hogan, 1995, p.16), constitutes a challenge to traditional methods and priorities in theology which is further sharpened by the employment of feminist pedagogical methods. The values of holistic and emancipatory epistemology and pedagogical practices, as espoused by feminist theologians and educators, can strain to breaking point the relationship between our educational and our theological models unless the content and form of theology itself becomes problematised.[2]

The orientation therefore of the teaching and assessment of this module is both theoretical and practical. The main assessment takes the form of a project on the general subject of 'the body', which combines a feminist critique of its chosen aspect with a critique derived from the perspective of Pastoral Theology, and brings the two perspectives themselves into mutual critique and engagement. Students are encouraged to produce work in negotiated forms other than the traditional essay (further criteria for the assignment are given below). One general pedagogical principle and two principles of feminist pedagogy have particularly informed the way I have sought to structure the assessment of this module.

Pedagogic principles

Methods of assessment shape the nature of the learning process

The content and method of the assessment cannot be divorced from the content and method of the teaching of the module as a whole. A teaching style which maximises student involvement and choice of study, which seeks to uncover student experience and engage this with wider experiential and theoretical perspectives and which encourages students to theorise their own experience, needs to reflect these priorities and procedures in the assessment required. The assessment must 'stimulate deep engagement with the learning process', as Sally Brown of the ILT has recently articulated.[3]

Marton and Säljö's study of qualitative differences in learning describes surface-level learning and deep-level learning in relation to students' grasp of the content of the subject studied. Crucially they show that students often make a strategic choice of surface or deep-level learning according to the method of assessment with which they are required to engage:

> The present investigations suggest that students may need to refocus their attention on the underlying meaning of what they are required to study and that this process could be helped by ensuring that the assessment procedures demand deep-level processing (Marton and Säljö, 1976, p.125).

I strongly share the view that 'deep learning can be assessed imaginatively with a little care and thought' (Brockbank and McGill, 1998), and would widen the range of discussion from Marton and Säljö's concentration on the deep grasping of the content of the subject, as expressed primarily in texts, to include dimensions of particular interest to feminist pedagogy, namely subjectivity and affectivity.

Two features of the 'Feminist Perspectives' assessment are particularly important here: the negotiated element and the invitation to creativity and engagement of personal experience. The requirement to plan their work, to negotiate topic and title, is embraced with great enthusiasm by some students and regarded as a somewhat daunting nuisance by others. The control given over the student's own learning, reflected at the point of assessment, is important in the encouragement of deep learning. Freeman and Lewis contend that '[g]reater participation in assessment is likely to raise students' feelings of self-worth' (1998, p.55). While this is indeed my experience I would also introduce the *caveat* that some learners find the level of freedom and control given to them initially threatening, and a supportive learning environment is important. Within the 'Feminist Perspectives' module the encouragement of the exercise of subjectivity through negotiation of the assessment is itself part of an overall feminist pedagogical strategy. The raising of levels of self-worth is evidently an important strategy in feminist pedagogy, but is not achieved without an appropriately supportive learning context which includes the integration of the whole learning experience within the module with the assessment procedure.

With regard to the invitation to creativity and the engagement of personal experience, pedagogical strategies are disrupted if this is reflected only in the module teaching and not in the assessment, or indeed only in the assessment and not in the module teaching. The procedures expected in the assessment should flow naturally from those engaged with during the classes and learning between classes, as indeed *vice versa* the procedures expected in the assessment will condition those engaged with during the module itself. For example, the theorising of students' own experience is encouraged in class discussion (a short time is set aside at the beginning of each class in which participants are invited to share their thinking and reflection since the last class, during which time much theorising of personal experience is developed) and is further invited in the assessment. A striking example is a piece of work based on the content and methodology of Melanie May's *A Body Knows* in which a female student explored her experiences of abuse, of depression, of baptism and of menstruation.[4]

It is important to locate this discussion of the connections between methods of assessment and the learning process in the context of a significant ambiguity felt within feminist pedagogy. That specifically feminist pedagogical literature is in general not especially interested in the realm of assessment may derive from a certain ambiguity, which I share, concerning the value of the practice of assessment itself.[5] As Virginia Woolf so eloquently says in her discussion of the ideal college for women:

> [W]hat could be of greater help to a writer than to discuss the art of writing with people who were thinking not of examinations or degrees [...] but of the art itself [...] Let us then found this new college; this poor college; in which learning is sought for itself [...] and there are no degrees (1984, pp.144-5).

The ambiguity then immediately surfaces as she contemplates the need for women to have 'BA' after their name to compete on equal footing with men in the job market.

Content and method are inseparable in feminist pedagogy

In 1995 I conducted a piece of research in the Cambridge Theological Federation into why so few students opted for the only module then offered in feminist theology (this was one of two undergraduate modules dealing with feminist or gender issues at the time). A key issue which emerged from this research, almost as a by-product, was the strongly held view of a small number of women students that tinkering with the curriculum, whether by introducing 'ghetto' feminist courses or by injecting feminist content into mainstream courses, was trivial. To change content while leaving in place methods of teaching across the board which contradicted the feminist critique was worse than useless, a hypocrisy. We needed, one woman articulated fiercely, to dismantle the whole edifice of authoritarian lectures 'done from the power-base of the teacher and received by the students'. 'The content' she said, 'is fine-tuning; structures are the key issues'. This points to something even wider than teaching style, to the whole ethos of the academic environment. The challenges which are embedded in the content of the feminist curriculum spill out to the whole educational process. If, therefore, the discipline of Pastoral Theology is to be open to the challenge of feminist pedagogy, those who teach and learn Pastoral Theology must be open to 'a total intellectual revolution in the concepts, perspectives and methodologies of the subject' which include the questioning of theological assumptions (Robinson, 1993). 'A feminist approach to Christian education' writes Carol Lakey Hess, 'embraces the messiness and dirtiness of discerning what the Christian message and life mean at this time' (Hess, 1996), and this includes wrestling with our understandings of God and of what it means to be a human being made in God's image. Feminist pedagogy in Pastoral Theology should enable such wrestling through its curriculum content and through its methods of teaching and assessment, through questioning, problematising, story-telling, dialogue and through the engagement of the affective and creative dimensions of learning. In the light of the way in which methods of assessment shape the learning process it is clear that these challenges extend to means of assessment and the form of the assessment is fundamentally important.

Feminist pedagogy must engage the affective and creative faculties as well as the discursively rational faculties

The teaching of the module invites students to examine their attitudes, values, emotions and 'gut knowledge' ('what the body knows'). Engagement with the creative arts as well as with discursive theory is strongly encouraged as a means to conduct this examination, widening the imagination and the available epistemological strategies, or 'ways of knowing'. Pastoral Theology involves reflection on the practices of faith communities, and theological education itself is a practice, so there is a high level of reflexivity in the practice of studying Pastoral Theology. Rebecca Chopp has identified three key features of feminist practices in theological education – narrativity, community, and symbolic patterning, for which she uses the metaphors of quilting and weaving (Chopp, 1995). The use of story, of communal reflection, of the recognition of both otherness and provisionality, encourage responsiveness and attention to complexity. They also encourage the engagement of the self in the process of learning, a reflection on personal attitudes and values, emotions and histories.

In order to continue and reflect these processes of student engagement (choice, involvement, integration of personal experience, creative and imaginative exploration and expression) I give the opportunity for the main piece of assessment to be presented in alternative forms – either by way of traditional essay or by way of drama, creative writing, liturgy, artwork or music. I include a controversial requirement that any non-discursive submission of this latter kind be accompanied by a written commentary of some kind explaining the piece. Below are those criteria for the assignment which are relevant to this discussion:

- The subject matter of the project must be related to theme of 'The Body'.
- The project should demonstrate an understanding of a feminist approach or approaches to its subject matter.
- The project should demonstrate an understanding of an approach or approaches to its subject matter from the perspective of Christian Pastoral Theology.

- The feminist approach(es) and the approach(es) of Christian Pastoral Theology should be brought into dialogue and mutual critique.
- The form of the project is open to negotiation with the course tutor. You will be expected to submit a title, initial bibliography and plan for your project, in written form, after a tutorial in Week 9 of the module.
- The length of the project should be 4,000–6,000 words (not counting references, bibliography and appendices, but including footnotes) or a negotiated equivalent.
- It is expected that where material which might not be self-explanatory to the examiners is used (e.g. in artwork or liturgy) an accompanying commentary will make its principles explicit.

Many students have taken up these options. Their work has been in the main immensely rewarding to them – one student described the experience as 'life-changing' – and also to me, but in so doing they have brought to light some problems with this kind of assessment.

Problems arising

The discursive explanatory element

This requirement poses two problems, one at a practical level, the other at a theoretical epistemological level.

The practical level I will illustrate the practical level problem by an example. The first time I taught this module a male student proposed that he present a piece of artwork which examined the attitudes to female sexuality within the Christian tradition in the light of a feminist critique. He chose to paint an iconographic and erotic portrait of the Annunciation to the Virgin Mary, through which he would examine and critique Christian attitudes to sexuality and the body. His portrait strongly suggested a woman masturbating. The production of this work was intensely emotionally and intellectually demanding, and also more time-consuming than he had expected. He found himself unable to produce an explanatory commentary which rose above the banal, although his visual artwork was anything but banal. He was simply too exhausted by the creative work. The mark he received did not truly reflect his originality or hard work.

I have found through experience that students fare much better when required to keep a diary or log as they go along, explaining the decisions they take, the rationale behind their production, the processes of connection, as these happen. This taps into the energy and creativity and real thought processes unleashed by engagement in the assessment, and avoids the production of a tame and lifeless addendum, which feels redundant to the student. This strategy was used most successfully the following year by a female student whose work took the form of a liturgical piece, designed for her own use at the time of a sterilisation operation, which took place while she was studying on the module.

Another possible strategy for assessing such work is the *viva voce* examination. As a dialogue mode it is a suitable vehicle for the uncovering and making explicit of what might otherwise be implicit or merely not observed in the submitted work. In a context, however, of dialogical teaching methods such as I have outlined above, the line between teaching and assessing is hard to hold in a *viva*, and consequently a lively and creative exploration of the subject can ensue which actually gives the student an advantage in assessment over her or his peers. Issues of comparability must therefore be considered.

The epistemological level At an epistemological level the question can be raised, and has been raised by students on the module, whether works of art should require any explanation beyond what is already expressed by them in their own medium. Besides which, it is clearly naive to assume transparency of meaning in a discursive, explanatory piece. However, as I develop further below, it is important that work be presented in a form which can be read according to its own conventions of meaning-expression by an appropriately qualified person. In addition, discursive explanatory writing often serves the function of encouraging the student to a higher level of reflectiveness and the ability to articulate this.

The need for such discursive explanatory comment would seem to come from three factors: the need to have work presented in a medium and a discipline with which the assessor is familiar, the necessity to have comparability of work offered for the assessment of a module, and the importance of ensuring a critical and evaluative element in the student's work. A creative presentation can encourage an 'advocacy mode' more characterised by passion than by critique. These factors lead on to further problem areas which are brought to light by the use of this kind of assessment.

The implications for methodological sophistication on the part of the student and of the assessor

The student I return to the example of the Annunciation picture. To present such a picture in iconographic form demands an understanding of the functions and conventions of iconography. The student needed this to express his ideas with any degree of sophistication, and the assessor needed this to understand and evaluate the work. This raises an issue which it is easier to deal with at the student level than at the the assessor level. I make quite clear to my students that a) they should only operate in a medium with which they are familiar already (so, for example, a student with a drama degree chose to produce a dramatic piece on the subject of domestic abuse) and b) that they must make explicit in the accompanying commentary the significance of the form of what is presented as well as the significance of content. To use a colleague's words, 'they must instruct the assessor regarding the artistic language they are using'. Within a full Women's Studies programme, as indeed currently is the case at Anglia Polytechnic University, students might expect training in a variety of methodologies and in interdisciplinarity, but even on a more modest single module such as *Feminist*

Perspectives I see no reason why an appropriately boundaried diversity, based on previously acquired skills and understanding, should not be encouraged.

The assessor But what of the assessor? She or he must grasp this 'artistic language' in order to make an appropriate assessment both of this piece of work in its own right, and of its place – its ranking – among the other work submitted. The assessor must have some means of ensuring comparability within the assessments, both within this module and within the whole award. This requires generalisable criteria for the assignment, applicable to and measurable within each diverse piece of work submitted, as well as requiring the assessor to be able to judge whether those criteria have been met within a given piece of work in a given genre. It has become clear to me that here is a prime case for collaboration amongst academics and for interdisciplinary cooperation. As a tutor of Pastoral Theology I cannot range into this kind of assessment unless I am willing to learn from and collaborate with not only tutors in Liturgy and other branches of theology, but also my colleagues in Art and Design, in Drama, in English studies and so on.

The implications for the tutor–student relationship

To invite students to produce work which engages their intimate self in a creative production is a risky business. It may unleash emotional and intellectual questioning, responses and even crises for which the tutor must accept some responsibility. Questions inevitably arise about the appropriateness of assessing such work, which become sharper if the tutor is also a marker. You can feel you are judging a person's inmost thoughts and concerns. The student who painted the Annunciation picture (some four years ago) told me on the telephone recently that it still 'haunts' him. Issues were raised for him about his role as a man in painting this, the reaction of friends who found it pornographic, the sense in which the painting had taken him over. Within this assignment concerning the body within a feminist pastoral theological perspective there has been some brave work. I have already mentioned the liturgy for women going through sterilisation, the drama about domestic abuse, the reflection on personal history and theology through body-knowledge. In all these cases students dared to face, reflect on and theorise their own experience in the context of what they were learning on the module. Another woman explored illness through her own experience of glandular fever. A gay man wrote a liturgy for the childless; a man who had recently become a father wrote a short story about hospitalisation and childbirth. The position of the men in this is controversial, as they felt acutely. They were upheld methodologically by the focus of the module on the interrelatedness of all forms of oppression, and ideologically by the commitment of the group to an ultimate vision of the affirmation of the shared humanity of all people.

My point is that such a participatory and holistic quest for the construction of knowledge, with such personal engagement on the part of the students, requires a particular kind of support from the tutor. Gill-Austern (1999) suggest five metaphors for the feminist teacher – the midwife, voice coach, storyteller and evoker of stories, contemplative artist, and reticent outlaw. These emphasise the supportive enabling, the creative stimulus, and the sustained attention which the tutor need to provide in a context such as the 'Feminist Perspectives' module. Moreover, the modelling of appropriately caring practices of professional relationship can be in itself an important aspect of pedagogy.

> These metaphors [...] evoke imagination for transformative possibilities in teaching that have an impact on students' self-understanding as they enter ministries of care in and beyond the church (Gill-Austern, 1999, p.151).

The need for support is particularly important where assessment is involved. This is not only because assessment of itself raises most students' anxiety levels, but also because, in a piece presented for assessment in an academic course, analysis and critical evaluation is expected. Analysis and critical evaluation demand a certain kind of detachment, which somehow has to be held in tension with the holistic involvement and personal commitment. In my experience tutors need to do the follow things:

Set firm boundaries and clear assessment criteria As mentioned, I give students a list of some ten criteria, against which their work will be judged.

Give support in choosing topic and method Freedom can bring either fear or a rash lack of sophistication. Clear support in structured discussion can overcome these problems.

Prevent uncontrolled engagement with the material This can be done by discussing work as it goes along and advising students clearly to avoid the topic or to restructure when there is a serious danger that that they are too engaged with the personal level of their material to be able to exercise critical judgement on it.

Be sensitive to the emotional dimension of the student's work Opportunity should be given to explore this with the tutor in so far as it relates to the assignment. Referral to someone else to talk through issues beyond our brief may be necessary.

Enable the student to exercise critical evaluation without 'betraying' their commitments A colleague recently expressed to me the difficulty of enabling a student to find that space for critical evaluation. The student was writing about something very important to her own life as a nun – '[she] is still at the love affair stage', my colleague said, 'critical evaluation in that situation is akin to treachery'. This relates to the question raised above concerning the 'advocacy mode', from which a student may be unable to get any critical distance. It is, however, not only a question of the personal nature of the material, but also a question of the nature of the intellectual discipline. The feminist perspective is in itself an 'advocacy perspective' with political and ideological commitments; this is clearly true in theology where feminist theology is seen as an advocacy theology, promoting the full humanity of women. Where appropriate we should at least encourage some reflexive comment, justifying the advocacy perspective. My final 'problem arising' concerns political and systemic matters.

The politics of gaining acceptance for such modes of assessment

The students   The key issue here for me is the necessity to protect students from being penalised by my interest in exploring feminist methodology. We have a responsibility to watch our students' backs for them in relation to the assessment process and its externally driven criteria and ethos. In a traditionally discursive subject such as theology assessment through the presentation of creative material has not been the norm. It is experimental and not by any means universally accepted. It is important not to use students as 'guinea pigs' or to sacrifice them on the altar of our ideological commitment to feminist practices.

The local educational establishment   The Cambridge Theological Federation offers awards via several different validating authorities, including Cambridge University and Anglia Polytechnic University. We also need our programmes to be validated by various denominational church authorities as approved courses leading to ordination for Christian ministry, since many students are ordinands. Each of these brings their own type of pressure to bear and has their own agenda about what theology and the assessment of theology should be about (I am not convinced that 'Benchmarking' will make much difference to this). The hard grind of justifying methods to colleagues and the necessity for a proper accountability for what is done in teaching and assessment is an ever present reality. The fact that different constituencies need different kinds of justification on different kinds of grounds should perhaps be welcomed as an invitation to multifaceted reflexivity (although it is sometimes more like a millstone round one's neck!).

The external assessor   I have found that a key person is the External Assessor, whose role locates him or her between the validating authorities and the teaching institution. Moreover, he or she is a representative of the wider community of scholarship in the subject area, whose opinions are highly rated by the Quality Assurance Agency. When I wrote my assessment criteria for 'Feminist Perspectives' I asked our then External Assessor for comment in advance, with the intention of forestalling criticism and protecting the students. He was in fact immensely encouraging, and has been able to make constructive criticism as the experiment has gone along from a position of understanding and acceptance. Because he was consulted from the beginning we have been able to tackle problems and difficulties in the appropriate assessment of work from the module from a basis of mutual understanding and commitment, even where our opinions have differed.

Developments in educational research and policy   The new emphasis on innovative methods of learning and teaching, which in itself commands different levels of assent in different institutions, and in departments within those institutions, is nevertheless a key issue in the current public agenda of Higher Education, and one which has a bearing on assessment. It is increasingly widely recognised that not only must assessment genuinely test the stated learning outcomes of a programme, but the form and method of assessment must be consonant with the form, method and values of the teaching and learning, since methods of assessment themselves shape learning. I hope that the energy and the public profile of the new Institute for Learning and Teaching will be an asset in attempts to reflect feminist pedagogy within forms of assessment.

Conclusion

I have sought to illustrate, through the examination of a specific MA module 'Feminist Perspectives on Pastoral Theology', how the principles of the coherence of learning and assessment and of content and method, together with a commitment to the engagement of the creative and affective faculties in learning, might be worked out in practice through a specific form of assessment at Masters level. I hope I have illustrated the immense fruitfulness of such an approach, as well as highlighting implications and problems, and offering some hints towards solutions.

Risk-taking which is responsible risk-taking is an important and necessary component of feminist pedagogy. Assessment is an area in which feminist pedagogy has not always taken a significant interest, except perhaps as regards issues of equal opportunities. Given the ubiquity of assessment in Higher Education, and the strong value put on it in contemporary society, it seems to me that those committed to feminist pedagogy should take a hand in shaping assessments which reflect the holistic and emancipatory values and practices to which we are committed. There is a need for argument and for advocacy of feminist pedagogical methods at all levels in respect of all educational practices, including assessment. And there is a need for transformative practice. I have a colleague with whom I am continually in dialogue concerning the merits of various teaching methods – and we have come to the conclusion that what he calls dangerous I call creative. Creativity is always risky, even dangerous, but without it pedagogy is infinitely the poorer and feminist pedagogy is impossible.

Notes

[1] *Daily Telegraph*, 7 March 2000.
[2] Bennett Moore, 1997-8. See also Hull, 1991, which examines specific problems of education in an ideological community like the church.
[3] *Times Higher Educational Supplement*, 29 October 1999.
[4] May 1995.
[5] See: Acker and Piper, 1984; Belenky *et al.*, 1986; Code, 1991; hooks, 1994; Chopp, 1995.

References

Acker, S. and D.W. Piper (eds) (1984), *Is Higher Education Fair to Women?* SRHE/NFER, Nelson, Guildford.

Belenky, M.F., B.M. Clinchy, N.R. Goldberger and J.M. Tarule (1986), *Women's Ways of Knowing: The Development of Self, Voice and Mind*, Basic Books, New York.

Bennett Moore, Z.E. (1997-8), 'On Copy Clerks, Transformers and Spiders', *British Journal of Theological Education*, 9 (3).

_____ (1998), 'A Midrash', *Feminist Theology*, 18.

Brockbank, A. and I. McGill (1998), *Facilitating Reflective Learning in Higher Education*, SRHE and Open University Press, Buckingham.

Chopp, R. (1995), *Saving Work: Feminist Practices in Theological Education*, John Knox Press, Westminster.

Code, L. (1991), *What Can She Know? Feminist Theory and the Construction of Knowledge*, Cornell University Press, Ithaca.

Freeman, R. and R. Lewis (1998), *Planning and Implementing Assessment*, Kogan Page, London.

Gill-Austern, B.L. (1999), 'Pedagogy under the Influence of Feminism and Womanism', in B.J. Miller-McLemore and B.L. Gill-Austern (eds), *Feminist and Womanist Pastoral Theology*, Abingdon Press, Nashville.

Hess, C.L. (1996), 'Education as an Art of Getting Dirty with Dignity', in C.C. Neuger (ed.), *The Arts of Ministry: Feminist-Womanist Approaches*, John Knox Press, Westminster.

Hogan, L. (1995). *From Women's Experience to Feminist Theology*, Sheffield Academic Press, Sheffield.

hooks, b. (1994), *Teaching to Transgress*, Routledge, New York.

Hull, J.M. (1991), *What Prevents Adult Christians from Learning*, Trinity Press International, Philadelphia.

Marton, F. and R. Säljös (1976), 'On Qualitative Differences in Learning: I – Outcome and Process; II–Outcome as a Function of the Learner's Conception of the Task', in *British Journal of Educational Psychology*, 46.

May, M. (1995), *A Body Knows: A Theopoetics of Death and Resurrection*, Continuum, New York.

Radford Ruether, R. (1983), *Sexism and God-talk*, SCM Press, London.

Robinson, V. (1993), 'Introducing Women's Studies', in D. Richardson and V. Robinson (eds), *Introducing Women's Studies*, Macmillan, Basingstoke.

Woolf, V. (1984), *Three Guineas* [1938], Chatto & Windus, London.

Chapter 13

Gendered Patterns in Writing and Degree Award

Becky Francis, Jocelyn Robson and Barbara Read

Introduction

There has recently been an increase in attention paid to issues of gender and achievement in the compulsory education sector. But less regard has been paid to issues of gender and achievement in the post-compulsory sector. However, student achievement at undergraduate level in Britain continues to show differentiation according to gender, despite the increased use of blind-marking in examinations adopted to counter discrimination. Some researchers have argued that such differences in achievement might be explained by the different writing styles adopted by male and female students. In relation to arguments raised elsewhere in this book, the notion that various writing styles are valued differently brings us back to the point that judgements, here relating to assessment, are not gender neutral. This chapter outlines the main arguments in the area of gender and undergraduate writing styles. It explores Francis's (1998) hypothesis that a bold and assertive style, more readily available to males, can be particularly rewarded and penalised in undergraduate writing, and it uses data from a study of undergraduate students' writing to test this theory.

Gender and undergraduate achievement

Over recent years, growing numbers of women have been participating in Higher Education, and indeed women undergraduate students now slightly outnumber men (Rees, 1999). Yet despite this shift in the gender make-up of the undergraduate student population, discrepancies in undergraduate achievement remain evident in the class of degree awarded to students. Of course, achievement is by no means the only area where gender differences are evident in Higher Education. Academic positions – especially prestigious ones – remain dominated by men (David and Woodward, 1998). Women students continue to be concentrated in the humanities, and males in science and engineering (Sutherland, 1994; Arnot et al., 1999). However, it is the issue of gender and achievement which we focus on in this chapter.

Men continue to be awarded more first class degrees than do women, although recent Higher Education Statistics Agency figures suggest a slight closing of this gender gap. As we report elsewhere (Francis *et al.*, forthcoming), there has been extensive research into this aspect of the pattern in gender and achievement. Many studies have sought to explain the reasons why more men than women achieve first class degrees. However, far less attention has been paid to the pattern at the other end of the achievement scale. Although more men achieve first class degrees, more men than women also perform poorly at undergraduate level. Table 13.1 shows the total UK figures.

Table 13.1 Class of first degree by gender: all UK universities, 1997/8

	First Class	Upper Second	Lower Second	Third Class/ Pass Without Honours	Unclassified Degrees	Total First Class
Female	9,395	62,687	46,189	8,152	9,023	136,503
Male	10,077	45,901	44,052	13,053	9,135	122,290

Source: HESA, 1999

Table 13.1 shows that despite women gaining slightly fewer first class degrees, they are actually awarded a greater proportion of 'good' first degrees (an upper second or first class honours award) than are men. That men more frequently gain first class honours degrees does have important implications. A first class degree is often required for postgraduate study, and consequently more men may have the opportunity to take up postgraduate studentships. However, the greater numbers of women than men gaining 'upper-second' awards are also significant. It is becoming increasingly common for employers of graduates in the UK to require that candidates possess a 'good' first degree. Those with first class degrees hold an advantage here. However, if the figures for first class and upper second class degrees in Table 13.1 are added together we can see that in 1998 more women achieved 'good' degrees than men did (over 72,000 women achieved 'good' degrees, compared to only 56,000 men). This, coupled with the point that fewer men than women achieve 'respectable' grades, demonstrates that the issue of gender and undergraduate achievement is one which affects both genders, rather than simply being a case of 'female disadvantage'.

Factors other than simple ability are at play here. For example, the subject studied at undergraduate level has a potential impact on grades awarded. It has been observed that because there are fewer 'right or wrong' answers in the humanities than in the sciences, there is a slimmer chance for humanities students to gain first class degrees than for science students (MacNabb *et al.*, forthcoming). As there are greater proportions of males studying science subjects, and females studying humanities subjects, it is argued that males are automatically advantaged in terms of the award of first class degrees (McNabb *et al.*, forthcoming). Yet the gendered trend in undergraduate achievement remains broadly consistent even within the humanities and social sciences. Concerns over discrimination at assessment have led to an increase in the practice of 'blind marking', where names are removed from students' work so that examiners do not know the student's gender or ethnicity. Because the majority of work submitted for final examinations is now 'blind marked', it tends to be assumed that the gendered pattern in achievement cannot be directly linked to overt gender discrimination in assessment. (Although it should be observed that some research has suggested that it remains possible to discern a student's gender through their handwriting and style; e.g. Keroes, 1990.)

Gender and undergraduate writing

There are a number of different possible explanations for the continuing existence of the gender discrepancy in undergraduate achievement, despite the practice of blind marking. One possibility is that male and female students have inherently different levels of ability. In the spirit of reflexivity concerning our own ideological positions in research (Weiner, 1994), the writers admit that as feminists who believe that gender differences are socially constructed, this essentialist hypothesis is not a line of inquiry that we would wish to pursue. It is also the case that there is no conclusive evidence of such inherent difference. Moreover, the concentration of men at both the top and bottom ends of the undergraduate awards refutes such essentialist arguments. An alternative explanation is that students write differently according to gender – and that gendered criteria are applied to students' writing. It is this possibility that our study has sought to investigate.

The notion that writing differs depending on the gender of the author is not new. 'Difference' feminists such as Hélène Cixous (e.g. 1990) have argued that men and women 'write the body', their writing style reflecting their (different) physical beings. Such perspectives can tie differences in writing to inherent, biological differences between the sexes. However, gendered writing styles have also been explored from social constructionist and social learning perspectives. Lakoff (1973) investigated women's speech patterns, maintaining that women's marginalised position in society is reflected in their less assertive 'women's language' (the characteristics of which include a greater number of 'hedges' and qualifiers, illustrating a lack of confidence). Later researchers argued that such features were not only characteristic of women's speech, but also of other disempowered groups: Lakoff herself came to endorse this view, maintaining that this style marked 'powerless' speech. This theory has been applied to undergraduate writing by a number of researchers examining gender difference (e.g. Keroes, 1990; Rubin and Greene, 1992). Moreover, such approaches are supported by arguments that a lack of confidence evident in female undergraduate writing causes their work to be awarded lower marks than their male counterparts (e.g. Martin, 1997).

It is a non-essentialist approach to the topic of gender and undergraduate writing which is pursued here. The research of Davies (1989; 1993) and Francis (1998b; 000) shows how children come to understand the world as gendered according to a relational binary code, or 'gender duality', as Davies terms it. Understanding that gender is central to a successful social persona, children (and adults) draw on gendered traits in order to delineate their gender identity. 'Masculine' characteristics such as bold assertion are in opposition to a construction of femininity which many women and girls take up as integral to their sense of identity (Francis, 1998b; 2000). Hence it would be no surprise if such gender constructions impacted on writing, reflecting the author's gender identity.

The gender dichotomy also underpins academic culture, and consequently impacts upon decisions about which kinds of knowledge, and approaches to knowledge, are considered academically worthwhile (Harding, 1990; 1991). A number of researchers have argued that the accepted academic writing style is assertive, self-confident and bold (Ainley, 1994; Martin, 1997); traits constructed as masculine. Hence Martin (1997) asserts that university marking criteria reflect gendered values, favouring masculine characteristics such as charisma, self-confidence, detachment, risk, and challenge in the award of first class grades. Researchers such as Clarke *et al.* (1994), Spurling (1990), and Martin (1997), have concluded that many female students are too cautious or timid in approach to adopt such an assertive style. Farrell (1979) maintains men are more antagonistic in their rhetoric, whereas women tend to avoid antagonism. Taylor (1978) found that female college students' work tended to be criticised for being insufficiently argumentative. Farrell (1979) and Roen and Johnson (1992) have consequently suggested that men's mode of writing may be more compatible with an academic style. Hence constructions of gender apparently place male students at an advantage regarding academic achievement.

However, the body of work which maintains that men are advantaged by a bolder writing style does not explore or explain why more men also gain third class and unclassified degrees. Clearly this apparently bolder approach among male students is not preventing comparatively high numbers from performing poorly. Francis (1998a) considered this problem, suggesting that the explanation might centre on other conventions of academic writing, as well as 'boldness'. For example, 'boldness' is only one facet of a first class writing style: the writing must also be lucid, considered, and carefully supported with references. Indeed, we would argue that without these features, a bold argument is likely to be penalised particularly heavily. Hence Francis (1998a) hypothesised that perhaps males who write boldly, but also articulately, fluently, and with references to support their argument, are likely to be awarded high grades. But conversely, men that write boldly but non-lucidly, or without any evidence to support their claims, might be awarded a particularly low mark.

Certainly, the findings of some studies lend credence to the suggestion that the delineation of traits such as consideration, diligence and self-consciousness as feminine (see Walkerdine, 1990), might to some extent aid women in their undergraduate writing. Flynn (1988) argues that women's writing tends to be affiliative rather than competitive or objectifying, and Rubin and Greene (1992) observe that this approach could make women's writing less confrontational and more open to the viability of other perspectives. They found that women are twice as likely to acknowledge other positions and view-points in their writing than are men. Obviously consideration and evaluation of other viewpoints is integral to academic writing.

The following discussion reports findings from a study which analysed students' writing according to gender and writing style. We shall discuss the extent to which our findings supported or challenged Francis' (1998a) suggestion that male students write more 'boldly' than do female students, and that in terms of achievement this bold style can be advantageous when it is successfully coupled with other conventions of academic writing, but damaging when it is not.

The study

The data discussed here is drawn from a study which examined undergraduate writing according to gender. The methods involved an analysis of essays written by undergraduate final year History students, and semi-structured interviews with students about their writing style and approach. Participants were drawn from History departments at four different London universities (including two post-1992 and two long-established universities). History was chosen as the discipline within which to examine students' writing, because similar proportions of men and women are represented on History courses. We examined one piece of work each from eighty-seven students. These pieces of work were all submitted as part of the students' final examinations, and were between 2,500 and 10,000 words in length. Unfortunately, few departments were willing to grant us access to students and their work, which resulted in the involvement of a far lower number of respondents than we had hoped for. The relatively small number of respondents gave rise to problems for our analysis, because of the small numbers in our sample achieving different grades: for example, only five men and three women achieved first class grades for their writing. This meant that in terms of a gender analysis, the numbers of students being compared within different grade bands was sometimes extremely small (especially at the extreme ends of the scale), and this made it difficult to generalise about gender and achievement.

Essays were analysed in terms of writing style (see Roen and Johnson, 1992). As we sought to analyse the tone or style of the work, we analysed each sentence, rather than word, categorising the sentences according to particular characteristics which have been traditionally gendered (Keroes, 1990; Lynch and Strauss-Noll, 1987). Our categories were: 'bold', 'tentative', and 'evaluative'. The categories 'bold' and 'tentative' were both divided into two levels. So, for example, statements which were assertive and unreferenced, but apparently reasonable, were categorised as bold; while statements which were aggressive, dismissive, or made outrageous claims were categorised as 'very bold'. Statements which were supported by references were not included in this analysis, as we sought to examine the instances where students brought their own argument, or 'something of themselves' into the essay.

Following our analysis of the written work, the respondents were then contacted and invited to take part in a telephone interview. Forty-five students agreed (eighteen men and twenty-seven women), and responded to a semi-structured interview which asked them about their writing styles and essay preparation. For a fuller discussion of our methodology, see Francis *et al.* (forthcoming).

Table 13.2 Examples of categories for 'gendered' writing styles

Category	Definition	Example Sentences
Bold 1	A rash statement; sentences which are not referenced, which are strongly stated, confront arguments head on, are powerful and direct statements of author's own opinion/view, clear over-statements, those which refute reservations and which may be characterised by their lack of qualifiers, lack of corroborative evidence, and/or use of superlatives/intensifiers and/or use of first person pronouns.	'Craddock also believed that many Africans in East and Central Africa were ridden [sic] with disease, and he gave other misinformed arguments about African people that in my opinion he knew nothing about.' 'There can be absolutely no doubt that Powell not only talks of difference but constructs it as well. Cosgrove completely fails to consider this.'
Bold 2	Sentences which are less bold but which are not referenced and which are clear assertions of viewpoint, draw explicit conclusions, follow a linear line of argument, state facts without qualifiers or superlatives; claims which build on work referenced elsewhere in the essay.	'There is no doubt that the political, and also economic situation of the Zulu people throughout this period had a strong influence [on] the writing of their history.' 'It is useful to remember that the Vietnam war was not fought for its own sake.'
Tentative 1	Sentences which are extremely tentative, hesitant admit to explicit reservations/ inadequacy of own point of view (e.g. 'I have attempted to show that ... '), which express extreme caution and tentativeness in phrases such as 'it is possible that ... ', or which combine two or more qualifiers (e.g. 'perhaps it could be seen that ... ').	'Powell in many ways gives a possibly more honest critique of liberal democratic states.'
Tentative 2	Sentences which are less tentative but still qualified (e.g. by using phrases such as 'appear to' 'can suggest' 'it could be argued that', 'may', 'there is evidence that' etc.)	'Britain did seem to suffer from its own race crisis because of the Suez crisis.' 'In this essay I will look at the way in which the book is written as well as trying to find out whether the book can be useful in understanding the struggle the natives of South Africa faced.'

Category	Definition	Example Sentences
Evaluative	Sentences which balance arguments, parts of arguments or points of view against each other, acknowledge alternatives and legitimacy of opposing views, have parallelism, acknowledge possibility, and which may be characterised by such phrases as 'on the one hand … on the other hand', 'alternatively', etc.	'Cuppers is of the opinion that Trier went into a catastrophic decline, whilst Wightman argues that there was no complete disruption in the town life to mark the end of Roman rule.'
Tentative + Bold	Sentences which combine manifest assertion of own opinion/new avenue of thought with a tentative phrase which does not successfully negate this boldness.	'I think in this period it is possible to see a revival of traditional conservative values, as you can see with attempts in 1959 to revive and reinforce obscure obscenity laws.' (B2 + T1)
		'Perhaps most convincing is the Reccon approach.' (B2 + T2)

The extent of difference in writing style according to gender

On analysis of the essays, the most noticeable point was that males' and females' essays were far more similar than they were different. This applied particularly to the categories which we had termed 'evaluative' (recognising and weighing up different arguments), and 'very tentative' (extremely cautious or nervous sentences containing repeated qualifiers or hedges): the male and female students' numerical use of these features was virtually identical. According to the literature (e.g. Lakoff, 1973; Rubin and Greene, 1992), both these categories would be expected to be used more frequently by women students. Of course, our study is limited by the relatively small number of respondents – perhaps a larger study would have found more gender – traditional results. Yet the almost identical use of evaluative and tentative sentences between male and female students was striking.

Our findings may illustrate an equal understanding of academic conventions by male and female students. Some previous studies in Higher Education which have focused upon women students' less assertive writing style appear to ignore other features of academic writing – some of which could be seen as traditionally feminine. Lakoff (1973) observed that certain features associated with women's speech – especially hedges – are characteristic of academic talk, for men as well as women. This is because of the cautious, evaluative approach adopted in academic discourse, arguably to present the speaker as 'objective' and her/his argument as a considered one. Rationality and 'objectivity' are prized in academia at the expense of emotion and subjectivity (Harding, 1990). The tentative style of academic speech and writing serves to present the speaker/writer as objective and considered, rather than as unassertive. Hence men's equal use of a tentative style may be due to their understanding of the requirements of academic convention. But it might have been assumed that as a tentative, cautious style is in opposition to dominant constructions of masculinity, this style would have been more difficult for men to adopt.

However, our analysis of students' writing did support the notion that more men than women tend to adopt a bold, assertive style of writing – although the difference in use of a bold style according to gender was not dramatic. Gender difference was particularly evident in students' use of a 'very bold' style; but there were relatively few instances of use of this style. Ninety-four 'very bold' sentences were found in male essays (125.4 after adjustments for essay length and gender parity), and seventy-four 'very bold' sentences were found in women's essays (89.2 after adjustments). Of the various categories that we analysed, the more mild version of 'bold' was the style adopted by far the most frequently in students' essays: there were 1590 counts of 'bold' sentences in male essays (averaging 41.9 sentences per essay by male students, after adjustments for essay length and gender parity); and 1607 counts of 'bold' sentences in female essays (averaging 37.8 sentences per essay after adjustments).

Clearly, this only constitutes a slight difference in the use of a 'bold' style according to gender. The most important point in our findings concerning the use of a 'bold', assertive style is that male *and* female students adopted this as the dominant approach in their academic writing, showing an understanding of academic convention. In their interviews, an identical proportion of male and female students argued that 'putting forward your own ideas' is what they believe examiners are looking for in a first class essay. On the other hand, not all these students claimed to adopt such an approach. Half of the male interview respondents claimed to adopt a bold or assertive approach in their writing, compared to only a third of female respondents (though again, the numbers concerned are small). So our findings here also support Rubin and Greene's (1992) argument that while students' writing bears far more similarities than differences according to gender, some areas of marginal difference support traditional gender constructions. As we have observed, researchers such as Spurling (1990), Clark *et al*. (1994) and Martin (1997) have claimed that men are more able to adopt the assertive, self-confident style necessary for academic writing (particularly for first class undergraduate writing). Our finding that men students used a 'bold' style slightly more often than women lends some support to this argument.

'Bold' writing, and achievement

In fact, frequent use of a 'bold' or 'very bold' style in students' essays by no means guaranteed a high grade. In our sample, three women and five men had achieved first class grades for the essays which we analysed (two of these women, and three of the men, went on to achieve first class degree awards). The female students in our sample who were awarded first class grades for their writing used fewer than half the number of 'bold' and 'very bold' sentences than did their five male counterparts. Indeed, these women's essays were characterised by an extremely low use of any of our stylistic categories, reflecting the way that the writing tended to be either essentially factual or conscientiously supported by references. The implication is that these women were awarded first class grades despite, or perhaps even because, they brought little of 'themselves' to their essay. This is interesting in light of the findings of Keroes (1990) and Taylor (1978), who argue that women's writing is characterised by a focus on the personal. Therefore, this removal of oneself from the writing could be expected to be particularly difficult for women to achieve.

There was some evidence that the more 'bold' and 'very bold' sentences that were used in an essay, the more the grade awarded decreased. This pattern was not consistent: for example, the male students awarded first class grades used a relatively large number of 'bold' and 'very bold' statements. (But again, we are only talking about five students here – in fact one of these students used 'very bold' statements more often than the other four put together, illustrating how easily the figures can be skewed when such small numbers are involved.) But as a general tendency, the use of 'bold', and particularly 'very bold' statements increased as the level of grade awarded decreased. Of course, many other factors besides style must be taken into consideration in the assessment of an essay. When considering undergraduate writing according to gender, it is important to remember that students are attempting to perform a particular type of writing. As Ballard and Clancy (1988) observe, part of the assessment of undergraduate writing is an evaluation of the extent to which students have produced competent writing and successfully adopted an academic style – and as we have argued above, this style is both considered and assertive.

But this finding does lend some support to the notion that the patterns in gender and achievement might be explained by the differing abilities of male students to use their bolder style competently within an academic framework. Students that present an assertive argument in a well-reasoned manner may be rewarded particularly highly, given the value placed on assertive argument in the academy (Bourdieu and Passeron, 1977; Spurling, 1990; Martin, 1997). But those who make bold claims with no clear rationale or supporting evidence may be penalised particularly heavily, because of their transgression of academic convention. The implication of this argument is that it is not the use of a bold, assertive style which guarantees a high grade, but rather the ability to adapt that style to fit academic convention.

A number of the students themselves suggested that the greater number of men gaining first class degrees could be explained by their greater use of assertion in their writing. When asked in their interviews to speculate on possible reasons for the gendered pattern in achievement at undergraduate level, four male and five female students suggested that men are bolder in expressing their opinions. For example, Sean argued that women are less ready to 'go out on a limb' in their written work than men. Hannah talked about the self-confident, bold approach of men in her seminar groups. She explained, 'some of the men would just come out with things that were totally off the wall {laughs} and I think they probably did that in their essays, they're not so cautious [...] they're braver'. Likewise, Fatima argued that men tend to be more confident and assertive. She also raised the issue of the impact of social class, saying of the male students from private schools on her course, 'They do seem to have an air of confidence that people who'd gone to state school were perhaps lacking in, because you do feel intimidated'.

The argument that men are more assertive in their writing was the argument provided second most frequently by students to explain the gendered pattern in achievement, preceeded only by the argument that fewer women gain first class degrees because of their many 'outside' commitments.[1] (That argument was given by eleven students, including eight women and three men.) Four further students (three female, one male) argued that fewer women gain first class degrees because they are more cautious and less confident than men, presenting the 'other side of the coin' to the 'men are more assertive' argument. (If these students' responses are included with the former students arguing that men are more assertive, this broad argument becomes the most popular explanation.) Of the students presenting the argument concerning male assertion, five students pointed out that this bold approach can either pay off, or go disastrously wrong, hence explaining the proliferation of men at both ends of the achievement scale. For example, when asked to explain why men are over-represented at both ends of the undergraduate achievement scale, Simon answers (boldly!), 'Oh, risk. A man will take a risk. A man will say something. And if you take a risk either it comes off and you're great, or it doesn't come off and you've got egg all over your face!' Likewise, Karen suggested, 'The lads that I saw at university tend to have very strong viewpoints, so they would probably assert themselves more all through the essay, therefore if they're right, they're right, and if they're wrong, they're completely wrong!'. She maintained that women are less assertive in their writing because they do not 'believe in themselves' as much as men. Louise maintained that men are 'not frightened of criticising people', but pointed out that if they do not support their arguments in their essays they will 'fall flat on their face'.

The arguments presented by these students support the notion that male students tend to predominate at both ends of the achievement scale because of their tendency to adopt a bold, assertive style: this style is favoured by examiners if the student 'gets it right', but leads to particularly heavy penalties if for some reason the student barks up the wrong tree. Louise specifies that the student must back up their bold argument, pointing out the consequences if they fail to do so. Hence her position particularly supports Francis' (1998a) hypothesis that students whose bold style is coupled with effective use of other academic conventions (e.g. good grammar and referencing) may be awarded particularly high marks; whereas students whose bold style is not coupled with such conventions may find that their bold style is penalised.

Discussion

The findings of our study show that male students were slightly more likely to use bold statements in their essays than were women. This supports much of the literature in the field. However, there was no evidence of correlation between greater use of a bold style and higher grade. This result questions the argument made by researchers such as Spurling (1990) and Martin (1997), that women's lack of assertion disadvantages them in the award of first class degrees. However, the small size of our sample means that this finding must be treated with caution. Moreover, commentators would rightly observe that the tone of the essay is obviously insufficient on its own to gain a particular grade: other factors, such as competency in writing skills, use of referencing and the like, all play a part in influencing an essay's success or failure. Nor is gender identity the only factor impacting on student writing: other aspects of identity such as ethnicity and social class may also have an impact. This demonstrates the complexity of discursive identification at play here. However, these considerations confirm the point that a bold tone, more often adopted by men, can only advantage them if other factors constituting a successful essay are also in place. Students must also achieve the tone and approach of professional academic discourse (a discourse which some writers have suggested is itself masculine, with its emphasis on rationality and objectivity, see Harding, 1990).

If it is the case that the use of a particular tone in undergraduate writing can impact on the mark awarded, it is arguable that male and female students should be provided with details explaining the desired academic style (as well as other conventions and features of a successful essay). Although a student's gender may impact on the relative ease with which they can adopt a particular style, a clear explanation of what is required would at least show students what they are supposed to be aiming for, and hence allow them to attempt to do so. However, our study revealed that many students felt that they had been given no guidelines for essay writing at all, let alone advice concerning the appropriate academic style. Half of the male respondents (nine), and nearly a third of the women (eight) said that they had been given no information at all concerning the sort of written work that would be well rewarded. A further four males and six females said that only very general information had been provided. Pauline said, 'I think with, um university essay writing it's more, how can I put it, a game of finding what the rules of the game are and then playing them in order to get a higher mark'. Her comments highlight the challenge for students of finding out what is required in essay writing, and how arbitrary it is whether or not they succeed in discovering 'the rules of the game'. Indeed, some students appeared never to have found out. When asked what tutors are looking for in a first class essay, Kathleen simply responded 'something I didn't have!', and further prompting revealed that she really was not sure. Wendy agreed that one 'never really knew what they were looking for', concluding that it was consequently 'pot luck' whether or not one was awarded a good grade.

This point was particularly illuminated by students' responses to our question asking whether they had seen their department's marking scheme. Only just over a quarter of respondents said that they had. As we discovered during the initial stage of our research, one of the two long-established university departments did not have a marking scheme at all, and the other only had a written explanation of how alphabetical grades were converted to percentages. (This latter department did, however, run essay-writing courses for students who wished to participate.) Even at the 'new' universities, students were evenly split as to whether they had or had not seen marking schemes, and those that had often argued that these were vague and therefore not very helpful. Although some students did mention information they had gathered concerning essay writing from optional writing classes, tutor feedback on previous essays, and marking schemes, over half the student respondents maintained that they had not been given sufficient detail about the expectations of teachers regarding student writing. As Karen commented, tutors did not help to 'steer you in the right direction, you had to do it yourself'.

Of course, the provision of access to a marking scheme or to detailed explanations of the appropriate academic tone does not help to address the power imbalance between students and lecturers which Lea and Street (1998) discuss and recommend that academics seek to change. Nor does the provision of such guidelines guarantee that students will act on that information. Indeed, only just over of half our respondents who had seen marking schemes said that these had influenced their writing. As Mike pointed out, 'reading it and putting it into practice are two different things'. However, if students were provided with specific information concerning the features of a successful undergraduate essay (including examples of an appropriate academic writing style), and the difference between various grades, they would have a far better chance of at least understanding what is required of them.

Conclusions

Our findings confirmed that male students use bold statements more frequently than their female counterparts, but we found less differentiation here than has been suggested by studies in the past. Moreover, there was no significant difference in students' use of tentative or evaluative approaches according to gender. Hence these findings question previous work which has suggested clear differences in academic writing styles, presenting women's writing as more cautious and evaluative, and men's as more assertive.

Having said this, our finding that men adopted a bold style *slightly* more frequently than women students does lend some support to previous literature in the area. Yet, the suggestion of some correspondence between the use of a bold style and a low grade warns against assumptions that men are necessarily advantaged by a bold, assertive approach to writing. The evidence of a particularly frequent use of 'very bold' statements in essays which achieved low grades lends some support to Francis' suggestion that those who write boldly but 'badly' are likely to be awarded low grades. However, her argument that those who adopt a bold (masculine) style alongside a competent use of English and conformity to academic conventions may be particularly highly rewarded in assessment was only partially supported. Although a high proportion of bold statements were found in the male students' first class essays, female students' first class essays reversed this trend – and the numbers involved were too small to test this effectively. Research with a larger sample of students will be necessary to test this notion further. However, bearing in mind the multitude of different possible factors which may impact on the award given to a student's essay (for example, identity factors such as gender, ethnicity, social class; competence in writing; the style adopted; and of course the opinion of the examiner, which in itself may be influenced by factors in their social identity), it will always be difficult to evaluate clearly the impact of particular factors on achievement. It therefore seems important that all students are helped to know what is required of them, by providing them with information and examples concerning successful academic writing and the way in which it is assessed.

Note

[1] A variety of explanations for the gendered pattern in undergraduate achievement were provided by students. Nine students offered explanations related to the greater conscientiousness of women: four women and two men suggested that men are either more lazy or more easily distracted than women. Three students suggested that men are 'less organised' than women. Only two – female – students provided essentialist explanations, suggesting that men are more technically-minded or more analytical than women.

References

Ainley, P. (1994), *Degrees of Difference*, Cassell, London.

Arnot, M., M. David and G. Weiner (1999), *Closing the Gender Gap*, Polity Press, Cambridge.

Ballard, B. and J. Clancy (1988), 'Literacy in the University: an "Anthropological Approach"', in G. Taylor *et al.* (eds), *Literacy by Degrees*, SRHE and Open University Press, Milton Keynes.

Bourdieu, P. and J. Passeron (1977), *Reproduction in Education, Society and Culture*, Sage, London.

Cixous, H. (1990), *The Body and The Text*, Harvester Wheatsheaf, London.

Clarke, P. *et al.* (1994), *Men and Women's Performance in Tripos Examinations, 1980–1993*, Cambridge University Press, Cambridge.

David, M. and D. Woodward (1998), *Negotiating the Glass Ceiling: Careers of Senior Women in the Academic World*, Falmer Press, London.

Davies, B. (1989), *Frogs and Snails and Feminist Tales*, Allen & Unwin, Sydney.

_____ (1993), *Shards of Glass*, Allen & Unwin, Sydney.

Farrell, T. (1979), 'The Female and Male Modes of Rhetoric', *College English*, 40.

Flynn, E. (1988), 'Composing as a Woman', *College Composition and Communication*, 39.

Francis, B. (1998a), 'Degrees of Gender: Gendered Patterns in Undergraduate Academic Success and Failure, and the Methodological Difficulties in Researching this Area', presented at Gendering the Millennium International Conference, University of Dundee, 11-13 September 1998.

_____ (1998b), *Power Plays: Children's Constructions of Gender, Power and Adult Work*, Trentham Books, Stoke-on-Trent.

_____ (2000), *Boys, Girls and Achievement: Addressing the Classroom Issues*, Routledge, London.

Francis, B., J. Robson and B. Read (forthcoming), 'An Analysis of Undergraduate Writing Styles in the Context of Gender and Achievement'.

Harding, S. (1990), 'Feminism, Science and the Anti-Enlightenment Critiques', in L. Nicholson (ed.), *Feminism/Postmodernism*, Routledge, London.

_____ (1991), *Whose Science? Whose Knowledge?*, Open University Press, Buckingham.

Higher Education Statistical Agency (1999), *Research Data Pack*, HESA, Cheltenham.

Keroes, J. (1990), 'But What do they Say? Gender and the Content of Student Writing', *Discourse Processes*, 13.

Lakoff, R. (1973), 'Language and Woman's Place', *Language and Society*, 2.

Lea, M. and B. Street (1998), 'Student writing in Higher Education: an Academic Literacies Approach', *Studies in Higher Education*, 23 (2).

Lynch, C. and M. Strauss-Noll (1987), 'Mauve Washers: Sex-Differences in Freshman Writing', *English Journal*, 76.

Martin, M. (1997), 'Emotional and Cognitive Effects of Examination proximity in female and Male Students', *Oxford Review of Education*, 23.

McNabb, R., S. Pal and P. Sloane (forthcoming), 'Gender Differences in Student Attainment: the case of university students in the UK'.

Rees, T. (1999), *Mainstreaming Equality in the European Union*, Routledge, New York.

Roen, D. and D. Johnson (1992), 'Perceiving the Effectiveness of Written Discourse Through Gender Lenses: the Contribution of Complimenting', *Written Communication*, 9.

Rubin, D. and K. Greene (1992), 'Gender-Typical Style in Written Language', *Research in the Teaching of English*, 26.

Spurling, A. (1990), *Women in Higher Education*, King's College Research Centre, Cambridge.

Sutherland, M. (1994), 'Two Steps Forward and One Step Back: Women in Higher Education in the UK', in S. Stiver-Lee, L. Malik and D. Harris (eds), *The Gender Gap in Higher Education*, Kogan Page, London.

Taylor, S. (1978), 'Women in a Double Bind: Hazards of the argumentative edge', *College Composition and Communication*, 29.

Walkerdine, V. (1990), *Schoolgirl Fictions*, Verso, London.

Weiner, G. (1994), *Feminisms in Education*, Open University Press, Buckingham.

Chapter 14

The Sea of Possibilities: The Learning Journal as Pedagogy of the Unconscious

Jennifer FitzGerald

Knowledge, we know, is not education until it has been internalised by the learner. One of the catalysts of the learning process is specific or personal relevance, a dynamic at the heart of feminist pedagogy. Yet this very relevance also creates difficulties. Not only do students bring their outside lives into the classroom, the classroom invades their outside lives, reverberating on their social, economic and psycho-sexual relationships at considerable personal cost. It is rational to refuse knowledge which calls into question the premises and structures on which one's daily life is predicated and which threatens one's closest relationships and dependencies. Thus even initially enthusiastic learners may resist the information with which they are confronted.

But the lid cannot be replaced on Pandora's box. Feminism has already thought

> the thing our traditional pedagogy has not wished to think, under the influence of a historically abstract and metaphysical 'humanism,' [...] how situations of race, class, gender, sexual orientation and social caste function in the production, reception, and interpretation of cultural works (Jay, 1987, p.786).

These questions enter the classroom and make uncomfortable demands on its participants. They also require a sophisticated methodology: unsurprisingly, recent commentators, including Christina Hughes in this volume, have explored the contributions of poststructuralism to pedagogy.

The feminist classroom is therefore a site of challenge, a cauldron of personal commitment and fierce resistance – sometimes in the same student. 'Unfortunately, the teacher's task is to make the student ill [...] to unsettle [her] complacency and conceptual identities' (Jay, 1987, p.790). Ignorance is not lack of information, but

> a radical condition, an integral part of the very structure of knowledge [...] it can be said to be a kind of forgetting [...] tied up with repression, with the imperative to forget [...]. it is an active dynamic of negation, an active refusal of information (Felman, 1987, pp.78-9).

If (in this context) ignorance is repression, should educators practise some kind of psychoanalysis? This suggestion is at odds with the rationalism upon which

Western education is founded. Feminist poststructuralism has demonstrated that logocentrism guarantees, and renders invisible, its own political interests while rejecting as 'irrational' (biased, partial) the politics of the Others it excludes (Ellsworth, 1992, p.98). A 'pedagogy of the unconscious' will therefore not only undo the student's defences against knowledge, but bring to the surface the repressed processes which implicate her in sexism, racism, classism, heterosexism, ableism.

How does the student access her own 'pedagogical unconscious', her resistances, positions, investments? How does the teacher-analyst facilitate the return of this repressed?

> The teacher, like the analyst, will have to conduct sessions that bring unconscious concepts, defenses, and desires into the realm of discourse, argument, and performance. Students may then discover how what they don't know that they think prevents them from knowing or thinking something else [...] we can teach the 'partiality' of knowledge – its incompleteness and its dependency on values [...] by disclosing the pedagogical unconscious as a structure of investments – an ideological discourse, if you will (Jay, 1987, p.790).

But how are these objectives achieved in the classroom? Magda Lewis, Elizabeth Ellsworth and Patricia Elliott analyse their own teaching experiences to identify strategies which 'make speakable and legitimate the personal/political investments we all make in the meanings we ascribe to our historically contingent experiences' (Lewis, 1992, p.186). A classroom in which interpersonal and interpolitical dynamics are addressed is perhaps the richest (and riskiest) arena for learning, where students and teacher engage in 'a sustained encounter with currently oppressive formations and power relations' as manifested in their immediate interactions (Ellsworth, 1992, p.100). These educators do not underestimate the unremitting confrontation and classroom conflict involved. They challenge their own investments as much as those of their students, they reflect on their own discomfort, admit failure – only to be spurred on to problematise further.

It is clear that hurt and anger accompany the exhumation of the most powerful interests and that the more a student feels threatened, the more she resists insight (Elliot, 1997, p.147; Tisdell, 1998, p.147). This is particularly likely to happen in the volatile circumstances of the classroom. Even the most alert teacher cannot calculate the impact on all her students, especially those who remain silent. In this essay I discuss a less ambitious strategy, which nevertheless can facilitate students' understanding not only of the world but also of themselves – of how their identities, assumptions, behaviour and relationships are constructed. The learning journal, familiar in Women's Studies as a means of integrating personal experience and academic learning, encompasses the affective dimension (Walker, 1998, p.64; Putnam, 1995). It can also bring unspoken assumptions, the students' own belief-system, to the surface (Dart *et al.*, 1998, p.258). Despite Kauffman's *caveat* that 'writing about yourself does not liberate you, it just shows how ingrained the ideology of freedom through self-expression is in our thinking' (Kauffman, 1997, p.1164), I hope to show that as a pedagogy of the unconscious the learning journal can play a part in deconstructing individualism.

The following discussion is based on learning journals which the author has assigned in two feminist courses over seven years at Queen's University, Belfast.[1] Students write a weekly entry after each class, responding to the course readings and discussions, but also drawing on their own experience and personal reactions. They are specifically encouraged to reflect and connect, making this an 'integrative' journal (Berry and Black, 1993). The entry is handed in at the next class; the student receives written feedback from the teacher three times during the course. The final entry is a review, in which the student reads the incremental record of her experience of the course, identifies difficult or defining moments and reflects on whatever changes she may have recognised in herself over the process.

The journal is characterised by perplexities, revisions, dramatic changes in mood.[2] Each entry is provisional, partial, likely to be interrogated by the entries that follow. It involves, as does the pedagogy of the unconscious, a 'different temporality of learning' from conventional paradigms:

> Proceeding not through linear progression but through breakthroughs, leaps, discontinuities, regressions, and deferred actions, the analytic learning process puts in question the traditional pedagogical belief in intellectual perfectibility, the progressist view of learning as a simple one-way road from ignorance to knowledge (Felman, 1987, p.6).

In this it resembles poststructuralism's 'subject in process', displaced over a range of diverse and inconsistent responses, discourses, positions.[3] The journal institutes a split between the writer, the self-as-subject, and the self she reflects on, the subject-of-knowledge (Jay, 1987, p.790). In the words of one student, it operates 'almost [as] an interactive device, allowing me to observe and analyze my reponses as they unfold [...], both cognitive and emotional'. This permits the writer retrospectively to acknowledge the discourses and positions which held sway at the time of the entry. The tutor's feedback functions as a reflective listener, acknowledging the student's feelings, drawing her attention to clues or conflicts buried in the journal-text, intermittently transforming the journal into a dialogue (Knights, 1998). It can also challenge her, 'dislocat[ing] fixed desires, rather than feed[ing] us what we think we want to know' (Jay, 1987, p.790). The feedback clarifies, expands, connects the points of difficulty with the larger course framework.

Because the journal validates affective as well as cognitive responses, it offers learners a space in which to question, engage with, object to or refuse new and disturbing ideas. When Marie Nolan took cognizance of her reactions, she was able to locate the source of her resistance:

> I think I may have identified another source of my problems in dealing with psychoanalysis which is I just find a lot of the theories very disturbing [...] I am astonished that it has taken me so long to consciously acknowledge these feelings [...] I think these feelings may have at least been partly responsible for my negative attitude toward psychoanalysis and my haste in dismissing many of the theories as abstract, far-fetched and obscure.[4]

Miriam McKeown recognised that her 'detached' approach was a hindrance; she began to 'acknowledge the need to accept ownership of my own doubts and insecurities relating to aspects of this course if I am to allow myself to learn effectively'.

These are essential, if limited, first steps in disengaging the 'active dynamic' of resistance. But what of the more powerful refusals of knowledge which feminist courses provoke? 'Women's resistance to feminism,' Lewis suggests, is 'an active discourse of struggle derived from a complex set of meanings in which women's practices are invested' (Lewis, 1992, p.188). Some of these meanings surface in learning journals: among the most resilient is the fantasy of autonomy, occluded by Western individualism and challenged by feminist poststructuralism.

The ontological assumptions underlying our personal experience and interactions are not easily scrutinised. It is hard to imagine otherwise what we have always taken for granted. Poststructuralism draws on psychoanalysis and linguistics to question fundamental notions such as the unified identity of the individual (conscious, rational, and independent) and the capacity of language to convey fixed, definitive notions of reality. It argues that the essential 'self' assumed by Western individualism and empiricism only appears autonomous and homogeneous because the forces that determine and disrupt it have been repressed into the unconscious. The 'individual' is instead conceived of as the subject of multiple, often contradictory and conflicting, discourses.[5] Not all feminist courses are poststructuralist, but it is unlikely that they can avoid the question of social construction. De Beauvoir's dictum, 'One is not born, but rather becomes a woman [...] it is civilization as a whole that produces this creature', is foundational to virtually all feminist critique (De Beauvoir, 1988, p.295). Implicit in this process is the ideology of individualism, with its discourses of free will and self-control.

Catherine Belsey's synthesis of the theories of Louis Althusser, Emile Beneviste and Jacques Lacan explains our investment in the 'obvious' assumption 'that people are autonomous individuals, possessed of subjectivity or consciousness which is the source of their beliefs and actions'. Even as we follow her analysis at an intellectual level and recognise this premise as 'the elementary ideological effect', we continue to feel its 'reality', since it constitutes the manner in which we live out our relationship with the world (Belsey, 1997, pp.658-9). While individualism interpellates us as subjects, convincing us of the voluntary nature of our participation in its practices, we rely on the idea of agency to shore up our defences against an arbitrary world. The middle-class, white, educated, prosperous Westerner lives a purposeful and comfortable routine, repressing the awareness of potential disaster, either personal (accident, unemployment, divorce, terminal illness) or collective (natural catastrophe, war) which could turn her 'reality' upside down. The belief that we can control our destiny through wealth (capitalism), science (knowledge, predicting effects through causes) or reason (empirical induction, logic) is an illusion, denied, sooner or later, by death. Under the delusion of democracy, we repress the social and political determinants of our 'choices' through the fantasy of autonomous identity.

For poststructuralist educators, unpacking this ideology and its discourses is a pedagogical imperative. However, I have not found any examination of how our investment in its fantasies can vary with age. This makes a significant difference to the ability of students, as opposed to teachers, to take on board the question of their positionality, as advocated by Jay, 1987, Ellsworth, 1992, and Tisdell, 1998.[6] Although there are substantial divergences between pre- and post-1992 universities in the United Kingdom and although Women's Studies attracts a disproportionate enrollment of mature students, it is still likely that the majority of undergraduates in any third-level classroom will be around around twenty years old. This is a critical developmental stage, a version of Lacan's mirror-stage, which renders them particularly susceptible to individualism:

> Lacan [...] uses the metaphor of the mirror to describe how the baby, at around the age of six months, first comes to perceive itself as a 'self', because it gains an integrated, coherent image of itself in the mirror. The child who experiences itself as physically uncoordinated and overwhelmed by emotions and phantasies over which it has no control – in fact, as 'all over the place' both physically and psychically – suddenly finds in the specular image reflecting back from the mirror, a satisfying and seductive image of itself as a coherent whole – a thing with edges. At this moment, the chaotic, unintelligible being that the baby up to then has experienced itself being, is magically transformed into a unified whole, though, of course, this is still of a very blurred, undefined and imaginary kind (Minsky, 1996, pp.144-5).

The crux of the mirror stage is that the baby – and the adult who replays this drama – both recognises and misrecognises itself. The image is a reflection of the viewer, but the image is much more coordinated, coherent and in control than the baby feels itself to be:

> We identify with something which looks like what we want to be, but this is also alien and separate from us [...] We misrecognize ourselves in the alienated image of what we want to be because this ideal image denies the chaos we feel in our own being (Minsky, 1996, p.145).

The toddler's insistence on autonomy – 'I can do it for myself!' – is the desire to achieve a control still out of reach; the teenager see-saws between the 'satisfying and seductive image' of adulthood – 'I am not a child! – and fears of inadequacy, rejection, failure. The twenty-something-year-old is deep in the process of establishing a singular, fixed identity, the 'ideal image [which] denies the chaos' she feels in her own being. This is recognised by advertisers targeting the fifteen to twenty-four year-old market: 'Young people want to establish their own identity [...] They want to be seen as something different, because the one thing youth hates is to be pigeonholed.'[7] This uniqueness is intimately bound up with the repression not only of disturbing emotions but also of the original symbiosis with her parents. In order to attain the status and identity of an adult, the young person consciously attempts to discard (some of) the values and lifestyle of her family of origin, in order to forge her own. The more recent the separation from the family, the more urgent the need to assert an autonomous, essential self.

If this is the case, then the 'young' student has a specific investment in resisting even straightforward social-construction theory, not to mention poststructuralism. This is borne out in my subjective experience of reading over

400 journals in seven years. There is some comparability, as students are assigned the same readings and discussion topics covered each week in the two courses, but also, of course, almost infinite variability, since each learner is encouraged to respond on the basis of her own experience and reflections. Accepting the unknowable factors which distinguish one student and one journal from another, this essay will address – anecdotally, through illustrations of a handful of pseudonymised journals – the difference age might have on the journal-writer's ability to unpack the fixed sense of 'self' and to recognise her position in a dynamic of discourses, interests and positions.

Based on this experience, I would hazard the generalisation that young adults can scarcely bear the idea that their identities are not self-generated, unique and under their own control. Students of thirty-plus, less invested in shoring up a unified, differentiated self, seem less threatened by the concept of the unconscious, the destabilisation of identity and meaning, the loss of autonomy and self-definition. Another factor may be the huge personal changes they have experienced since they decided to return to education, leaving behind the life and identities they have known. Although the younger age-group need to believe in 'choice', the freedom to determine their own lives, university for them is often an unquestioned progression from school. Re-entry into education prompts mature students to reflect on how 'free' their earlier 'choices' have been.[8] Since many of the older students I encounter enter third-level through Access courses – alternative modes of entry to Higher Education for non-traditional students – the experience of feeling oneself changing has been in process some time before they enter my classroom (Wilson and Hill, 1997). This may be particularly true of women who come to Access having already taken take courses in community women's groups.[9]

Age is therefore only part of the explanation: the personal experience of changing is another. If the pedagogy of the unconscious aims at exploring the intimate ways in which our identities are discursively constructed, it is worth taking these differentials into account. The remainder of this essay will compare journals by young adults and by mature students. The first set of comparisons will examine the reactions to social constructionism, and the second set will focus on journals confronting poststructuralism.

Encouraged to respond personally to feminist course content, students often adapt the journal into a 'confessional' form (Berry and Black, 1993). Twenty-year-old Maggie Doyle admitted to herself in its pages that she was bulimic for the first time, and that 'I cannot go outside of my home without wearing make-up [...] because without my make-up or mask, I feel unattractive.' This opened up the question of social construction:

> I believe that society is partly to blame by constantly penetrating [*sic* for perpetrating?] such high expectations of women to be thin and beautiful [...]. I guess I cannot blame society completely, for I myself may be partly to blame, by trying to conform to their expectations, much against my own body's will. However, I know I will never change and that society has in some way shaped my views on beauty and the body.

Every time the journal brings her close to realizing how, by internalizing social norms, she has become their agent, she reverts to discourses of individual freedom and self-control:

> Now I understand that I should not care what other people think [...] but should make my decisions according to what will make me and those close to me happy. Nobody else's opinion matters.

Maggie directs her energies to establishing a differentiated identity; acknowledging the ideological formation of her 'own opinions' and values is much too great a threat to this process. Her journal, however, registers the struggle involved in asserting what isn't quite proven.

Nuala Maguire (twenty-two) is even more persuaded of the efficacy of self-consciousness:

> I agree that it is not pleasant to have to question certain aspects of one's character or patterns of behaviour which you had believed were an inherent part of you. However [...] once these constructs of conditioning are revealed to us we can then set about resisting or subverting them.

This reflects an intense need to believe in the autonomy of the self, even in the face of the homogenizing processes of consumer culture:

> Consuming is after all one of the chief pleasures in life [...] if we are aware of how this consumer culture functions we can consume from a position of power.

Bernadette Shaw (twenty-one) goes in the opposite direction, blaming herself for lacking the 'strength or [...] self-confidence [...] to assert my own individual identity.' A rape victim, at first she felt that 'by writing painful experiences in my journal [...] I was somehow writing them away'.[10] Unsurprisingly, issues of power and resistance loom large in discussing social construction:

> Perhaps it was the first time I had consciously recognised the extent to which I, my body, thoughts and actions are socially constructed. I felt a body double, a duplicate, a mass product that this powerful machine called society spits out to tow the line. I was a propaganda sponge that had readily accepted everything without once questioning the implications this had for myself. Had I betrayed ME, had I been TRUE to my own desires and needs?
> [...] I hope that I can learn to accept my constructed self as being part of me, it is me, I can modify it, mould it into the direction I want to take it but I can never rid myself of it. I realise that I cannot wipe the slate clean, and in some regards it hurts.

Attracted, like Nuala, to easy solutions, she nevertheless resisted their blandishments: 'I wish there was some magic formula to follow but unfortunately I don't think there is one'.

Educators point out that learning which is 'appropriated in a very personal way' can be integrated 'into our sense of identity' (Boud *et al.*, 1998, p.33). In these extracts, each journal-writer simultaneously recognises, and resists, the notion that what she identifies as her 'true' self is a product of social conditioning. Perhaps young women find the loss of autonomy so hard to contemplate because at some, repressed, level they feel its fragility. Too few male students take these courses to make meaningful gender comparisons, but it is fair to generalise that they seem to use the journal to negotiate a sense of male guilt (and occasional anger at being 'made' feel guilty), while young women's journals dramatise an ambivalence between what they want to believe and what they suspect – and deny (as in Elliot, 1997).

The following three journals written by students aged thirty-one to forty-six begin with the same assumptions but follow a different trajectory. Forty-six-year-old Miriam McKeown's early entries employ liberal discourses. These ceased to convince as her own independence, so salient during her rebellious adolescence, came under pressure. Her journal brought to the surface the extent to which she internalised the desires of others as her own: the separate identity on which she prided herself actually depended on repressing her attachment to others. She reflected on the hidden agenda of liberalism:

> Allowing everyone the right to make their own choices suggests impartiality while it may simply be a way of skilfully avoiding confrontation [...] I think I saw myself as unconventional, pursuing my own goals regardless of others' disapproval – what rubbish!

Thirty-four-year-old Caroline Morgan's journal acknowledged how she projected her own fears onto other women, in the wake of being abandoned by her mother as a child. Seeing aspects of their unconscious reflected back in their journals, both students gradually identified how their personal investment in ideological positions influenced attitudes which they would otherwise have considered reasoned and objective. Annie Ryan (thirty-four) recognised that her desire to give her children a 'perfect childhood' was a fantasy emerging from the chaos she had experienced consequent on maternal schizophrenia. Reading about nineteenth-century constructions of female madness triggered off a new exploration of her mother's mental illness:

> Recently I have been looking at my world through different lenses, but I can't quite get things into focus. You see, I'm starting to wonder if my mother was mad at all – and that seems like such a mad thing to say. If my mother wasn't mad, then who am I? My mother's madness has had such a definitive influence on me, that if I question its existence then I think I might be questioning my very identity.

Initally, Annie took the role of 'the self-as-subject' while her mother became 'the subject-of-knowledge', but as the latter merged with the former, she became her own subject:

> The attempt to understand my mother has blurred with my attempts to understand myself and this has blurred with my attempts to understand psychoanalysis, patriarchy, feminism, deconstructionism. In the past I have wondered what my identity is – always feeling that I never really had one, I thought that I never felt sure of myself because I never had a stable female role model. Now I believe that our identities are not fixed; we

keep on and on deconstructing and reconstructing ourselves. Our lives are like texts that we keep re-reading, meanings keep shifting; there is no final point at which we can say we have discovered a 'self'.

She has arrived at cognitive understanding which often evades students faced with poststructuralist theory. These learners use their journals to articulate their struggles with counter-intuitive notions and an unfamiliar epistemology. How younger and older students deal with the emotional challenges of poststructuralism can be gauged by the following comparisons.

Elaine Johnston's resistance to the deconstruction of her unified identity is typical of other twenty-one-year-olds: 'What is the point in destablizing all I believe in to trade my beliefs for the – to me – ridiculous theory that there is no certainty, no truth, no life?'

> My whole concept of 'me' was questioned [...] I concluded that if to be a humanist is to believe that I am me because I know myself, then I must be a humanist [...] as the class ended I pulled my own beliefs closer about me and determined to make up my own mind before listening to any other off-the-wall theories, which was how I saw the anti-humanist theory.

The contrast with Hugh Stewart (thirty-one) could not be more stark. Reflecting retrospectively on a heated personal exchange with a friend and fellow-student, he began to unpack, and theorise, his investment in discourse:

> I realised my criticism of her criticism of 'me' was simply an example of us adopting a subject position – our identities fit the profile of oppressed woman and misunderstood man, and we simply played out the role [in] the system of signification those profiles dictated. Later we agreed that each of us carries around our own baggage or 'shadow', and that, more importantly, we can't escape it completely, regardless of efforts at self-consciousness. It is as though we can be aware of the existence of an ideologically motivated system, but cannot do anything about our assigned role within it. This 'assigned' aspect is important, I know, for it is an acknowledgement of the constructed nature of identity, and to a large extent, experience.

Another factor which differentiates mature students is class: young adults from a working-class background already participate in the middle-class enterprise of Higher Education; by contrast, older students may identify very consciously through previous life-experience as working-class.[11] Hugh's self-questioning brought him face-to-face with his considerable investment as a member of 'an underclass, disenfranchised, insignificant':

> What has kept me going right through, more than anything else, is the 'certainty' that people like me, poor, uneducated, low in self-confidence, etc [...] simply do not do what I'm doing. This pioneering mission is my investment in discourse [...] My guess is that my choice of the object position in this discourse of class and economy actually suits whatever (not so unconscious) heroic idea of struggle my own history makes attractive [...] I feel I slip into the ease of such discourse – it posits me as oppositional to something, a very comfortable position from which to complain of others affecting me while I myself can get by doing as little as possible about my position.

Even as this essay attempts them, I realise how insidious such comparisons are: the variables which stimulate Hugh Stewart's or Miriam McKeown's self-analysis are incalculable. Also, any such bringing to consciousness is inevitably partial (Ellsworth, 1992, p.103): in almost every journal, a student prepared to address privilege or oppression with regard to one position resists similar knowledge with respect to another category. The one positionality which is rarely mentioned out loud is the most contested amongst classroom participants. Religious/political/ cultural identity is for the most part unspoken. Such repression is both deeply pathological and pragmatic, holding for the whole of Northern Irish society. Our 'culture of silence' has meant that political matters are only discussed with those who are known to be 'on the same side' (Lampen, 1995, p.78).[12] Recent legislative changes have lifted the lid somewhat, but most undergraduates have been educated along denominational lines: university is the first place where they meet their religious/political counterparts. They are therefore likely to censor themselves in the mixed company of the classroom. Pedagogic strategies for addressing such deeply contentious topics are still awaited. Most colleagues, having learnt through experience that open debate on this subject leads to categorical statements without reciprocal listening, displace the discussion metonymically onto other contested identities.[13] The privacy of the journal permits some reflection on these issues, although they do not surface very frequently. Part of the equation includes the teacher's perceived postionality and the student's sense, or lack, of 'safety'.

Indeed, poststructuralist pedagogy turns the spotlight most emphatically on the privilege, interests and position of the teacher. In attempting to implement a pedagogy of the unconscious, I aim to facilitate open and relaxed debate in the classroom, as well as to provide extensive feedbacks to each student. In both I introduce my own positionality and experience self-reflexively, and address insensitivities and mistakes when they come to my notice. The journal acts as a feedback mechanism in the other direction, as the students respond to classroom interactions. No doubt only a minority will take this risk, but it introduces at least a modicum of two-way private communication. My greatest commitment is the time I spend on each feedback, amounting to twice as many hours per week as I spend in the classroom.

The journals compared above illustrate trends the author has identified in young adults and mature students, but it would be misleading to suggest strict uniformity across age. Siobhan McDonald's frustration with the proposition that 'language defines the world rather than the world defining language' was typical of students of any age seeking 'a universal, unquestionable, world-changing argument' which would silence their opponents. The journals of some students in their early twenties also demonstrate a firm grasp of poststructuralist epistemology, and not only at the cognitive level. Both his age (twenty-two) and his gender threatened to subvert, but in the long run intensified, Martin Robertson's self-questioning:

> As I read this again [...] I think 'Oh dear! Oh dear! This is sixth form angst stuff – get back to coherence, rationality, closed discourse. This all sounds so soft, it's not you.' [...] I'm a man – I'm the one who can enter the symbolic and run with it.

Without achieving the specificity of self-analysis of Hugh Stewart's journal, Martin 'ran with' the destabilizing insights he had acquired:

> However, I think/feel a change has been made; the journal has led me to use/discover more of myself, and become more aware of my beliefs, hopes, fears, prejudices that I hold. In many ways my discourse has been deconstructed. I've been forced to read my own silences [...]
>
>   My position, my life – the parts I can identify – have been constantly questioned. Where do 'I' stand? How do I identify as an 'identity'? How do I speak?

Another exception – but perhaps indicative of her mid-position, at age twenty-five – is Felicity Roche, for whom disorientation proved liberating:

> These theorists [are] simply trying to widen the scope of vision as much as possible to allow us to question, challenge and explore for ourselves. Why conform? Why not explore? Why not jump off the rock of certainties into the sea of possibilities – if you look back you just might find that that rock was only made of crumbs anyway. It may be wet and cold in that sea and frightening to have no grip on solid ground, but you could get to like swimming.

Claims for the efficacy of the learning journal as a pedagogy of the unconscious are necessarily modest. This essay has argued, on the basis of the author's anecdotal experience, that it can provide students with a means of 'explor[ing] the *connection between* who they are as individuals and the structural systems of privilege and oppression [...] that partially inform how they think' (Tisdell, 1998, p.139). However, young adults, at the developmental stage of establishing a separate identity, are more resistant to, and more distressed by, such a challenge. Mature students may be predisposed to it, not only by age but by life-changing processes set in motion through their re-entry to education.

'Like psychoanalysis, education can only begin with self-doubt, and its disciplinary self-analyses should be interminable', says Jay (1987, p.790; Felman, 1987, p.88). The 'interminability' of learning is integral to the journal process:

> This may be the end of the journal, but I think that in many respects, for me, it is only the beginning (Caroline Morgan).

> Our lives are like texts that we keep re-reading, meanings keep shifting; there is no final point at which we can say we have discovered a 'self'. So, while this may be my final journal entry, the learning has not finished (Annie Ryan).

> It can always be otherwise and never reach an end (Martin Robertson).

Encouraged by the journal 'to take the kind of risks that make them grow', many of these students are ready to 'jump off the rock of certainties into the sea of possibilities'.[14]

Christina Hughes' paper, 'Pedagogies of, and for, Resistance', at the Feminist Pedagogies conference (included in this collection) was particularly relevant to my own concerns. I have incorporated readings suggested by her paper into the finalised version of my own essay, with due acknowledgement. I should also like to thank Myrtle Hill, who read an earlier version of this essay, and above all my journal-writing students, for permission to quote from their journals and for letting me share in their self-learning.

Notes

[1]   These courses are cross-listed for English and Women's Studies: 'Women, Culture, Texts' focuses on popular culture; 'Women, Discourse, Theory' on poststructuralism.

[2]   The following description of a typical learning journal can only be validated by reading a sample of the journals in full. This would not, however, replicate the open-ended, incremental experience of writing the journal or the teacher's experience of reading and responding during the course of the journal's composition.

[3]   One has, however, to allow for the distorting effect of the journal as summative assessment. Assessment shifts the writers' awareness from themselves to the examiner; they will be more averse to taking risks; they will reveal less and stabilise the text more, 'turn[ing] the messy process of learning into a polished performance' (Gibbs, 1995, p.34). On the other hand, students inevitably prioritise summatively assessed work; a formative journal, however desirable, would not get written. The criteria for summative assessment include: reflection, the process of learning, range of theories, applying content to one's own experience or practice, creativity, originality.

[4]   Journals are quoted with permission of their authors, whose names have been changed.

[5]   Discourses are 'not [...] philosophically coherent thought systems but rather [...] clusters of ideas, notions, feelings, images, attitudes and assumptions that, taken together, make up distinctive ways of thinking and feeling about things, of making a particular sense of the world' (Dyer, 1986, p.19).

[6]   Although Tisdell's students average thirty-eight years old, she does not highlight how their age helps or hinders poststructuralist self-analysis. Slotnick *et al.* do examine differences between young adults and mature students in developing identity, but the identity they are discussing – commitment to a professional career – renders their analysis irrelevant to my purposes.

[7]   David Hieatt, Anti-Corp Advertising Agency, quoted in Hutton, 2000, p.32.

[8]   Many thanks to Myrtle Hill for bringing this crucial factor to my attention.

[9]   There were already over 200 women's groups (urban and rural) in Northern Ireland in the early 1990s (McWilliams and Killmurray, 1997, p.2). Women's Studies is sometimes offered as an Access course.

[10] Given the subject matter of feminist courses, it is not surprising that a number of students disclose personal traumas they have experienced in their journals. On reading such an entry, I see the student privately as soon as possible. I clarify that the journal cannot be the place for dealing with, as opposed to mentioning, such painful memories, and direct her to the appropriate agencies and the Student Counselling Service. I respect the decision of those who decide not to follow through these contacts, but I remind them that I am not capable of giving them professional help. I also remind the student that she can delete that particular reference from the journal before submitting it for summative assessment.

[11] Many thanks to Myrtle Hill for reminding me of this fact.

[12] During the 1981 hunger strike, when political tension in Northern Ireland was at a high pitch, I was asked by a fellow citizen of the Republic of Ireland what my colleagues

thought of the hunger strike. My answer – 'We never talk about it' – was symptomatic of this communal survival strategy.

[13] Colleagues teaching Northern Irish politics, for whom displacement is not an option, develop various classroom strategies such as role playing but can still be faced with (telling) silence. (Dr Graham Walker, personal communication.)

[14] Prof. Felicity Riddy, University of York, external examiner for the learning journal 1993-5, personal communication.

References

Belsey, C. (1997), 'Constructing the Subject: Deconstructing the Text', in R.R. Warhol and D. Price Herndl (eds), *Feminisms: An Anthology of Literary Theory and Criticism*, Macmillan, Basingstoke.

Berry, E. and E. Black (1993), 'The Integrative Learning Journal (or, Getting Beyond "True Confessions" and "Cold Knowledge")', *Women's Studies Quarterly*, 21.

Boud, D., R. Keogh and D. Walker (1998), 'Promoting Reflection in Learning: a Model', in D. Boud, R. Keogh and D. Walker (eds), *Reflection: Turning Experience into Learning*, Kogan Page, London.

Dart, B.C., G.M. Boulton-Lewis, J.M. Brownless and A.R. McCrindle (1998), 'Change in Knowledge of Learning and Teaching Through Journal Writing', *Research Papers in Education*, 13.

De Beauvoir, S. (1988), *The Second Sex*, Pan Books, London.

Dyer, R. (1986), *Heavenly Bodies: Film Stars and Society*, St.Martin's Press, New York.

Elliot, P. (1997), 'Denial and Disclosure: An Analysis of Selective Reality in the Feminist Classroom', in G.R. Leslie and L. Eyre (eds), *Dangerous Territories: Struggles for Difference and Equality in Education*, Routledge, London.

Ellsworth, E. (1992), 'Why Doesn't This Feel Empowering? Working Through the Repressive Myths of Critical Pedagogy', in C. Luke and J. Gore (eds) (1998).

Felman, S. (1987), *Jacques Lacan and the Adventure of Insight: Psychoanalysis in Contemporary Culture*, Harvard University Press, Cambridge, MA.

Gibbs, G. (1995), 'Diaries, Logs and Journals', *Assessing Student-Centred Learning*, Oxford Centre for Staff Development, Oxford.

Hughes, C. (2000), 'Pedagogies of, and for, Resistance', in this volume.

Hutton, W. (2000). 'The State I'm in at 50', *Observer*, 21 May.

Jay, G.S. (1987), 'The Subject of Pedagogy: Lessons in Psychoanalysis and Politics', *College English*, 49.

Kauffman, L. (1991), 'The Long Goodbye: Against Personal Testimony, or an Infant Grifter Grows Up', *Feminisms: An Anthology of Literary Theory and Criticism*, Macmillan, Basingstoke.

Knights, S. (1998), 'Reflection and Learning: the Importance of a Listener', in D. Boud, R. Keogh and D. Walker (eds) (1998).

Lampen, J. (1995), *Building the Peace: Good Practice in Community Relations Work in Northern Ireland*, Community Relations Council, Belfast.

Lewis, M. (1992), 'Interrupting Patriarchy: Politics, Resistance and Transformation in the Feminist Classroom', in C. Luke and J. Gore (eds) (1998).

Luke, C. and J. Gore (eds) (1998), *Feminisms and Critical Pedagogy*, Routledge, London.

McWilliams, M. and A. Kilmurray (1997), 'Athene on the Loose: the Origins of the Northern Ireland Women's Coalition', *Irish Journal of Feminist Studies*, 2.

Minsky, R. (1996). *Psychoanalysis and Gender: An Introductory Reader*, Routledge, London.

Putnam, D. (1995), *The Journal Project: Dialogues and Conversations within Women's Studies*, Second Story Press, Toronto.

Slotnick, H.B., M.-H. Pelton, M.L. Fuller and L. Tabor (1993), *Adult Learners on Campus*, Falmer Press, London.

Tisdell, E. (1998), 'Poststructural Feminist Pedagogies: the Possibilities and Limitations of Feminist Emancipatory Adult Learning Theory and Practice', *Adult Education Quarterly*, 48.

Wilson, C. and M. Hill (1997), *Women and Access: Opportunities and Constraints*, Research Report no.4, Institute of Continuing Education, Queen's University, Belfast.

PART V
OVERSEAS PERSPECTIVES

Chapter 15

Assessment of Caring: A Feminist Curricular Transformation

Mary S. Erickson

Introduction

The purpose of this article is to describe how the faculty at the State University of West Georgia integrated the perspectives of caring and feminist teaching strategies into its nursing curriculum. The focus of the new curriculum is to provide activities to enhance student satisfaction and learning: activities that enable students to learn how to care for themselves and others. The university is a state-funded institution governed by the Board of Regents. Located fifty miles from Atlanta, Georgia, it attracts students primarily from the southeastern United States. The nursing programme, which grants baccalaureate degrees, has a student body that includes 10 per cent male and 20 per cent minority students.

The impetus for curricular change was twofold. The first impetus was the unhappiness of the faculty with the old, traditional ways of teaching nursing and treating students. The second impetus was curricular change suggested by the National League for Nursing (NLN), an accrediting agency for nursing programmes in the United States. Although some changes that we have made are designed only for professional programmes, others could be applicable to a wide variety of disciplines. Since the late 1980s, one theme that has dominated discussion among nurse educators is that caring must be explicit in health care policy. Watson (1988), a nurse theorist, states that:

> in order for nursing to be truly responsive to the needs of society and make contributions that are consistent with its roots and early origins, both nursing education and the health care delivery system must be based on human values and concern for the welfare of others. Caring outcomes in practice, research, and theory depend on the teaching of a caring ideology (p.32).

Resolutions at NLN conventions reflected relationships between caring as a core value in nursing and the need for reform in nursing education: a total curricular revolution. Other major reasons for this revolution were that caring could be learned by students experiencing caring practices with faculty, and that schools of nursing should move away from a content-driven curriculum. Critical thinking and holism also become important key concepts as we strive to prepare practitioners for the future.

Philosophies of caring

Noddings (1984) argues that human caring and the memory of being cared for forms the foundation of our ethical responses. One needs to have the experience of being cared for and to have had the value of caring instilled in the past in order for one to be capable of caring. Five perspectives of caring have been identified: caring as a human state; caring as a moral imperative; caring as an affect; caring as an interpersonal relationship, and caring as a nursing intervention (Morse, 1990).

Jean Watson describes three factors that are considered part of the science of caring. The first factor is the cultivation of sensitivity to ones self. Those not sensitive to their own feelings find it difficult to be sensitive to the feelings of others. This was why we began to encourage students to learn to care for themselves. The second factor is the development of a helping-trusting relationship. The quality of ones relationship with others is an important element in determining caring effectiveness. This factor provides the basis for the promotion of group cohesiveness. The third factor is the use of problem-solving for decision-making, because systematic problem-solving allows the nurse to practice the science of caring. This factor provides a norm for the teaching of critical thinking (Watson, 1979).

After reviewing various definitions of caring and after discussion of personal beliefs, the faculty developed the following philosophy for our nursing programme:

> Caring, as a basic way of being, is central to nursing and means that people and inter-
> personal concerns matter. The concept of caring is a major theme in the process of
> becoming a knowledgeable, compassionate individual who is able to respond to human
> needs. Caring for self and others also involves self-awareness and belief in personal
> empowerment. Caring is learned by experiencing caring practices between students and
> teachers, students and students, and nurses and patients (State University of West
> Georgia, 1998).

After development of the philosophy, we began to change our curriculum based on the concept of caring. Evaluations of the curriculum during and after its development helped us to understand that we had indeed also created a curriculum based on concepts of feminist scholarship partly because of our concern with 'the connection between content, process, and teaching approach' (Heinrich and Witt, 1993, p.120).

Traditional education

Prior to this curriculum revolution, traditional nursing education was often considered rigid and hierarchical, contrary to the egalitarian ideas often associated with feminist education and contrary to what the NLN was now calling for. As we developed our curriculum, we also identified other issues that seemed related to the more traditional forms of education. A continuing problem in nursing is that the profession is often viewed as having little solidarity. Nurses devalue each other or the profession to those entering it. Keen suggests our non-caring stance may be related to who we are (women, primarily) and what we do (undervalued work). She believes the oppression directed at nursing by more powerful groups in the medical care system is similar to the oppression of women in a patriarchal society, and this oppression is a major reason why we in turn treat each other so poorly (Keen, 1991).

Nurses often devalue patients too. Riemen (1986) analysed patient descriptions of non-caring nurse-patient interactions. She agrees that nurses respond in non-caring ways because nurses are rewarded for efficiency: for getting the job done. Nurses become attuned to monitoring machines while the patient becomes a secondary attachment. When students have not been assisted in learning to care for themselves, it is indeed hard for graduates to easily learn to care for others.

Traditional nursing education also devalues students. Freire (1970) describes the banking concept of education which is often education of oppressed groups. In this type of education, the teacher makes deposits into the students' minds, and the teacher also makes the decision about what to learn: thus students are taught to submit to the will of others. Hedin and Donovan (1989) also equate traditional nursing education with education of the oppressed. Caring as an integral part of nursing, and learning as the result of the sharing of power have not been part of the traditional teaching/learning environment.

Feminist education

Nursing faculty are not the only ones to struggle with new philosophies of teaching and learning. Feminist scholars also call for a shift in education that values not only theoretical understanding, but personal experience and emphasises a connectedness between learners and between subject and learner. 'Feminist teaching methods allow participants time alone to reflect and time together to discuss and to learn from one another' (Heinrich and Witt, 1993, p.120). As we restructured our curriculum, we realised that we were adopting feminist teaching strategies.

Four major feminist techniques used in our new curriculum include self-disclosure, journaling, dialogue, and empowerment. In our restructuring, we were attempting to legitimise our students' voices by encouraging dialogue with others in a safe environment, by helping students feel important and cared for, and by promoting learning through reciprocal communication with faculty.

Curricular change

One strategy in our new curriculum is the use of journals so that students might share reflections and insights. We also thought some students might initially be more comfortable with disclosure through writing than through face-to-face contact. Through the use of the journal, we encouraged the change from 'power over' to 'power to'. Students become empowered as they share and work together and as they realise they can think and are capable of discovering their own answers. Hawks and Hromek (1992) believe that empowerment encourages autonomous decision-making and increases feelings of self-worth.

And we have attempted to promote the sharing of feelings within a safe structured environment. The environment we chose is the caring group. Beck studied written descriptions of caring experiences between nursing students. She concluded that 'students need to have a sense of being cared for to nurture their own ability to care for others and that nursing students can be caring role models for each other' (1992, p.22). The focus of our caring groups is to enable students to learn to care for self and others while developing self-awareness and empowerment within a safe, nurturing environment. Specifically, we wish to help students identify caring and non-caring behaviours, strengthen coping skills, group problem solve, and to have some time for fun. Groups, composed of ten students and a faculty facilitator, meet five hours per semester. Based on student requests, the group stays together for the length of the programme.

Guidelines are established by the group regarding attendance, participation and confidentiality. The time allotted to caring groups is included in clinical laboratory hours. Caring groups are not therapy groups. Students understand that if problems arise, students may be referred to other services on campus such as the counselling centre. Groups use a variety of strategies including games to get to know one another, trust-building activities, positive affirmation and relaxation techniques.

In addition to journaling and the caring group, we have also restructured our schedules so that we have smaller sections to promote class interaction. We have decreased our content with the expectation that students are to come to class prepared. We have decreased the amount of class time devoted to lecture to provide for more group activities and emphasise both critical thinking and the linkages between theory and personal experience.

Caring is not about solving all of the students' problems. Students make decisions for a variety of reasons. Problem-solving for decision-making is a factor in the science of caring and must be encouraged. Mayeroff writes that 'In caring for a person, for instance, there are times when I do not inject myself into the situation. I do not take a stand one way or the other. I do nothing' (1971, p.1). Students can be helped to problem-solve and to see the possible results of their decisions. After giving support, the right choice for faculty may be to 'do nothing'.

Assessment of curricular transformation

Assessment of our curricular changes continues. Questions that are currently being explored include the following:

- Does participation in caring activities translate into caring behaviors in the clinical area? Guynn *et al.* (1994) report that students identify themselves as more caring after the caring curriculum experience, and Grams, Kosowski, and Wilson (1997) found that students expressed an intention to recreate the caring group experience in future practice settings. Evaluation by employers in the clinical areas are ongoing.

- Is the caring curriculum a true retention strategy? Thus far, our data indicate that it is, but more data is needed for evaluation. The faculty, however, believes that if students are happier, they will stay and tell others about our programme. Perhaps then the caring curriculum can become not only a retention strategy but also a recruitment strategy.

- Do caring groups have the same meaning for culturally diverse students? Kosowski, Grams, and Wilson (1997) found that the groups do increase cultural sensitivity and consciousness, contribute to academic success, and encourage personal and professional growth among our international students.

- What are the implications for faculty who are involved in the caring curriculum and specifically, the caring groups? A study in progress identifies the most positive aspects of the curriculum change for faculty as the connection formed with students and the egalitarian environment that we are working to achieve. Negative aspects reported include difficulty making tough decisions related to grading and progression when we know our students personally, the time involved in planning and conducting caring groups, and the 'burden of caring' which occurs when we feel powerless to help our students with problems beyond our expertise.

Through integration of principles of caring and feminist scholarship, we believe we have built a trusting community, empowered our students, and made a contribution to the science of caring. In the process, we have also created a more satisfied, enlightened faculty. However, more research is needed to determine how to help faculty learn to care for themselves as they continue to care for students.

References

Beck, C.T. (1992), 'Caring Among Nursing Students', *Nurse Educator*, 17.

Freire, P. (1970), *Pedagogy of the Oppressed*, tr. M. B. Ramos, Continuum Publishing, New York.

Grams, K., M. Kosowski and C. Wilson (1997), 'Creating a Caring Community in Nursing Education', *Nurse Educator*, 22.

Guynn, M., C. Wilson, B. Bar, K. Rankin, J. Bernhardt and C. Hickox (1994), 'Caring Groups: A Participative Teaching/Learning Experience', *Nursing and Health Care*, 15.

Hawks, J.H. and C. Hromek (1992), 'Nursing Practicum: Empowering Strategies', *Nursing Outlook*, 40.

Hedin, B.A. and J. Donovan (1989), 'A Feminist Perspective on Nursing Education', *Nurse Educator*, 14.

Heinrich, K.T. and B. Witt (1993), 'The Passionate Connection: Feminism Invigorates the Teaching of Nursing', *Nursing Outlook*, 41.

Keen, P. (1991), 'Caring for Ourselves', in R.M. Neil and R. Watts (eds), *Explorations in Feminist Perspectives*, National League for Nursing, New York.

Kosowski, M., K. Grams and C. Wilson (1997), 'Transforming Cultural Boundaries Into Caring Connections', *Journal of Nursing Science*, 2.

Mayeroff, M. (1971), *On Caring*, Harper & Row, New York.

Morse, J., S. Solberg, W. Neander, J. Bottorff and J. Johnson (1990), 'Concepts of Caring and Caring as a Concept', *Advances in Nursing Science*, 13.

Noddings, N. (1984), *Caring, a Feminine Approach to Ethics and Moral Education*, University of California Press, Los Angeles.

Riemen, D.J. (1986), 'Noncaring and Caring in the Clinical Setting: Patients' Descriptions', *Topics in Clinical Nursing*, 8.

Tanner, C.A. (1990), 'Caring as a Value in Nursing Education', *Nursing Outlook*, 38.

Watson, J. (1979), *Nursing: The Philosophy and Science of Caring*, Little, Brown & Co., Boston.

_____ (1988), *Nursing: Human Science and Human Care*, National League for Nursing, New York. State University of West Georgia Department of Nursing.

_____ (1998), *Philosophy*, Carrollton, Georgia.

Wilson, C., K. Grams and M. Kosowski (1997), 'Caring Groups in Nursing Education: Creating Caring Connections in Nursing Practice', *International Journal for Human Caring*, 1.

Wilson, C. and C. Hickox (1995), 'Caring Groups: An Experiential Teaching/Learning Strategy', in P. Bayles *et al.* (eds), *The Web of Inclusions: Faculty Helping Faculty*, National League for Nursing, New York.

Chapter 16

Feminist Pedagogy and International Studies

Karen J. Vogel

Introduction

Although theories about experiential education, student-centred learning, and feminist pedagogy have found application in many university and college classrooms, these approaches have been slow to come to international studies and comparative area studies curriculum. A nationwide study in the United States in 1994 found that little progress had been made in the pedagogy of these fields of study. Students were unprepared for the 'new challenges and the many opportunities presented by the dynamic post-Cold War international environment' (Goodman, *et al.*, 1994). International studies programmes and area studies courses in political science in particular needed to do 'much more' than just deliver content; they needed to find a way to engage students, to encourage global awareness, and to better train international experts, professionals, and activists. Since the post-Cold War era presented increasing dilemmas related to definitions of citizenship, identity, representation, and political power, many of these courses also required better methods for asking and answering questions about inclusiveness both in domestic as well as international politics.

In this essay, I argue that using feminist pedagogy, including elements of experiential education and student-centred learning, in international studies courses is an effective way to meet this need. Feminist pedagogy provides a framework for developing critical thinking skills, connecting students to their learning, and fostering social understanding and political engagement. Drawing on student comments from class journals, assessment forms, and class assignments, I suggest that student-led discussions and interviews, simulations, case study research, and out of class volunteering with non-profits and international governmental and non-governmental organisations can help students develop tolerance, global awareness, and the desire to get involved in their local communities and the world.

Feminist pedagogy, student-centred learning, and International Studies in the US

Feminist pedagogy, student-centred learning, and experiential education often share theoretical approaches to learning and teaching. For example, the 'student-centred' approach includes theories that suggest student understanding and awareness of social and political issues can be promoted through pedagogies which foster learning in a social setting or social constructivism (Stage, *et al.*, 1998). Similar pedagogies which trigger an awareness of students' social conscience or that encourage recognition of the possibilities for social transformation through action can also increase student learning and engagement with the subject (Freire and Faundez, 1989). Still other research which focuses on multiple intelligences (Gardner, 1983) and varied learning styles push us to consider new methods of education which move away from traditional lecture and toward collaborative learning and student participation in activities both in and out of the classroom (Stage, *et al.*, 1998). Such ideas closely relate to the feminist pedagogic agenda of creating more democratic classrooms, using students as learning resources, and fostering a sense of caring for students as individual learners.

Related to the 'student-centred approach' is experiential learning. Described as both a method of instruction and a process for learning, experiential education can be defined as 'immersing students in an activity (ideally, closely related to course material) and then asking for their reflection on the experience' (Clements, 1992; Cantor, 1995). Learning activities like these push the student to engage directly with the subject being studied and may take place in either a work or service setting (Kendall, *et al.*, 1986). Of primary importance in creating learning is the reflection and analysis on the part of the student during and after the activity, connecting the experience to academic study or course readings. These activities are similar to the feminist pedagogical tendency to seek validation of personal experience and to enhance theory-building and student participation in creating knowledge. However, experiential education by itself has often been criticised for not paying close enough attention to the centrality of gender and race in educational structures and processes (Kenway and Modra, 1992; Gore, 1991). Often experiential education tends to focus more on the process of learning than on what is being learned and why.

Although feminist pedagogy draws on some of the methods of experiential education and student-centred learning, what differentiates feminist pedagogy is the additional practice of foregrounding assumptions about knowledge that are often assumed to be value neutral. In other words, feminists ask for justification of what may have been previously backgrounded assumptions about a particular concept, method, or discipline (Myers and Tronto, 1998). Feminist pedagogy goes beyond trying to just understand how students learn or what will foster greater social awareness. Feminist pedagogy provides a fruitful method for asking questions about how we know what we know and what biases may exist in that knowledge.

As Myers and Tronto (1998) explain, feminist pedagogy recognises the categories of selectivity and situatedness in exposing bias. Selectivity refers to the idea that in Western intellectual traditions 'the part has mistaken itself for the whole'. For example, many Western men who wrote about democracy in the 1700s and 1800s may have kept slaves, believed women to be unequal, and dismissed people from Asia as uncivilised (Minnich, 1990). These writers argued for democracy for themselves, but not necessarily for everyone else. The question is not about their accounts of democracy, but rather their lack of recognition of bias. These writers and philosophers did not question whether their partiality influenced their beliefs about who should be considered a citizen or not. Similarly, in international studies or comparative politics, one needs to be aware of who or what is defining concepts and policy-making and for what purpose. In other words, to what extent do scholars and political leaders miss part of the picture?

Situatedness comes from accounts of feminist philosophers of science such as Sandra Harding (1991) who argues that the place from which one conducts scientific research always influences what one comes to know. We have to be careful not to be too oblivious to how our knowledge may be influenced by our own perspectives. As Harding and others observe, 'what people think they know to be true may in fact be mere chimera in their narrowed field of vision. Broadening their base of knowledge, then, requires people to broaden the perspectives from which they look at knowledge' (Myers and Tronto, 1998). Again, in international studies and comparative politics, we need to be aware of the standpoint of people doing research as much as the position of people making important foreign policy decisions. In order to examine international issues more fully, we must be aware of broader, multiple perspectives.

In the United States, these techniques have been evolving since the 1970s and largely have appeared in undergraduate (four-year colleges) and graduate level Women's Studies courses (Hoffman and Stake, 1998). Only recently, perhaps within the last five years, have feminist pedagogical techniques appeared in other more 'traditional' disciplines such as political science. The advantage of using multiple teaching and learning strategies is that students can develop a richer, deeper understanding of topics and at the same time connect them to their own experiences. In the case of intenational studies and comparative politics, content no longer is distant or abstract. Students feel that they can engage in questioning bias and theory-building as well as participate in actual events and activities related to international studies.

Building connections inside and outside of the classroom

Since the early 1990s, I have been experimenting with various feminist pedagogical techniques in my university courses which are cross-listed in political science and international studies. (Some of these methods have been documented elsewhere. See Vogel, 2000.) These courses range from introductory seminars for first year students to classes for seniors or students majoring in the social sciences. Although I teach at a small liberal arts university in the upper Midwest of the United States, variations of these methods could be employed at any university or college with similar programmes or areas of study. These strategies may be used as well at community colleges or two-year institutions to introduce students to collective learning, group discussions, and reflective practice. One constraint might be class size. Such pedagogical methods tend to work best in classes no bigger than twenty to twenty-five students. If these methods were to be used in larger classes, arrangements would need to be made for special discussion sections or 'workshop' settings to provide a more 'comfortable' atmosphere and closer contact among students and instructors.

In whatever course I teach, I begin by setting the stage for what we will be doing both inside and outside of the classroom together. I start by identifying some general learning goals in my syllabus. The learning goals might include enhancing critical thinking skills, developing discussion techniques and working with others, learning about strategies of multilateral negotiation, gaining confidence about asking questions and pursuing answers, improving writing skills, or increasing skills of theorising and reflection. Although I often prescribe the general topics and readings we will cover, I do not detail all the information that I expect students to learn. I let students know that they will have opportunities for contributing to our syllabus and for reading on their own. The students will also have some time for exploring related theories and interests which the students may develop during the course of the semester.

Next, like Jean Fox O'Barr (1994), I believe an important step in the classroom is building links between the students and their own knowledge as well as between the students and the new material they are reading. Usually on the first day of class, I have students interview each other and share the results of that interview with the rest of the class. During the interview, I ask students to exchange names, majors, and other information; usually I ask them to find out from each other whether they are interested in foreign languages, if they have travelled to another country, or if they have had an experience living in another culture (Vogel, 2000).

Frequently, American students in the Midwest have been no farther than the Canadian border, but many times, other international students are in class who can talk about their backgrounds. Students may also be in class who have participated in international exchange programmes prior to college and can share some of their experiences. Students of different ethnic backgrounds may additionally talk about their experiences living in different regions of the US. As the semester unfolds and we read histories or descriptions, theories and analyses of international politics, students use this early discussion experience to locate themselves in the larger discourse of international studies; they link what they are learning with questions they have about their own lives and cultural experiences. These conversations often open the door to discussions of race, class, and gender issues in their own countries as well as abroad. As one student noted in her journal, 'I have been impressed with our class discussions [...] We are breaking down some of the walls that we have built up. Makes me believe there is hope in ending the ignorance and racism that sometimes exists on our campus and in the world' (Student Journal, Spring 2000).

In assigning class readings for courses about government and politics in Europe, Asia, or other parts of the world, I choose readings which give a flavor for that region through the voices of writers from those areas. I also include articles or books from authors who may represent a minority view or alternative voice to the dominant culture in a particular country or region. Incorporating as many points of view as possible gives students an opportunity to talk about how information is presented and the strengths and weaknesses of various interpretations. By also using readings and texts with different methodologies (e.g. personal narrative versus quantitative analysis), students gain multiple insights to problems and discover new ways to process knowledge.

Another method for engaging students in international topics is to include an assignment during the semester which encourages face to face interaction and interviews with international students on campus or in the community. I have used this exercise in my international studies/political science seminar for first year students. Usually within the first half of the semester, students are asked to meet with an international student outside of class, preferably someone who came to Minnesota in the last two years. Conducting a half-hour interview, students must ask several questions: What did the international student find strange or interesting about their first visit to the US? What was different from home or familiar? Were there any misconceptions that were dispelled by seeing the US for themselves? Did they or do they still have any experiences with sexism or racism? And how is this different or similar from social or traditional practices at home? After the interview, students in the first year class are asked to write up the results, discussing what was said and some of their own impressions of the meeting.

The results of this assignment are multiple. First, American students have a chance to hear about what it is like to be an international student in another country. Second, they often get to hear about the social, political, or cultural practices of people in a different state. Third, the international students have a chance to share their knowledge and experience with the American students and perhaps to form friendships on campus which otherwise might not occur easily. Fourth, students are given the opportunity to think about their own prejudices, confronting stereotypes and misconceptions about people from a different ethnic background. And finally, the assignment often prompts curiosity and interest in learning more about other people and political systems around the world. As a typical first year university student noted in her self-assessment essay at the end of the semester, 'I was so happy to do the international student interview assignment; it was a life-changing experience. I learned as much about myself as I did about the person I was talking to' (Student Assessment Essay, Fall 1999).

Another way to encourage interests in international issues is to have students participate in simulations, policy workshops, and country case study research. In particular, I use these methods of active, student-centered learning in my course on Government and Politics of Western Europe. At the beginning of the term, students may choose a country which is currently a member of the European Union. This country is their 'case-study' for the rest of the semester, using what they learn in their research about this state in tests, policy position papers, and class discussions. During the last two weeks of class, students then use this knowledge to participate in a simulation of the debates of the European Council of Ministers, representing the country they have researched all semester long. Students must represent accurately the position of their state, taking into account who controls the governments and the country's economic, social, and political circumstances. They must take the country's 'point of view' rather than arguing strictly from their own personal perspective on the issue at hand. In this way, students are challenged to look at issues in a different way, to develop problem-solving skills, and to seek common ground for discussion even when national interests seem very far apart.

The results of the case study research and simulation are that students become directly involved in the material and carry their interests beyond the classroom. Frequently students who take this course develop such an interest in the European country they have studied they go on to pursue further work through independent research and study abroad.

Using simulations and case study research can also be done through participation in Model United Nations programmes. Throughout the United States and parts of Europe, universities and colleges host conferences where students can simulate the decision-making apparatus of the United Nations. At my institution, each year we send a team of college students to the national Model United Nations conference held in New York City. The students spend a week representing a particular country and engaging in multilateral negotiations. The opening ceremonies of the conference are usually held in the General Assembly Hall of the UN building, and during the conference, students hear guestspeakers from various UN agencies and related non-governmental organisations (NGOs). The experience provides an excellent opportunity to learn about other countries, the operations of international organisations, and the role of the United States in these activities. During our preparations for the conference, we debate, analyse, and critique theories about international governance, integration, and leadership, often raising questions about power, human rights, gender and politics.

Connecting the local and the global

Along with class readings and student-centred projects, greater awareness of community and global issues can be achieved by collaboratively designing, with students and local international organisations, experiential learning activities which take students out of the classroom and off campus. For example, in my course on International Organisations, I have students volunteer thirty to sixty hours at the American Refugee Committee, the Center for Victims of Torture, the Minnesota International Center, Women Against Military Madness, the Minnesota Chapter of the United Nations Association, or the Minnesota International Institute. Working with these organisations, we devise activities where students learn about the work of these groups and the global issues they address. Often these issues involve human rights, conflict resolution, and treatment of women. In addition to the volunteer hours and regular class time, students are required to write about their experiences and to research the history, operations, and programmes of the organisation. In this way, reflection, theorising, and experience are all built into the learning process.

The professor largely chooses the organisations although sometimes students have suggestions about which organisations might interest them. I attempt to choose organisations which are open to working with students of all genders and which will give the students the best variety of experiences. A few weeks prior to the beginning of the semester, I contact officials at each organisation to discuss with them their expectations for students as well as my expectations for the projects. The organisations are then asked to evaluate the volunteer work of the student during the term and to share that evaluation with the students and me. Any written work, such as applied research, completed by the student is also made available to the organisation if desired.

Volunteering at locally based international organisations, while simultaneously studying globalisation, the role of women in international organisations, and human rights, helps students discover that global topics may have local dimensions and vice versa. Through their papers and journals, students are pushed to connect theory and practice, and they are involved in their own learning processes. This involvement, as well as the off-campus experience, automatically changes the teacher–student relationship. I am no longer the sole authority or provider of knowledge on a subject; the development of knowledge, in this case on international topics, is a shared activity among students, community organisations, and faculty member.

In the traditional international studies or political science classroom of the past, power to distribute knowledge or to guide the direction of inquiry resided only with the instructor. Such power meant that the professor determined what was to be studied and how it was to be studied. In fields for years dominated by men in the United States, this power often meant a limited discussion of women's roles in the international arena or even acknowledgment that a feminist lense for the studies of these areas might be possible. Clearly the use of feminist pedagogy alters the distribution of power in the classroom, opening the door for students of all genders to participate in an intellectual discourse. At the same time, the discourse itself in international studies and political science is gradually starting to change and to acknowledge the presence of inclusiveness issues within the discipline as well as in the regions and international topics which we study.

Conclusion

In the early 1990s, disengagement and disenchantment with international studies and comparative politics curriculum were identified as key problems in the American university system. This essay has argued that feminist pedagogy, combined with elements of experiential education and student-centred learning approaches, provides a solution to these dilemmas by moving beyond traditional, lecture-driven methods of teaching and learning. In the case of courses in international or regional studies on topics such as International Organisations, Transitions in Postcommunist Central and Eastern Europe, Government and Politics of the European Union, or Diplomacy and the United Nations, the whole point is to get students to recognise bias and to participate in the theory-building process. We want them to build a connection between themselves and what is going on in the world. Feminist pedagogy places critical thinking and the exploration of bias at its center while at the same time exploring new ways to enhance student learning through student-led discussions, simulations, and out-of-class volunteering. These methods meet the needs and goals of international studies in the United States by helping students to enter 'another's shoes', to learn more about inclusiveness and political power, and to develop greater sensitivity to transnational issues in general. The best feminist pedagogical techniques draw on experiential education and student-centred learning, while at the same time providing a framework for critical theoretical study.

References

Cantor, J.A. (1995), *Experiential Learning in Higher Education: Linking Classroom and Community*, ASHE-ERIC Higher Education Report no. 7, George Washington University, Washington, DC.

Clements, A.D. (1992), 'Experiential Learning Activities in Undergraduate Development Psychology' in *Teaching of Psychology*, 22.

Freire, P. and A. Faundez (1989), *Learning to Question*, Continuum, New York.

Gardner, H. (1983), *Frames of Mind*, Basic Books, New York.

Goodman, L.W. (1994), *Undergraduate International Studies on the Eve of the 21st Century*, Association of Professional Schools of International Affairs, Washington, DC.

Gore, J. (1990), 'What Can We Do for you! What Can "We" Do for "You": Struggling Over Empowerment in Critical and Feminist Pedagogy', *Educational Foundations*, 4.

Harding, S. (1991), *Whose Science? Whose Knowledge? Thinking from Women's Lives*, Cornell University Press, Ithaca.

Hoffman, F.L. and J.E. Stake (1998), 'Feminist Pedagogy in Theory and Practice: An Empirical Investigation', in *NWSA Journal*, 10 (1), Spring.

Kendall, J. and Associates (1990), *Combining Service and Learning: A Resource Book for Community And Public Service*, 1, National Society for Internships and Experiential Education, Raliegh, North Carolina.

Kenway, J. and H. Modra (1992), 'Feminist Pedagogy and Emancipator Possibilities', in C. Luke and J. Gore (eds), *Feminisms and Critical Pedagogy*, Routledge, Chapman & Hall, New York.

Minnich, E. (1990), *Transforming Knowledge*. Temple University Press, Philadelphia.

Myers, J. and J.C. Tronto (1998), 'Truth and Advocacy: A Feminist Perspective', *PS: Political Science and Politics*, 31 December.

O'Barr, J.F. (1994), *Feminism in Action: Building Institutions and Community Through Women's Studies*, University of South Carolina Press, Chapel Hill.

Stage, F.K., P.A. Muller, J. Kinzie and A. Simmons (1998), *Creating Learning Centered Classrooms: What Does Learning Theory Have to Say?*, ASHE/ERIC, Higher Education Report, 26 (4).

Student Journal, Spring 2000.

Student Self-Assessment Essay, Fall 1999.

Vogel, K.J. (2000), 'Connecting Students with the World: Experiential Education and International Studies', *Hamline Review*, Hamline University, St Paul, Minnesota.

Chapter 17

Queer Theory and Lesbian Politics in the Community College

Allison Green

Introduction

In the ongoing discussions and debates about lesbians in academia – as faculty members, as instructors in the classroom, as students, and as the subjects of research and scholarship – community colleges have been neglected. Community colleges, common across the United States, are institutions where students may attend their first two years of higher education, earning an Associate of Arts degree, or a one- or two-year vocational programme, earning a certificate to work in a position such as dental assistant or travel agent.[1] The invisibility of the community college in these discussions of lesbian identity and queer theory is, I argue, a class issue. Community college faculty are marginalised because of whom we teach and whom we are assumed to be. Yet, the conditions of our institutions allow us to foreground issues of identity and representation for students early in their academic careers, long before students at four-year institutions may encounter them. Furthermore, our institutional conditions can allow us to bridge the divide between theory and politics, which is at the heart of disagreements over lesbian identity and queer theory. Thus we have significant experiences to contribute to these debates. In this article, I examine the context of community colleges relative to debates over queer theory and lesbian identity, using as a case study an experience I had teaching a course combining freshman composition with sociology on the theme of gender.

A house of difference

The invisibility of the community college in the lesbian identity/queer theory debates is evident in two recent anthologies on issues for lesbians in higher education, neither of which considers the significance of community colleges in any substantial way. The editors of *Lesbians in Academia: Degrees of Freedom*, Beth Mintz and Esther D. Rothblum, explain who is not in the anthology and why: for space considerations, narratives from lesbian graduate students and job-seekers were not included; closeted lesbians from Christian and military institutions, not surprisingly, did not submit manuscripts at all. The editors are pleased, however, with the resulting diversity, which they describe as including 'type of academic setting'. They do not explain why community college instructors are not represented, but the oversight is significant. If *Lesbians in Academia* contains no community college instructors, 'academia' must not include two-year colleges. *Tilting the Tower: Lesbians Teaching Queer Subjects* (Garber, 1994) contains papers from a few community college instructors, but the authors never explicitly discuss the impact of their type of institution on their subjects.

This lack of visibility is clearly a class issue. It is not hard to find popular depictions of the community college: in the film *Good Will Hunting*, to identify just one example, Robin Williams plays the backwater community college instructor with a heart of gold who lectures to dimwitted, gum-snapping students who clearly are not 'real' college material. Williams is considered a failure for teaching at such an institution. The students are there because they could not get into better colleges; they will earn their minimally respectable A.A. degrees so they can do the unimportant work of fixing the cars and cutting the hair of the professionals who earned rigorous degrees at universities. Such depictions apparently blind even those who hope to 'capture the variety and complexity that comprises life for lesbians as academics' (Mintz and Rothblum, 1997, p.3).

Yet the community college is better positioned to be a site for contested meaning and social transformation than the university. If there is a 'house of difference' in higher education, to paraphrase Audre Lorde, then surely it is more likely to be the community college than any other type of educational institution.[2] I do not want to oversimplify or overstate this. Certainly the community college is as prone to racism, sexism, classism and heterosexism as any other institution. Certainly it can be profoundly conservative. But the potential is there in community colleges for a radical disruption of traditional conceptions of knowledge and higher education. At the heart of this potential is the ability of the community college to challenge the dichotomy between theory and politics, which, in the form of queer theory and lesbian identity politics, are central concerns for lesbians in the academy.

Theory and politics: still dichotomised

In 'Queer Theory: The Monster that Is Destroying Lesbianville', Lynda Goldstein summarises the tensions between lesbian identity politics and queer theory in the academy. On the one hand, lesbians are becoming increasingly visible in the classroom, in the curriculum and on the faculty, thanks to years of hard, often painful, work. On the other hand, queer theory has emerged to question the very notion of a stable identity, potentially undermining these efforts. As Goldstein notes, 'playful, performative, irreverent queer theory seems only to make a mockery of the very real and difficult conditions of our academic and home lives within a variety of communities' (1997, p.264). The emphasis of queer theory seems to be on performativity over lived reality, on texts rather than people, on abstract and apolitical musings instead of efforts to improve lesbians' lives. Says Goldstein: 'No coherence. No utopics. Bi? Trans? Straight? Gay? Lesbian? Whatever, queer theory responds. Get over categories' (1997, p.267). But

Goldstein argues that queer theory is no monster out to destroy lesbians. Yes, some queer theory is lightweight and simplistic; yes, queer scholarship's ability to make money for publishers, especially the scholarship on popular culture, can eclipse other work on gender and sexuality, thus lessening the opportunities for lesbian academics in other fields to publish and achieve tenure. But, Goldstein suggests, queer theory at its best sets the stage for true coalitions across race, class, gender and sexuality; it is revolutionary, unwilling to accept a place for lesbians at the academic table, preferring to upend the table and set about feeding everyone. In that sense, queer theory is political and is about people.

Goldstein's bridging of queer theory and lesbian identity politics is a welcome addition to the discussion. Lisa Duggan has also mapped some of this terrain, especially as it concerns her scholarship on the history of lesbians in the United States. She conceives of herself as a 'translator – of activist concerns in academic settings, and of intellectual/theoretical arguments to further concrete political projects' (1998). She rejects the queer theory versus identity politics stance as simplistic and suggests that it is sometimes used to mask political and generational conflicts among academics.

Yet the schism continues to complicate discussions about the roles, research and pedagogy of lesbians who teach in higher education. And, although the focus in these debates is queer theory and lesbian identity, the larger issue is the general one of theory versus politics. We can look to debates about women's studies for the same kinds of conflicts. For example, here is Wendy Brown on the viability of women's studies:

> If the mission of women's studies is understood as primarily political, and as willingly sacrificing intellectual coherence to its political project, who will teach in such programmes and what kind of teaching will it be? [...] Many contemporary feminist scholars currently have limited traffic with women's studies programmes – they may cross-list a course or two, or allow their names to be affiliated with the programme, but remain peripheral to the curriculum and governance of the programme. Conversely many women's studies programmes are staffed by a disproportional number of faculty with an attenuated relationship to academic research and writing, but whose political devotion to feminism and pedagogical devotion to the students is often quite intense (1997, pp.96-7).

In Brown's conception of women's studies, political and pedagogical 'devotion' are necessarily counterpoised against intellectual rigor. The same distinction could be applied to the activities of lesbians in the academy. Those who give considerable time and energy to their work as role models for lesbian students, as visible challenges to straight students and as activists for curricular and institutional change, it might be argued, are committing the double crime of allowing themselves to be distracted from their own scholarship and ignoring current scholarship in queer theory by replicating the fallacy of the unified lesbian subject. Community college instructors, too, fare poorly under this conception: we spend more time teaching than faculty at universities and we are rewarded for teaching, not scholarship, therefore we must be 'sacrificing intellectual coherence to [our] political project' (Brown, 1997, p.96).

If we are to reconcile the apparently competing claims of queer theory and lesbian identity politics, then we must return to some very basic tenets. Theory without politics is elitist and classist; it is the luxury of those who are not battling every day for their survival. And politics without theory is anti-intellectual and thus likely to be shortsighted at best. In order to recognise and act on this dynamic nature, we need to reconceptualise the academy as a place where theory informs politics and politics informs theory in all ways and at every level. We cannot artificially separate the academy, as intellectual sphere, from the 'real world', as political sphere.

Again, it is useful to consider the debates in women's studies. Leora Auslander suggests a binary conception of theory and politics when she states that there is a 'crisis of constituency' in women's studies programmes today (1997, p.18). The first women's studies scholars had been full-time activists, she notes, and as they joined the academy, they had 'a sense of accountability to a movement and to people beyond the academy' (1997, p.19). But activism was exhausting, and universities became a 'refuge' (1997, p.19). As a result, 'A paradoxical consequence of gaining some large measure of respectability and legitimacy within the academy is that we have become less engaged with the world outside of it' (1997, p.19). This is a false dichotomy, and nowhere is this more obvious than in the community college.

Bridging theory and politics

Auslander's discussion of women's studies activists presumes that there is an academy and there is a real world. But, at the community college, we are the real world. That is, we are demographically more like the real world than most universities. Community colleges have open-admissions policies – virtually anyone may enroll. At my college, an applicant must merely be eighteen years old and have a high school diploma or its equivalent.[3] In fact, there is no application process; students simply enroll in classes. They do not compete with other students for admission. In addition, students are not penalised for poor grade point averages in high school or at other colleges. Although some courses, such as freshman composition and college-level math, require students to pass entrance examinations, many other courses have no prerequisites, and, while a student is taking remedial writing or math courses, she may begin working toward her A.A. immediately. Furthermore, the tuition is much lower at Highline than at any of the regional four-year institutions.

What this means is that the student body at a community college is likely to be more demographically diverse than at a four-year institution – in terms of class, ethnicity, first language and age. More students at community colleges than at other institutions of higher education are the first in their families to attend college. Our students often feel like outsiders to academia – and they are. This sense of themselves as outsiders gives them a perspective on higher education that can potentially keep them grounded in practice while they are being introduced to theory.

More specifically, our students tend to have a sense of themselves as having multiple, conflicting and shifting identities. Consider the leadership of our club for gay, lesbian, bisexual and transgender students, which I helped a group of students start in the spring of 1996. Of the four club presidents I worked with, before passing the advisor role to a colleague, not one of them was what we might think of as the typical college student – someone just graduated from high school, with plenty of financial aid, working only to earn spending money. Our first president was a white, middle-class ex-marine in her late twenties who was earning her paralegal certificate after a work injury to her back. Our second president was in her early twenties, white, working class, deaf; the state vocational rehabilitation office paid her tuition as long as she was in a one-year certificate programme, such as child care, and did not try to get an A.A. degree. Third was a Chicana grandmother in her mid-thirties. And fourth was a middle-aged white man in a state worker retraining programme who had been dishonorably discharged from the military for being gay. All of these students were interested in claiming a gay/lesbian identity and in putting in time to increase visibility on campus. At the same time, all had other identities that often claimed their time and energy: mother, grandmother, Deaf, returning student, Chicana, poor, working class. These competing identities often 'won out' – three of the four presidents were in office for two quarters or less before leaving the club to take care of other obligations. And for every one of these students, there are likely dozens at Highline whose gay, lesbian, or bisexual identity is not enough to propel them into organising around it.

Perhaps our students do not have the luxury to identify primarily as gay, lesbian or bisexual (few seem to define themselves as 'queer'). A white, nineteen-year-old middle-class student with no children, whose ethnicity and class are largely invisible to her, may find it relatively unproblematic to claim her lesbianism as an identity to organise around. If she is a women's studies major at a four-year institution, she will, we can hope, expand her understanding of identity and recognise her class and ethnicity. But for many of our queer students, issues of poverty, racism, family obligations, even ageism, are competing with sexual identity for time and energy. If the purpose of queer theory is, as Goldstein argues, 'to subvert expectations [about sexuality and] open up possibilities for multiplicity', then our students already have access to a very concrete understanding of that theory (1997, p.267).

Another reason that community colleges are well positioned to bridge politics and theory is the fact that we are two-year institutions. Many of our students will never transfer to a four-year college; Highline is their only exposure to higher education. Those of us who are concerned with social justice know that we cannot assume our students will study issues of gender, class, race, ethnicity and sexuality in specialised, upper division courses, and so we build those issues into our 100- and 200-level courses. Furthermore, students at this level can benefit from studying these issues just as much, if not more, than advanced students. For example, students at Highline can take their introductory sociology class with a focus on Hip-Hop music and culture.[4] Hip-Hop culture, with its critique of racism, police brutality, and economic injustice, becomes the central focus of study. For many students this may be the first time they have found an important aspect of their lives deemed serious enough for academic scholarship. This course allows students to learn the basics of an academic discipline through familiar material – and it allows them to critique assumptions of what is acceptable for academic study. For students who participate in Hip-Hop culture, this experience can be as transformative as the experience of lesbians who take their first queer theory class and find that their experiences are central and not marginalised.

Of course, another reason faculty at Highline teach topics that might be expected only at upper-division and graduate levels is that, if we do not teach them now, we will never teach them. For those of us who majored or minored in women's, ethnic or gay/lesbian studies, we have to incorporate the books, articles, films and other materials that changed our lives into our introductory courses – or never teach them at all.

Maria Gonzalez, writing in *Lesbians in Academia* about the overemphasis on coming out in the classroom and the underemphasis on bringing lesbian issues into the general curriculum, argues:

> There is some very strong evidence within this collection of writings that lesbians are being coopted into the academy. Their work in queer theory and gay and lesbian studies is not filtering broadly into the curriculum but ghettoised and tokenised into marginal spaces. For those who challenge this description, I respond with the question, 'Is lesbianism discussed in the introductory classes of English, history, or biology?' (p.235).

For Highline the answer is 'yes'. Lesbianism is being addressed at least to some degree in introductory sociology, political science, general humanities, literature, ethnic studies, anthropology and geography classes. To summarise, we are motivated to raise issues of sexuality in introductory courses because of the conditions and pressures of the two-year institution: many students will end their higher education at this level and will have no further opportunity to study sexuality at a higher level; our students benefit from learning about issues of sexuality; and as instructors we have no other opportunities to teach material that has been transformative for us.

For all of the above reasons, sociologist Derek Greenfield and I developed a course called 'He Said/She Said: The Social Construction of Gender', in which we created a curriculum designed to challenge students' notions of gender and sexuality.

Liquid nitrogen

Derek and I taught 'He Said/She Said' in the fall of 1998 to forty-five students, who earned five credits of introductory sociology and five credits of introductory (freshman) composition. The book that sparked the discontent was *S/he* by Minnie Bruce Pratt, a lyrical memoir about life on the transgender borders that undermines and explodes traditional conceptions of gender. Throughout the course, issues of sexuality and sexual identity arose numerous times, but, I will argue, it was the combination of my presence as an out lesbian and the use of Pratt's radical text that ignited student action. Furthermore, this student activism was a good outcome –

even a desirable one – which demonstrated to students the power of agency and resulted in transformative experiences for at least several of the students and possibly more.

I first came out in class in a discussion of Carol Tavris's *The Mismeasure of Woman*, in which I pointed out the heterosexual bias in the book, using my own experience. As always, students did not react overtly. But my openness had an impact: shortly thereafter, three students came out to the class (two others came out to me but not to the class). Students who were uncomfortable with homosexuality did not indicate their disapproval either verbally or nonverbally in the classroom. At least one straight student, 'Rick', responded positively. He had lesbian housemates and told me it was 'cool' that I had come out to the class. This established a rapport between us that was useful later, when he was disturbed by *S/he*.

About two-thirds of the way through the quarter, we were scheduled to begin reading *S/he*. Derek and I were expecting some resistance, but we were caught by surprise when, the week before readings in the book were even assigned, several students voiced concerns in class: 'Why are we reading this book?' 'It's pornography.' 'I started reading it and I can't.' It is not often that students read books ahead of due dates, but no doubt they were drawn to chapters such as 'Cock', 'Penis', and 'Fuck'. Derek and I listened to the concerns and reassured students that they did not have to like the book. There would be plenty of opportunities to discuss their concerns during seminars.

From class discussions and student evaluations, I estimate that about a third of the students strongly objected to the book, but one student was extremely troubled. 'Beth' appeared in my office one day to say she would not read *S/he*. Beth was a white woman in her mid-thirties who had been using the course to explore issues of childhood sexual abuse and her failed marriage to an African American man. I asked her why she did not want to read the book, and she referred to the introduction in which Pratt explains how she left her husband for a woman and was denied custody of her sons because she was a lesbian. Beth said that her own mother had abandoned her for a woman when she was a child. Very agitated, Beth said: 'My mother preferred pussy to us children!' Eventually our discussion became heated, and I told her we would have to take this up at another time when we were both calmer. She angrily left my office. For weeks thereafter she refused to make eye contact with me, and she later met with my division chair and organised a meeting of students outside of class.

'Marie', an immigrant from Tonga with a conservative Christian faith, also expressed concerns about the book early on. One day in class, we asked students to write down questions they would have for Pratt. Students met in groups and shared their questions. Marie was in a group with 'Sam', a student in the state's Running Start programme, which allows high school students to go to community college. When we asked the class for volunteers to read their questions, Marie asked Sam to read his. It included the phrase, 'nympho, homo, lesbo, porno'. After a silence, several students challenged Sam's use of words, and a tense discussion ensued.

The next morning Marie appeared at my office, crying. She had gone to work after class the day before and there had been a newspaper column by conservative

Christian evangelist Billy Graham on her desk with the message to refrain from judging others. She had been wrong, she said, to encourage Sam to read his comment. It was hateful and judgmental, and she had realised that Christianity was not about hate. I hugged her as she sobbed.

Thereafter, Marie, not Beth, became the liaison between the angry students and instructors. The students, after meeting outside of class, asked for an all-class forum. The day of the forum, Marie began by stating that we were not there to call people names or vent angry feelings; we were there for constructive discussion. Whenever a student in the ensuing two hours edged toward inflammatory language, Marie stepped in and calmly redirected their comments. The forum ranged over a number of issues, from perceived unfairness in grading to concerns about a lack of gender 'balance'. Some men and a few women thought we had spent too much time on women and not enough time on men. They even used, as support, the fact that we spent more time on lesbian issues than gay male issues. In fact, we had taken great care to distribute class time, readings and videos equally between women and men. But some students are so used to the privileging of men that true gender balance feels disproportionately tipped toward women. Furthermore, I have encountered in student evaluations in other classes the perception that lesbianism is getting too much attention in class merely because I am out in the classroom. This objection is ironic given the lack of lesbian visibility in the general curriculum.

Not all students objected to the book. Several strongly supported it, including 'Rachel', who had announced on the first day of class that she wanted to be a sex researcher and was collecting oral histories of sexual experiences. Several female students, older by about ten years than most of the other students, had not heard of the meetings outside of class and were surprised at the level of anger. They voiced support for our use of the book. Many students, mostly women, argued that we had not overemphasised women's issues at the expense of men's.

Afterwards, Beth came to talk to me for the first time in weeks. I told her I would not talk without a third party present, and we arranged to meet with a campus counselor. In the course of that meeting, which lasted an hour and a half, Beth acknowledged that her discomfort with Pratt and her fury at her mother had coalesced in anger at me. I represented lesbians in general and her lesbian mother in particular. Once she had acknowledged this she apparently felt better and, at the end of the session, asked me for a hug! When I ran into her again a year later, she told me that the course had been an important learning experience for her.

I am convinced that it was the combination of my being out and the radical nature of the book that lead to the upheaval in our classroom. I had named myself 'lesbian', unsettling enough for some students but fixed, quantifiable. I have come out numerous times in classes before, and never has there been such a reaction. In our class, too, until we began reading *S/he*, students who were uncomfortable with my openness were able to manage their discomfort and continue to participate. The book, however, describes a fluid, unbounded sense of sexuality and gender that upended everything the students had known. Had both Derek and I been straight, students may have objected, but they would have been able to see the sexuality in the book as 'other' rather than as 'in their midst'. They could have dissociated themselves from the material more easily.

At the same time, it wasn't just any material about homosexuality that bothered students – it was Pratt. We also used E. Lynn Harris novel, *If This World Were Mine*, which is about a group of African American friends, one of whom is gay. Central scenes in the book involve explicit gay sex, and not one student complained about it. In fact, most students loved the book. Students who were engaged with *S/he* and supported our use of it pointed out this contradiction to other students during the class forum. But Harris's novels are on the best-seller list for a reason – they offer an uncomplicated, unthreatening version of sexuality. Pratt does not.

I believe this upheaval was useful and meaningful for students. As a group, students took their education into their own hands; as individuals, at least two students, Beth and Marie, underwent personal transformations. Furthermore, the effects rippled beyond the class. When the director of student programs, Diane Anderson, met with student government officers, who had been asked by some of our students to 'do something' about our class, she asked if they thought this situation would be different if the book under discussion were about race. This led to a thoughtful discussion among them about sexuality in the curriculum.

It might be argued that students were responding out of homophobia and therefore their activism was regressive rather than progressive. However, one of the arguments students kept voicing was that the book was not 'appropriate' for college study, and Derek and I were able to respond to this comment by helping students question assumptions about what is and is not academic, what is inside and outside the curriculum and why. The controversy was ultimately positive because it brought implicit assumptions into the open so they could be addressed, and it provoked students to take ownership of their education and voice their concerns. We cannot challenge our students to think critically and deeply about topics that are almost never addressed critically by the society at large and not expect strong resistance. However, active resistance is much more productive than other forms, such as apathy, giggling and cheating. Students who actively resist can be challenged to articulate their ideologies and level of knowledge, to listen to diverging ideologies and absorb new knowledge, and to synthesise what they are learning with what they already know. Such synthesis clearly occurred for at least some of our students.

I should note that our staff and administrators are largely supportive of classes such as 'He Said/She Said'. Derek, for example, was in the tenure process then and has since earned tenure. Without such support, it would be much harder for us to allow the flames of controversy to burn, confident that students would benefit in the end.

'Rick', the student who had called me 'cool' after I came out, but who had been very disturbed by *S/he*, stopped me on the sidewalk a couple of months after the class had ended. 'Allison', he said, 'I had a dream about you'. Uh-oh, I thought. He said, 'We were here on campus, and we were drunk. And there was a monster truck rally going on in the pavilion. And then the ground turned to liquid nitrogen'. 'Cool', I said. I do not know to what extent the ground of sexuality and identity turned to liquid nitrogen for our students, or for how long. But I know that we stimulated a level of thinking, discussion and, in at least a few cases, transformation that is often considered impossible in 100-level courses. The community college provides fertile ground for a dynamic synthesis of politics and theory. And although we do not have all the answers, we do have a kind of experience that has been seldom heard, a kind of experience that gives the lie to the dichotomy. At our best, we live up to our name, community college, and we combine theory and politics in order to transform individuals and society.

Notes

[1] Students attend community colleges, which are also called two-year and junior colleges, primarily for two reasons: 1) tuition is lower and class sizes are smaller than at the public universities and 2) community colleges have 'open-door' admissions; anyone may enter, although students need to pass placement tests to begin college-level courses in math and English. For students who have done poorly in high school, the community college offers courses to bring their skills to college level and a way to improve their grade point averages for admission to four-year institutions. In the Seattle area, the University of Washington has opened branch campuses that offer only third- and fourth-year courses, specifically for students who have spent their first two years at community colleges.

[2] Quoted in Pagenhart, 1994, p.177.

[3] International students have additional requirements, such as an English examination if English is not their first language.

[4] Derek Greenfield developed and teaches this course.

References

Auslander, L. (1997), 'Do Women's + Feminist + Men's + Lesbian and Gay + Queer Studies = Gender Studies?', *Differences*, 9.

Brown, W. (1997), 'The Impossibility of Women's Studies', *Differences*, 9.

Davey, D. (1984), 'Davey D's Hip Hop Corner', <http://www.daveyd.com> (25 July 2000).

Duggan, L. (1998), 'Theory in Practice: The Theory Wars, or, Who's Afraid of Judith Butler', *Journal of Women's History*, 10.

Garber, L. (ed.) (1994), *Tilting the Tower: Lesbians Teaching Queer Subjects*, Routledge, New York.

GenderWatch, <http://www.softlineweb.com/softlineweb/genderw.htm> (12 May 2000).

Goldstein, L. (1997), 'Queer Theory: The Monster that is Destroying Lesbianville', in B. Mintz and E.D. Rothblum. *Lesbians in Academia: Degrees of Freedom*.

González, M. (1994), 'Cultural Conflict: Introducing the Queer in Mexican-American Literature Classes', in L. Garber (ed.), *Tilting the Tower: Lesbians Teaching Queer Subjects*.

Harris, E.L. (1997), *If This World Were Mine*, Anchor Books, New York.

Mintz, B. and E.D. Rothblum (eds) (1997), *Lesbians in Academia: Degrees of Freedom*, Routledge, New York.

Pagenhart, P. (1994), '"The Very House of Difference": Toward a More Queerly Defined Multiculturalism', in L. Garber (ed.).

Pratt, M.B. (1995), *S/he*, Firebrand Books, Ithaca, New York.

Tavris, C. (1992), *The Mismeasure of Woman*, Touchstone, New York.

Chapter 18

A Feminist, Collaborative Process of Academic Development

Valerie A. Clifford

The New Zealand scene

New Zealand has not escaped the economic rationalism that has engulfed many Western countries. Universities are beset by rising student numbers, the diverting of government funding to the vocational tertiary sector, staff redundancies, loss of job security, axing of courses, large increases in student course fees and the restriction of student allowances. Universities strive to become entrepreneurial (an oxymoron to many academics), competing for money through consultancies, research funding and full fee-paying, overseas students, technological delivery being pushed as a way of competing for on- and off-campus students. Meanwhile NZ students have a collective student debt of $NZ3.24 billion and commonly work part-time to fund their studies.

While female students now make up just over half of the undergraduate population, institutionalised sexism still leads to poor ratios of women to men postgraduates and staff. Women earn less than their male colleagues as they get appointed to lower positions and lower rungs of the pay scales (even allowing for qualifications and publications). In 1991 women academics made up 22 per cent of full-time academics and 48 per cent of part-time academics. However, only 11 per cent of full-time Senior Lecturer and above positions were held by women and only 14 per cent of the part-time senior academic posts (Brooks, 1997). These figures show little change over the 1990s.

It was amidst this climate that a group of women academics generated the time to think deeply about their personal educational philosophies and to research their own teaching.

Introduction

For feminists the current pressures on universities offer exciting opportunities. In New Zealand the increase in student numbers has raised the number of women students to equal that of men students, and increased the diversity of students attending tertiary education, from within and from outside our country. Students from other cultures enter tertiary education with different frames of reference, goals and expectations. Some of these students challenge the Western, scientific, patriarchal traditions of our universities and so join the feminist voice in demanding change. Decreasing government funding and market pressures make accommodation of culturally different students a priority for universities. This has placed a new emphasis on the teaching role of universities and on academics to understand the nature of learning and teaching (beyond the Socratic method), and to be adequate practitioners of these theories. Concepts of socially constructed knowledge and the feminist validation of personal and emotional knowledge jostle with male, rationalist beliefs in the integrity of facts. Concepts of active learning and student-centred learning grate against the didactic lecture mode where students are viewed as empty vessels to be filled with facts pre-digested by the lecturer.

Despite these pressures to create new curricula and introduce new pedagogies the university culture appears resistant and change has been minimal. This is the challenge that we (a group of women working in a traditional New Zealand university) grasped.

A feminist, collaborative process for academic development

We offer you a feminist collaborative process for academic development. We call it a feminist process because we, as women, feel comfortable with it and it fits with the ideas that abound on women's ways of thinking, working and learning (Gilligan, 1982; Belenky *et al.*, 1987; Clifford, 1998). We do not see it as 'women only' ground. It would be exciting for our ideas to be picked up regularly and used by men and women to benefit students and the whole academic system:

> It is a long road to social change and yet we need to go it and we need company along the way, or at least, I do. It can all be undone so fast [Barbara].[1]

We have positioned this process in the context of a traditional university environment, in New Zealand, where changing teaching styles can be very difficult. Disciplines have historical, pedagogical traditions attached to their embedded theories of knowledge and staff and students often hold entrenched expectations. Change involves disrupting the theory of knowledge of the discipline and supporting excursions into pedagogical innovation in hostile environments. The rhetoric in universities now is all about quality teaching and change yet little is being done to support academics faced with these stressful demands. Academic development has also already developed a history and tradition of exposing academics to dollops of pedagogical theory and practice with little follow-up support for the ideas to be put into practice:

> I think that I wasn't aware how much energy, effort and anxiety, and how little support there is in the university environment, to change your teaching style. The rhetoric may be that it is quality education and that we are moving towards student-centred education but it seems to me to be very difficult to actually do that [Janet].

Academic developers need to find new ways of being catalysts for change and for offering ongoing support through the change process. Brookfield (1995) has written inspirationally about the use of group work, in the form of structured critical conversations about teaching, to help teachers 'learn what they do', and others have advocated the building of ongoing, cross-discipline, facilitated groups as the most effective form of academic development (Davis *et al.*, 1989; Maher and Tetreault, 1994; Sandler *et al.*, 1996), but what stays with us is often the difficulties rather than the successes. The difficulties caused by multiple layers of assumptions, expectations and uncertainties (Miller, 1990), the differences in disciplinary epistemologies and pedagogies, in feminisms, the pervasiveness of our competitive culture (McLeod *et al.*, 1994; Jipson *et al.*, 1995) and the lack of time in busy lives to work with group processes and to work through the competing ideologies and practices (Miller, 1990; McLeod, 1994). As a group we faced all these challenges and found ways through them.

We are going to take you into our group and show you the challenges, the frustrations, the awakenings, the successes and the disappointments of our venture, and to feel the supportive functioning of the group. With this experience we have been inspired to start other groups to bring about change and hope that we can similarly inspire you.

The group

We are university lecturers in physiology, bioethics, religious studies, psychological medicine, academic development and education. We were drawn together by a university wide email from Val (academic developer) and Janet (education) seeking others interested in exploring, in a group situation, the relevance of feminist pedagogy to disciplines across the university. Of the fifteen women who initially responded, nine settled down to work formally together as a research group, six of us seeing the project right through. As feminists we wanted to know what it might mean to take feminist pedagogy out of the discipline of Women's Studies and into disciplines not usually identified as feminist. Together we explored the parameters of feminist pedagogy and dared each other to try new roles in the classroom, to introduce new curriculum, to stand up to peer antagonism and student resistance. We intellectually challenged each other's views and beliefs while emotionally and practically supporting each other in our new teaching endeavours. The group, as a mechanism for initiating and sustaining pedagogical change, became as important as the projects themselves, as without the group the projects would not have existed. It has been a transformative project. Our teaching has changed. We have changed and we live in the hope that, as a result of our projects, our institution might be slightly different.

The university where we were working had a history stretching back into the last century and was the main economic driving force of a small, rural city with a strong conservative, Scottish, Presbyterian heritage. The university was dominated by its medical school and the culture was strongly patriarchal and research orientated. Only 11 per cent of the senior academic staff (senior lecturer and above) were women (Department of Statistics, 1993). Some departments had no female academic staff and others only one or two. Women academics were, therefore, often isolated, with little opportunity to discuss, and receive support for, innovative ideas in curricula and pedagogy. Students resisted change to traditional teaching practice, afraid that it would adversely affect their marks. They also resisted taking on responsibility for their own learning which involved more time and effort on their part.

From the beginning the commitment to the group was exacting for all of us; fortnightly two-hour meetings plus preparation. We met, we read, we talked, we argued – and we took the ideas that we had discussed and tried them out in our teaching. We came back and talked and read some more and thought through the implications of our work, and wrote about them. We thought each week about pulling out of the group but it was too important, too interesting. We really cared about our teaching, we really cared about being feminists, and we wanted the two to interact. This group was about life-long learning, being teacher-researchers, getting a research grant, gaining ethics committee approval, reviewing literature, being innovative, taking action, analysing and publishing. And fun!

We looked at our teaching through our own lives, interviewing each other about our development as teachers, transcribing our own lives and offering the transcripts to all of the group. This deepened our knowledge of our divergent experiences of life and increased our empathy for each other's standpoints as women. It started us talking about our teaching, helped us find a common language, as we struggled with concepts, recognised our prejudices and understood our enlightenments. Our children's more recent educational experiences added to our own.

We read the theoretical literature. We circled round and around critical pedagogy, feminist pedagogy, post-structuralism, post modernism. We defined and redefined and wondered about 'gynagogy'. We held our classrooms and curricula up against these ideologies and vowed to pursue change.

We worried about our students' resistances; their silences, absences, arguments, collusion and bad evaluations. We agonised about our colleagues' disapproval; if we were jeopardising our applications for tenure and promotion; our vulnerability in the next restructuring and redundancy rounds. Group members dropped out as pressure mounted to concentrate on 'proper' research in their disciplines. Yet along the way, the group provided a forum in which career paths could be analysed, experiences exchanged, plans made and moral support activated. We energised each other to take up the challenge of introducing feminist teaching.

The projects

We gave birth to our individual projects painfully after several months of labour. Janet's project encompassed whole curriculum change. She had been developing it for several years and was up and running before all of us. Judith wanted to care for her students while introducing potentially disturbing alternative readings of biblical texts. Jean invited her students to come to some understanding of their professional relationship with pregnant women. Val questioned her assumptions about journalling as a feminist approach to assessment. Barbara wanted her students to recognise the political nature of their education. Sunny experienced the hierarchical imposition of an innovative curriculum which challenged teachers' traditional living theories of practice.

A constant question throughout the group discussions was why we labelled our pedagogical practices as feminist rather than critical (Luke and Gore, 1992; Gore, 1993). As we prodded and poked our data, and lifted up the corners to see what might lie hidden beneath, we wondered what it all meant. Jean's students said she was still a good teacher despite being a feminist. Janet's students were asking highly politicised questions about the education system. Val's students seemed to overlook gender as a category of analysis in their teaching. Judith's students produced moving, creative poetry and prose. Barbara met up-front student resistance and Sunny found her students either felt threatened or mystified by the nature of her enquiry. We needed to find some way of drawing out what we were learning from our projects.

Making sense of it all

We found Kenway and Modra's (1992) continuum, which moves from personal consciousness raising, through the development of critical consciousness (analyzing the personal as social/theoretical constructs) to political action, useful for positioning our projects.

Kenway and Modra argue that feminist educators still focus too much on consciousness raising which can become 'reflection without action' (p.156). They advocate critical analysis of situations in order to become empowered and move to action. They challenge feminist educators to look beyond their 'lively' classrooms to analyse what transformations are, or are not, taking place for the students. As interactive teaching and experiential learning become commonplace, the theorising of gender can be overlooked.

We used the continuum as a structure in which we placed our projects. In positioning ourselves in terms of our projects rather than our personal feminist beliefs we have become aware of the discrepancies between our beliefs and our level of feminist functioning in our professional lives. The strength of the cultures of the traditional scientific discipline particularly allowed little room to change curriculum or teaching strategies.

We placed Jean and Barbara's work first as examples of personal consciousness raising. They were both trying to make room for the personal within the scientific paradigm and were both stepping outside their 'brief' in the eyes of their colleagues and their students. Jean wanted her physiotherapy students to see pregnant women as more than bodies and wanted them to start to think about the language and power relationships of health professionals with their clients. Barbara sought, through negotiated assessment, to raise her students' consciousness of the political nature of their education and met up-front student resistance.

Judith's project (McKinlay, 2000) showed a moving between the personal and analytical as she invited students to listen to each other and to the voices of scholars. She carefully thought through her role as facilitator as she balanced the tensions generated in the classroom by emotional as well as critical and creative responses. She tried to allow space for her students to 'try on' different readings of the texts.

Sunny, Val and Janet's projects were examples of prompting action among colleagues and students. Val (Clifford, 2000) asked her students (who were university lecturers) to use learning journals and group feedback to critically reflect on their own learning and plan future action. Sunny worked with medical students in a new problem-based learning curriculum, to develop the capacity to self-reflect and connect with their emotional knowledge. Janet successfully prompted the critical questioning of the gendered nature of curriculum through a pedagogical environment emphasising critical enquiry and student-centred learning.

The Kenway-Modra framework brings together our eclectic experiences of feminist pedagogy. We have struggled with the project at many levels: our own identification with feminism, understanding the constructs of feminist pedagogy when coming from a non-education discipline, the non-acceptance of feminist orientations in our academic communities, reconceptualising our discipline knowledge from a feminist perspective, and imagining different classroom and assessment strategies. We have become critically reflective teachers and we can use the lens of feminism to talk about personal conscientisation, critical conscientisation and feminist praxis in our teaching.

The real success of the projects for all of us has been the development of a critically reflective group, one which showed us a different way of working. We found that the group could be supportive and demanding, nurturing and critical, inspiring and sustaining. This feminist process of professional development is embedded in women's collaborative ways of working, and challenges people at any stage of their unfolding to work with others to push their own boundaries of understanding and practice.

The group is so important that we need to unpack the complexities of the group process to give you an idea of how it worked for us, to explore the nature of the support that the group provided and what we learnt from the experience.

Unpacking the process

Commitment

The fortnightly meetings, the running of the research projects, analysing the data and writing up were a tremendous time and energy commitment. This sort of commitment is not freely given or easily extracted from busy academics on purely intellectual grounds:

It takes time to collaborate. In any team project it takes time to get to know people personally. It takes a lot more time to work in a team than to run a project by yourself [Janet].

There have to be strong inducements in the situation. In a presentation on collaboration Dawn Francis (1998) spoke of the need for 'passion' for people to find and sustain enough quality time to commit to a topic. In this case feminist pedagogy was the initial intellectual interest. We were intrigued, curious, wanted to know more about feminist pedagogy, wanted to know where we fitted with the pedagogy and with the institution. For us the passion lay in working with a group of women on a woman's topic, in woman's ways. Our gender gave us some common language and understanding of where we were coming from:

I kept in the group because it was all women. We talked about things that mattered to me. Men do disturb the dynamic. It felt safe to be robust in conversation. I did not need to watch my back in case the males needed things to be interpreted to them to keep them on-line and safe to have around [Barbara].

A chance to work with other women. A chance to look into other women's working situations. But also there was a sort of release, you were with people who 'understood' and had 'been there' or 'were there', a safe haven in a way [Jean].

This made the group a 'safe haven' where we could say the feminist words, expose our ignorance or where we could be vociferous, even argumentative about issues without being put down.

The group also provided a chance to network with other women around the university:

It was safety. It gave me a chance to work with senior women [...] often talked about going for research grants and jobs [...] personal networking. As well as bringing the personal into our teaching, the group also brought the personal into our professional lives [...] It was a chance to get out of my own department. It gave me a network and the group became important for support. It was a chance to open other windows [Janet].

Support

For us the women-centredness of the project was an initial and an on-going imperative to belong to the group. After the initial flush of enthusiasm the hard work set in and what kept the group together was the support that we offered each other. We lived through the reviews of group members seeking tenure, the demands being made on us by university committees requiring 'token women', and the shortage of women postgraduate supervisors. We experienced the belittling of our research areas and the appropriation of our teaching innovations. We realised that as a group we could mentor each other. We were using the group to analyse the position of women in tertiary institutions, understanding what it meant to be a feminist and a feminist teacher, and seeing the potential for action through the group:

It kept me sane in a very demanding period of my work [...] the group probably played a part in helping me come to a clearer analysis of what was happening to me at work [...] the project helped me reflect on what it meant to teach within a patriarchal discourse, the possibilities for political action and curriculum change. The year was a continual discussion between internal and external aspects of my life [Barbara].

So while working to bring the personal into our teaching, through our struggles with feminist pedagogy, the group was bringing the personal into our work lives, providing mentoring in many different aspects of research, teaching and university governance that women often do not receive (Shapiro and Farrow, 1988; Neville, 1988; Collins, 1992; Ozga, 1993; Baachi, 1993; Brooks, 1997):

We are talking about academic mentoring [...] Val wanted academic mentoring to be like one of these groups, for there to be a whole lot of groups where people got together and did this sort of thing. I think it rarely happens [Jean].

The combination of working on something exciting and meaningful together while providing such a high level of personal support proved irresistible:

It was my feminist pedagogy group, where I belonged and I could explore these ideas [Janet].

Legitimation

This mentoring fuelled the need to meet together, but the excuse to spend work time at the group meetings had to be academically legitimate. Researching feminist pedagogy did not impress some of our (male) colleagues and their innuendoes made some members of the group twitchy. We found that being involved in a research project, with a university research grant and a goal of publication impressed our skeptical male colleagues. These were terms of reference that our colleagues recognised as academic and authentic. The university research grant meant that the topic was legitimate and the research methodology of an acceptable 'scientific' standard. The goal of publication meant that our work would be subject to peer review. These aspects also legitimated the project in our own eyes because we take our roles as academics seriously and have careers in the field. We also enjoy learning, being intellectually challenged and seeing our ideas work in practice:

It felt like a bit of a luxury to me [...] I was continually having to justify two hours [...] then there was the response of my colleagues, just a bunch of women sitting around talking about their periods or something [Jean].

Democratic processes

Co-facilitation As the project espoused feminism we (Val and Janet) were very careful to choose a group structure that was based on the principles of democracy and egalitarianism. Our choice of the roles of co-facilitators gave the group two initiators and guides. We called the first meeting and offered a one-page preview of what the project might look like. From that meeting on everything that was done was negotiated in the group. We facilitated the discussions, checking that the agreed agenda for each meeting was worked through and that everyone was fully involved. We fed ideas and resources into the group, as did the other group members. We organised basic necessities for meetings like the room, photocopying, tea and coffee, the group microphone and tape recorder, all things that make a meeting happen:

> That was another thing that was rewarding about the group, that it was so equal, and so I became more confident [...] as my situation became more apparent [...] people weren't critical of me [...] instead they tried to encourage me to read and learn and that was amazing, the group had a life of its own [Jean].

> I really value what they have and they in turn value what I have and I feel that is so appropriate for a focus like feminist pedagogy to have a kind of respect and egalitarianism and understanding of where people are coming from [...] it fitted our philosophy in the pedagogy that we were using them ourselves in the group [Janet].

Co-facilitating the group increased the reality of democracy in the group as no one person was seen as 'leader'. It also offered us, as facilitators, the advantage of support, allowing us the chance to debrief after the meetings. We checked out our perceptions of the interactions in the group and discussed ways of approaching situations. We had had different pedagogical careers and different histories with members of the group. This was invaluable in understanding some group interactions and being innovative about dealing with them. At an organisational level it was an insurance that all those small jobs still got done when one of us was away. It also meant that when Val moved to another university it was a natural progression for one of the other group members (Barbara) to move into the role of co-facilitator with Janet:

> As a facilitator it was great to have someone to talk through the process with regularly and to swap perceptions of what was happening [...] they were amazingly different at times [...] and at the analysis end, has been great to have someone on board to evolve the book outline with [Val].

As the project evolved so did the dynamics of the group and the roles of the facilitators. We had originally thought that, as facilitators, we would interview each of the group members about their educational autobiographies. We soon began to feel uncomfortable with this idea as it would place a lot of knowledge (and therefore power) in our hands when it would be more appropriate for it to be shared in the group. The collective drawing up of the interview schedule, the mutual interviewing that took place and the sharing of scripts forged strong links between us all early in the group's history. It seemed a natural progression for us (Val and Janet) to also become involved in research projects so that we faced the same struggles, and support in our research, as the other members of the group.

Way of working The way of working in the group was important. The group negotiated the agenda and timelines. Our initial task was to decide ways of proceeding and writing a research proposal and funding application. This demanding work was intertwined with the enjoyment of developing of our educational autobiographies. We spent several months vociferously debating literature in the area and encouraging each other to formulate research projects:

> The material was new to me [...] I learnt from listening to discussion [...] just loved being part of a group that was doing something where you could come back and talk about what you were doing on equal terms and then go away again for another session to think about it again [...] that place to come and reflect in a body I thought was invaluable and I would love to have similar experiences to do the same sort of thing [Judith].

As we struggled with the realities of our projects we supported and gave feedback to each other. As the projects neared completion we brought different insights to help make sense of the rich qualitative data which some of us had not handled before. The substantive writing took place over the summer 'break' and the scripts were chewed over at an all-day retreat in February. Polishing of the scripts has been done by email and fax.

A strong focus on the task is evident here but it was all embedded in our personal conversations, support and laughter.

Challenges

The group was not all plain sailing. Julie McLeod *et al.* (1994) wrote about the difficulty of working with people with different theories and practices and found that gender was not enough to bind the class together. We wonder what has been the dynamic between the six of us to keep us together, and what dynamics had made the others drop out? All the women who left had very good pragmatic reasons for doing so, but so did those who stayed. The tensions between departmental politics, the politics of teaching and personal feminism were played out differently for all of us.

One original group member consistently challenged the worth of the work of the group and sought to marginalise us, as facilitators, from the group. This challenge to the power of the facilitators to act as spokeswomen for the group made us constantly re-evaluate our roles as co-facilitators. The role of facilitator is a very privileged one and requires maintaining a level of honesty with the group and ourselves about happenings and opinions and for each member to feel comfortable with that level of honesty. The resistance from one member could have effectively paralysed the group but, for us, it provided an ongoing challenge to live up to our espoused feminist principles. So, although uncomfortable, the interaction also enriched the group:

> It strikes me in this environment how inadequately we cater for collaborative professional development [...] it has to happen by example and it has to happen by

collaboration. Val didn't work as an expert in this group, people didn't look up to me as an expert either, I had the opportunity to work alongside the group [Janet].

I think that the really important thing about the group was that we were all confident women in different ways. So I don't think, even if Val had wanted to be an expert she couldn't have been the expert because I am sure people like x would have immediately sat on her and said, 'No I don't see it like that' [Jean].

As the group members developed their knowledge of the potential functions of groups and their experience of the group processes, two members took the process and started and facilitated other groups based on the ideas of collaboration and facilitation and are, in turn, introducing others to the process.

Conclusion

I will never stand up and teach again without having this project in the back of my head [Jean].

We hope that institutions looking for ways of initiating and sustaining change will recognise, in the process presented, a way of exciting staff to drive change. For staff involved with change, this offers a way of being in control of change and being supported during the process, while establishing networks across the campus as the basis of friendships and future collaborations.

Our project shows the unfamiliarity of academics from non-humanities disciplines with educational frameworks theorising pedagogy. To them education language and concepts are as impenetrable as science/technology is to those in the humanities:

I remember when I first came how completely foreign the whole discussion seemed to be to me. I was completely and absolutely ignorant and I found that really quite devastating. I guess one of the really important things about the group has been the learning and in particular the realisation of different ways in which people teach [...] so it gave me an incredible amount of confidence [Jean].

Universities need to recognise the strength of the paradigms of different disciplines and their impact on the courage of staff to be different. The patriarchal organisation of the institution itself allows little room to question deeply embedded histories. The immersion of colleagues and students in these cultures does not easily allow for exploration of change at Departmental, School or course level. Trying to introduce pedagogical change by ourselves leaves us in unsupported positions when challenged by students. Innovation often starts when we have a gut feeling about our students and our teaching but we do not know the theory that supports that feeling and are inarticulate about what we are doing and why, so we do not impress our students or our colleagues. With this group we have found a way of moving forward constructively with those feelings, of being able to step out from the crowd, and invite our students on a journey with us. We know that if it does not work out that there will be a reasoned explanation and lessons learnt rather than public belittlement and an erosion of confidence:

> I will always be grateful for this project as it helped break through some of that loneliness of the woman/feminist academic, helped me to identify some dynamics and passions and to make some different choices [...] helped give me a safe context, affirmed my reality and analysis as in 'not crazy' and hence helped me to survive and move on with some sense of self esteem [Barbara].

> I have learnt from the project that professional development and learning to teach is much more successful in an on-going collaborative group rather than an expert training session that comes together infrequently [Janet].

The collaborative process illustrated here offers an opportunity for all academics to focus on educational philosophies, to explore them in the company of others, some struggling with new jargon and new frameworks and some familiar with them. The group allows academics to make a commitment to put ideas into action, while receiving feedback on their ideas and implementation, from supportive colleagues. The process then encourages an analysis of the innovation and dissemination of the ideas to colleagues. In this way the possibility of pedagogical change spreads:

> Unless you have a group like this I would probably be much less likely to sit and think about what I am doing and then change things readily. The support of the group and learning that you can come back actually allowed what might have been a passing thought to become something that you did [Judith].

The diversity of learning through this collaborative process has been immense. It would not have been possible for us to have gained this wealth of knowledge and experience on an individual project. From our project there are now six of us who can work with the process and see its promise. As an academic development process, to bring change to a tertiary education institution, this process offers long term benefits in not only getting innovative pedagogy projects up and running but in also giving staff skills that are essential to their teaching role and valuable in other areas of the university's work. This process truly develops the 'academic' in us all, while building networks across the campus and providing grass roots challenges to the university to focus on change in the areas that matter educationally:

> I think the ghost of this group will fly out [Jean].

Institutions need to give recognition and support to innovative change processes. Some universities have supported the development of Graduate Certificates in Tertiary Teaching opening up one way for staff to begin to explore educational praxis. On-campus courses offer a regular forum for discussion and an on-going support group for feedback on participants' investigation of their teaching. While many universities fund their staff to attend these course few allow time release for study (personal knowledge of the New Zealand and Australian university sector), a vital component for success.

For those not yet able to commit to a formal course of study, or in institutions that do not provide access to a course, the Action Learning Programme at the University of Queensland offers an exciting example of another way for institutions to support pedagogical innovation (Tertiary Education Institute, 1996). The Programme uses group processes to focus on pedagogical change, and is fully supported by the university in terms of finances, sponsorship and recognition of participation. Institutional support for our project came in the form of research grants (from the University of Otago and the University of Canberra). Other ways to support collaborative processes of academic development are through facilitator training and acknowledgement of the time involvement.

Recognition is another important aspect of institutional support for change and although promotion criteria now include pedagogical endeavours universities have to be seen to be implementing this change before the university folklore, that currently diminishes teaching, will change.

The challenges now are to explore (1) the portability of these processes, and (2) the embedding of such processes in institutional policy. Being now part of a regional university, where twelve island groups mingle, the question arises of the appropriateness of the process to other cultures. In New Zealand we were a group of Pakeha (European) women and the cultural differences that challenged us were those of our academic disciplines. Will the cultural differences based on ethnicity be greater than those of our disciplines? Will ethnic groups known for the collective orientation of their cultures find these learning processes quite natural? Will commitment, motivation and legitimation be crucial issues for the success of the groups? What will be their passions? How is the role of facilitator seen here? Will the university support this innovative process of professional academic development?

If universities are serious about their commitment to quality teaching and learning and supporting pedagogical innovation, they also need to support creative processes for achieving those ends.

Special thanks to Janet Soler, Barbara Nicholas, Jean Fleming, Judith McKinlay and Sunny Collings for participating in this project, for your amazing collegiality, for your permission to write about our work together and for your constructive comments on this chapter.

Note

[1] All quotes are from tape transcripts of group meetings, including a meeting reviewing the experience.

References

Baachi, C. (1993), 'The Brick Wall: Why so Few Women Become Senior Academics', *Australian Universities Review*, 36 (1).

Belenky, M.F., B.M. Clinchy, N.R. Goldberger and J.M. Tarule (1987), *Women's Ways of Knowing. The Development of Self, Voice and Mind*, Basic Books, New York.

Brookfield, S.D. (1995), *Becoming a Critically Reflective Teacher*, Jossey Bass, San Francisco.

Brooks, A. (1997), *Academic Women*, SRHE/Open University Press, Buckingham.

Clifford, V.A. (1998), 'A Patient-Centred and a Doctor-Centred Practice – a Viable Concept?', in C. Waddell and A. Petersen (eds), *Health Matters*, Allen and Unwin, Sydney.

_____ (2000), 'Journalling: Is This Feminist Assessment?', *Cornerstones: What do We Value in Higher Education? Proceedings of HERDSA Annual International Conference July 1999*, Melbourne.

Collins, J. (1992), 'Disciplining Academia: Women Academics and Possibilities for Change', *Women in Leadership Conference*, Edith Cowan University, Perth.

Davis, F., A. Steiger and K. Tennenhouse (1989), *A Practical Assessment of Feminist Pedagogy*, La Direction des Services Pedagogiques, College Vanier, Quebec City.

Department of Statistics (1993), *Educational Statistics*, Department of Statistics, Wellington, New Zealand.

Francis, D. (1998), 'An Issues Paper on Collaboration', Keynote address presented at *CUTSD Annual National Teaching Forum*, Canberra.

Gilligan, C. (1982), *In a Different Voice*, Harvard University Press, Boston.

Gore, J. (1993), *The Struggle for Pedagogies*, Routledge, New York.

Jipson, J. *et al.* (1995), *Repositioning Feminism and Education*, Bergin & Garvey, Westport, Connecticut.

Kenway, J, and H. Modra (1992), 'Feminist Pedagogy and Emancipatory Possibilities', in C. Luke and J. Gore.

Luke, C. and J. Gore (1992), *Feminism and Critical Pedagogy*, Routledge, New York.

Maher, F.A. and M.K. Thompson Tetreault (1994), *The Feminist Classroom*, Basic Books, New York.

McKinlay, J. (2000), 'Match or Mismatch? Attempting a Feminist Pedagogy for a Course on Biblical Criticisms, *Teaching Theology and Religion*, 3 (2).

Mcleod, J., L. Yates and K. Halasa (1994), 'Voice, Difference and Feminist Pedagogy', *Curriculum Studies*, 2 (2).

Miller, J.L. (1990), *Creating Spaces and Finding Voices. Teachers Collaborating for Empowerment*, State University of New York Press, New York.

Neville, N. (1988), *Promoting Women: Successful Women in Educational Management*, Longman Paul, Auckland.

Ozga, J. (1993), *Women in Educational Management*, Open University Press, Buckingham.

Sandler, B.R., L.A. Silverberg and R.M. Hall (1996), *The Chilly Classroom Climate. A Guide to Improve the Education of Women*, The National Association for Women in Education, Washington, DC.

Shapiro, G.L. and D.L. Farrow (1988), 'Mentors and Others in Career Development', in L. Larwood (ed.), *Women's Careers: Pathways and Pitfalls*, Praeger Press, New York.

Tertiary Education Institute (1996), *The Action Learning Programme 1996, Information Booklet*, University of Queensland, Australia.

Chapter 19

Women's Executive Development in Australian Higher Education

Colleen Chesterman

Introduction

The Australian Higher Education sector has undergone major structural changes over the past fifteen years. In 1987, a unified national system, consisting of thirty-seven publicly funded universities, was created out of a previous binary system of universities, institutes of technology and colleges of advanced education. Over the same period there have been marked changes in student and staff numbers, in conditions and with a tightening of the funds available from the central government, fee-paying courses and fee-paying overseas students have increased. The sector is widely seen as under considerable strain. Student numbers, for example have increased from 441,000 in 1989 to 686,200 in 1999. Staff numbers have not increased proportionately: indeed in the eight years to 1999, academic staff decreased by 8.8 per cent to just over 30,000 and general (non-academic) staff decreased by 6 per cent to 40,000. Staff numbers increased only for those in casual employment, now 11,600 (Department of Employment, Training and Youth Affairs – DETYA, 2000). The research projects discussed later in this paper suggest that women, particularly in the academic stream, are disproportionately represented in part-time and casual employment. As in other sectors historically, the increase in female numbers in academic work has been accompanied by a devaluing of the work performed.

During these years women undergraduate students have consistently outnumbered male undergraduate students in Australian universities, and their academic performance and achievements are generally higher as well. This is also true for high school students where girls outperform boys and have stronger retention rates to the completion of the final year of secondary school. However, the position of women staff in Australian universities is far from equal when compared to that of their male colleagues.

This inequality is puzzling in light of the fact that Australia has had in place a strong legislative framework that makes discrimination against women and girls unlawful, in both employment and education. Equity legislation was introduced through the 1980s in a number of states. Additionally since 1986, universities in Australia have been covered by the provisions of the federal Affirmative Action (Equal Employment Opportunity for Women) Act, amended the Equal Opportunity for Women in the Workplace Act 1999. This Act requires organisations to put into place programmes designed to assist women employees achieve equity and overcome the effects of past discriminatory practices, both direct and indirect. Organisations detail their progress in a public annual report, which also describes special programmes and any steps taken to overcome entrenched barriers to equality. This Act is administered by the Equal Opportunity for Women in the Workplace Agency <www.eowa.gov.au>.

There are also national (and in some cases, state) policy frameworks or acts to ensure the development of educational, and in some areas employment, equity plans for other specified groups, staff and students, including people from non-English-speaking background, Aboriginal and Torres Strait Islanders and people with a disability. In response to this legislation and policies, all Australian universities have specialist equity staff and equal opportunity units.

Yet despite the strength of the legislation, the existence of a range of programmes and action plans and a long and documented history of action for equal employment opportunity for women staff, the situation in Australian universities at the end of 1999 showed a continued pattern of inequity in women's employment in universities. An examination of statistics shows that women staff experience inequality, particularly in their representation at more senior levels. 1999 statistics on the proportions of men and women in the different general staff grades demonstrated a funnelling syndrome by which women are concentrated in lower graded occupations (DETYA, 1999).

Table 19.1 Percentage of general staff levels by sex, Australia 1996 (fte)

Higher Education Worker Scale Levels	Women %	Men %
HEW Level 4 and below (support staff)	69	31
HEW Levels 5-9 (Middle Management)	51.8	48.2
Above HEW Level (Executive)	26	74

Despite the marked discrepancy shown at the senior executive level, it is important to note that the percentage of women at executive level has increased from 26 per cent in 1996 (Probert *et al.*, 1998).

DETYA statistics also show differences between male and female academics, with women academics dominating the lower grades and men the senior levels, as shown in Table 19.2. This table shows both tenurable and limited term positions.

Table 19.2 Percentage of academic staff levels by sex, Australia 1999

Level in Academic Scale	Women %	Men %
Below Lecturer	50.4	49.6
Lecturer	42.7	57.3
Senior Lecturer	27.8	72.2
Above Senior Lecturer	15.4	84.6

Four major research reports have recently provided compelling evidence of gender inequity and these have been usefully summarised by Sullivan (1999). Castleman *et al.* (1995) studied payroll data from ten universities in South Australia and Victoria and showed that women lagged behind men in achieving permanency and seniority. Deane *et al.* (1996) investigated women's disadvantage in research. They showed that success in gaining research support was based on a complex interaction between the institutional profile (whether traditional universities or new technology-based universities), the discipline of the researcher and the seniority of the applicant. Women's lack of success was founded in their concentration in non-traditional universities, in newer disciplines such as nursing or creative arts and in junior levels or casual employment.

Burton (1997) undertook a major survey of all Australian universities to tease out the major issues blocking equal opportunity in employment. She placed particular emphasis on the 'masculine culture' of Higher Education institutions. She defined culture as reflecting not only values and priorities but also the structural arrangements in which they became embedded. She identified in universities 'employment terms and conditions, policies, practices and reward structures (that) historically have been organised around the cluster of characteristics, attributes and background circumstances typical of men' (pp.17-19).

In another major national study Probert *et al.* (1998) identified significant disadvantages experienced by women in Higher Education in relation to pay equity, permanency and classification. This report was particularly useful in describing and documenting the different experiences of women in general (non-academic) and academic streams, using both DEETYA statistics for 1997 and their own extensive survey. In relation to general staff, the study produced powerful quantitative evidence that, even when qualifications, level of employment and length of tenure were controlled, there remained a significant pay differential between men and women. Indeed women administrative staff were consistently found several classification levels lower than male administrative staff with identical qualifications and years of service. The study suggested that 'there is little coherence across the sector in the way work responsibilities are distributed between classification levels raising the possibility that areas dominated by women are under-valued or not recognised at all in the current job classification system'. In analysing the data for academic staff Probert *et al.* emphasised that women academics with the same qualifications and the same number of years working in a university had the same classification levels as their male colleagues. The factors that limited academic advancement however were those that had more impact on women than men, such as late entry, career breaks and domestic responsibilities. Specifically women academics typically begin and/or finish their doctoral qualifications later, are more likely to work part time for a period or throughout their careers, and tend to have more career interruptions than male academics, linked to women's responsibilities for dependent children. Women academics' lower classification levels and therefore lower remuneration compared to their male colleagues was due to two specific factors; less years overall in university employment and being less likely to have a PhD. A lower proportion of women (36 per cent) hold PhDs than men (56 per cent) and women had had 8.9 years of employment in a university compared with men's 13.8 years. The promotional criteria in Higher Education thus embodies indirect sexual discrimination, in that the disadvantage to women academics' position relative to their male colleagues arising early in their career, often due to them bearing and caring for children, but compounds and accumulates over time and throughout their careers. Women academics are less likely to have the advantage of mentoring by an eminent senior scholar and are less likely to have strong international networks which will enhance academic careers.

The research reports demonstrate as well the lack of women in senior management. As documented in the reports by Burton and Probert the numbers of women in senior management positions in universities in Australia, while growing, are still so unrepresentative as to provide evidence of continuing systemic and cultural barriers to women's progress. Universities in Australia have attracted significant criticism for their lack of inclusive managerial structures and development opportunities for senior women. (Ramsay, 1995; Higher Education Management Review Committee, 1996). The lack of diversity in management has negative implications for universities' future viability and capacity to respond to change.

There have been a number of national calls for the sector to address the issue of equity more concertedly, leading to the establishment in 1994 of the National Colloquium of Senior Women Executives in Australian Higher Education. The background to the establishment of this lobby group and network is outlined by one of the founders Eleanor Ramsay in ATN WEXDEV (1999b, p.72). In 1998, the Colloquium prepared a paper based on the findings of the recent research reports and approached the Australian Vice-Chancellors' Committee (AVCC), arguing that the sector as a whole should take greater responsibility for ensuring that women in both academic and administrative fields were able to meet the strong qualifications barriers demonstrated by the sector. The AVCC responded and in July 1999 adopted an action plan until 2003 targeting specific improvements in the situation of women in Higher Education. The Action Plan (AVCC, 1999) has three main elements:

- to exert the AVCC's leadership to promote the achievement of gender equity in Australia;
- to develop strategies based on research for overcoming barriers to gender equity for university staff;
- to refine the AVCC and university staff development services to target gender equity more effectively.

The Action Plan also commits each of Australia's universities to undertake its own specific actions in support of the plan. The AVCC will review progress against the plan each year, will ensure equal representation of women on committees and delegations and will sponsor more detailed research including analysis of career paths of selected groups of general staff and a study of career supports and weighting given to teaching and research in academic promotion.

Existing leadership programmes

The AVCC Action Plan did not emerge in a vacuum. A number of Australian universities, in addition to their equity programmes, run Women and Leadership and/or Women and Executive Development programmes. Fifteen of these programmes are summarised in a publication by the Australian Technology Network Women's Executive Development Programme (ATN WEXDEV, 1999c). This booklet analysed the different foci of the projects, in relation to target group, number of participants and aims and objectives. The discussion enabled practitioners to consider what aspects of the programmes worked most effectively, what problems had arisen and what were the best ways forward for women's leadership programmes.

A programme based on the existence of a network to encourage women's participation in senior women is the Australian Technology Network Women's Executive Development Programme (ATN WEXDEV), of which I am National Director: The ATN is a consortium of five leading Australian universities (Curtin University of Technology; Royal Melbourne Institute of Technology University; Queensland University of Technology; University of South Australia; University of Technology, Sydney), located in the five mainland states of the Australian continent, which have signed an agreement to operate cooperatively on areas of shared interest. They have combined to run ATN WEXDEV, a strategic career development programme designed by and for senior women on the academic and general staff. ATN WEXDEV has operated since 1996. Until 1998 it was supported by Commonwealth funding to strengthen executive development in Higher Education; this funding was matched by the five universities. Since 1999 the five universities have taken over responsibility for the programme at both national and local levels.

It is interesting that this initiative came from technology universities. It is commonly assumed that they have traditionally masculine leadership cultures, because of their strong links with industry and industry-based funding sources, and reflecting the dominance within their structures of industries in which women are poorly represented, such as engineering, mining, business and information technology. On the other hand, there is limited concrete and systematic evidence of such a bias and indeed, the large-scale mergers that dominated Australian universities in the 1980s incorporated education and nursing faculties, with higher representations of women at senior levels, into all five institutions. The ATN universities demonstrate a shared commitment to valuing diversity and ensuring gender equity. All have strong equity and equal opportunity units and they are rated as leading edge performers by the Commonwealth Affirmative Action Agency. Indeed it is suggested that it is common that such relatively recent institutions may be less bound by tradition:

Within countries, such as the UK and Australia, where former Polytechnics and Colleges of Advanced/Higher Education have become universities in recent years, these institutions generally seem to have a better record in appointing women, at all levels of the academic hierarchy, than the older research-oriented universities (CHEMS, 1998, p.22).

The original focus of WEXDEV was women at the senior levels within each institution, Deputy and Pro-Vice-Chancellors, Deans and Associate Deans, Heads of Departments and Administrative Units. This involved 125 women from the five Universities. In 1998 the target group for the Programme was expanded to provide developmental opportunities for women at the junction of middle and senior management, increasing the target group to over 450 women. The programme has also established a separate stream for sixty indigenous women working in the universities, to connect them through an e-mail network and to enable them to choose those programme elements most appropriate to their development. Since the publication of the AVCC Action Plan ATN WEXDEV has been more closely integrated with leadership programmes for all women staff in all the universities.

Objectives of the programme

The structure of the ATN provides a unique and effective context within which to work on the issue of under-representation of women in senior university management. The five universities together provide a near-national network, and, located as they are in five different States, they are able to collaborate without prejudice to their need to be increasingly competitive. Their similar histories and academic profiles ensure some commonality, but they are sufficiently varied in their characteristics as to provide a very wide range of learning opportunities for the programme participants. The ATN WEXDEV programme consciously attempts to build links between academic and administrative staff through two key strategies.

The programme uses the potential of the network across the Australian continent, using inter-institutional collaboration to break down individual, institutional and geographic isolation. It also builds on the strong links that the ATN Universities have established with business, industry, government and community organisations have been targeted to provide different examples of contemporary management and to generate opportunities for senior executive development.

ATN WEXDEV aims to create synergies between individual and organisational benefits so that capability (individual learning needs) and context (intra-institutional issues) are addressed simultaneously. In 1999 the Management Committee affirmed four objectives, with the focus moving from the individual, through the institution, the network and the wider society. The objectives highlight the importance of working collaboratively with other organisations to ensure that the overall objectives are fulfilled:

- To enhance personal professional development opportunities for senior women to gain appropriate skills and experience for emerging management opportunities.
- To support the growth of organisational cultures that value diversity and encourage improved representation of women in senior executive positions.
- To build on the tangible benefits of the collaborative network between ATN universities by providing significant cross-institutional activities for senior women.
- To strengthen strategic alliances with other organisations, nationally and internationally.

The ATN WEXDEV model is not a tightly designed programme in which a group of aspiring leaders is recruited and structured and sequenced training provided. It accepts that the senior women to whom it is directed already have significant managerial and personal responsibilities. Hence the programme offers flexibility and the opportunity to choose between a number of elements that women can tap into at different times, with different levels of commitment. This has the disadvantage that women do not form a cohesive collegial group. On the other hand it does provide choice and the advantages that can be derived from being part of a wider group.

Opportunities offered by the ATN WEXDEV programme

Some activities have been designed to help improve the culture and environment of universities for women. Others aim to focus on meeting the objectively assessed or personally felt professional development needs of individual women. Yet there is no dichotomy between these aims. The programme aims to develop the synergies between the contextual, systemic and cultural issues on the one hand and the professional development needs of individual women. A woman taking part in these activities gains important management experience and information, developing her individual capacity and confidence, while simultaneously raising the visibility of senior university women. The programme also assumes that improving the organisational culture for women requires work with both women and men.

Personal professional development The programme provides, in each university, a range of activities for personal professional development, including skills analysis, workshops and mentoring, in the context of the strategic priorities of the participants' organisations.

Senior executive placements In these participants undertake a month-long project of benefit to high-performance national or international organisations in business, industry, Higher Education or the public sector to observe how other organisations deal with current management issues.

Seminars and workshops Each university provides a range of local seminars and meetings in which important professional issues are explored and skills developed. These have included financial management, ethics and committee skills. In addition occasional national seminars are held, designed to provide up-to-date management theory and high-quality training in areas including entrepreneurialism and knowledge management. Seminars and workshops are also designed to strengthen inter-institutional networks as universities can send representatives to other states or to a national conference or workshop.

Networking Networking in order to link women within and across institutions is an essential component of the programme, to share information and also to set up structured group discussions on subjects of strategic importance. The Programme uses both a Home Page (http://www.uts.edu.au/oth/wexdev) and an e-mail Discussion List to link participants, providing information on programme opportunities, stimulating discussions and canvassing views on the future of the programme. Networking is also important on a face-to-face basis, informal and formal, and the programme has increased cross-institutional communication and collaboration.

Implementation of the programme

ATN WEXDEV is administered by a national Management Committee comprising senior staff from each of the five ATN universities. A National Office has been established, with a part-time Programme Director and a part-time Executive Assistant. In the collaborative style of the programme, the National Office was based in Melbourne at RMIT from 1996 to 1997 and from mid-1997 to the present in Sydney at UTS.

Each university has nominated an Institutional Contact, working part-time, with responsibility for promoting the programme, identifying core participants, building links between the ATN WEXDEV programme and other institutional initiatives for their women employees and managing the implementation of ATN WEXDEV within their own institutions. Each university also has a University Implementation Committee, convened by a senior woman, which brings together all areas with a role in gender equity including equal opportunity, staff development and teaching and learning groups. This ongoing contact is important in ensuring that there is coherence and full coverage in the programmes provided by these divisions and a joint opportunity to identify areas of difficulty. The programme operates on continued contact between the National Office and the university institutional contacts and we are gradually cutting back on the role of National Office so that the programme and its cross-institutional links become embedded in each centre.

Evaluation of the programme

During the three-year operation of the ATN WEXDEV programme, there have been two evaluations. The first focused particularly on participants' experiences of the programme. Participants indicated that they had enhanced their knowledge and skills on issues of management and leadership, had the opportunity to extend their experience in senior positions and had strengthened their professional networks. The second focused on the success of embedding the programme within each institution and expanding to women in middle management and to indigenous women. The programme has shown itself to be innovative, flexible and substantial. It has gained committed support from senior university management and high visibility among the women in the target group. Through their involvement women believe they have had the opportunity to influence organisational cultures so that they are responsive to the employment patterns and career priorities of all women staff. During 2000, there was a special focus on seminars such as research development for women academics who have been less likely to be involved in executive development programmes than women administrative staff.

Within the general picture of inequity in Australian universities, the ATN universities perform well. The proportion of all academics who are female in ATN is at or above the national average; the proportion of senior academics who are female is higher than the national average and that the ratio is well above national average. We know that the proportion of *all* general staff who are female in ATN is above 50 per cent but below the national average, but that since 1996 the proportion of *senior* general staff who are female has increased significantly more than the national average increase and that there has been a marked increase in the feeder group to senior executive management. In one of the universities over 50 per cent of the senior administrative staff are female. We are cautious however about drawing too many inferences from what are still low numbers in a constantly evolving situation. Nonetheless it was pleasing that by November 2000, two of the five universities had female vice-chancellors, important role models for other women.

Key characteristics of the programme

The ATN WEXDEV model of senior executive development for women has an innovative design based on experiencing different and changing environments to gain positive developmental benefits and networking to establish a critical mass of senior women.

Experiencing different and changing environments

Each element of WEXDEV provides women with opportunities to go outside their institutions and to experience different organisational and management cultures and hence develop a capacity to manage change. This is most clearly exemplified in senior executive placements in which they experience approaches being taken in other sectors to strategic issues that are now challenges for universities. Many discussions on the list are designed to encourage positive responses to changes, so that participants set goals, adjust to circumstances, and bring teams with them.

Building a critical mass through networking

The importance of networking has become more apparent through the four years of the programme. Research suggests that as women rise in the university hierarchy, their peer support falls away and they become isolated from other women. It is also suggested that although women are good at networking, the networks they establish are not as powerful as those of their male colleagues (M. Rothstein and L. Davey, 1995, pp.20-25). There is some evidence that women in particular are more likely to use networks to foster relationships, support one another and share concerns about women's disadvantage, rather than to further their careers (H. Clark, J. Chandler and J. Barry, 1996, p.9). The focus of ATN WEXDEV on women's professional development and on cultural change within organisations provides a clear encouragement to direct networking activity towards targeted goals. The 1997 evaluation showed that many of the women felt quite isolated in their own university setting and praised the opportunities 'to network with colleagues in other states and in other areas of university activity.' On the list women acknowledge the importance of being part of a larger group, of sharing experiences and building links with other individuals that might provide a basis for collaborative activity. Some have used the list to develop informal mentoring relationships.

Conclusion

Extending the network beyond institutional and sector boundaries has been important in building links with significant other organisations working on women's executive development, which in turn has validated the skills of women in Higher Education, for example through their appointment to boards. WEXDEV has also been successful in gaining a grant from the Australian Government, through its development agency AusAid, administered by the International Development Programme, to work with senior women in South African Higher Education to build a similar informal training and support network.

The Vice-Chancellor of RMIT University pointed out at a recent ATN WEXDEV conference that networks offer a powerful way of achieving critical mass and access to the economies of scale necessary for successful competition, while at the same time maintaining institutions at a manageable size and allowing local responsiveness. 'But networks are a new form of organisation and represent a new way of relating – there are no roadmaps about how to do this' (ATN WEXDEV, 1999b, p.10). The ATN WEXDEV programme provides an example of a 'micro-climate' within which the critical mass of women at relevant levels has increased participants' sense of effectiveness and impact both as individuals and as a group. Women can look across all five universities for powerful role models.

Women's executive development has been established as a priority on the ATN strategic agenda, with the recognition that this is not a marginal activity, but one that is vital for the enhancement of the overall management capacity and strategic planning of the ATN universities. Its success is demonstrated by the Vice-Chancellors' commitment of funds to maintain the WEXDEV National Office, combined with a commitment to establish the structural and organisational basis to foster broader collaboration between institutionally-based women's leadership programmes within the ATN, so that programmes developed at one institution may be presented at others, or that universities may combine to develop relevant programmes.

Women involved in WEXDEV, at each individual university and across the five universities, know that they are part of a large grouping through which they can gain advice and support when needed. They feel more positive in relation to their personal visibility, importance and voice within the university. Moreover, perceptions of the capacities and capabilities of women have markedly improved. Senior ATN women as a result have an increased awareness of the value they add to their institutions, of the limitations of mono-cultural organisations and of women's potential as change-agents. They are provided with opportunities to recognise their own leadership potential. WEXDEV demonstrates the power of conversation and dialogue in informal networks to establish cultures of support, to gain information and insight and to effect change in the dominant cultures of Higher Education.

An earlier version of this work was published in the proceedings of the 'Winds of Change: Women and the Culture of Universities' conference held at University of Technology, Sydney, 13–17 July 1998.

References

ATN WEXDEV (1999a), *A Model for Women's Executive Development*, ATN WEXDEV, Sydney.
_____ (1999b), *Networking and Collaboration*, ATN WEXDEV, Sydney.
_____ (1999c), *Women and Leadership in Higher Education in Australia*, ATN WEXDEV, Sydney.
Australian Vice-Chancellors' Committee (1999), *Action Plan for Women Employed in Australian Universities, 1999 to 2003*, AVCC, Canberra.

Burton, C. (1997), *Gender Equity in Australian University Staffing*, Department of Employment, Education, Training and Youth Affairs, Canberra.

Castleman, T., M. Allen, W. Bastalich and P. Wright (1995), *Limited Access: Women's Disadvantage in Higher Education Employment*, National Tertiary Education Union, Melbourne.

Clark, H., J. Chandler and J. Barry (1996), *Too Scattered to Provide a Critical Mass*, Papers of 1996 SCOS Conference, UCLA, Los Angeles.

Commonwealth Higher Education Management Service (1998), *A Single Sex Profession: Female Staff Numbers in Commonwealth Universities*, Association of Commonwealth Universities, London.

Deane, E., L. Johnson, G. Jones and N. Lengkeek (1996), *Women, Research and Research Productivity in the Post-1987 Universities: Opportunities and Constraints*, Department of Employment, Education, Training and Youth Affairs, Canberra.

Department of Education Training and Youth Affairs (2000), *Selected Higher Education Statistics 1999*, DETYA, Canberra.

Higher Education Management Review Committee (1995), *Report of the Committee of Inquiry/Higher Education Management Review*, Australian Government Publishing Service, Canberra.

Probert, Belinda, P. Ewer and K. Whiting (1998), *Gender Pay Equity in Australian Higher Education*, National Tertiary Education Union, Melbourne.

Ramsay, E. (1995), 'The Politics of Privilege and Resistance' in A.M. Payne and L. Shoemark (eds), *Women, Culture and Universities: A Chilly Climate*, University of Technology Women's Forum, Sydney.

Rothstein, M. and L. Davey (1995), 'Gender Differences in Network Relationships in Academia', *Women in Management Review*, 10 (6).

Singh, J.S. (1997), 'Women and Management in Higher Education', *ACU Bulletin*, Association of Commonwealth Universities, London.

Sullivan, M. (1999), 'Status of Women in Australian Universities – Myths and Realities', *Australian Feminist Studies*, 14 (30).

Chapter 20

The Troublesome Concept of Merit

Sandra Harding

Introduction

Gender inequality within the academy and outside of it has been well documented (Kanter, 1977; Burton, 1991; Tomaskovic-Devey, 1993; Bacchi, 1993; French and Harding, 1996). Varying explanations exist concerning the core of the problem and many possible solutions have been advanced. For the most part, however, our universities aggregate around a particular prospective solution to the problem: the application of the concept of merit to drive recruitment and promotion decisions. However, this concept is loaded. It raises more questions than it answers.

In this chapter, I outline an argument that seeks to explore the concept of merit against a more socially-embedded understanding of social inequality by standing outside of the dominant theoretical perspective of neoclassical economics that drives a merit-based solution. I look at the issue of gender inequality from other theoretical perspectives and, in so doing, I come to a very different conclusion about the likely success of a merit-based solution to inequality. This process of using multiple perspectives to inform our understanding of a particular phenomenon is called 'triangulation'.

'Triangulation', as a social science concept, refers to the process of looking at a problem from more than one angle (strangely enough, not necessarily three angles) in order to learn more (Jary and Jary, 1991). This is a useful process as, by moving between alternative, often competing explanations for some phenomenon, new insights often emerge and the limitations of the original insights become apparent. This is not to deny the original insights, but instead to put them in perspective, to permit of other explanations of the social phenomenon under study. Triangulation provides the basis for elaborated understanding.

Using this broader theoretical framework, I seek to demonstrate that the application of merit as an 'objective' criterion to fix gender inequality will not work as long as women remain at a structural disadvantage as a result of their social production and reproduction roles. This argument is embedded in a broader understanding of the nature of business, work and social organisation, moving beyond the narrow neoclassical economic theoretical perspective that is more commonly brought to bear and that makes sensible a reliance on the concept of merit to set inequality to rights. In other words, merit as a solution emerges from this dominant paradigm, this dominant theoretical perspective about how the world works. But there are competing explanations of economy and society and these permit of an alternative understanding of gender inequality in the academy. Such an approach offers an elaborated understanding that provides the basis for innovative and creative solutions to the poor placement of women.

To this end, my argument is presented in three parts. First, I examine the basis for particular explanations of economy and society. There are many perspectives that I could bring to bear, but I confine myself to a variety of classical views. I place neoclassical economics in historical perspective by exploring competing theoretical perspectives that were developed in reaction to it. My aim in this first section is to provide the necessary theoretical backdrop for my later, specific challenges to the concept of merit as an objective criterion that will set inequality to rights. In the second section, I employ this theoretical backdrop to explain inequality at work, focusing on the troublesome concept of merit and looking to alternative approaches to redressing this inequality. I argue that the poor placement of particular social groups, like women and other minorities, in our business organisations and academia cannot be understood using a neoclassical economic framework. We must go outside this dominant view in order to better understand why such poor placement occurs and what can be done to redress this. In the third section, I make some final observations and draw conclusions based on the foregoing discussion.

Competing explanations of economy and society

Neoclassical economics is rooted in the work of Adam Smith (1776). According to this perspective, the market is competitive and business organisations operate best when allowed to interact in free and unfettered competition. Society is not as important as individuals, 'atomised' individuals, who each make quite independent choices for, or against, some particular product or service. The idea is that such choices are made using particular criteria, like price, quality and availability, and the organisation that delivers the best mix of these 'wins' the support of consumers. To achieve this, business must maximise efficiency (inputs to outputs): the most efficient organisation wins under free market conditions. In this way, according to this particular theoretical perspective, some producers are appropriately rewarded over others.

This perspective is based on a series of simplifying assumptions like perfect information, rational action and free entrance into and exit from the market. It also relies on an 'invisible hand' to set things right. A key tenet of this perspective is that, left alone, the market itself is efficient and will deliver the best result for society.

Moreover, this theoretical perspective marries individualism and the idea of a meritocracy to explain how society works. According to this perspective, individuals act in the market as rational, independent players and, as far as their placement in society is concerned, individuals only succeed through their own talents and hard work. Race, ethnicity, gender and social class are irrelevant in this view of the world. There is an open social system, meaning that an individual's placement in society is not constrained by anything other than that person's own merits. The key idea is that anyone can move up the social hierarchy if they choose, if they work hard enough.

Under neoclassical assumptions, workers are recognised only as a factor of production that must be controlled and manipulated to deliver greater and greater efficiencies. Work is hard and will be avoided. Workers, as factors, must be both compliant and productive. Classical management theory, like that espoused by Taylor (1911) and Gilbreth (1919), rely on these sorts of notions of business, work and organisation. Taylor's 'scientific management', in particular, relied on a separation of control and execution: managers think and control while workers do, that is execute the task.

As a theoretical perspective, neoclassical economics is optimistic, perhaps overly so. Certainly classical theorist Adam Smith expected wealth to be generated without end under free market conditions. Society as a whole would benefit from the upward spiral of economic growth delivered by the free-flow of market forces as needs were met in the marketplace and efficient owners became richer and rewarded workers by sharing this wealth with them, to the greater good of all. There is an explicit judgement here that owners and workers who succeed do so through their own merits, and will be rewarded in proportion to their merit.

Neoclassical economics has become the dominant paradigm promulgated by most business schools and most of the disciplines that drive their approaches are embedded within it. It is also the dominant paradigm in the West, in general. But this is not to suggest that this is the only, or even the best, explanation of economy and society. Alternative explanations also inform our understanding.

In general, these alternative perspectives developed in reaction to neoclassical ideas. Karl Marx ([1867] 1918) offered one of the earliest reactions to Smith's theory. He thought Smith was brilliant (McLellan, 1990), but Marx, living in England during the Industrial Revolution and writing some eighty years after Smith, did not see the upward spiral of wealth for all that Smith had so optimistically predicted. Instead he witnessed the horrors and atrocities of life in the sweatshops and 'satanic mills' of the time. Marx, philosopher, revolutionary and, then, social scientist, set himself the task of trying to figure out what went wrong: why Smith's perfectly reasonable theory did not result in wealth for all and a universal increase in the quality of life.

In the end, Marx ([1857-8]1965; [1867]1918) argued that the system of production itself, the free market or capitalism, is the problem. It sets people against one another as only some people (capital) have ownership and control of the means of production, while others (labour) have only their labour to sell. Under free market conditions, as producers try to become the most efficient and responsive in their industry, it is rational for owners/managers to try to extract as much from workers as possible and give them as little as possible in return. This would not work in the long-term, according to Marx, as not only would workers become wretched in such a system, but they could no longer afford to buy the very products they produce. Without a mass consumer market, business itself would collapse. This is the key contradiction in capitalism that Marx thought would lead, ultimately, to the destruction of that system of production. Moreover, Marx argued that capitalist society is inherently unequal, by virtue of the existence of the power differential between these two groups: capital and labour. A meritocracy cannot exist where whole groups in society, particular labour in his view, begin at a disadvantage. To suggest that everyone has an equal chance to move up the social system, to accumulate wealth, is simply a deception, according to Marx. There is important contemporary scholarship in this tradition. Much of this later work is focused on exploitation at work, in particular, on the consequences of the separation of execution (doing the work) and control (thinking about, planning and supervising the work) (Braverman, 1974; Burawoy, 1979, 1983, 1985; Friedman, 1977). Power and control are key constructs in this tradition and later scholarship worries a great deal about the social and political principles at work in business, work and organisation. Later theoretical development in explanations of business, economy and society reacts to the work of both Smith and Marx. Among these others, I highlight the work of Max Weber, Critical School theorists and feminist theorists.

As far as the study of formal organisation is concerned, Weber is most famous for his analysis of bureaucracy (Weber, 1968). All first year business students learn about this important 'ideal type.' But Weber's work on bureaucracy represents a fragment of his larger inquiry. Like Smith and Marx, Weber was really trying to solve a bigger puzzle through his scholarship: he, too, was trying to understand the nature of society and social change. He wanted to understand why our particular economic system (the market/capitalism) arose where it did, in the West, and when it did rather than at some other time and place. In the end, he identified a range of factors that were present in the West, and absent in the East, that accounted for the development of capitalism. Structural factors include: calculable law, capital accounting (to determine income yielding potential), markets and geographic proximity (Weber, 1927). Moreover, Weber argued that religion spurred the development of capitalism. He argued that the development of Protestantism aided the rise of capitalism as it included in its key ideas notions of the moral worth of hard work, acceptance of one's God-given station in life, frugality and the accumulation of wealth as proof of one's chosen status (Weber, 1958b, 1927).

Particularly relevant to the notion of a meritocracy, Weber also argued that society is layered and people reside at different locations in the social stratification system depending on their economic class (similar to Marx), social honour or status and political power (Weber, 1968). Movement up the hierarchy is possible, but it is not simply a matter of individual effort and hard work and most remained roughly where they started. Coming back to notions of bureaucracy, Weber (1958a, 1968) was very pessimistic about humankind's future. He suggested that bureaucracy, with its routinised systems, files, and hierarchy of control, was technically the most efficient form of social organisation and would come to displace all other forms. He anticipated that, increasingly, business would be run by large bureaucracies because of the technical and economic efficiencies they permit. This worried him greatly. It is not that he did not like economic efficiency. Instead, he was concerned that single-minded pursuit of this economic principle was propelling this criterion for action into centre stage. He was most concerned that, ultimately, society would lose the ability to judge social action and organisation on anything but purely economically-rational grounds. In fact, he saw that we were coming to value the economic criterion of efficiency so highly that it was becoming the only legitimate basis for action. Under these conditions, making decisions based on grounds like equity or justice cannot be understood to be rational. Weber's analysis led him to the conclusion that humanity is trapped in the iron cage of a narrow and distorted economic rationality and there is no way out.

Weber's perspective on work and organisation has also been picked up and developed by modern scholars. In fact, two different groups have emerged. The first group comprised people we label organisational psychologists today (for example, Mayo, 1945; Katz, Maccoby and Morse, 1950; Katz and Kahn, 1966; Whyte, 1951, 1959). They examined what happened in workplaces that took as fact neoclassical economic assumptions about workers being mere factors of production and sought to explore the effect that working, say, on an assembly line, would have on people. This group explored the consequences of economically-rational bureaucracy, economically-rational business practice, on people within the enterprise. They sought to demonstrate that workers were not merely objective factors of production, that power and informal relationships exist within organisations and these condition work effort and productivity. Workers can be engaged or dissociated, encouraged or discouraged by what happens in their organisations.

The second group following Weber does not have the same 'behaviouralist' agenda. This second group look to flesh out the concept of bureaucracy itself, to see whether the characteristics ascribed to it by Weber (1968) exist in modern organisations and to explore the impacts of these. Scholars focussed on the structural correlates of organisation (Woodward, 1958); how best to organise within them (Burns and Stalker, 1961; Lawrence and Lorsch, 1967; Galbraith, 1973); the environment in which such structures are embedded (Hannen and Freeman, 1977, 1984, 1988; Aldrich and Pfeffer, 1976; Aldrich and Marsden, 1988; Carroll and Delacriox, 1982; Carroll, 1984); and how organisations interact with their environments (Pfeffer, 1972a, 1972b, 1973; Pfeffer and Salancik, 1974, 1978; Child, 1972; Burt, 1980, 1983; Miles, 1982; DiMaggio and Powell, 1983; Baum and Oliver, 1991, 1992). A significant contribution in this tradition highlights the existence of a monopoly or core industrial sector, populated by large bureaucracies that operate under conditions of muted competition as they control their markets in important ways, and a competitive industrial sector populated by small, aggressively competitive enterprises that have no such control (Baran and Sweezy, 1966; Hodson, 1978; Baron and Bielby, 1980) and primary and secondary labour markets within monopoly and competitive industrial sectors (Edwards, 1979), respectively. Much work continues in this tradition today. Two more sets of scholars are important to my critique: Critical School theorists and feminist theorists.

Critical School folk (Horkheimer and Adorno, [1947] 1972; Habermas, 1984) and two important forebears (Gramsci, 1971 and Lukacs, [1923] 1971), provide critical insights into the nature of social organisation. Gramsci and Lukacs both wrote in the 1920s. They both tried to explain why, despite the atrocious conditions under which much of the Western world lived, workers did not revolt and usher in a new society as Marx had optimistically hoped. Lukacs ([1923] 1971) came to the view that most people were kept happy enough, through access to sufficient food and entertainment, not to seek to change the basis of society. Gramsci (1971) argued, similarly, that it had become conventional wisdom that economy and society is naturally unequal and competitive, that it is good and proper that some people are wealthier than others and that this is merely their just dessert for their talent and hard work. According to these theorists, things do not change even under difficult conditions where whole groups are systematically disadvantaged as these same people fail to see how things could be otherwise. Gramsci called this taken-for-granted, conventional wisdom that dominates our thought and action a 'cultural hegemony'.

Critical School theorists, like Horkheimer and Adorno ([1947] 1972) and, more recently, Habermas (1984), picked up on this idea of a cultural hegemony, and Habermas, in particular, has set himself the task of trying to work out how this overly economic-rational view of the world might be challenged. His solution is startling. Habermas argues that what we need is more rationality, not less. To rely only on an economically rational view of the world – precisely what neoclassical economics does – is to consider valid only one of a number of equally valid bases for social action. At the moment, we judge social action and explain the nature of organisation and gender inequality using only economic principles. More particularly, we judge most social action on the basis of its economic efficiency. The more economically efficient the answer to a particular problem, the better. This is what counts. But, as Weber (1968) argued, there are other bases that we can use both to judge social action and to guide notions of the appropriateness of social organisation. These other bases include truth, truthfulness and rightness (social justice). Habermas (1984) argues that we need more rationality not less, and certainly not more of the narrow and, consequently, distorted rationality that only judges action using economic criteria that dominates our thinking at the present time. In a similar vein, I have argued that at least one particular type of alternative business organisation, now and in the past, works to three sets of principles – social, political and economic – in contrast to sole pursuit of restrictive economic principles that drive 'traditional' business (Harding 1996, 1998). In short, the perspective generated by Critical School theorists brings to bear a good dose of social and political awareness to our understanding of economic activity.

Feminist theory adds value in a similar fashion. There is no single feminist perspective. There are many feminisms (Walby, 1990). I shall briefly explain three of them – liberal feminism, socialist feminism and radical feminism – to demonstrate that different insights about the world of work, business, and its impact on women and minorities, can be gleaned from each of them. Liberal feminism is more closely aligned with a neoclassical economic view of the world. This perspective argues that women must catch up, indeed will catch up to men as they prepare themselves and remain in the workforce for similarly lengthy periods of time (Reskin and Padavic, 1994). However, there is the problem of 'homosocial reproduction': organisational managers and leaders choose managers and leaders who replicate their own characteristics as this is a way in which trust is generated (Kanter, 1977). To be the same sex, to have negotiated the same school system, to speak the same language, to look the same is to create a degree of trust and confidence between a successful manager and his (rarely her) protégé. Oftentimes, those women who do succeed are those with whom men are most comfortable. These are often women in their own image who are expected to perform in the job in much the same way that a man would (Wajcman, 1998), regardless of any additional responsibilities for which women still take the lead, such as social reproduction roles like child care and domestic duties.

By contrast, socialist feminism has strong ties to Marxism. Class is the main issue and women's poor performance as far as acquiring senior managerial posts is concerned is an artefact of class differences. According to this logic, women do not own and control the means of production and, therefore, they are subject to those who do. Under these conditions, women, like disenfranchised male workers, are subject to the whims and fancies of the controlling elite.

Radical feminism argues a deeper issue. Radical feminists cite the importance of sexuality and do not dismiss the notion of misogyny, the hatred of women. According to this perspective our society is dominated not only by capitalism as a system of production, but also by 'patriarchy' as a system of domination (Walby, 1990). Women, simply because they are women, have been denied full participation in society (Bennett, 1988, 1991; Walby, 1990) and it is not in mens' best interests to change this (Reskin, 1988).

Where does all this get us? There are competing theoretical perspectives about how society operates and should operate. These notions or perspectives reflect competing theoretical positions about social organisation. None of these theoretical positions can be labelled as the truth. Theories are never proven (Feyerabend 1988). However, some theories do seem to explain more than others, and on this basis, we certainly can have a preferred perspective, properly the one that seems to explain more of what happens in the world around us.

In combination, the work of three classical scholars, Smith, Marx and Weber, and their followers, provides the context for much scholarship and practice in organisations today. Yet, even though all three are important, one perspective remains dominant. Neoclassical economics, as economic rationalism, lies at the heart of the current, popular understanding of the nature of organisational life. The notion of a meritocracy is inextricable linked to a neoclassical economic view. How does a broader view of business, work and organisation help us? In general, a broader view brings to bear a more sophisticated view of social inequality. It is time to establish the insights generated by this broader view.

The troublesome concept of merit

Merit as a solution to inequality is embedded in a neoclassical economics theoretical perspective. This is why it is troublesome. It is linked to a series of limiting assumptions about the way the world works. Individualistic, meritocratic and competitive notions of social stratification embedded in neoclassical economics imply that those who have 'made it' to date have done so solely through their own efforts: that there has not been any leverage supplied by race/ethnicity, class, or gender. From this perspective, inequality is not a problem, in fact it is never a problem. Instead, it is a natural consequence of individual aptitude and action. In other words, neoclassical economic assumptions require that those who have not succeeded have only themselves to blame.

This is a problem as inequality attached to whole groups does exist in the world – and at work. Yet this dominant view about the way the world works provides no way of understanding poor placement in society, indeed poverty or discrimination, for these groups as the theory operates at the level of the individual. When faced with an individual instance of inequality, the assumption is that the individual concerned has not tried hard enough to reach the top. Following this logic, poor placement for whole groups, like women and other minorities, can only be understood on the basis of poor effort by individuals in this group. This is particularly worrying as, when faced with whole groups that seem to suffer poor placement, an individual-level explanation like that offered by neoclassical economics implies that the demerits of the individual are somehow transmitted to the whole group. It implies that all members of these groups are somehow unworthy and this brings a disturbing biological reasoning to bear.

Under neoclassical economic, individualist assumptions, strategies to redress inequities are simply not sensible. Inequality attached to social groups on anything other than merit-based grounds is incomprehensible so there can be no reasonable basis upon which to propose strategies for redressing the inequality attending the position of women and minorities, in management ranks, the academy or in a segmented market more generally. Targets or quotas would not be fair as the most meritorious candidate for recruitment or promotion may miss out in favour of a less qualified other.

Alternative theoretical perspectives take us much further. They make it easy to understand that an objective meritocracy, where individuals are located along a social hierarchy solely on the basis of individual aptitude and action – on their own merit – is not possible. There is no even playing field. There is no objective place to stand. People are located at positions in the socioeconomic hierarchy as much by their gender, race/ethnicity and class as by their individual merits. Under such conditions, to judge on 'merit' is a nonsense as not all groups have a chance to be equally meritorious. To be female, non-white and poor is to be at a disadvantage when decisions are made on some supposedly objective, merit-based criterion. Judged on merit, women who must juggle both social production and reproduction roles, find it much harder to percolate through to senior positions.

Moreover, this poor representation of women at these senior-most levels is not simply a matter of choice. There is an argument that women choose family or family/career or career, in this way making an active decision on their career trajectory. While many women choose to commit to family, the argument runs, many successful men have made a career choice, often with the help of supporting partners who take primary responsibility for the domestic domain, subjugating their own extra-domestic goals in support of this choice. However, alternative theoretical perspectives indicate that, in many cases, such 'choices' are an illusion. Social structures and expectations reinforce the position of whole groups in society. In this case, women remain primarily responsible for social reproduction roles and this severely constrains the choices women may make. While individual women may have some choice, particularly those who through the seniority of their position can afford to pay for childcare and domestic assistance or who do not have a family or who receive the support of a partner who elects to subjugate his/her extra-domestic goals to that woman's career, general social expectations mean that most women's choices are tightly constrained. They must negotiate both social reproduction and production roles, taking the lead in domestic and family matters, even as they seek to measure up against supposedly objective merit-based criteria.

As Burton and Ryall (1995, Chapter 18) point out, gender is a critical organising principle in our society and we need to understand this at its base. Feminist theory helps a great deal in this. Race/ethnicity and class are equally important organising principles and we must move beyond a neoclassical economic, merit-based frame to understand this. All of the alternative theoretical perspectives developed in reaction to neoclassical views support this richer understanding of social inequality. Successful strategies for increasing the number of women in senior roles in academia, like accepting applications in the first round only from suitably qualified women (Bacchi, 1993) are sensible from these alternative theoretical perspectives. While such strategies may cause great angst, they are likely to represent one of the few possibilities for increasing the participation of women at the senior-most levels.

Along similar lines, it is impossible to reconcile a concern for the management of diversity with individualist, neoclassical economic assumptions. Diversity ought to take care of itself under these conditions. Indeed, the notion of the management of diversity itself posits that this is something done by some objective, monocultural group (white/male/middle class). Yet, management itself is, or ought to be, a part of this diversity. Again, the limiting assumption is that those who do best will reach the top, others are clearly not as deserving and ought not be helped to such positions.

If redressing the poor placement of women and minorities has any intrinsic worth at all, it will be critical to develop and promulgate a different construction of inequality at work, based on alternative theoretical perspectives, so that diversity and equality have a fighting chance. However, radical feminist theory suggests that this will not happen easily.

The difficulty of shifting away from current merit-based approaches is underscored when we consider alternatives to the *status quo*. One approach may be to fundamentally redefine 'merit', perhaps even eliminating it from our lexicon, so that recruitment and promotion decisions can be made on other bases. This approach would require universities to 'reality check' current recruitment/promotion criteria, involving a review of existing positions and ranks with a view to establishing what is actually required to perform these roles competently. The idea is to establish criteria for competence. This would mean challenging assumptions like, for example, the candidate with the most publications 'wins' when all that is really required is evidence of some appropriate level of productivity. Moreover, continuous service may not be as important as the calibre or quality of that service. Once a pool of competent candidates has been established, recruitment/promotion decisions can be made on other, appropriate and work-related criteria. Remedying the under-representation of particular groups may be one such criterion. The core idea here does not involve appointing individuals who are not competent to undertake a particular role. Rather, it is about accurately specifying the role and then selecting amongst competent candidates on other, relevant criteria. Another alternative is to turn this process on its head. For example, if women are underrepresented in a particular area, the approach may be to invite applications in the first round only from women (Bacchi 1993). This latter approach constitutes the sort of direct and unapologetic affirmative action that is, in all likelihood, necessary to ensure appropriate levels of participation by women and minorities in senior positions. Whether approaches like these are best described as redefining merit or eliminating merit is open for debate. Irrespective of this labelling, such approaches are only sensible if we dismiss the notion of a meritocracy currently aligned with the dominant hegemony of economic rationalism. As it stands, the concept of merit is troublesome as the idea that fair and objective judgements can be made and rewards allocated solely in proportion to worth, to individual merit, is, at best, naive and, at worst, a deception.

Alternative perspectives encourage a broader view of social organisation and inequality that permit of strategies aimed at delivering equitable outcomes. By contrast, neoclassical economic assumptions and the troublesome concept of merit, as currently operationalised, work against any improvement in the status of women and other minorities.

Conclusion

Triangulation from a range of alternative bases provides important insights on the problem of the poor placement of women in the academy. Neoclassical economics, the theoretical perspective from which a merit-based solution is sourced, is not socially embedded – this is why it is troublesome. It provides no way of explaining why certain groups are concentrated in more or less advantaged positions in society, except to argue that they must not be as talented or hardworking, or worthy as those who reside in more advantaged positions. It provides, therefore, no sensible basis for establishing strategies to redress such inequalities. In short, this perspective takes a free market, rational individual action and a meritocracy that delivers rewards in proportion to worth as given.

Alternative perspectives recognise that work, organisation and inequality are socially-embedded and contrived at many levels. Individuals in society do not act in a purely rational, mechanical fashion, individually weighing the costs and benefits of their purchase or employment choices. There are limits to the application of a purely economic form of rationality where neither a perfect market nor perfectly rational actors exist. To assume otherwise is to deny or play down the importance of anything that is not economic in nature. More to the point, inequality exists and does not merely reflect 'natural' differences in talent and hard work. Class, gender, and race/ethnicity operate to lever some into higher status positions, while others are not so advantaged, particularly women, the poor and racial/ethnic minorities. Notions of an even playing field that uses objective, merit-based criteria to allocate people to places in the social and economic hierarchy are too idealistic in the same way that notions of a truly free market are too idealistic. The playing field is simply not even. Some groups (male, white, middle to upper class) start in an advantaged position. The field is biased towards their success.

We must take gender inequality seriously, but when we move beyond the series of simplifying assumptions that are neoclassical economics we can understand its nature more broadly and understand that solutions, like 'merit' that work to the same logic will not solve this problem. We need to think far more deeply and constructively than this.

An earlier version of this work was published in the proceedings of the 'Winds of Change: Women and the Culture of Universities' conference held at University of Technology, Sydney, 13-17 July 1998.

References

Aldrich, H. and P.V. Marsden (1988), 'Environments of Organizations', in N. Smelser (ed.), *Handbook of Sociology*.

Aldrich, H. and J. Pfeffer (1976), 'Environments of Organizations', *American Journal of Sociology*, 2.

Bacchi, C. (1993), 'The Brick Wall: Why So Few Women Become Senior Academics', *Australian Universities Review*, 36.

Baran, P.A. and P. Sweezy (1966), *Monopoly Capital*, Penguin, Harmondsworth.

Baron, W.T. and J.M. Beilby (1980), 'Bringing the Firms Back In: Stratification, Segmentation, and the Organization of Work', *American Sociological Review*, 54.

Baum, J.A. and C. Oliver (1991), 'Institutional Linkages and Organizational Mortality', *Administration Science Quarterly*, 36 (2).

_____ (1992), 'Institutional Embeddedness and the Dynamics of Organizational Populations, *American Sociological Review*, 57 (4).

Bennett, J. (1988), 'History that Stands Still: Women's Work in the European Past', *Feminist Studies*, 14.

_____ (1991), 'Misogyny, Popular Culture and Women's Work', *History Workshop Journal*, 31.

Braverman, H. (1974), *Labor and Monopoly Capital: The Degradation of Work in the Twentieth Century*, Monthly Review Press, New York.

Burawoy, M. (1979), *Manufacturing Consent: Changes in the Labor Process under Monopoly Capitalism*, University of Chicago Press, Chicago.

_____ (1983), 'Between the Labor Process and the State: The Changing Face of Factory Regimes Under Advanced Capitalism', *American Sociological Review*, 48.

_____ (1985), *The Politics of Production*, Verso, London.

Burns, G. and G.M. Stalker (1961), *The Management of Innovation*, Tavistock, London.

Burt, R.S. (1980), 'Models of Network Structure', *Annual Review of Sociology*, 6.

_____ (1983), *Corporate Profits and Cooptation*, Academic Press, New York.

Burton, C. (1991), *The Promise and the Price: The Struggle of Equal Opportunity in Women's Employment*, Allen & Unwin, North Sydney.

Carroll, G.R. (1984), 'Organizational Ecology', *Annual Review of Sociology*, 10.

Carroll, G.R. and J. Delacroix (1982), 'Organizational Mortality in the Newspaper Industries of Argentina and Ireland: An Ecological Approach', *Administrative Science Quarterly*, 27.

Child, J. (1972), 'Organizational Structure, Environment and the Role of Strategic Choice', *Sociology*, 6.

Dimaggio, P. and W. Powell (1983), 'The Iron Cage Revisited: Institutional Isomorphism and Collective Rationality in Organizational Fields', *American Sociological Review*, 48.

Edwards, R. (1979), *Contested Terrain*, Basic Books, New York.

Enterprising Nation (1995), 'Report of the Industry Task Force on Leadership and Management Skills' (The Karpin report), Australian Government Publishing Service, Canberra.

Feyerabend, P. (1988), *Against Method*, Verso, London.

French, E. and S. Harding (1996), 'Management Models for Implementing EEO in the Workplace: Strategies and Structures, No Simple Solutions', paper presented at Australian and New Zealand Academy of Management Meetings, December.

Friedman, A.L. (1977), *Industry and Labour*, Macmillan, London.

Galbraith, J. (1973), *Designing Complex Organizations*, Addison-Wesley, Reading, Massachusetts.

Gilbreth, F.B. (1919), *Applied Motion Study: A Collection of Papers on the Efficient Method to Industrial Preparedness*, Macmillan, New York.

Gramsci, A. (1971), *Selections from Prison Notebooks*, New Left Books, London.

Habermas, J. (1984), *The Theory of Communicative Action, Volume One: Reason and the Rationalisation of Society*, tr. T. McCarthy, Bacon Press, Boston.

Hannan, M. and J. Freeman (1977), 'The Population Ecology of Organizations', *American Journal of Sociology*, 82.

_____ (1984), 'Structural Inertia and Organizational Change', *American Sociological Review*, 49.

_____ (1988), 'The Ecology of Organizational Mortality: American Labor Unions, 1836-1985', *American Journal of Sociology*, 64.

Harding, S.L. (1996), 'Alternative Production Regimes: The Challenge of Karpin', *Journal of the Australian and New Zealand Academy of Management*, 2 (2).

_____ (1998), 'The Demise of the Mondragon Cooperatives', *Australian Journal of Social Issues*, 33 (1).

Hodson, R. (1978), 'Labor in the Monopoly, Competitive and State Sectors of Production', *Politics and Society*, 8.

Horkheimer, M. and T. Adorno, ([1947] 1972), *Dialectic of Enlightenment*, Herder, New York.

Jary, D. and J. Jary (1991), *Sociology*, Harper Collins Dictionary, New York.

Kanter, R.M. (1977), *Men and Women of the Corporation* (New York: Basic Books).

Katz, D. and R.L. Kahn (1966), *The Social Psychology of Organizations*, John Wiley, New York.

Katz, D., N. Macoby and N. Morse (1950), *Productivity, Supervision and Morale in an Office Situation*, Institute of Social Research, Ann Arbor, University of Michigan.

Lawrence, P.R. and J.W. Lorsch (1967), *Organization and Environment: Managing Differentiation and Integration*, Harvard University Press, Boston.

Lukacs, G. ([1923] 1971), *History and Class Consciousness*, Merlin Books, London.

Marx, K. ([1857-8] 1965), *Pre-Capitalist Economic Formations*, Introduction by E. Hobsbawm International Publishers, New York.

_____ ([1867] 1918), *Capital*, William Glaisher, London.

_____ (1990), *Karl Marx: Selected Writings*, D. McLellan (ed.), Oxford University Press, Oxford.

Mayo, E. (1945), *The Social Problems of Industrial Civilization*, Harvard University Press, Boston.

McLellan, D. (1990), *Karl Marx: Selected Writings*, Oxford University Press, Oxford.

Miles, R. (1982), *Coffin Nails and Corporate Strategies*, Prentice Hall, New Jersey.

Pfeffer, J. (1972a), 'Size and Composition of Corporate Boards of Directors: The Organization and Its Environment', *Administrative Science Quarterly*, 17.

_____ (1972b), 'Merger as a Response to Organizational Interdependence', *Administrative Science Quarterly*, 17.

_____ (1973), 'Size, Composition, and Function of Hospital Boards of Directors: A Study of Organization-Environment Linkage', *Administrative Science Quarterly*, 18.

Pfeffer, J. and G.R. Salencik (1974), 'Organizational Decision-Making as a Political Process: The Case of a University Budget', *Administrative Science Quarterly*, 19.

_____ (1978), *The External Control of Organization: A Resource Dependence Perspective*, Harper & Row, New York.

Reskin B. and I. Padavic. (1994), *Women and Men at Work*, Pine Forge Press.

Smith, A. ([1776] 1937), *The Wealth of Nations*, Random House, London.

Spenner, K. (1993), 'Labor-Management Firms', Triangle Area Organisational Stratification Seminar, Department of Sociology and Anthropology, Raleigh, NC.

Taylor, F.W. (1911), *Shop Management: The Principles of Scientific Management*, Harper and Row, New York.

Tomaskovic Devey, D. (1993), *Gender and Racial Inequality at Work: The Sources and Consequences of Job Segregation*, ILR Press, New York.

Wajcman, J. (1998), *Managing Like a Man: Women and Men in Corporate Management*, Allen & Unwin, St Leonards NSW.

Walby, S. (1990), *Theorizing Patriarchy*, Basil Blackwell, Oxford.

Weber, M. (1927), *General Economic History*, tr. F. Knight, Greenberg, New York.

_____ ([1918] 1958a), *From Max Weber*, H.H. Gerth and C. Wright Mills (eds), Oxford University Press, New York.

_____ (1958b), *The Protestant Ethic and the Spirit of Capitalism*, tr. T Parsons, Scribner, New York.

_____ (1968), *Economy and Society*, vols 1 and 2, G. Roth and C. Wittich (eds), University of California Press, Berkeley.

Weick, K. (1969), *The Social Psychology of Organizing*, Addison-Wesley, Reading, Mass.

Whyte, W.F. (1951), 'Small Groups and Large Organizations', in J. Rohrer and M. Sherif (eds), *Social Psychology at the Crossroads*, Harper, New York.

_____ (1959), *Man and Organization*, Richard D. Irwin, Homewood, Ill.

Woodward, J. (1958), *Management and Technology*, HMSO, London.

Index